EVERYMAN, I will go with thee,

and be thy guide,

In thy most need to go by thy side

PLATO

Born at Athens 428 B.C. After the death
of Socrates (399) he spent some years
travelling, and visited Cyrene, Egypt and
Sicily. Returning to Athens in 386 he established himself as head of the Academy,
where he spent the remainder of his life
except for two more journeys to Sicily (367
and 361). He died in 347 B.C.

PLATO

The Laws

TRANSLATED WITH
AN INTRODUCTION BY
A. E. TAYLOR, M.A., D.LITT., LL.D.
*formerly Professor of Moral Philosophy
in the University of Edinburgh*

DENT: LONDON
EVERYMAN'S LIBRARY
DUTTON: NEW YORK

Par 225/4/10/67

NO. 275

CONTENTS

INTRODUCTION

THE *Laws*, to-day the least generally known of Plato's major compositions, is in some respects his most characteristic work. As he tells us himself, in his great seventh *Epistle*, he had felt himself called from his early manhood to the life of the statesman. It was the tragedy of his life, as he saw it, that he had come into the world in an age in which Athens had no longer any important part to play in history and had lost the fundamentally sound *moral* without which no people can play any part in history worthily. An Athenian conscious of the vocation to statesmanship could only discharge his appointed service to Athens, Greek civilization, and humanity at large, in an indirect way; he must give himself to the work of education. If a younger generation, or rather the prospective leaders of such a generation, could be trained in sound views of conduct and duty, something could thus be done towards the production of the right kind of public man, should a happier and healthier state of public morality ever provide such a man with his opportunity; and since the quality of all others most necessary in such a statesman is capacity for true thinking and sane judgment, the proposed education must go to the roots of the matter: the true statesman must think rightly about the ultimate things, God, man, and their relations to one another. His thought, to be just, must be trained in the most exacting discipline of the severest sciences. This is why Plato founded the Academy as a school for statesmen, and why mathematics and metaphysics were the foundations of the Academic education. The reason, in fact, why the true statesman must begin his education with 'geometry' is that his work will require him to be a realist, in the best sense of the word, and not a romantic or sentimentalist. The school for statesmen thus became an institute for the prosecution of the most abstract of the sciences; this is why Plato seems in so much of his later writing to be preoccupied with topics so very remote from what we call 'practical' interests. In the *Laws*, as Burnet has said,[1] we see him coming back as

[1] *Platonism* (University of California Press, 1928), p. 94.

an old man of about seventy to the matters which had always been nearest to his heart, after more than thirty years in which he had in the main been precluded from dealing directly with them.

So far as the modern reader knows anything of Plato's views on those to him the most important of all matters, religion, law, education, he knows about them chiefly from the *Republic*, a work in the main probably some thirty years earlier than the *Laws*, where they are treated much less fully, and always under the restrictions imposed by the fiction that the interlocutors are men of an earlier date speaking in the days of Plato's childhood, or possibly actually before his birth. The *Republic* has more to say about education than about religion, and vastly more than about law; but even about education it can only tell us what Plato was thinking at the age of about forty; we know from the *Laws* in much fuller detail what views he held after an added thirty years of experience and meditation. Without them, Plato's immense influence on Christian theology in its primitive period would be largely inexplicable, while his services to the scientific study of jurisprudence would be entirely unknown to us. The dialogue adds little of importance to our knowledge of Plato as a thinker on metaphysics and the philosophy of the sciences; it is the one work which gives us the full measure of Plato the practical thinker and the originator of so much that is best in the 'institutions of modern civilization'.

The date of the composition of the *Laws* is fixed by the following considerations. It is manifest that the passage in Book IV (711 *a–b*), where the principal character of the dialogue speaks of the opportunities which would be afforded to a high-minded political reformer and legislator by co-operation with a 'tyrant', or autocrat, of the right stamp in a way which implies first-hand knowledge of the conditions of life under an autocrat, is an allusion to Plato's own experiences during the period when he was, against his own judgment, attempting to fit Dionysius II for his position at Syracuse, and that the events alluded to already belonged to the past. The work must therefore belong to a date later than the year 360 B.C., when Plato returned from Syracuse for the last time. The composition of so long a work, especially one involving so much preliminary study of the details of Attic and other systems of laws, by a man of advanced old age must have covered a long period, and we may fairly

suppose it to have extended over most of the time between
Plato's last return from Syracuse at the age of sixty-seven or
sixty-eight and his death as an old man of eighty or more in
348–347 B.C., all the more that the tradition of later antiquity
was that the text was never finally revised by the author,
and the work only put into circulation by his scholars, apparently after his death.[1] It is, apparently, the unrevised state
of the text which accounts for the presence of a number of
small inconsistencies in matters of detail as well as for various
irregularities of grammatical construction which are not to
be readily explained by transcriptional error on the part of
scribes. We may thus think of the work as in progress
during the whole of the interval from some date in or after
360 B.C. until Plato's death, except for whatever time must
be allowed for the composition of that short supplement the
Epinomis, if, as I myself incline to hold, that is the work of
Plato, and not, as is thought by many contemporary scholars,
of his pupil, Philippus of Opus, the reputed transcriber of
the *Laws*.

The personnel of the dialogue is exceedingly simple. There
are three speakers, all elderly men: an unnamed Athenian,
who is assumed to have had experiences, like those of Plato
himself at Syracuse, of life in a city under a 'tyrant', and to
represent the views of an organized group of scientific thinkers
whom we recognize as the Platonic Academy; a Cretan named
Clinias, and a Spartan called Megillus. Of the former we
learn that he is a citizen of Cnossus, once the 'capital' of
Minos, and has a family connection with the famous medicine-
man and prophet Epimenides; of the latter that he belongs to
a Spartan family in which the office of *proxenus* of Athens is
hereditary. These facts are intended to explain the readiness
shown by both to communicate their business to an Athenian
and ask his advice on it. The dramatic situation presupposed
is only fully explained in the closing words of Book III.
The Cretans, who have resolved to refound a city which has
long been deserted, have entrusted the necessary business to
the inhabitants of Cnossus, and they, in their turn, to a body
of ten commissioners, of whom Clinias is chief. Clinias and
his friend, who have fallen in company with the Athenian, are
walking, on a day of midsummer, from Cnossus to the cave

---

[1] See *Plato, the Man and his Work*, pp. 464–5. If, as seems probable,
Isocrates V 12 is an allusion to the work, the *Laws* must have been in
circulation within a year or so of the author's death.

of Dicte, the traditional birthplace of Zeus. Their conversation turns upon the purposes and merits of the traditional
legislators of Lacedaemon and Cnossus, Lycurgus and Minos.
As the Attic visitor proves himself by his observations to be
an expert in jurisprudence and constitutional theory, the
scheme for the new Cretan foundation is disclosed to him,
and the conversation develops into a complete outline
of a proposed constitution and legislative code for the
projected city.

It has been said that the dialogue shows Plato to have had
no personal familiarity with Cretan topography. If this is
true, it is nothing to be surprised at. The manifest object of
the whole work is to serve as a model for scientific students
of jurisprudence and politics who may be called upon to act
as advisers to the practical statesman engaged in founding
a new community or remodelling an old one. The revival
of old societies and the constitution of new ones was, in fact,
one of the outstanding features of the last quarter of a century
of Plato's life, the period which opens with the breaking of
the Spartan power at Leuctra by Epaminondas in 371 B.C.
Among the first consequences of the victory were the re-
constitution of Messenia as a political community, and the
foundation of Megalopolis as a centre for political life in
Arcadia. Plato is credibly said to have been invited by
Epaminondas to act in person as the author of a constitution
and code for Megalopolis, but to have excused himself (Diogenes Laertius, III, i, 23). It is certain that assistance was
asked from and rendered by his pupils in the Academy in
numerous similar cases. To quote Plutarch (*adv. Colot.*,
1126 *c–d*): 'Plato sent Aristonymus to the Arcadians, Phormio
to Elis, Menedemus to Pyrrha. Eudoxus and Aristotle wrote
laws for Cnidus and Stagirus. Alexander asked Xenocrates
for advice about kingship; the man who was sent to Alexander
by the Greek inhabitants of Asia, and did most to incite him
to undertake his war on the barbarians, was Delius of Ephesus,
an associate of Plato'. The eleventh extant Platonic epistle
is a probably genuine reply, belonging to the same period as
the inception of the *Laws*, to a request for assistance in a
similar task from the distinguished Academic mathematician
and statesman Laodamas of Thasos.[1] According to accepted
Greek conceptions a newly constituted state should be furnished with a written constitution and a code of jurisprudence

[1] See J. Harward, *The Platonic Epistles* (1932), p. 228.

from its first inception.[1] The object of the greater part of the *Laws* is to give expert advisers from the Academy, called in to assist in undertakings of this sort, a model for their procedure.

It is this immediately practical purpose which, more than anything else, explains the difference of atmosphere between the *Laws* and the much better known *Republic*. The city imagined in the *Republic* is partly a Utopia; we are plainly given to understand that the author himself does not think of it as anything likely ever to take actual shape in the workaday world. The aim of the dialogue is throughout ethical rather than political, to answer the question how a good man differs from a bad one, and to impress upon us the lesson that, for time and for eternity, 'it's better being good than bad'. The ideal city, with its philosophic kings and virtuous soldiers, is only introduced on the ground that in the life of a whole 'nation' the issues of right and wrong, which are so easily confused if we limit our observation to the life and fortunes of the individual, can be read on the large scale, so that 'he who runs' may read them. A few fundamental principles of the highest importance are explained and insisted upon, but details are, quite properly, not provided for us. What Plato gives us in the *Laws*, on the other hand, is a carefully thought-out scheme, often going, for illustrative purposes, into quite minor details, of the kind of constitution and the sort of legal code to which a truly philosophic statesman might look for the preservation of a high and sound *moral* in the life of an actual Hellenic community in the middle of the fourth century before our era. It is important for the right understanding of the work to appreciate the point that Plato was, like his contemporary and rival, the publicist, Isocrates, convinced that the palmy days of the traditional city-state were over; if Hellenic civilization were to be preserved at all, it would have to be by political institutions of some novel type. Under the transparent fiction of a legislation for 'Magnesia' he is putting before the younger men who will actually be called upon to devise these institutions his views of the principles on which the work must be done, if it is to have permanency and value. This explains some features of the system which would look singularly out of place if we thought of it as actually intended for any society likely to arise in

---

[1] Cf. the amusing passage in Aristophanes' *Birds* (1035-1057), in which a hawker arrives with regulations from Athens for the new 'city in the clouds'.

such a backwater of civilization as Crete, such, for example, as the numbers of the contemplated society, which impressed Aristotle [1] as extravagantly great, the assumption that it will be a centre of advanced scientific research, and the careful provision made in Book XII for keeping it in touch with the whole intellectual and moral life of the Hellenic world. We cannot tell how far Plato may have had premonitions of the way in which the entrance of the Macedonian power was to lead to the general diffusion of Hellenic civilization; the moral and legal principles he lays down are no other than those which might have been formulated by a thinker aware of the near advent of the 'Hellenistic' age and concerned that its task shall be properly executed.

Plato's work is ostensibly, like many other later books which have made history, a treatise on the principles of jurisprudence; it might well bear the same title as a well-known volume of Hegel's lectures, *The Philosophy of Law*, or be named like one of the works of Pufendorf, *The Duty of a Man and Citizen*. For the complete investigation of the subject he finds it necessary to construct both what we might call a theory of the constitution and a comprehensive legal code. We have to consider, *first*, how a civilized society should be constituted, through what organs the various functions of public life, deliberative, legislative, executive, judicial, should be exercised, and what should be the powers of these different bodies, and their relations to one another; *second*, what statutes should be laid down for the conduct of the members of society towards the community and towards each other, and what penalties prescribed for their infraction. This body of statutes will further require to be arranged on a logical plan in which *public* law, dealing with offences against the community as such, is properly discriminated from *private* law, which is concerned with the conduct of individual citizens towards one another, and this latter again subdivided into the *law* of *torts*, which is concerned with the award of compensation for damage, and the law of *crimes*, by which punishment is awarded for infringement of rights. The intellectual labour involved in a first attempt at systematization of this subject-matter may perhaps be gauged from the fact that the elementary and fundamental distinction between a civil action for damages and a criminal prosecution for violation of rights has to be made clear and defended at length by Plato himself;

[1] *Politics*, II 1265 *a* 13 ff.

it was not clearly recognized in the Attic jurisprudence of his own age, and, if the reigning exegesis of the chapter of the *Nicomachean Ethics* which deals with *justitia directiva* is sound, was not properly appreciated by Aristotle, even with Plato's treatment of the problem under his eyes.

The excogitation of a system of political institutions and a legislative code is, however, the least part of the work of the philosophical jurist as Plato conceives it. Before these particular tasks can be entered upon, the end to which all government and all law are relative has to be rightly understood. That end is the promotion, throughout the community, of the highest type of personality attainable, 'complete goodness'. If the authors of any people's institutions set a false or confused idea of personality before themselves, the institutions they create and perpetuate will reflect the perversions and incoherencies of their ideals, the national life of the people in question will be stunted or distracted. The foundations of constitutional and legal theory have thus to be laid in a sound and thoroughly thought-out doctrine of conduct; 'politics' must be throughout an application of the principles of a true 'ethic'. This is all the more necessary, since the true function of law in the community is not to threaten or punish, but to direct. In any society, there is an element, a minority, which has no desire to lead the good life; there are those who will only keep out of mischief from dislike of its unpleasant consequences, and the law can do nothing for such persons but issue an order, and take care that non-compliance with that order shall be made sufficiently disagreeable. But the mass of decent citizens do at heart prefer doing the right thing to doing the wrong; only they are commonly confused on the question what particular thing is the right thing, and when they know what it is, their real desire to do it cannot always be counted on to prevail against temptation. The primary business of the lawgiver with such persons is to give them direction and encouragement. This is why Plato holds that the laws of a truly philosophical code must not be so many bare 'imperatives', each provided with its penal 'sanction'. They should be introduced, as the different sections of his own specimen legislation are, by 'preambles' in which direction and encouragement are combined. The law-maker must appeal to our intelligence by pointing out the reasons why the line of conduct he prescribes is the right one, and to our worthier emotions by enlisting our sense of

honour, manhood, chivalry, on the side of his proposals and
awakening a genuine repugnance against the breach of them.
This is why when we come at last, in the ninth book of the
Laws, to the systematic code-making, the ethical 'preambles'
occupy so much more space than the statutes to which they
are nominally prefatory.

Further, the extent to which a given society can hope to
achieve 'complete goodness', and the methods by which it
will best aim at that ideal, are inevitably conditioned by its
inheritance of traditions and its material 'environment'. It is
idle to attempt to construct a code or a constitution *in vacuo*
and without reference to the antecedents and the economic
condition of the persons who are to live under them, and, in
a given case, antecedents and economic conditions may be
such that the ideally best is not 'humanly attainable'. The
truly philosophically-minded man of affairs will never be
'practical' in the vulgar sense of being content to aim at
anything lower than the best which it is open to him to attain, but what that attainable best is will always be largely
dependent on the composition of the society for which he
is working, and its general economic possibilities. Hence,
in the illustrative example of the fictitious 'Magnesian'
colony, we are carefully provided with information about the
provenance of the future citizens, and the size, topography,
and produce of the territory they are to occupy, before any
attempt is made to provide for their public life.

There are two other outstanding features of Plato's thought
in which it is like our own, and singularly unlike the habit of
mind of the Roman lawyers of whom much of his code must
remind us. The typical Roman lawyer cared nothing about
science or intellectual education, and he was not religiously-
minded. The interest of religion for him was simply that it
can be made into a useful implement for the maintenance of
social order. Plato thought very differently. To know truth,
he held, is the prerogative by which man is set above all the
works of God which surround him, and it is his only prerogative, at once intellectual and moral. Knowledge of the
true scale of good and evil is, in fact, the one sure and infallible preservative against the practical neglect of good or
commission of evil, and such knowledge—as a real personal
possession—only comes as the crown of an arduous discipline
in true thinking pursued resolutely to its end. This is why
Laws VII, Plato's most mature and considered discussion of

education, insists that every free-born citizen shall receive an adequate training in the elements of the sciences, and maps out the stages of such an education from its very beginnings, why the Minister of Education is to be the *premier ministre* of the community, and why we learn in *Laws* XII that eminence in geometry and astronomy, as well as proved virtue and sincere piety, will be demanded of all candidates for a place on the permanent Committee of Public Safety to which the Academic statesman will look as the sheet-anchor of his constitution. There is no possible divorce, according to Plato's view of the matter, between the understanding of the order of nature around us, and the understanding of the order which God requires us to bring into our own thoughts and acts; the spirit of 'knowledge and understanding' is not to be disjoined from the spirit of 'wisdom and godly fear'. In the closing pages of the whole work with their contrast between the secularism of the earliest Greek cosmologists and the devouter spirit of the more mature Academic science we are reminded of the familiar saying of Francis Bacon that a little knowledge may lead to atheism, but deeper knowledge conducts a man back to God. On the ear trained to perceive such things the one sentence strikes like an anticipation as the other like an echo of the *Christus magister ad omnia* of Augustinianism. Hence it is not surprising that the two books of the *Laws* of outstanding interest should be just the two which deal with matters entirely outside the sphere of the jurist as conceived by the Roman lawyers; the seventh with its programme of higher education, and the tenth, where the doctrines of a 'natural' or 'philosophical' theology make their appearance, for the first time in the history of European thought, as truths claiming to be capable of 'demonstration by natural reason'. In both cases philosophical theory is made the basis for demand for practical institutions which were only to take actual shape in later ages. In the seventh book we are introduced to the secondary school or *Lycée* as an institution in which the various branches of higher education are to be co-ordinated in a single establishment adequately provided with its staff of publicly remunerated expert teachers. In the tenth, Plato has, for good and bad, introduced to the European imagination the conception of the Inquisition, a tribunal commissioned to take account of 'heretical pravity', and empowered to use all the resources of the 'secular arm' for its repression.

The *Lycée* and the Inquisition may perhaps be said to be the most striking instances of Plato's anticipations of institutions destined to have an important history in later ages; but there is a third which should be added to them. We should miss the point of the disquisitions of Book III on the history of the Peloponnese, Persia, and Athens if we neglected to note that they are all intended to enforce a doctrine of constitutional theory which had never been uttered before, and which its author holds to be of capital importance—the doctrine of the necessity of the 'balance of the constitution'. It is one of Plato's most important original discoveries that good government is impossible where the plenitude of sovereign power is concentrated in the hands of a single person, or a single body of men. The well-being of a society depends upon the combination of respect for legal order, good will of all to all, and the sense of personal responsibility for the good or bad conduct of the 'nation'. This combination can only be secured where there is a proper division of the powers of sovereignty; to speak more precisely, what is needed is a constitution combining the two elements of 'monarchy', personal authority and initiative, and 'democracy', popular control of affairs, by some rational scheme of 'division of powers'. In view of the prominence given to this thesis in *Laws* III, it is not too much to call Plato the author of the doctrine of constitutionalism. We might even venture on the *mot* that the first 'Whig' was neither, as Johnson once declared, the devil, nor, as Acton maintained in correction of him, St. Thomas of Aquinum, but Plato. (The Whig strain in Thomas's *de Regno* is, in fact, itself influenced by the *Laws* through Aristotle's *Politics*.) It has been the fashion in the earlier years of the present century to disparage the so-called 'compromise' of the Briton, with his ingrained respect for a 'constitution', by comparison with the more 'logical' intransigence of the 'Latin' royalist or republican. The experience of an age in which 'dictatorships' of various kinds are being experimented in with such dubious success may perhaps incline us to agree with Plato that it is not the truest wisdom to ride half-truths to death.

In view of the intricacy of the argument of Plato's most elaborate work, and the length of the digressions in which the writer is fond of indulging, it will be well to prefix at this point a general synopsis of the whole book. To appreciate its real unity of purpose it is necessary to keep in mind one character-

istic of the writer which shows itself more or less markedly in
all but his briefest dialogues. Like Burke, as described by
Goldsmith, Plato loves 'to wind his way into his subject like
a serpent', and the trick is the more unavoidable that the
form of his works is dramatic; they profess to be stylized
reports of conversations. Hence he commonly begins at some
considerable distance from his main theme, with remarks of
a kind which might naturally be made in an actual colloquy.
For the same reason, the positions taken up in the earlier
stages of the conversation are frequently intended to be
subject to a good deal of modification as the discussion proceeds, and as often as not they are meant only half in earnest.
It is only when we turn back from the end of a dialogue, and
read the opening pages a second time, that we can fairly judge
either of their precise bearing, or of the proportion of jest
which the writer is mingling with his earnest. In the *Laws*,
a work of unusual length by a man who has reached old age,
and a work which has never received final revision, these
characteristics are particularly noticeable. The preliminaries
are, as we cannot avoid feeling, rather unduly spun out;
it is harder than usual to know just how much allowance to
make for the playful element in them, and the transitions to
the graver central themes are not managed with Plato's earlier
artistic address. Some of these blemishes would presumably
have disappeared if the text had been submitted to a final
revision; none of them is at all surprising in a work which
cannot have been begun until its author was at least close on
the age of seventy. Their presence, which in the last century
tempted a few scholars to speculate rashly about incompetent
editorial tampering with an *opus postumum*, is really rather
evidence of the scrupulous fidelity with which the transcription
of Plato's text has been carried out.

The whole argument of Books I and II, like that of *Republic* I, is intended as preliminary to the systematic treatment of Plato's main theme. The dramatic situation is that
an Athenian student of law and constitutional theory has
fallen in with an elderly Cretan who is taking a long day's
walk in the company of a Spartan friend; the common interest
of all three in what would now be called 'the social problem'
provides a natural subject for the conversation with which
they propose to occupy themselves during the day. The
question propounded is whether there is a discoverable central
unity of purpose underlying the characteristic institutions of

xx   THE LAWS OF PLATO

Sparta and Crete, and if so, whether this purpose is that which the highest statesmanship would set before itself. The answer, from the Cretan or Spartan point of view, is that the institutions of both communities tend to one definite end, and that the end which ought to inspire all legislation, the promotion of *virtue* or *goodness*. The fundamental fact about public life is that every 'city', or political society, is engaged in an undeclared but permanent *warfare* against all rivals; almost in the words which Hobbes was to use so many centuries later, an independent society is in the 'state of nature' relatively to all its neighbours, and the state of nature is one of 'war of all against all'. Consequently the 'public good', the object which a statesman or legislator admittedly ought to have before him in all his institutions, is definable as victory in this warfare, and the supreme business of a citizen is to be an effective combatant in it. Virtue, therefore, being simply efficiency in the discharge of this supreme business, is reducible to *valour*, the distinctive excellence of the fighting-man. Now the whole aim of the famous Spartan discipline and the similar institutions of Crete is to make the citizen a first-rate man-at-arms, and the institutions of Lycurgus and Minos are thus beyond criticism; they are consistently devised with a view to the production of the type of personal character which we can see to be the one thing needful for a combatant in the unending warfare which is human life.

Plato dissents *in toto* from this 'militaristic' philosophy of life. In his view, the supreme victory which has to be won by any man, or any society of men, is a triumph over an *internal* enemy, the conquest of the worse elements within the community, or the personal self, by the better, and this conquest is not completed, in either case, by the mere rout or expulsion of the worse element. It is only fully won when harmony is effected by the voluntary subjection of the worse to the direction of the better. Hence it is peace and not war which is the best state for the community, or for the soul of the individual, and the enactments of the legislator will therefore have peace, not war, as their ultimate object. From such a point of view, wisdom, *sophrosyne* (sobriety of soul), justice (reverence for rights), are the supreme virtues; the mere valour of the fighting-man can only take the fourth rank. It is therefore manifest that there is a fundamental vice in the famous Spartan discipline. All its provisions aim at fostering one single part of 'complete goodness', and that the part to which we have just given the lowest place. What is more, 'complete goodness' is so close a unity that when one subordinate element in it, valour, is treated as the whole, that element is itself misconceived. By aiming exclusively at the production of this single virtue, the Spartan system comes only to promote the less important half of valour itself. The Spartan learns to bear himself bravely in the presence of danger, pain, difficulty in the field, because he is made to face them all as part of his education; he never acquires that further moral courage which is identical with *sophrosyne*, power to face exposure to the temptations of a position which affords a man full scope for the indulgence of his craving for pleasures, riches, dominion, without disgracing himself; and the reason why this lesson is never learned at Sparta is that these are temptations which the young Spartan has never been made to encounter as part of his regular training. Hence the reputation of Spartans with the outside world is an ambiguous one. They are famous all the world over for their courage in danger and pain, but the perverse sexual practices encouraged by their 'barrack-room' mode of life, and the relaxed morals of their women, are also notorious.

The main contribution of the First Book to the argument is contained in these three propositions: that a state should be permanently organized with a view to peace, not to war; that to be so organized it must make '*complete* goodness' its ideal of character for its citizens; that the moral training which is to issue in such complete goodness demands exposure to the seductions and blandishments of our 'pleasant vices'. 'Pleasure' is no more to be mastered by running away than danger or pain. The practical importance of this point leads to its long and half-playful illustration by the particular case of the right treatment of convivial wine-drinking. It is, of course, impossible to approve of the unrestrained toping of many non-Hellenic people and some Hellenic societies. On the other hand, Plato does not admire the Spartan prohibition of all social use of the bottle. A wine-party, if properly conducted, that is, if the *convives* are under the control of an older master of the feast, who is not himself carried away by their merriment, and can therefore see to it that the drinkers 'behave like gentlemen', may be made a valuable training-ground for the practice of modesty and sobriety. It is an excellent discipline to be thus artificially placed in a situation where it is easy to forget the demands of decorum and modesty, and to be expected to acquit oneself well in that situation on pain of disgrace. Plato understands, as we might expect, that the young man who has never been allowed to run any risk of exposure to the seductions of the 'bottle' is not likely to distinguish himself by sobriety if ever he finds himself in the position to indulge himself. But he is, of course, more concerned for the general principle he is enforcing than for the particular application of it. The painful experiences of the thirty years which followed upon the collapse of Athens and the rise of Sparta to a dominant position at the end of the 'Decelean War' had shown only too conclusively that no Spartan in a post of responsibility outside Spartan territory could be trusted not to abuse the opportunity to gratify lust, avarice, the itch for meddling domination. The reason, Plato holds, is that the Spartan has never been exposed to these temptations and learned to resist them; he has had no chance to deserve the commendation pronounced by Scripture upon the man 'who hath had the power to transgress, and hath not transgressed'. It is, further, the misfortune of the central authorities who have to pick the occupants of such posts that their choice has to be made in the dark, between candidates none of whom have given previous proofs of their moral qualifications. Under a different and wiser social system the citizen would have the benefit of discipline in the control of appetite, and the magistrate the advantage of valuable information about the strong and the weak points in the characters of his subjects.

The Second Book of the *Laws* opens with the remark that there is still a third social benefit to be derived from the properly regulated use of wine, though we cannot say what this is without discussing the whole problem of the use of music and poetry as a vehicle of early moral education. (The connection of the two problems is, in fact, as artificial as ingenious, and we should probably not take it as more than half-serious). Plato is, indeed, dealing once more with the theme already treated in the third book of the *Republic*, the cultivation of a child's moral sense through its taste and imagination, but the familiar topic is handled with a psychological thoroughness to which the *Republic* affords no parallel. As yet nothing is said of the cultivation of the child's intelligence and understanding; that is to be the main theme of Book VII, which, in its turn, presupposes the results of the present discussion. We have to lay it down as the foundation of a sound paedagogy that a child's first experiences in life are its feelings of pleasure and pain, and that education itself may very properly be said, at this stage, to be simply 'learning to feel pleasure and pain about the right things', a declaration which called forth the unqualified applause of Aristotle.[1] More precisely we may define this simultaneous education of taste and of character through taste as 'a drawing and guiding of the young to the rightly uttered discourse of the law' (659 d), that is the spontaneous formation of a moral and artistic taste for just what an older and matured judgment will recognize as good. The possibility of such a training is provided by the two facts that a child, like other young animals, cannot keep quiet, but is always jumping and shouting, and that in man, by the gift of God, these originally random movements and noises can be transformed into tuneful and rhythmical song and dancing. Hence Plato asserts with perfect seriousnes that the whole aesthetic and moral training of the child can be brought under the head of education in the 'choric art', the art of song accompanied by the strains of the lyre and the movements of an appropriate *ballet d'action*. (Even 'gymnastics', the general training of the body, so far as this can be made part of a really young child's education, is got under this rubric by regarding it as one subdivision of 'dancing', the art of bodily movement.) The aim of the whole educational process is to exclude from the first all possibility of the not uncommon divergence between taste and judgment which leads a man to find pleasure in art which his judgment pronounces to be bad, or to get no pleasure from what his understanding recognizes as good. The child is to learn to like just what he will in due time find to be good art, and to dislike what a maturer judgment discerns to be bad. If this is to be effected, the maintenance of a sound taste and true canons in music and the connected arts will have to be made a prominent function of the public authorities; there must be a complete abandonment of the widely entertained view that there are no fixed standards of good and bad in music, good music meaning simply that which, at any time, is found pleasing by the majority of an audience, and the best musician the composer or performer who is most popular and most successful in 'putting it across'. It will be the duty of the State to discover the true standards for the various forms of musical composition, and to canonize them to the exclusion

[1] *E. N.* 1104 *b* 11.

of all others, and that this can be done is sufficiently proved by the stereotyped conventionality of Egyptian art (656 *d e*). (It is worth noting that Plato commits himself to no opinion on the *merits* of these Egyptian conventions in art. He merely appeals to the example of Egypt as proof that the permanent maintenance of artistic canons is possible, and commends the serious attention which that people have given to the problem.)

Plato's acceptance of the standing Greek conviction that music is the most 'imitative' of all arts, and that what it 'imitates'—or, as we should say, represents or suggests—is 'moods of the soul' prevents him from feeling that there is any difficulty about making a training in musical taste also a training in moral taste. Music being an 'imitative' art, it is essential to good music both that the object it 'imitates' should be beautiful, and that it should imitate that object rightly. The requirement that the imitating should be rightly done demands a complete harmony in the tone of all the constituents which enter into it, words, melody, rhythm, time, movements of the ballet. On this side of the matter the result to be obtained is one which we should call 'aesthetic', and the defects in contemporary music against which the attack is directed are sins against a refined and austere artistic taste. The stipulation that the 'mood of soul' which the music 'imitates' must be genuinely beautiful brings in the moral side of the conception. To Plato, as a true Greek, the 'ugliness' of conduct which is morally out of place is the most immediately salient fact about it, and the 'beauty of holiness', if the scriptural phrase may be permitted, is something much more than a metaphor. To judge by the tone of much of our literature, we are less sensitive on the point; we seem slow to perceive ugliness in wrong-doing as such, or even ready to concede the 'artistry' of great wickedness. It may be a wholesome discipline to consider carefully whether this difference of feeling may not be due less to a confusion on Plato's part between the beautiful and the morally good than to a certain aesthetic imperceptiveness on ours.

The connection between this discussion and that which preceded it is externally effected by the reflection that if 'music' is to be the business of the whole community, every generation within it must take its part in the 'singing'. There will have to be 'choirs' of old men, no less than of young men and children, and all of them will have to do their singing with gusto and verve. This is more than we can expect of the elderly, even if we confine their performances to the family circle, unless they are allowed to rejuvenate themselves temporarily for the task by the judicious aid of the wine-cup. These remarks should probably be taken as more than half playful. Even in Book II itself there are hints that the 'singing' of the old men is meant to be done more with the understanding than with the voice; their real service to the 'music' of the community is that they inspire the anthology of 'national melodies'. When the subject is taken up again in Book VII, the actual compilation of this anthology is made the business of the Minister of Education and his advisers, all of whom are men of years and experience, and we may fairly take what has been said in the earlier discussion about the older men and their singing as replaced, for serious purposes, by these more specific arrangements. Perhaps it is not far-fetched to suggest that Plato's real thought is that the besetting fault of anthologies compiled for the youthful by their seniors is to be too 'grown-up', and that a Committee of Selection is likely to avoid this fault more successfully if it comes to its work warmed by a reasonable quantity of good wine?

With Book III we enter on the direct discussion of the main problem of the constructive statesman, what a 'city' is and how it arises. What Plato does in this book is to apply the 'genetic' method to the interpretation of Greek history from its legendary beginnings down to his own day. By a study of the way in which law and constitutional order arise in a society we are to discover their functions and the conditions requisite for the permanent and successful discharge of them. This is 'philosophy of history' in its first inception; in the extant literature of the ancient world we hardly meet with another example of the same kind and quality until we come to St. Augustine's *de Civitate Dei*. The handling of what may be called 'pre-history' is notable for its judgment and sanity. Only the briefest summary of Plato's treatment can be attempted in this introductory essay.

We have no trustworthy information about the actual beginnings of our civilization, but we may fairly represent them imaginatively by considering what would happen if a natural cataclysm destroyed the whole of a community with the exception of a few shepherds and goatherds, who might escape, for example from a deluge, owing to the remoteness and inaccessibility of their position. All the arts of civilization would naturally be lost, and with them all records of earlier times, and it would be many generations before they would be recovered. There would be at first only a few rude family groups with no means of intercommunication, and none of the implements of industry, and the life of these groups would be pastoral in character. They would live on the products of their herds, and having no 'portable property' to quarrel about would be orderly and peaceable. Their form of government, if we can call it so, would be 'patriarchal', like that ascribed by Homer to his Cyclopes. In process of time, as the first difficulties of the situation were overcome, there would be a formation of larger social groups, the recovery of agriculture, and the first beginnings of 'enclosures', all still in the uplands, and out of danger from any recurrence of the deluge which had destroyed the earlier civilization. The first beginnings of legislation and political sovereignty would appear with the formation of a common rule of life for such a society out of the traditions brought to it by each of the minor coalescing family groups. When the memories of the old catastrophe had been still more completely forgotten, men would come down to the plains and begin to build larger cities, like the Ilios of Homer's poems, and even to venture on the water again. All this would lead to an age of accumulation of wealth, to warfare, and the rise of rich, ambitious, and powerful monarchs equal to serious military undertakings. We should, in fact, find ourselves in the 'heroic age' of which the *Iliad* gives us a generally faithful picture. (It is this section of the *Laws* from which Aristotle has drawn his formula for the course of historical evolution: 'first the family, then the village-community which grows out of the family, then the full-blown city-state, originating out of the village-community'.)

With the traditional story of the war against Troy and the events which followed it, down to the Dorian conquest of the Peloponnese, we are at last in the region of fairly continuous history, and begin to discover the lesson history has for us. The main point is that the Dorian conquest, which ended an age of general upheaval due to a 'world-war', provided a unique historical opportunity for a statesman, if there had only been a man with the genius to profit by it. The invaders had acquired a new territory, they had no ancient traditions or vested interests to tie their hands, and so they might have established a state which could have held its own against time and against all outside rivals. They plainly misused their advantage, for, though they are said to have set up a federation of three kingdoms, Sparta, Argos, Messene, all pledged to mutual support, two of the three were in time reduced to impotence or subjection by the third, and the old rule of life, which was in fact dictated by the position of the Dorians as a conquering minority in the midst of a hostile population, has only survived at Sparta. And we can 'after the event' see at once where the great mistake was made. The three kingdoms tried to assure their own permanency by a mere compact that in the case of innovation being made, whether by monarch or by populace, in any one of them, the other two would unite to suppress it. The truth which was thus ignored is that the permanent well-being of every state demands a 'balance in the constitution', a *division* of the powers of sovereignty between several parties; concentration of sovereignty in the same hands is always fatal. In the absence of this internal division of sovereignty in the individual states, there was no adequate check on the temptation natural to the monarchs to 'extend the prerogative'. If Sparta has retained much of the old institution, it is because she has been fortunately preserved by the 'division of power'. Providence, or fortunate circumstance, gave an opening for this in the events which led to the division of the kingship between two houses; a wise statesman—this, of course, means Lycurgus— carried the process a step farther by the creation of the γερουσία, or senate, in which the kings had only an equal voice with other members, and the division was made still more complete at a later time by the institution of the powerful magistracy of the ephors. The Spartan constitution has thus become a mixed one, as Plato holds that a sound constitution should be.

We are carried a step farther by a comparison of the history of Persia since the days of Cyrus with the contemporary history of Athens. Such a comparison indicates that the two indispensable elements between which a sound constitution must be in a balance are *personal rule* (monarchy), and *democracy* (popular control). At the time of Cyrus both these necessary elements were present among the Persians as well as among the Athenians. Since that date the element of popular control has disappeared among the Persians; the government has become a complete autocracy, and the consequence is that Persia is now only strong and formidable 'on paper';

there is no true loyalty in the Persian subject, since he really has nothing to be loyal to. At Athens, the old respect for personal character and official authority has been lost in a complete rule of the 'mob'. In both cases the source of the mischief has been ignorance of the true principles of education. Every Persian prince since Darius I has been 'born in the purple' and 'spoiled' in early life by women and eunuchs, who treat him as a superior being whose caprices may never be 'crossed'. At Athens the evil began when the uneducated were encouraged to think their own judgment in music and the drama as competent as that of the educated; the delusion that one man's opinion has the same weight as another's soon spread from the sphere of art to that of politics. In Persia no one is now seriously trained to command; at Athens no one learns how to obey. The moral for the intending legislator is that every salutary government must combine the two factors of 'monarchy' and 'popular freedom'. There must be authority, but the authority must not degenerate into regimentation; there must also be individual freedom and initiative, but the freedom must not be anarchical. Plato is thus opposed on principle to the (falsely so-called) 'logic' of the *doctrinaire* with his clamant demands for 'all or nothing'; 'half the loaf' is to his mind not merely 'better than no bread'; it is commonly, as Hesiod had remarked, better than the whole loaf; *intransigence*, authoritarian or democratic, he holds, can only end in the undoing of the State. It is in this spirit that we find him in the eighth *Epistle* urging 'compromise' on the contending parties at Syracuse. 'Let the one side enjoy freedom *under monarchical rule*, and the other supreme power in the form of a *responsible* monarchy, with the laws holding absolute authority not only over the other citizens but also over the kings themselves'.[1] The philosophical principle of this doctrine of political 'compromise' is that stated, not for the first time in Plato's maturer writings, at *Laws* IV, 713 *e* ff. Absolute and unfettered sovereignty, or dominion, over human conduct is the special prerogative of God, our unseen Master, and the surrogate or vicegerent of God in the historical world is not the caprice of either monarch or populace, but *reason* speaking in the accents of *law*. (As a recent eminent British philosopher has said, the characteristic function of law is not compulsion, but direction.) The worth of the principle thus laid down, we are told, may be tested by

[1] Epp. VIII, 355 *e* (trans. Harward).

the experiment of taking it as the foundation of a complete constitutional and juridical system for the 'city' Clinias is, as we now learn, to found.

The topographical inquiries about the situation and character of the territory to be assigned to the imaginary 'city' with which Book IV opens are meant to serve more than one purpose. As we have said already, part of Plato's object is to enforce the practical point that the legal and constitutional institutions most appropriate to a society must be in keeping with its natural 'environment', its economic resources, and the composition of the population; the building of a Utopia in fairy-land is not work for a practical statesman. Further it is intended to indicate the kind of natural conditions which, in Plato's opinion, give the constructive statesman the best chance to establish the finest type of national life. This is why we are asked to imagine that the available territory is varied enough to yield all the main staple requisites of bodily existence, but not fertile enough to make production for the foreign market possible. It is also why access to the sea, the great high road of commerce and inter-State politics, is assumed to be difficult. With the assumed conditions, the city will be self-supporting, and there will be nothing to encourage the influx of large numbers of aliens engaged in commerce, like those who congregated in the Athenian Piraeeus. The economic basis of existence will thus be agrarian, not industrial, and this, it is assumed, will make for sound national *moral*; the danger that the spirit of the community may be 'commercialized' is reduced to a minimum. The composition of the population will have every chance of remaining uniform, and there will be little risk of the perturbing influences of the outer world on national traditions of life and conduct.

Another grave risk excluded by these initial assumptions, and naturally prominent in the thought of an Athenian philosopher, is that the growth of a large volume of sea-borne commerce might lead to the rise of a navy, and this to the appearance of the spirit of aggressive 'imperialism'. This, as Plato holds, is what had happened at Athens. The Athenians were driven by their geographical and economic situation to develop their naval strength, and their possession of a powerful fleet then led them into that policy of overseas 'expansion' which ultimately undermined the public *moral* and brought about the downfall of the Periclean democracy.

This should explain why Plato excludes, as conditions which the wise statesman will regard as ill suited to his purpose, just those which we are tempted to think favourable to the rise of a 'great people'. National greatness, as he conceives it, is not a matter of wealth or dominion, but exclusively one of intellect and character, and the kind of character he rates highest is strong, tenacious, and deep-rooted, without any taint of facile 'cosmopolitanism'. His citizens, so unlike the Romans of the early Republic in their intellectual and artistic interests, are to resemble them in the *gravitas* and *pietas* of their moral temperament, and to secure this result, he is willing to sacrifice all opportunity for the playing of what the world at large counts a 'distinguished part' in history. In fact, as he is careful to tell us more than once, we should need to see life through God's eyes before we can venture to say which parts in life are distinguished and which undistinguished, or even whether there is much real difference in distinction between one part in the comedy and another. *Our* concern is only to sustain that part for which we have been cast well. We have also to remember that Plato, like Greek philosophers in general, does not take *time* very seriously. He is not stirred, as a more modern thinker might be, by the vision of a people's life as an adventure, through an innumerable series of generations, into the unknown with the prospect of un-ending 'progress' towards ends which cannot be discerned in advance. He is, of course, aware, as he several times says, that no system of law and politics can be brought into the world perfect *omnibus numeris*. Many necessary supplemen-tations and corrections will have to be made in his own pro-posals by the light of experience of their working, and at the cost of preliminary experimentation. Yet he repeatedly speaks of this provisional and experimental stage as one which should be of short duration; we are apparently to think of the authorities of his 'city' as needing less than a generation for the experiences which would justify them in declaring their institutions definitely inviolable.

We are to imagine ourselves, then, in the ideal position of having a perfectly free hand to propose whatever institutions and laws we judge most conducive to the end the true states-man has in view, the promotion of 'complete goodness'. It is, to be sure, hardly possible that any actual legislator will ever be so fortunate as to enjoy this complete freedom of action, but we may conceive that miracle to happen if a supremely wise and experienced statesman should have the opportunity of co-operation with an 'autocrat' at once young enough and intelligent enough to appreciate his ideals and conceive an enthusiasm for them, and morally noble enough to put his absolute power at the statesman's disposal (and so to use it for the suppression of itself). This is not, indeed, the situation in which our three speakers are imagined to find themselves, since Clinias will, of course, have to get the approval of the authorities of Cnossus, and ultimately of the Cretan communities at large, for his proposals. The meaning is simply that from this point in the argument we are to *feign* ourselves free to recommend any institutions and enactments which we judge best for the statesman's purpose, to frame an ideal, without concerning ourselves with the question how far we are able to enforce it. We are to be told, to borrow Butler's phrase, what 'conscience' would effect, 'had it power as it has manifest authority', what reason, 'the surrogate of God', pronounces as law. And the first step we shall have to take will therefore be that of laying down the principles of *moral* 'valuation' upon which the whole of a rational system of law and political organization ultimately depends. The speaker accordingly imagines himself to be in the position of a legislator with plenary authority speaking to the whole body of prospective citizens, and addressing them upon the principles of right living.

The ethical discourse on the whole duty of man, which opens at *Laws*, IV, 715 *e*, does not reach its completion until we are near the middle of the following book, though it is interrupted early in its course (at 718 *d*) in order to explain its precise function. The concern of the law, which is the embodiment of reason, is not simply with the seriously-minded, but with the whole body of citizens, most of whom are at heart on the side of decent living though they need direction in difficulties, and are often seduced into misconduct by their lower nature. Hence it is not enough to formulate a number of imperative statutes sanctioned by penalties for their infringement, in the fashion of the empirical physician who merely orders the patient to swallow his prescriptions with a threat of the consequences of neglect. The physician of the soul should attempt to enlist the sensible patient as an ally in his treatment by explaining the grounds on which it is based and encouraging co-operation with it. Each section of the 'code' should therefore be introduced by a preamble in which the moral grounds for the subsequent enactment will be explained, and a suitable appeal made to the subject's judgment and 'better feelings'. In particular, the present discourse on the principles of right living at large must be taken as such a prelude to the whole body of legislation which is to follow upon it.

The key-note of this latest version of Plato's ethics is struck in its famous opening sentence. 'God eternally pursues the even tenour of his way', and Justice is God's attendant. To be happy a man must follow Justice and God with a 'humbled and disciplined' soul, and to 'follow' God means to be like God, who—and not man, as Protagoras had said—is the true 'measure' of everything. To be like God, then, is to lead the life of right 'measure', and the first principle of this life is to have a true scale of moral worth. Reverence, or honour, is to be paid to its recipients in their proper order, and the proper order is to give the first place to the gods of the world of the living and the patron deities of the city, the second to the gods of the dim world beyond the grave, the third to 'daemons and heroes'—or as a Christian might say to 'angels' and canonized saints—the fourth to departed ancestors in general, the fifth to our still living parents, and only the sixth to ourselves and the men of our own generation. In connection with duty to parents, in particular, we must observe due proportion in the discharge of it. In life we can never do too much for them; we are to put not merely our purses, or our bodily labour, at their service, but to cherish them with the deepest affections of the heart. When they are dead, modest observances which 'keep their memory green' are better than wasteful sepulchral rites followed by forgetfulness. When we come to the respect proper to be shown to ourselves and our contemporaries, the essential thing is to remember that a man's soul must be held in higher honour than his body, and his body than his possessions. Hence it is dishonouring my own soul to care for enjoyment, riches, power, or health more than for virtue or wisdom, and dishonouring my body to prefer wealth to health. Moreover, neither extraordinary physical superiority nor vast wealth is, speaking generally, for a man's good. The first breeds vanity or gross lusts, the second luxury and laziness. The middle condition in both respects is the best for a man. The main rules for right conduct to others are two: In our relations with our fellow-citizens we should be careful to rate the benefits we get from them higher, the services we render them lower, than they do themselves. And in relation to the 'alien', who is outside the circle of equal legal citizenship, especially the alien who appeals to us in the name of religion, the 'suppliant', we should be even more 'on our honour' to behave well than towards a fellow-citizen, since nothing is so hateful to God and man as the taking of advantage against the defenceless.

There are, further, certain guiding principles which can be laid down for a man's conduct in matters which cannot be commanded or forbidden by positive statute (Kant's 'duties of imperfect obligation'). One such principle is that the quality above all others required in all situations in life is ἀλήθεια, 'genuineness', 'staunchness', 'loyalty'. Another is that it is good to practise this and all other points of virtue in one's own person, better to go farther and bring the misdeeds of others under the notice of the authorities, best of all to give 'authority' active support in the chastisement of offence. Rivalry in such active practice of 'goodness' is, in fact, the one form of emulation which ought to be universally encouraged, just because the aim of each competitor in this case, and in this case only, is to communicate a good as widely as possible, not to engross it to himself. The good man's zeal for justice will, however, be combined with a merciful spirit. He will treat the 'remediable' transgressions of his fellows mercifully, because he knows that no one does evil for its own sake, and he will be sedulous to avoid not only all hysterical emotionalism, but the deadly and insidious vice of 'partiality to self' in his judgments (which Plato, like Butler, regards as 'plain dishonesty').

Since it is, after all, men and not gods with whom the statesman has to concern himself, and—as even Kant was careful to recognize—the desire for a pleasant existence is universal in humanity, the ethical preamble ends with a consideration of our 'interested obligation to virtue'. Plato, unlike Hedonists of the type of Mill, rests the case for the superiority of virtue to vice on ground entirely independent of 'hedonic consequences'. But he is fully ready to add that virtue is not only more appropriate to the 'dignity of human nature' than vice; it is also, in point of fact, attended by a 'surplus of pleasures over pains', if once the rules for calculating the respective 'lots' of pleasures and pains are correctly formulated and the sum worked right. The rules are that we desire pleasure and have an aversion to pain; the state of absence of both is not positively desired, but is preferred to pain. A balance on the side of pleasure is positively desirable, a balance on the side of pain undesirable; an exact counterpoise of the two leaves us indifferent, though we should acquiesce in it by preference to a balance on the side of pain. The 'dimensions' to be considered in computing the items of the account are 'number' and 'size' (i.e. frequency, duration, intensity). Now if we compare the life corresponding to each of the four commonly recognized 'cardinal virtues' with that answering to its contrary vice, we find that there is less excitement in the first than in the second; its pleasures, and its pains also, are less intense. But the pleasures of virtue are both more frequent and more lasting than the pains, the pains of vice more lasting and more frequent than those of virtue. A man of judgment will not overrate excitement, and on this ground he would pronounce that even in respect of 'hedonic consequences' virtue really has the advantage over vice; the way of the transgressor really is hard, though Plato is careful not to confuse its hardness with its moral badness.

We find ourselves at last, as we are approaching the middle of Plato's Fifth Book, on the threshold of the work of actual social and political construction. The construction itself will exhibit a twofold character. We have to provide (*a*) a systematic body of *legislation*, (*b*) an *executive* of magistrates and official boards to carry this legislation into effect. The magistrates are, so to say, the warp, the general population the woof, of the fabric the statesman will have to weave, and the threads of the warp must be the stronger of the two; the executive must be constituted in a way which will ensure that its members shall be men of tested superiority of understanding and strength of character. In the subsequent elaboration of details, the legislation and the provision of an executive naturally proceed, in the main, *pari passu*; each principal set of regulations for the life of the community is accompanied by a consideration of the official machinery by which it can be satisfactorily enforced. But before we can proceed with either part of our task in detail, there are certain outstanding features of social organization which we must take as fixed once and for all and permitting of no modification, and the second and larger half of Book V is concerned with the specification of these social 'invariants'.

First of all, in this static and agrarian community, the number of households, or 'hearths', must be kept constant, to ensure that no grave social revolution shall arise from either over-population or under-population. Over-population would lead to unrightful expansion at the cost of neighbours, under-population to inadequacy to national self-defence. Of course, the number of households necessary and sufficient in an actual case will depend on the size of a state's territory, but for purposes of illustration, it is taken hereafter to have been fixed at 5040. (The choice of the number is based on the practical ground that it has been formed by multiplying together the successive integers from 1 to 7, and thus is divisible by every integer less than 10, as well as by 12. This is an important practical point because it may be desirable for various purposes to divide the population into more than one set of groups constituted on different bases, and it is purely for illustration of this advantage that the particular number 5040 is chosen.)

Next, there are practical reasons why the basis of our society should not be 'communistic'; the private family and its property will have to be fundamental institutions, and in this respect a feasible ideal for realization by ordinary humanity will depart from the Utopia of the *Republic*. The aged Plato is reluctant to make this concession, as he shows by repeating his earlier doctrine that there should be no private interests whatever in a perfect society; there, the very phrase 'my own' should not be heard. But such a condition of existence, we are now told, is one for 'gods or sons of gods', not for common flesh and blood. For ordinary humanity we must fall back on a system of universal 'peasant proprietorship'. Each household will have its strictly inalienable 'estate', which must be handed down undivided to a single heir in each generation, and this will be made a point of religion. The heir will be a son chosen as fittest for the position by his father; daughters will be provided for by marriage, and to ensure that they shall not miss this provision, it will be the law that dowries may neither be offered nor accepted. The working of the system obviously requires that the average family shall be one son and one daughter, and Plato tries to secure this by encouraging adoptions on the part of citizens who have no sons, or have been bereaved of their sons. Tendency to over-population, if it appears, will be met, in case of need, by the sending out of colonies, and unavoidable depopulation from unforeseen epidemics and the like, by a reluctant incorporation of new settlers.

Economic inequalities cannot be altogether prevented, but they may be kept within reasonable bounds by a series of wise regulations. The inalienable patrimonies will, in the first instance, be made as nearly as possible of equal value, and a careful exhaustive survey of the territory, marking their boundaries, must be preserved in the public archives. Commercialism will be strictly checked by a regulation based on Spartan practice and recommended again at the beginning of the nineteenth century by Fichte in his *Geschlossener Handelsstaat*, a work akin in many ways to the *Laws*. The state will have its own currency, which must be one of tokens with no intrinsic value, and it will be illegal in a citizen to own foreign currency. Credit will be prohibited—a device for checking the rise of inequalities of fortune already mentioned in the *Republic*—and, as we want men to live by their own exertions, not on the automatic return of investments, and still less by 'speculation', there will be no toleration of lending on interest. It follows that such differences in 'personal' property as can arise under such restrictions will, in the main, be due to the legitimate exercise of intelligence and industry. They should, however, be further kept within limits by a device suggested to Plato by Solon's division of the Athenians into four property-classes. Plato proposes a similar division, the fourth, or poorest class, possessing nothing beyond their patrimony, the first or richest being allowed to own four times the annual yield of the patrimony. Any increment of wealth beyond this upper limit will be escheated to the Treasury, or, as we should say, subject to an income-tax of one hundred per cent. It will be found inevitable that certain important executive posts should be reserved for members of the wealthiest classes, and we shall thus, though reluctantly, have to allow a man's 'stake in the country' as well as his personal qualities, some influence in the distribution of offices.

For administrative purposes the population should be divided into twelve tribes, and the 'capital' into twelve corresponding districts, in order that various administrative duties may rotate conveniently through all these divisions in the course of the year. Consequently, care will be taken to see that the total real and personal wealth of these tribes is as nearly equal as possible, the capital will be situated in a central position, and every patrimony will be divided into one half situated closer to, and another half more remote from it; in the combination of these 'half-sections' to form patrimonies everything will be done to ensure the utmost possible equality. A further point, on which Plato was apparently the first to insist, is that, to prevent small dishonest gains, the state must insist on a rigorous standardization and inspection of all coins, weights, and measures.

With the Sixth Book we come at last to the constitution of the most important magistracies and administrative boards. The most important of all ordinary magistracies is that of the νομοφύλακες, or 'Curators of Law', a body which Plato has adopted from Athenian practice, but with great extension of its powers. It is to consist of thirty-seven members of proved intelligence and character, who must be over the age of fifty and below that of seventy. Their functions are to watch over the interests of the law in general, to keep the register of properties, and penalize and 'black-list' citizens guilty of fraudulent concealment of income, to act alone, or in concert with others, as judges in the trials of grave offences. They are to be elected (by votes given in writing and signed with the voter's name as a safeguard against electoral irresponsibility) by a process which has several stages. The number of thirty-seven is got by allowing three representatives to each 'tribe', and adding an odd man to prevent equal division of opinions.

The 'representative chamber' of the scheme, as we may call it, is the Executive Council. Its function is not legislation, but the issuing of administrative decrees, and it is elected by a process ingeniously devised to give all property-classes equal representation, while excluding class friction and 'wire-pulling'. In the first stage of the election an equal number of representatives are chosen from all four classes, but with the provision that while members of the richer classes are bound under a penalty to vote for the representatives of all four, the poorest class are free, if they please, to abstain from voting in the choice of their own representatives. The effect would be that the votes of the poor would have a preponderating effect at this stage in the selection of the representatives of the rich, those of the rich in the choice of representatives of the poor. The unduly 'class-conscious' member of any section would thus have little chance of election. In the second stage the number of the elected from each class is reduced to one-half, by a vote compulsory on all citizens. Finally, half of the names which have survived this stage of the proceedings are chosen by lot, and we are thus left with a Council of three hundred and sixty members, drawn in equal numbers from each property-class, who may fairly be presumed to be capable of working together harmoniously for the general good, one-twelfth of the whole body forming the acting committee for each month of the year. Bodies of minor importance whose constitution and functions are dealt with are the Urban Commissioners and Rural Commissioners (ἀστυνόμοι and ἀγρονόμοι), of whom the former are answerable for the maintenance of order within the capital, and the proper condition of its streets and buildings, the latter for the general good order of the rural districts, and the Commissioners of the Market (ἀγορανόμοι). Provision has also to be made for the military and religious needs of the state by careful regulations for the appointment of cavalry and infantry officers of various grades, and priests and other functionaries of both sexes for the numerous temples, 'chapels', and shrines of the city. More characteristic of Plato than the provisions under these heads (which are largely taken, with suggestions for improvements, from the actual practice of Athens) are the regulations which follow upon them for the State appointment of functionaries to supervise education in 'music' and 'gymnastic', and to preside over public competitions in both, as well as of the Minister of Education, who, as has been already said, is the most important and responsible public servant of all. To secure the fitness of this 'Prime Minister' for such a post, it is laid down that he must be a man of over fifty with children of his own, and shall be elected, for a term of five years, out of the body of 'Curators of Law' by the votes of all the rest of the magistrates. This preliminary enumeration of indispensable officials ends with some weighty remarks about the importance of the 'temporary magistracy' with which the members of a jury are invested in the law-courts; the detailed provisions by which Plato hopes to make the rendering of justice a more solemn, responsible, and considered procedure than is possible under the Attic system of large popular dicasteries are reserved for a later stage in the argument. We turn next to consideration of the actual legislative code by which the life of a morally healthy society should be regulated.

Since the foundation of social order in the community is a

wholesome family life, and marriage is the institution upon which the family depends for its inception, Plato's 'legislation' begins with the regulation of *marriages*. It is fundamental that marriage should be regarded as a solemn duty to society, and that public duty should be a man's principal guide in the selection of a wife for himself or a husband for his daughter, and this gives a profounder reason for the prohibition of dowries of which we have already spoken. It is also a reason why extravagant expenditure on wedding festivities and all irresponsible feasting and unseemly merriment on such occasions should be repressed. The procreation of children is a solemn duty to religion and society and is not to be taken in hand 'lightly or wantonly, to satisfy men's carnal lusts and appetites'. Incidentally also the peace of the household requires us to lay down from the first a right rule for the treatment of *servants*. The right rule is that, for the sake of both parties, a master must be even more scrupulously fair and just in his treatment of his servant than he is in his behaviour to his own equals, but must be no less careful not to compromise his position as master by unbecoming familiarities or indulgences; his word must be law to the servant. Again, the right note of seriousness must be struck from the very beginning of married life. The early days of marriage must not be spent as a prolonged 'honeymoon' holiday. Not only must the young husband take his place daily at the public table with other men, but women also must be taught to live constantly under the eye of the society to which they belong. Since they are morally frailer than men, they, even more than their husbands, must be safeguarded by knowledge that their daily life is open to public inspection. They also must have their public table, though no such institution has been tried even at Sparta, and such control of the 'private life' of the weaker sex has been generally believed impossible. The rudiments of civilized morality can only be attained by the effective control of the keenest primitive appetites, hunger, thirst, sex, and the control will not be effective unless it extends equally to both sexes. The 'civilization of woman by man' is therefore an imperative social task.

Since the married pair are to regard it as a bounden duty to society to present it with worthy offspring, it is next proposed to institute a board of ladies, appointed by the magistrates, who will supervise the conduct of a married couple in this matter, and have a general control over such parties for the first ten years of their married life. This control will be exercised in the interests at once of morality and of eugenics. The board will counsel married people against heedless propagation, and if marriages remain sterile will arrange for their dissolution on equitable terms. It will act under the 'curators' as a conciliator in conjugal dissensions, and there will be penalties for those who are contumacious to its remonstrances. It will also take care that serious violations of conjugal fidelity are penalized. Finally, the state will be careful—as no actual Greek city of Plato's time was—to keep an accurate public record of all births and deaths; such a record is absolutely necessary if there is to be proper observance of the laws fixing the age for marriage, military service, qualification for the various official posts. The age for marriage is fixed by Plato himself as between thirty and thirty-five for men, between sixteen (or according to a later passage, eighteen) and twenty for girls; a man's liability to military service is, as at Athens, to begin at twenty and cease at sixty; if women are given 'war work'—a point to which Plato will return later on—it should be after they have borne their children, and before they reach fifty. No man under thirty, or woman under forty, should be appointed to any office.

With Book VII we reach Plato's most careful and final treatment of the social problem in which he was more interested than any other, that of universal *education*. The unfortunately better-known treatment of *Republic* III is a mere sketch in comparison with this more mature discussion. There must, of course, be public supervision from the outset; nothing must be left to the caprice of the individual householder, and the work cannot be taken in hand too early, since it is in the initial stages, when an infant body and mind are most readily plastic, that wrong treatment will do most mischief. Plato, in fact, begins 'education' even before birth by laying it down that it is the duty of the expectant mother to take all the exercise required for the well-being of the child in her womb. When the infant has been born, the authorities must see to it that the nurse gives it all the air and exercise needful, and especially that it is kept from hurting itself by walking too early; it must, before everything else, 'grow straight'. The general principle to be observed is that a baby should live as though it were 'always at sea'; it must be dandled and danced, and must be kept from being frightened by being sung to. (This is meant to lay the first foundations of brave and steadfast *moral*.) Also a baby must be kept placid, and not allowed to become fretful or passionate. (This is meant as a basis for the development of *sophrosyne*.) At the age of three, children may begin to receive judicious correction, and will take to playing various games. They should be left to invent these earliest games for themselves, but should, from three to six, be brought daily to play with one another under the superintendence of ladies appointed by the magistrates, who will thus see to it that their nurses are bringing them up properly. At six lessons may be begun, and the girls will be segregated from the boys. The boys must be taught to ride and to use such weapons as bows, darts, and slings, and the girls should be taught as much of the same things as is possible, care being taken that all the children are trained to use either hand indifferently. As this training in 'gymnastic' advances, it will specialize in the two branches of dancing and wrestling. Of wrestling we may note that only the stand-up sort which is useful as training for warfare has any educational value; 'trick' wrestling is useless and should not be encouraged. Similarly, the dancing which is specially appropriate is the dance in armour, which has its value as preliminary preparation for future military training.

Music—the earliest vehicle for the training of taste and intelligence—requires fuller treatment. Plato accordingly repeats what he had already said in Book II about the 'imitative' character of music, and the danger of unwholesome innovations in musical fashions. It is now made a function of the 'Curators of Law' to see that the desirable types of musical composition are invested with the sanction of religion, and that no innovation upon them is tolerated. Tragedy is thus, as in the *Republic*, banished from Plato's society. The State cannot permit the festivals of its gods to be polluted by choruses who are declaiming against the conduct of these very gods and wailing in a fashion only in place in a funeral dirge. Or, to put the point more generally, the legislator will say to the dramatist: 'I too am busied in the making of a drama of real life in which the actors are the citizens of the State themselves, and I cannot permit any competition by stage-plays composed in a different spirit and inculcating very different lessons.'[1] Poets must be made to understand that their work is prayer, and that, since they often do not

[1] Compare 800 *c* with 817 *b*.

themselves know what are the true blessings for which we should pray, they must go to the law for the knowledge. The poet must not be allowed to circulate any verses which have not first had the approval of the Curators. It will be the State's duty to compile a suitable anthology of new and old poetry, and the compilers must be men of sound taste who have already reached the mature age of fifty, if the young are to be imbued with the right taste for austere and high art. (Thus Plato, in the *Laws*, is the first author of the proposal that the State should impose a 'censure' on literature, as of so many other proposals which were only to be put in practice, for evil or good, in much later ages.) He now proceeds with the details of the education to be built up on this basis of sound aesthetic and moral taste, to design, as he puts it, the ribs of the vessel of which he has already laid down the keel. The importance and novelty of the regulations he is on the point of introducing explains his emphatic repetition of the thought that, even if human life is no more than a game for God's entertainment, our business, as the living pieces in the game, is to play it well, and that this means that peace, not war, is our great business, because it is only in peace that we can devote ourselves to the chief concern of life, *education*.

If we are serious with education, we shall need *schools* with proper buildings, adequate grounds, and expert teachers. As these teachers will need to receive regular salaries from the State for their support, in fact, will need to live by a profession, they must, in accord with Hellenic sentiment which Plato shares, be aliens.[1] And daily attendance at these schools will have to be compulsory for both sexes. (We shall not realize the full novelty of the proposals which are being made here if we take them to be mere repetition of the demand familiar from the *Republic* that education shall be a matter of public concern and shall be extended to both sexes. What the *Laws* adds, as an entirely new conception, is, as Burnet has said, the notion of the *secondary school*, a permanent establishment for the higher education of the young by a duly organized and co-ordinated staff of expert teachers provided with all requisite equipment and collected in one establishment. Such schools first meet us in history as actual institutions of the Macedonian age, and presumably their appearance is due to the influence then wielded by members

[1] They must come from other Hellenic cities. It is not meant they that will be 'barbarians'.

of the Academy as the recognized authorities in education and jurisprudence. The thoroughgoing systematization of secondary education is thus an ideal directly derived from Plato.) We should not let ourselves be disturbed by attacks on our proposals for the education of *girls* as paradoxical: there are parts of the world where the outdoor labour supposed by Athenians to be so peculiarly 'man's work' is regularly done by women, just as the experience of Sparta shows that women can wrestle, if they are trained to do so, though even the Spartan women are not trained, as we shall expect ours to be, to be of real service for national defence. We shall insist that the women of the city must at least be able, in case of necessity, to repel raiders from its walls.[1] Since the economic scheme of our community ensures abundance of leisure to all citizens, it must be understood that this leisure is not to be wasted in lust and laziness, but filled with the strenuous activities of a life directed towards the fullest bodily and mental achievement. The citizens will be expected to rise early, and waste no precious hours in unneedful sleep. For this reason public as well as private business should be transacted in the first hours of the day, and boys should be taken to school before daybreak. A school-boy is the most unmanageable of all young animals, just because he has in him a 'spring of intelligence', which does not run clear as yet. Hence, special attention must be paid to his *moral*. As to the subjects of education, *arithmetic* enough must be learned for the ordinary business of life, elementary *astronomy* enough to understand the Calendar, and enough of *music* to know how to tune one's lyre, and these studies, with reading and writing, will suffice up to the age of sixteen, if we allow the first three years of this period for the reading and writing, and the second three for the learning of the lyre, care being taken that the sharp boys are not allowed to push on too fast, or the dull permitted to lag behind. The only difficult problem during these years is the selection of suitable prose reading (verse has been already dealt with). Sound books on law and morals may, of course, be read, but there is a difficulty about other kinds of prose. (The difficulty is that, in Plato's time, the available prose consisted for the most part of the works of Ionian men of science, and for reasons presently to be explained, the moral

[1] There is an evident allusion to the panic-stricken behaviour of the Spartan women when Epaminondas was threatening Sparta after the battle of Leuctra, recorded also by Aristotle (*Pol.* 1269 *b* 37 ff.).

and religious tone of this literature is unwholesome.) The whole problem will therefore be remitted to the Minister of Education, acting with the advice of experts nominated by himself.

Over and above the more elementary studies just enumerated there remain, as subjects for 'higher education', three branches of knowledge in which all free men ought to have some proficiency, *arithmetic, geometry, astronomy* (going beyond the very rudimentary knowledge required for understanding the Calendar). One cannot expect many young people to attain a really advanced standard in these subjects, but we may require all our pupils to learn at least as much as is commonly acquired in Egypt without any difficulty. In Egypt there are games which teach the players to discover the factors of numbers and to manipulate fractions, and we may use problems of this kind to lead up to the recognition of the existence of 'incommensurable' lengths, areas, and volumes, a subject on which even the dabblers in mathematics among the Greeks are discreditably ignorant. (The suggestion is thus that one subject to be included in secondary education in the later 'teens' should be 'irrational magnitudes', 'algebra up to quadratic equations', as the phrase is nowadays.) Astronomy should also be pursued far enough to give a proper understanding of the uniformity of the movements of the planets and of their true relative velocities in their orbits.[1] Plato's secondary education has thus a scientific and not a humanistic foundation. We should, of course, remember that it could not well have been otherwise; the Greeks were not linguists, and if they had been, could not have found much literature other than their own to repay study. A humanistic 'higher education' in such conditions would have been predestined to superficiality. The book ends with an awkwardly-placed section on the value of *field-sports* as an educative discipline. The only field-sport Plato would encourage is the sort of hunting which involves active exertion and endurance, the chase proper. Netting and snaring, and for a different reason, sea-fishing, should be prohibited.

The contents of the Eitght Book are a little difficult to classify. Provision is first made for the placing of the whole daily life of the society under the religious sanction by providing each month and day with its appropriate ritual of *worship*. Since

---

[1] On the precise correction of current astronomical theory hinted at here see the note *in loco*, at *Laws,* 822 *a.* Cf. also Burnet, *Greek Philosophy,* *Part I.* 345-9.

the athletic and musical sports and contests for which provision has already been made will, of course, be part of this
worship, this provides an opportunity for laying down regulations for the contests which will mark special festivals, as well
as for the regular monthly military exercises by the militia.
Plato would have the more special 'contests' take the place
filled in actual contemporary life by the great pan-Hellenic
'games', but would reconstruct the programme of events.
All the competitions should be in exercises which have a real
military value, particularly in rapid evolutions in full military
accoutrement, and, since these sham fights are to be a training
for the real thing, they should involve actual danger.   Plato's
principles require that girls shall take their part in all these
performances so far as their physique will allow; but he admits
himself unqualified to make any more specific recommendation
on this head.

These remarks lead up to an important matter of ethical
principle upon which Plato lays very great stress.   Is there
not real danger of a relaxed *sexual morality* in a society where
the young men and women have ample leisure from severe
toil and associate so freely in 'sports' and other pursuits?
Plato's view is that there is no danger if we can but establish
the right social tradition.   The right rule is that 'homosexual'
relations must be absolutely suppressed as unnatural, and the
normal sexual impulse confined strictly within the bounds of
monogamous matrimony.   He admits that most persons will
think the proposal Utopian, but urges that they are mistaken.
The example of famous athletes shows that strict and lasting
continence is possible, and we may fairly expect our citizens
to do as much for the crown of virtue as boxers have often
done for an Olympic garland.   The complete repression of
incestuous desire in civilized society shows how effectual the
moral and religious sanction can become, and the problem is
therefore the simple one of creating the same sort of social
tradition against fornication as already exists against incest.
Even if we never quite attain this ideal, we may at least
hope to attach a stigma of disgrace to all detected irregularity.
Plato's rule in matters of sex is thus precisely what the half-
educated among us reject as the 'ascetic' Christian standard,
and this ought not to astonish us.   No serious Greek moralist
ever took the 'romantic' view of sexual relations.[1]   The

[1] See the admirable remarks of E. R. Bevan, *Christianity* (Home University Library), p. 53 ff.

physical conjunction itself was looked on wholly unsenti-
mentally as a merely animal function in which a man temporarily abdicates his personal dignity and becomes grossly
ludicrous, though in practice, in view of the insistence of the
appetite, such self-forgetting received an easy indulgence.
The attitude of Rabelais towards such things is more in
keeping with Hellenic feeling than the *erotomania* of Swinburne
or the sentimentalism of Shelley. In the demand Plato makes
for continence he is only asking that his countrymen shall
make their practice conform to recognized moral theory;
there is no hint in anything he says of the distinctively
Christian conception of the sanctification of bodily functions
themselves to a spiritual end.

The remainder of *Laws* VIII, now that the topic of the personal conduct of citizens has been disposed of, is taken up
with a consideration of the most important regulations dealing
with *torts* and disorders likely to arise in an agrarian community, and their prevention. Under this head are considered
such matters as encroachments on boundaries, diversion of
water-courses, the ownership of stray animals, and we are
given a significant hint (843 *e*) that the provisions introduced
are largely borrowed from those of existing Attic law. The
illustrative examples used to elucidate the principles on which
Plato desires to lay stress are often the same which we meet
again in Justinian's *Institutes*, and later still in Grotius's
de Jure Belli et Pacis. In this connection we have also a
discussion of the regulation of *markets*, and the terms upon
which aliens may be allowed to practise an industry. The
main object of the proposed regulations of the market is to
secure that all transactions shall be on the basis of immediate
payment and that there shall be no 'higgling' about prices.
The seller is to have his fixed price and to take neither more
nor less. Plato's object, like Ruskin's in *Fors Clavigera*, is
not so much to keep the seller from asking too much as to
prevent him from getting rid of inferior wares, at a pretended
'sacrifice'. Aliens are to be allowed to enter the territory
freely, without being required, as at Athens, to pay any poll-
tax, provided they have an industry by which to support
themselves, and are willing to obey the laws of the State,
but they must normally depart with all their property after
twenty years; right of permanent settlement will be granted
only as a reward for special services done to the State. (It
must be remembered that it is a consequence of the previous

prohibition of trade to Plato's citizens that *all* industry will be in the hands of aliens; the citizen population will consist entirely of land-owners and their 'hands'.)

With the Ninth Book we come to *criminal jurisprudence*, and it is part of Plato's high originality that the distinction between criminal law and the civil law of torts is made for the first time on a clear and intelligible principle. The fundamental distinction which Plato misses in all existing legal procedure is that between a *tort*, the mere infliction of loss or *damage*, which can be sufficiently met by an award of *compensation*, and a *crime*, the violation of a *right*, which requires that the offender should, besides making good any loss he has occasioned, suffer a *penalty*. The defect charged here on Attic and Hellenic procedure is that in the place of this vital distinction it sets another which is not adequate for judicial purposes, that between the voluntary and involuntary causing of damage. Plato regards this distinction as philosophically vicious, in view of the Socratic thesis, which he fully accepts, that *all* wrong-doing is in the last resort due to error, and so involuntary. But apart altogether from the issues raised by the Socratic 'paradox', the distinction, as he is careful to point out, is in any case not the one relevant for the purpose of the jurist. In deciding whether a case before the courts is one for mere award of compensation or for the infliction of a penalty, the vital question is not whether the defendant has acted voluntarily or not, but whether he has merely caused loss or violated a right. Until this point is grasped, it is impossible to draw any clear distinction between a civil action and a criminal prosecution. Naturally, when the distinction between a tort and a crime has been once made, the further subdivision of crimes according to their gravity requires the distinction between a criminal act done with intent to commit the particular violation of right, and one done with intent to commit a lesser, or possibly a graver, offence. (Thus bodily wounding may be inflicted with intent to maim, or with intent merely to inflict a disfigurement, or with intent to kill, and each of these crimes, to be punished justly, requires a different sentence.) Hence in the details of his criminal code Plato is careful to take into account the precise nature of the culprit's presumable intention, as well as the distinction between the crime of sudden violence, committed under provocation or emotional excitement, and the premeditated crime of violence, and between both and the crime of craft. He has also to allow for differences in the status (as citizen, resident alien, slave) of criminal or victim, or of both. In effect, the section of the *Laws* which opens with Book IX is plainly meant as a model of a really scientific criminal jurisprudence, covering all the main branches of violation of public and private right.

In the selection of penalties for various offences, what strikes a reader familiar with actual Attic practice most forcibly is the comparative frequency of the penalty of death for the more serious offences, and the still greater frequency of fairly long terms of imprisonment. Death was not a usual penalty at Athens, except for certain grave offences against the State, and imprisonment of a citizen, except in the form of temporary detention of an offender sentenced to a fine, was as good as unknown. The frequency of imprisonment for a year or longer in Plato's code is, from the Athenian point of view, though not from ours, a singularity. The penalty of death, we must remember, is not, on Plato's own principles, really the 'extreme penalty'. He regards it as a more merciful procedure to dismiss the 'incurable' offender from the world than to let him linger on in a state of moral wickedness, and in the degradation and misery of an imprisoned convict. A modern reader is likely to be unfavourably impressed both by the free use made of corporal punishments, particularly when the offender is an alien or slave, and the exceptional severity with which all crimes committed by a slave on a free person are treated. We need to bear in mind both that Plato does not share the modern sentimental view of corporal punishment as peculiarly degrading to the victim, and that in any society where the servile status is recognized, crimes committed by a slave on the free have something of the character of mutiny. The list of crimes actually dealt with in *Laws* IX opens with certain grave offences against the State as a whole, which are all to be visited with death when the culprit is a citizen: *sacrilege, high treason* in the form of direct attempts to subvert the constitution, *treasonable practice* with the foreign enemy. They are to be tried by a court composed, much on the model of the Athenian Areopagus, of the 'Curators of Law' and the magistrates of the preceding year, and miscarriages of justice are provided against by the provisions that every member of the court must declare his personal judgment on the case, and that the proceedings, unlike those of an Athenian trial, must be spread over three days. Grave crimes against the *person* of the individual citizen are next treated in a descending order of magnitude, *homicide, maiming, wounding* with intent to kill, bodily *assault*.

In *Laws* X, historically in many ways the most significant part of the whole work, Plato appears as an innovator in a twofold way. The book is the foundation of all subsequent 'natural' theology,[1] the first attempt in the literature of the world to *demonstrate* God's existence and moral government of the world from the known facts of the visible order. It contains also the first proposal ever made, so far as we know, to treat erroneous beliefs about God and the unseen world as crimes, and to erect an inquisition to suppress 'heretical pravity'. At Athens, as in other ancient societies, 'impiety', that is overt disrespect to the established *cultus*, was, of course, a serious offence, but it seems clear that no mere expression of opinion about such matters was regarded as criminal. The treatment of Socrates himself is a striking illustration of this point. It is plain that the real offence of Socrates in the eyes of the democrats who brought him to trial was his supposed *incivisme*. This is what was meant by the 'corruption of the young' alleged against him. The real meaning of the further charge of 'practising novel religious rites' seems never to have been explained by the prosecutors themselves, and the one thing which can be said about it with any confidence is that it is not a charge of holding 'heretical *opinions*'. Moreover, as we learn from Plato himself, Socrates came near being acquitted, and could clearly have made sure of it if he had been willing to adopt a more deferential tone in his 'defence'. Plato could become the author of the proposal to 'persecute' for opinions precisely because he held that there are certain beliefs which are poisonous to the moral life of society, and that these beliefs can be proved to be false. His position in the matter is precisely that to be taken up later by the medieval Christian Church, except that he appeals to science and not to an authoritative supernatural revelation. Hence it is difficult, if one grants his premisses, that certain beliefs are known to be at once false and morally poisonous, to dispute his conclusion that the State is false to its duty if it allows the poison to be disseminated.

---

[1] The adjective *natural* in this connection meant, in the first instance, simply *philosophically true*. The implied contrast is not with supernatural revelation, but with the imaginative fictions of poetic mythology and the socially useful fictions embodied in the religious Calendar of the State. The *name* is directly due to the great Roman antiquary, M. Terentius Varro, for whose views, see Augustine, *de Civ. Dei*, VI, 5.

The particular beliefs which are of this poisonous kind, and tend, if left unrepressed, to issue in practical evil living, are, according to Plato, three: (1) simple *atheism*, the denial that there are gods of any kind, a doctrine which he treats as identical with the 'naturalistic' theory that the world, including the minds in it, is the product of the purposeless movements of corporeal elements; (2) the doctrine that there are gods, but that they are wholly *indifferent* to human conduct—deism, as we might now call it; (3) the doctrine that there are gods and that they exercise a judgment on men's conduct, but that the impenitent sinner can *escape the judgment* by prayers and sacrifices. Of the three, the first, simple atheism, is morally the least reprehensible, the third far the worst. It is better to believe in no God at all than to believe in careless gods, and better to believe in careless gods than to believe in venal gods. Plato's own conviction is that he can demonstrate the falsity of atheism, though the demonstration is neither brief nor easy, and that the further refutation of the two morally graver heresies is a simple matter when once the existence of gods, or of a God, has been established.

Before proceeding to the refutation of the atheist, it is necessary to show that we understand his position and the motives for his incredulity. Plato's view is that atheism is the product of two historical factors, the corporealism of the early Ionian men of science, who assumed that the order of nature can be accounted for on 'mechanical principles' without any appeal to intelligent design or purpose, and the 'sophistic' theory of the purely conventional and relative character of moral distinctions. Both doctrines, he holds, will be completely refuted if he can show that all the 'motions' of body are caused by prior 'motions' of soul; in that case 'artifice', intelligent purpose, will actually be the source of both 'nature' and 'chance'; it will be impossible to maintain that the great fundamental categories of a rational morality are merely the 'subjective' illusions of beings who are themselves 'products of unguided evolution'. What has to be shown is, in fact, to put it quite simply, that minds or souls, not bodies, are 'what there is to begin with' (892 c).

The proof that the order of nature itself presupposes intelligent guidance turns upon an analysis of the notion of κίνησις, *motion* or *process*. The all-important point is that all motion is of one of two kinds; it is either 'motion which can move other things but cannot set itself moving', i.e. *imparted* or *communicated* motion, or 'motion which can move itself as well as other things', that is, *self-originated* motion. And it is clear that, in the order of causality, merely communicated motion presupposes, at however many removes, self-originated movement of something as its source. Now when we see anything which clearly exhibits self-originated motion, we always say that that thing is *alive* (ἔμψυχον), or, what comes to the same thing, that there is ψυχή, *soul*, in it, and these two expressions are strictly equivalent. In other words, the *definition* of soul is simply that it is 'the movement which can originate itself'. To say, as we have just said, that communicated movement implies pre-existing self-originated movement therefore means that the 'motions of soul', that is, 'tempers, wishes, calculations, true beliefs, purposes, memories' are the ultimate sources and causes of all 'mechanical' motions, none of which are self-originating. Soul, or mind, is thus shown to be the cause of all cosmic motion, as had already been argued more briefly in the *Phaedrus* (245 c–e).

Next, to account for the actual movements in the universe there must be more than one soul. (This means that Plato's doctrine is not pantheism but a theism of some kind.) There must be at least two souls in existence, and there may be as many more as are needed to account for the facts. For in the world as we know it there are both order and regularity, and also irregularity and disorder. Hence we cannot account for the facts as one and all due to a single 'best soul'; there must be one or more souls which are not completely wise or completely good. But the study of astronomy shows us that the dominant all-pervasive movements in the universe are strictly orderly and regular; partial disorder is everywhere overruled. Hence the supreme soul must be a perfectly good soul, that is, it must be God. The appeal made to astronomy as the science which most convincingly reveals a perfect wisdom at the heart of the world-order, an appeal which reminds us, with differences, of Kant's famous sentence about the 'starry heavens above and the moral law within', is further illustrated by some interesting remarks made in Book XII about the difference in spirit between the secularism of the earliest Ionian science and the devoutness characteristic of the Academy. According to Plato, it is precisely because the astronomers of the Academy are so much better acquainted with the strict regularity with which the complicated motions of the heavenly bodies—he is thinking specially of the planets—

for all their complexity conform to very precise mathematical law, that they cannot avoid confessing the presence of a supreme directing intelligence. So long as it could be supposed that a planet really is, as the name suggests, a 'wandering' star, a vagabond of the cosmic spaces, there might be some excuse for the irreligious cosmologist, and more excuse for the popular suspicion that the pursuit of cosmology predisposes to unbelief, but an 'undevout', Academic astronomer would be 'mad'. The true suggestion of a scientific astronomy is that, to put Plato's thought in Kantian terminology, the 'kingdom of nature' is itself part of a wider 'kingdom of ends'.

There are several points in connection with the preceding argument which should be remarked. (1) We note that *evil* as well as good is expressly said to be due to 'souls'. This excludes the doctrine of the later popular Platonism, according to which an independent 'matter' is the ultimate source of evil. (2) God (or the gods) is definitely said to be a soul, and a soul to be 'a motion which originates itself'. The fundamental difference in theology between Aristotle and Plato is precisely that Aristotle insists on getting behind such a source of motion to a still more ultimate '*unmoving*' mover. The activity of Aristotle's God is strictly immanent within himself: it is an activity of unbroken self-contemplation; *out-going* activity is essential to the God of Plato. He is then, as Aristotle's God is not, a Providence, and in a real sense, a Creator. (Whether he is also a Creator in the full Christian sense is a more difficult question, and our answer to it will depend on our interpretation of the difficult and figurative *psychogony* of the *Timaeus*.) In any case Plato is absolutely in earnest in the ascription of purpose, design, and foresight to God. (3) Formally the argument disregards the question, never felt by the Greeks to be specially important, whether there is only one god or many gods. But the recurrence of the phrase, 'the best soul', shows at least that there is, in Plato's theology, one soul which is supreme in the hierarchy of good souls and will therefore be God in a sense in which no other can be called so. The relation between this soul, the one which is responsible for the supreme 'orderly movement' in the universe, and the lesser souls responsible for the minor uniformities, such as the several orbits of the planets, is never explained, any more than Aristotle ever explains the relation between his supreme 'unmoving mover' of the universe and the 'unmoving movers' of the individual

'spheres' of his astronomical system. For the practical purpose of the *Laws* it is found sufficient to argue that the whole
course of events is controlled by a perfect wisdom, without
elaborating a speculative theology in detail. (4) The Platonic
'argument for the being of God' is the so-called 'cosmological
proof' which starts with the fact of the existence of a world
of definite structure as a datum to be explained; the character
of this datum is such that the proof based upon it also in-
corporates within itself the so-called 'argument from design'.
The reasoning is thus *a posteriori* in the scholastic, and only
proper, sense of the phrase, an inference from effect to cause.
There is no trace in Plato, and, I believe, none in Greek philosophy generally, of the strictly *a priori* or 'ontological' contention that the denial of the divine existence is a meaningless
self-contradiction.

The refutation of the two graver heresies now becomes a
very simple task. The belief that God (or the gods) is (or
are) indifferent to our conduct is natural in a mind which
has too much native piety to acquiesce in atheism, but is
shocked by the spectacle of apparently successful wickedness.
Divine indifference could only be due to inability to regulate
human affairs, to conviction that they are too insignificant to
deserve attention, or to the pride which regards itself as
superior to so humble a task. But impotence, ignorance of
the real significance of the apparently trivial, conceit, are all
incompatible with the character of a perfectly good soul.
And we can readily see that the moral government of the world
and everything in it can be sufficiently secured by the establishment of a single very simple law. The identification of
the soul with a self-originating movement has, in fact, incidentally established the imperishability of all souls, as the
Phaedrus had argued. Such souls are imperishable because
they have the sufficient and necessary condition of their persistence within themselves. If we suppose then that God has
established the simple law that souls, so to say, 'gravitate'
towards the society of their likes, it follows at once that, in
the endless succession of lives and deaths, each man's soul
steadily makes its way to the company of the like-minded;
each of us therefore in the end 'does and has done to him'
what it is fitting that such a man should do or have done to
him. This is the 'judgment of God' which it is impossible to
escape. The worst heresy of all, that which represents God
as actually bribed by sacrifice or flattered by formal devotion

THE LAWS OF PLATO

into winking at iniquity, can be set aside still more summarily
as charging the 'best soul' with the immorality of a hireling
shepherd whom the wolf has bribed to connive at the mangling
of the flock.

All this natural theology belongs, of course, not to the
actual law against irreligion, but to its preamble. The
proposed statute itself is a stern one. Overt maintenance of
any of the proscribed doctrines is to be brought to the notice
of the magistrates, and a magistrate neglecting to take action
will himself become liable to prosecution for impiety. The
cases are to be tried before the court already instituted to deal
with capital crimes, and in the case of each heresy a distinction
must be drawn between the minor guilt of the offender who is
otherwise a man of virtuous life, and the worse guilt of the
offender who aggravates his impiety by evil living. The less
guilty 'virtuous heretic' must in every case be confined for
not less than five years in the House of Correction, where he
is to converse with none but members of the 'Nocturnal
Council'—a body to be described more fully in the closing
book of the *Laws*—who will reason with the prisoner on his
errors. A second conviction is always to be followed by
death. For the worst 'infidel' of all, the impostor who trades
on the credulity of simpler folk by founding superstitions and
immoral cults, in which he himself does not believe, Plato
proposes what he regards as a severer treatment. Such men
are to be kept in life-long strict imprisonment in a solitary
'convict prison', where they will be secluded from all human
society; at death they are to be denied burial. In fact,
they are treated as 'dead in law' from the time of conviction.[1]
This law is followed by another, a kind of 'Conventicle Act'
intended to protect society against such religious impostors.
No shrines or sacrifices shall be permitted except those belonging to the public worship of the State; there are to be no
'oratories' in private houses, and all persons wishing to offer
any kind of sacrifice must do so at the public altars, through
the public minister of religion, and with the established ritual.
Only so can society at large be prevented from being implicated
in the impieties of fraudulent 'priestcraft'.

[1] These provisions involve one of Plato's most interesting anticipations
of very modern practice, his proposal for a grading of prisons. He would
have (1) a house of detention for the safe-custody of arrested persons
whose cases have not been disposed of; (2) a house of correction for the
ordinary offender who is serving his sentence; (3) a peculiarly close and
solitary prison for the worst criminals of all. Thus he anticipates the
distinction between the 'cells' the county gaol, and the convict prison.

Book XI is concerned with a series of enactments against less serious offences. It deals in succession with the law of *treasure-trove*, the prevention of dishonesty in *buying* and *selling*, the regulation of *retail trade* and *innkeeping*, the terms on which *piece-work* of all kinds should be contracted for and remunerated. Then follow elaborate regulations about *testamentary dispositions*, succession to an estate where there has been no testament, the *guardianship* of orphans, which is to be carefully controlled by the State, and the treatment of *family dissensions* of various kinds; the law will be particularly stringent in enforcing proper respect for parents and for the aged in general. The next offence to be dealt with is the causing of hurt by *noxious drugs*, with which Plato classes the employment of philtres and charms of all kinds; this last crime might be ignored in a society of perfectly rational beings, but it has to be taken into account in communities where the current belief in the sorcerer's powers makes him dangerous. After a paragraph dealing with *robbery* and *larceny*, Plato proceeds to dwell on the necessity of public enforcement of proper supervision of the *insane* and *imbecile*. The law must hold their sane relatives responsible for their custody. Finally, *begging* must be rigorously suppressed by law, though it must also be recognized as a public duty to see that no one, not even a slave, who is out of employment from no fault of his own shall starve. The book closes with rules about the admissibility of evidence in the courts, and the penalizing of *perjury*. The litigiousness which, as we see from Aristophanes and the orators, was a common Athenian failing, is checked by penalties for *vexatious prosecution*; Plato even makes the offence capital in cases where the prosecutor's motive is shown to have been personal gain. In a similar spirit he proposes to check the abuse of the calling of a professional λογογράφος, or composer of speeches for intending litigants, by making the 'advocate' in vexatious suits liable to the same penalties as his employer. Many of the detailed provisions of this section of the *Laws* can be shown, and more may be suspected, to be founded on the Attic jurisprudence which Plato is trying to correct where he finds it unsatisfactory.

With Book XII we return to the subject of public law. Penalties are imposed for various forms of misconduct on the part of *ambassadors* or public envoys, and *embezzlement* of the public funds—an offence which was always charged on Athenian politicians by their opponents—is struck at by the

enactment that the punishment for so grave a breach of
trust should always be death, irrespective of the amount
of the defalcation.   Then follow injunctions dealing with the
importance of strict military discipline, the penalties to be
enforced for insubordination, the distinctions which may be
awarded for good service, the excuses admissible for failure
to execute military orders, and the creation of a military
tribunal to deal with such matters.

The adequate discharge of duty by all magistrates is to be
secured by adopting the Attic practice of requiring every
magistrate, on the expiry of his term, to submit to an *audit*
(εὔθυνα).   Plato has given special care to the appointment of
the Board charged with the conduct of these audits.   The
members must be over the age of fifty and under seventy-
five, and are to be chosen, with peculiar solemnity, by universal
suffrage, each voter giving his vote for the person whom he
regards as, on his whole record, the best and most capable of
his fellow citizens.   The process is to be repeated until only
the required number of names remain uneliminated.   In the
first instance a board of twelve members will be thus appointed,
afterwards it will be sufficient to elect three new members
annually.   Membership of this Board is the highest honour
which can be conferred on a citizen of Plato's State, and is
attended by exceptional marks of distinction, in particular by
a public funeral.   He is careful, however, to provide for
appeals against its decisions, and requires any member of it
whose action is quashed on such an appeal to be removed
from his post.   Incidentally, in the course of this discussion,
Plato testifies at once to his own high sense of the importance
of veracity and to the shortcomings of Attic practice in the
matter of truth-speaking, by refusing to allow oaths to be
taken by citizens in the course of legal proceedings; the permission of an oath to litigants, he thinks, as mankind go, is
no better than an incentive to the impiety of perjury.

Nothing has been said as yet about the intercourse of our
citizens with the rest of the Hellenic world.   Plato does not
desire to encourage the spirit of 'cosmopolitanism', nor to
expose the national *moral* to the influences of a vast influx
of aliens.   On the other hand he disapproves of the Egyptian
and Spartan churlish antipathy to 'foreigners', and is anxious
that his city shall be kept well abreast all social and intellectual 'progress'.   Accordingly, while he would not allow
foreign travel to citizens before they have reached the age of

fifty, and requires them even then to procure the licence of the State for it, he desires men of a mature age and proved character to visit other societies in quest of any institutions which may be judiciously transplanted. Such travellers must, on their return, make a report of their observations to the 'Nocturnal Council', a kind of standing Committee of Public Safety, which is charged with general supervision of all affairs and required to be in perpetual session. It is a select body composed of the members of the Board of εὔθυνοι, who have just been spoken of, the ten senior Curators of Law, the Minister and ex-Ministers of Education, and an equal number of co-opted younger assessors between the ages of thirty and forty. One of its important duties will be to receive the reports of returning travellers, and exercise its discretion in the introduction of social institutions and of branches of research upon which they have reported favourably. (Thus, for all its self-sufficiency, the city is not to become a moral or intellectual 'backwater'.) Similarly, there will be careful control of the temporary admission of alien visitors into the State. Visitors who come in the course of trade, or on their own private affairs, will be hospitably lodged and protected from injurious treatment, but will not be allowed opportunities of personal intercourse with private citizens beyond what their business makes necessary. But the State will give active encouragement to responsible foreign visitors whose object is to impart or receive lessons in true statesmanship. They will be honoured guests of the nation, and every door will stand open to them.

The pages which immediately follow deal with a variety of legal points. Here, and in the awkward insertion of the section on field-sports at the close of the seventh book, we see more noticeably than anywhere else in the *Laws* evidence that the work has not received its final arrangement. Rules are laid down in rapid succession about the giving of *bail*, the conditions on which one man may search another's house or property for stolen goods, the term of undisputed possession which will create a title by *prescription*, the proper penalties for such different offences as violent interference with the appearance of a party to a law-suit or his witnesses, or of a competitor in the public 'sports', the receiving of stolen goods, the taking of presents by public servants for the performance of their official duties—a crime which Plato would always punish with death. Next comes a law directed against the waste of wealth on a costly and vulgar *religious ritual*. Plato would permit only wood or marble as the material of images used in public worship, and only plain draperies of white as vestments, and would set a strict limit to the sums which may be expended in this way. For household purposes he would allow no images. There remain now only two topics to be treated of to complete the outline of the *corpus juris*. One is the regulation of *procedure* in the case of suits between private citizens. (Such regulations as we have already met were concerned with cases in which the interests of the State itself were concerned.) Plato's object here is to provide a double possibility of *appeal*. He would have such disputed claims referred in the first instance to an arbitrator appointed by the parties. An appeal is to lie, at the discretion of either party, to a local court of the sectional division to which the parties belong, and again from this body to one of the higher courts which have already been instituted, but the penalty incurred if the disputed decision is sustained is increased at each stage. The details of the arrangements which will be necessary we may learn from considering the sound existing precedents in other societies—an indication that here, as elsewhere, Plato is drawing upon Attic practice—and from our own experimentation. Directions are then given for the steps which should be taken to enforce compliance with the decision finally reached. The other matter about which nothing has been said, beyond a very general warning in Book V against waste and ostentation, is the disposal of the bodies of the *dead*. Interment should not be permitted within the walls, nor in any part of the territory which can be used to raise agricultural produce. The monuments erected to the dead must be inexpensive and unostentatious, and provide room only for the briefest of inscriptions. In the interests of the living, funeral expenses will be kept down to a modest sum by statute, and to encourage the true view of the soul as the real self, and discourage superstition, there must be no prolonged lying-in-state of a dead body, and no elaborate and public display of lamentation as it is borne to the tomb. There is to be no 'keening', and the mourners must be outside the walls before day-break.

Plato has now completed the survey of a proposed political constitution with its legal code. But there is still one thing to be done which he regards as of supreme moment. It is not enough that a society should have good laws, unless there is somewhere within that society a competent body charged with incessant vigilance over their perpetuation. There should be in the body politic a member which corresponds in this way to the head, the seat of intelligence and the senses which most directly subserve intelligence, sight and hearing, in the natural body. The peculiarly select 'Nocturnal Council' is manifestly a promising organ for this purpose: its older members, chosen in the way which has been described, may fairly be regarded as the intelligence of the community; the specially gifted younger men whom they co-opt as their assessors should render them the same sort of services which the trained senses of sight and hearing render to an animal's or a man's intelligence in the task of self-maintenance. The 'Nocturnal Council', then, will be charged with unremitting supreme surveillance over the maintenance of the national life. If it is to discharge this trust it must, of course, understand that there is a fundamental unity of aim running through the whole fabric of law and constitution, and it must be under no mistake as to what the one aim which the life of the State has before it is.

Now we know that this single aim of public life is 'complete goodness', and we know again that such goodness manifests itself in four great typical forms (the so-called 'cardinal virtues' of the *Republic* and *Laws*). So it will be impossible to understand the single aim of a rightly ordered social life without understanding how these four things can be one, and this one thing four. The members of the supreme 'Nocturnal Council', therefore, will not be fitted for their responsibilities unless they have been thoroughly trained in the power to 'see the one in the many and the many in the one'. (This is the standing description in Plato of the supreme philosophical discipline for which his formal name is 'dialectic'. The 'dialectician' is just the thinker who can see how a single great principle exhibits itself in a whole system of manifestations without losing its unity, and how a whole varied range of different facts are manifestations of one single principle, and yet are *different* manifestations.) And if the members of our council are to be capable of understanding in this way how *goodness* can be both one and many, they will need to have been systematically trained in the same kind of insight in other fields of knowledge. (Thus, though the name 'dialectic' is not used in the *Laws*, Plato makes exactly the same demand for the thing as he had done in the *Republic*.

It is an error to say he has lowered his intellectual demands, or that he contemplates the possibility of a practical states- manship which is content with an inferior substitute for the insight required of the 'philosophic kings' or 'complete guardians' of his earlier work.) And we may add something more. We must, of course, also demand from the body which is to be the 'sheet-anchor' of our constitution a *godliness* resting on *knowledge*. In other men we may be content with a mere *fides informata* which takes its religion on the State's authority, but not in our ultimate guardians: their religion must be a matter of personal *knowledge*. Now we saw, in our reply to the atheist, that to see the truth of theism a man has to know two things. He must know what the soul is, that it is the 'movement which originates itself and all other movement', and he must know the truths of mathematical astronomy, which *prove* the wisdom and goodness of God. Hence we must require complete mastery of mathematical astronomy, as well as right understanding of the metaphysical status of soul, as an indispensable qualification for member- ship of our supreme council. Consequently our State must provide for an education in science which goes far beyond anything that was contemplated in our remarks about secondary education.

At present we are not even in a position to speak definitely about the particular studies which will be required. (Plato means, as was the fact in the fourth century, that the 'higher mathematics' is making rapid and unforeseeable progress, and for that reason no precise programme can be laid down for it.) But we can at least say that without the highest attainments in the 'new sciences' no man will be intellectually qualified for the work he assigns to his 'Nocturnal Council', and without such a body in the State there is no guarantee for the effective- ness or permanency of the most wisely devised institutions. It is significant that in the closing pages of the book, the name 'curators' or 'guardians' of the law, originally given in Book V to a body of vastly inferior qualifications, is trans- ferred to this new council, much as in the *Republic* the name 'guardians' is first given to all the soldiers of the State and then restricted to the comparatively few who prove intellectually fit for the higher office of 'philosopher-king'. The members of the 'Nocturnal Council', in fact, answer closely in the *Laws* to the 'philosopher-kings' of the *Republic*. The main differ- ence is that in the later work, owing to the great advances which had been made in mathematics in Plato's lifetime, by associates and friends of his own, there has been a considerable rise in the standard of mathematical intelligence which he requires as a condition of reaching the most responsible post in the commonwealth. It is probable, as Burnet has said, that Plato was looking to pure science for more than it has to give, but his convictions were absolutely sincere, and he never wavered in them. It is interesting to find him, in a letter of practical advice written probably when his mind was already engaged on the problems of the *Laws*, telling a correspondent that unless there are persons in a society capable of undertaking the duty of 'sovereign control' of the *moral* of the whole daily life—that is, of discharging the functions he lays on his 'Nocturnal Council'—it is useless to devise laws and institutions for it.[1]

It is certain that the *Laws* is the latest of all Plato's writings, unless we accept as genuine the little dialogue *Epinomis*, declared by its singular title to be meant as a supplement, or appendix, to the major work. It has been common among scholars, for the greater part of a century at least, to depreciate this work, and to ascribe its composition to Plato's pupil, the Academic Philippus of Opus, said by tradition to have been the amanuensis or transcriber of the *Laws*. This ascription is still vigorously maintained by many of the foremost Platonic scholars of Germany in particular, such as C. Ritter, Wilamowitz-Moellendorf, Werner Jaeger, and others. To the present writer, as to a minority of better scholars than himself (e.g. Hans Raeder, Professor Burnet), the alleged evidence against Platonic authorship drawn from vocabulary and diction seems singularly inconclusive, and the charges of inferiority in thought made by many critics to be illusions based on misconception of the writer's real meaning. Frankly, I think it more likely that any increased infelicity of expression is due to advancing years and infirmity on the part of Plato than to maladroit imitation by a disciple. But the reader should be warned that this, though I hope it may yet prove to be the sound, is not the accepted view. In any case, the *Epinomis* seems, from the first, to have been circulated along with the *Laws*, and to have passed through the hands of the personal disciple who gave the larger work to the world, and may therefore be presumed to represent, at least in its main position, the thought of Plato. Its main interest is that it tells us a

[1] *Ep.* XI, 359 *a–b*.

little more, if we can trust it, than we should otherwise know about the advanced mathematical studies demanded at the end of the *Laws* of all aspirants to membership of the 'Nocturnal Council'. The main point is that the whole *corpus* of mathematics must be put on a philosophical basis by the constitution of a thoroughly rational science of number, which will begin with the study of the 'natural integers', and develop from that as a foundation the doctrine of quadratic and cubic surds, as well as that of 'progressions' or series. Scientific geometry and stereometry have really nothing in principle to do with land-surveying and gauging, and the names they bear in ordinary language are therefore ludicrously inapposite. Both are really parts of the science of number, the one dealing with quadratic and the other with cubic surds. A full exposition of the meaning of this remarkable passage is the less necessary, as the reader may be referred to the excellent translation of the *Epinomis* by J. Harward.

The comparative neglect of the *Laws* is really a modern aberration. No work seems to have had a more potent influence on the political thought of ancient philosophers from Aristotle downwards. A great German scholar, recently deceased, once, indeed, made the hasty remark that Aristotle never did more than 'turn over the leaves' of the book. But no one can have known better than Wilamowitz that to 'turn over the leaves' of an ancient papyrus roll was a physical impossibility; a book of the fourth century B.C. had to be read continuously or not at all. That Aristotle had read the *Laws* very thoroughly is shown by frequent echoes of it in his own *Ethics*, and more conclusively still by the treatment of political and educational principles in his *Politics*. Burnet's commentary on the *Nicomachean Ethics* is specially deserving of commendation for the attention given in it to Aristotle's reminiscences of the *Laws*. The elaborate study of the structural growth of the Aristotelian *corpus* which has been so fruitfully initiated within the last two decades by such scholars as Jaeger, von Arnim, Mansion, has, perhaps, so far not yielded many results which can be assumed to be absolutely assured. But it does seem to be already definitely established by these investigations that all the more theoretical part of the *Politics*, the books which treat of the political, economic, educational institutions of the 'ideal' commonwealth, are directly inspired by the *Laws*. Aristotle's 'ideal state' is just the city of the *Laws* made more commonplace and left without its 'sheet-anchor', the 'Nocturnal Council' of God-fearing mathematicians.   No divergence of opinion as to the precise relation between this part of the *Politics* and that in which Aristotle treats problems of *Realpolitik* in the 'positivistic' temper of a Machiavelli affects the trustworthiness of this inference.

Writers of the Hellenistic and Graeco-Roman ages who show knowledge of Plato treat the *Laws* as a perfectly familiar work: some of its great moral and religious utterances, notably the sentences about the 'following of God', with which the general preamble to the legislation is introduced in Book IV, are among the favourite quotations of the Christian Fathers.   In the West, direct acquaintance with the book was inevitably interrupted as the knowledge of Greek died out in the 'Dark Ages'.   But, as I have already said, through the *Politics* of Aristotle the main principles of the Platonic 'constitutionalism' left a deep impress on the political thought of the great men of the thirteenth century.   Direct familiarity with the *Laws* appears again when the revival of learning makes Greek texts once more accessible.   The ill-acquaintance of nineteenth-century writers with the book presents a striking contrast with the knowledge of it habitually shown by the great line of 'Platonizing' divines and moralists who were the chief glory of seventeenth-century Anglicanism.   In the last century itself there is one great and splendid exception to the general neglect of the work in our literature.   To Ruskin, that *anima naturaliter Platonica*, the *Laws* made a special appeal, as we see from the incorporation of long and important passages into *Fors Clavigera*, itself, perhaps, the most Platonic of great modern works on 'politics' in the noble Hellenic sense.

Whether and how far the book has had the effect on the actual practice of legislators for which Plato was hoping is another question.   It has once at least been proposed to put the whole scheme of the *Laws* into operation as it stands. The philosopher Plotinus [1] obtained from the Emperor Gallienus the grant of a ruined city in Campania which he dreamed of restoring under the name Platonopolis, and administering by the 'laws of Plato'.   (This can hardly mean 'on the lines of the *Republic*', since a detailed scheme of law and a definitely constituted body of magistrates are essential to the proposal, and the *Republic* provides for neither.)   Fortunately, more practical advisers persuaded the emperor to withdraw

[1] Porphyry, *Vit. Plot.* 12.

the permission for an adventure with which Plato himself would have had no sympathy.

The synopsis already given will have shown how curiously fertile Plato's work is in suggestions, major and minor, of new constitutional, legal, and educational departures, and how many of these departures have only been put into practice in quite modern times.[1] The 'practical man', in modern times, has, often to his own loss, known little or nothing of the political thought of the ancient world. It is safe to say that most of the 'reforms' which we can find anticipated in the *Laws* have been adopted by later statesmen and lawyers on their own merits without any consciousness that the authority of Plato's name might be invoked for them. It may be doubted, again, whether any recollection of the *Laws* predisposed Christian divines and statesmen to the ominous step of making false theological belief a penal offence, and creating an authority to repress it. No doubt, as Dr. E. R. Bevan has recently said,[2] the influence of Greek philosophy as a whole is very largely responsible for this attitude. If the Old Testament supplied examples of the merciless destruction of idolators, Judaism seems to have known hardly anything of

---

[1] It may be worth while to insert a list, which could probably be extended, of some of the more outstanding original contributions of the *Laws* to 'politics'. I would specify first, as most important:

(1) The clear enunciation of the principles of 'constitutional' or divided sovereignty in Book III.

(2) The provisions of Book VII about the training and education of infants, children, and young persons, which amount to recognition of (*a*) the importance of orthopaedics; (*b*) the principles of the kindergarten; and (*c*) of the higher secondary school.

(3) The definite creation of 'natural theology' in Book X.

(4) The constitution in Book IX of criminal jurisprudence as a distinct branch of law, by the side of the law of civil torts.

To these might be added as of secondary, though still great, importance:

(5) Recognition of the necessity of an official survey and registry of all titles to real estate (Book V),

(6) And of the official enforcement of a uniform standardization of all weights and measures (ibid.).

(7) The gradation of the various prisons of the State (Book X).

(8) The careful regulations dispersed through Books IX, XI, XII, to secure the proper conduct of judicial proceedings, and to prevent hasty and irresponsible verdicts.

(9) The recognition of the public duty of encouraging science shown in the regulations of Book XII about intercourse with other societies. The full measure of Plato's detailed achievement in jurisprudence will only be apparent when some scholar with the requisite specialist knowledge has undertaken the hitherto imperfectly executed task of comparing *seriatim* the provisions of the later books of the *Laws* with the extant remains of Athenian jurisprudence.

[2] *Christianity* (Home University Library), p. 109.

the penalization of opinions or beliefs, as distinct from overt practices or incitement to overt practices. Intolerance of speculative error came to the Church from the philosophical schools, not from the synagogue. But how far this intolerance was simply part of the general atmosphere of the schools, how far it may have been fed by special recollections of Plato's drastic way with the heretic in *Laws* X, is another question. If soluble at all, it could only be answered by a specialist with a knowledge of the literature of the early Christian centuries which the writer of these lines does not possess.

On the other hand, the appearance of the 'secondary school' as a regular institution in the Hellenic cities of the 'Alexandrian' and 'Graeco-Roman' ages at least suggests almost irresistibly that one of Plato's great inspirations must have borne pretty direct fruit. If so, the modern world has to thank Plato for its two most important educational institutions. The Academy was the first 'incorporated' university in the world's history, and continued to be one for nine hundred years, until the Emperor Justinian closed it, as an act of Christian propaganda, in A.D. 529. It seems more likely than not, that the *Lycée* also is the creation of Hellenistic statesmen trained on the principles of the *Laws*.

It is even possible that Plato's work in jurisprudence has at least contributed to the origination of what we call Roman law, and so to the construction of all modern legal systems, though the evidence here is not so complete as we could wish. The way in which the derivation was effected seems to have been, generally speaking, this: The immediate source out of which the Roman lawyers elaborated their science was, as is well known, the edict of the *praetor peregrinus*, which embodied the principles upon which the praetor proceeded in dealing with cases in which one party or both were non-citizens, and therefore not entitled to the application of the cumbrous traditional *jus Quiritium*. These principles, those of the so-called *jus Gentium*, appear to have been borrowed very largely, as was only natural, from the already existing legal systems of the highly developed Greek cities with which the Romans were early brought into contact, and the study of Hellenistic *papyri* is gradually disclosing to us the existence in the Hellenistic age of a large body of law common to Greek cities at large. A widely diffused system of this kind, of course, implies a common source somewhere in a single mind, or in a group of minds working in association and with common inspiration, and it is hard to point to any body existing in the Hellenistic age which satisfies the conditions of a common keen interest in the theory of jurisprudence and a common impulse except the Platonic Academy. In this indirect way, the Roman law, which is either the avowed foundation, or one of the principal constituents, of the existing law of all European peoples, certainly seems to owe its own origin largely to the great philosopher who has been too often mistaken for a kind of 'beautiful but ineffectual angel' blinded by 'excess of light'.

It only remains to explain very briefly the principle upon which the present translation has been made. The text pre-supposed throughout is that of Burnet, for the use of which I am indebted to the proprietors, the Delegates of the Clarendon Press. It has been my aim not to depart from Burnet's text without recording the fact. Where I have thought it no more than an even probability that a departure may be right, I have preferred to acquiesce in the printed text.

I have made constant use of the Latin version of Ficinus, and the excellent commentaries of Stallbaum, C. Ritter, and Dr. E. B. England. I owe numerous suggestions to the very happy passages of translation frequently interspersed in Dr. England's work, of which I have ventured to make the free use I am sure he would have allowed me were he still living. I have naturally consulted the text and rendering of Dr. R. G. Bury (in the Loeb Library). More than once, when I thought I could not better the turn given to a phrase by Dr. Bury, I have allowed myself to follow him. I owe much gratitude to my old friend, Mr. W. L. Lorimer of St. Andrews University, for his encouraging help with the difficult passages.

A. E. TAYLOR.

SELECT BIBLIOGRAPHY

EDITIONS. Complete Works: A. P. Manutius and M. Musurus (Aldine Ed.), Venice, 1513; H. Stephanus and J. Serranus, Paris, 1578; G. Stalbaum, 1850; C. F. Hermann, 1851–3; I. Bekker, 10 vols. (Greek and Latin), 1816–23; J. G. Baiter, J. C. Orelli and A. G. Winckelmann, 21 vols., 1839–1841; R. B. Hirschig and C. E. C. Schneider, 1856–73; M. Schanz, 12 vols., 1875–9; J. Burnet, 5 vols., 1899–1907.

TRANSLATIONS. F. Sydenham, 1759, 1776; T. Taylor and F. Sydenham, 1804; H. Cary and H. Davis, 1848–52, 1900; W. Whewell (Dialogues), 3 vols., 1859–61; B. Jowett (Dialogues), 3rd ed., 1892; H. N. Fowler, W. R. Lamb, R. G. Bury, and P. Shorey, 12 vols. (Loeb Library), with text, 1919–37.

GENUINE WORKS. *Hippias Major, Hippias Minor, Jon, Menexenus, Charmides, Laches, Lysis, Cratylus, Euthydemus, Gorgias, Meno, Protagoras, Euthyphro, Apology, Crito, Phaedo, Symposium, Phaedrus, Republic, Parmenides, Theaetetus, Sophistes, Politicus, Philebus, Timaeus, Critias, Laws.* Separate editions and translations of the foregoing dialogues are numerous. Opinion is divided as to the authenticity of *Epinomis*. It is safe to admit the *Epistles* as genuine, with the exception of I and XII which are undoubtedly spurious. Plato's will (Diogenes Laertius, III. 41–3) is certainly authentic; but the great majority, if not all, of the 32 epigrams attributed to him in the *Greek Anthology* are by other hands.

CRITICAL. F. Zeller: *History of Greek Philosophy*, 1881; W. Pater: *Plato and Platonism*, 1893; E. Barker: *Greek Political Theory: Plato and his Predecessors*, 1918; P. E. More: *The Religion of Plato*, 1921; A. E. Taylor: *Platonism and its Influence*, 1925; *Plato, the Man and his Work*, 1926; R. C. Lodge: *Plato's Theory of Logic*, 1928; C. Ritter: *The Essence of Plato's Philosophy* (trans. E. Alles), 1933; F. H. Anderson: *The Argument of Plato*, 1935; R. L. Nettleship: *The Theory of Education in Plato's Republic*, 1935; R. Demos: *The Philosophy of Plato*, 1939; *Plato's Academy: the Birth of the Idea and its Rediscovery*, 1939; J. Wild: *Plato's Theory of Man*, 1946; G. C. Field: *The Philosophy of Plato*, 1949; N. R. Murphy: *The Interpretation of Plato's Republic*, 1951; Sir W. D. Ross: *Plato's Theory of Ideas*, 1951.

BOOK I

A VISITOR FROM ATHENS; CLINIAS, A CRETAN; MEGILLUS, A LACEDAEMONIAN

[N.B. In the references the small letter after the page number refers to the section and line in Burnet's text.]   Steph.

Ath. To whom is the merit of instituting your laws ascribed, 624 gentlemen? To a god, or to some man?

Clin. Why, to a god, sir, indubitably to a god; in our case to Zeus, in the case of Lacedaemon, to which our friend here belongs, I believe, according to their own story, to Apollo. That is so, is it not?

Meg. Certainly.

Ath. You mean that Minos, just as Homer relates, used to repair to a conference with his father every ninth year,[1] and that his legislation for your Cretan cities was based on his father's oracles?

Clin. So our local story has it. It adds the further detail that Rhadamanthys, the brother of Minos—the name will, of course, be familiar to you—was conspicuous for his justice. Well, as we Cretans insist, it was his ancient administration of our 625 judicial business which earned him this deserved reputation.

Ath. An honourable distinction indeed, and most appropriate to a son of Zeus. But as you and our friend Megillus have both been brought up under such venerable legal institutions, I trust you will not find it disagreeable to spend the time, as we walk this morning, in conversation on questions of politics and jurisprudence. The distance from Cnossus to the cave and chapel of Zeus is, I understand, quite considerable, and there are presumably shady resting-places, such as the sultry season demands, on the way, among the lofty trees, where it will be a comfort, at our age of life, to make frequent halts and entertain one another with discourse. Thus we may reach the end of our long journey without fatigue.

Clin. To be sure, sir, there are groves of prodigious fine,

[1] *Odyssey,* τ 179, ἐννέωρος βασίλεος Διὸς μεγάλου ὀαριστής.

I

tall cypresses farther on, as well as meadows, where we can take a rest.

Ath. I am glad to hear it.

Clin. No doubt you are, but we shall all be gladder still when we come to them. Well, let us make our start, and good luck go with us!

Ath. With all my heart! Come now, tell me, what is the purpose of your laws in prescribing your system of common meals and physical training, and your distinctive accoutrements?

Clin. Why, in the case of my own countrymen, sir, I take the purpose to be very obvious. As you can both see for yourselves, Crete, as a whole, unlike Thessaly, has not a level surface. This is, of course, why the Thessalians rely by preference on cavalry, but we on rapid infantry movements, since with us the ground is uneven and better adapted for training in these manœuvres. On such a terrain a soldier must naturally be lightly accoutred, and not carry a load as he runs; consequently, bow and arrows are felt to be recommended by their light weight. These arrangements, then, have all been made with a military purpose, and it is warfare, if I am to speak my own conviction, which our lawgiver kept in view in all his dispositions. For instance, his reason for establishing the common meals was presumably that he saw that when the whole population are in the field, that very circumstance compels them to take their meals together, through the campaign, for self-protection. He meant, I believe, to reprove the folly of mankind, who refuse to understand that they are all engaged in a continuous lifelong warfare against all cities whatsoever. Hence, if a force must take its meals together in war time, for the sake of self-defence, 626 and post relays of officers and men to act as its guards, the same thing should equally be done in time of peace. In fact, the 'peace' of which most men talk—so he held—is no more than a name; in real fact, the normal attitude of a city to all other cities is one of undeclared warfare. By reflection on these lines you will discover that our Cretan legislator constructed the universal scheme of all our institutions, public and private, with a view to war, and transmitted his laws to us for observance in precisely the same spirit. It was his conviction that there is no benefit to be got from any other possessions or associations, where there is a failure to maintain supremacy in the field; all the advantages of the vanquished pass to the victors.

Ath. Your training, sir, would appear to have given you an admirable insight into the institutions of Crete. But you might be a little more definite on one point. As to your test of a well-constituted city; I understand you to be saying that such a city must be so equipped as to be victorious over its rivals in warfare? Am I right?

Clin. Most decidedly, and I fancy our friend here will be of the same mind, too.

Meg. Why, my good man, what other answer would you expect from any Lacedaemonian?

Ath. Well, possibly this is the right test in comparing cities with cities, but there may be a different test for the comparison of village with village?

Clin. Not at all.

Ath. The same test holds good?

Clin. Certainly.

Ath. Well, and when we compare one household in our village with another, and one man with one other man? The same test still holds?

Clin. The very same.

Ath. And the individual man? Must we think of him as related to himself as foeman to foeman, or what are we to say in this case?

Clin. Ah, my Athenian friend! (I would rather not say 'Attic', for I think you deserve to take your appellation by preference from the goddess) you have made the position all the more incontestable by this reduction of it to first principles. The more readily, then, can you satisfy yourself of the truth of what has just been said: humanity is in a condition of public war of every man against every man, and private war of each man with himself.

Ath. And pray, how are we to understand that?

Clin. Why, here, sir, is the field in which a man may win the primal and subtlest victory, victory over *self*, and where defeat, defeat by *self*, is most discreditable as well as most ruinous. There lies the proof that every one of us is in a state of internal warfare with himself.

Ath. Then suppose we invert the argument, thus. If each individual man is master of himself, or, alternatively, mastered by himself, may we, or may we not, say that a family, a village, a city, exhibit this same feature? 627

Clin. You mean that they may be masters of, or again mastered by, themselves?

Ath. Exactly.

Clin. Again a very proper question. The facts are beyond

doubt, particularly in the case of cities. Any city where the better sort are victorious over the masses and inferior classes may properly be said to be mistress of herself and be rightly congratulated on the victory; where the reverse happens, we must speak in the opposite sense.

Ath. The question whether worse is ever really master of better is one we shall do well not to raise, since it calls for fuller consideration. Your present assertion, as I understand, comes to this: an unrighteous majority may sometimes make a combined effort to subdue by violence a righteous minority of their kinsmen and fellow-citizens; when this attempt succeeds, the city may properly be spoken of as enslaved to herself, and called bad; when it fails, we call her good, and say that she is mistress of herself.

Clin. This language certainly sounds paradoxical, sir, but we cannot withhold our assent.

Ath. Now stay a moment, and consider a further point. There might be a great number of brothers, with the same father and mother, and it would not be remarkable that the majority of them should prove unrighteous and only a minority righteous?

Clin. Not in the least.

Ath. Nor would it be seemly for you and me to press too minutely the point that such a household or family can be said as a whole to be worsted by itself when its wicked members triumph, and to be its own mistress when they fail. The aim of our present inquiry into current language is to examine, not the propriety or impropriety of its phraseology, but the objective truth or falsehood of a theory of legislation.

Clin. Truly said, sir.

Meg. Yes, excellently put so far, as I agree.

Ath. Well, let us go on to a further point. These brothers of whom I have just spoken might conceivably have an adjudicator to decide between them?

Clin. To be sure they might.

Ath. Now which would be the better adjudicator? One who exterminated all the bad brothers and enjoined the better to govern themselves, or one who put the government into the hands of the good, but spared the lives of the worse and brought them to voluntary submission to this government? There might be still a third degree of merit in an adjudicator, if we could find one who would take in hand a family at variance
628 with itself, reconcile its members for the future by his regulations,

without the loss of a single life, and keep them on permanent amicable terms.

Clin. And this third sort would be far and away the best of adjudicators or lawgivers.

Ath. But, mark you, in all the regulations he gave them, he would be legislating with a view to the clean contrary of war.

Clin. That much is true enough.

Ath. Then what of the man who organizes a city? Is it with a view to external warfare he would order its life? Would he not much rather pay regard to the internal warfare which arises, from time to time, within the city, and is called, as you know, *faction*—a kind of war any man would desire never to see in his own city, or, if it broke out, to see appeased at once?

Clin. Obviously he would.

Ath. Now which of two courses would one prefer? That peace should be restored by the victory of one party or the other to the faction, and the destruction of its rival? or rather that friendship and amity should be re-established by a reconciliation, and the citizens compelled to bestow their attention on an external enemy?

Clin. Why, any man would prefer the latter issue, for his own city.

Ath. A lawgiver, no less than another?

Clin. Why, of course.

Ath. And any legislator will have the best as the object of all his enactments?

Clin. Undeniably.

Ath. But the best is neither war nor faction—they are things we should pray to be spared from—but peace and mutual good will. And thus a victory of a city over itself turns out, it would seem, to be not so much a good as a necessary evil. It is as though one fancied that a diseased body which has been subjected to medical purgation were at its best in that condition, and ignored a body which has never stood in need of such treatment. So, if a man takes a similar view of the happiness of the city, or indeed, of the individual man,—I mean, if external wars are the first and only object of his regard—he will never be a true statesman, nor will any man be a finished legislator, unless he legislates for war as a means to peace, rather than for peace as a means to war.

Clin. Your argument, sir, has the appearance of being sound; yet I am very much mistaken if the institutions of Lacedaemon,

*C 275

as well as those of my own country, have not the latter as their one serious end.

629   *Ath.* Very conceivably they have, but our present concern is to submit them to calm inquiry, rather than obstinate contention, as we are convinced that their authors have the same interests at heart as ourselves. We may begin, if you will kindly assist in the examination, by an appeal to the words of an enthusiast for warfare, Tyrtaeus, an Athenian by birth, and a naturalized fellow-citizen of our friend from Sparta. He says, you will remember, that he would 'make no reckoning or count' of any man, no matter how vast his wealth, or what his advantages—and he makes a pretty full enumeration of such advantages—unless he proves himself at need a first-rate warrior. You are sure to have heard the verses, Clinias; as for Megillus, no doubt he has them at his fingers' ends.

Meg. Naturally.

Clin. We know the lines in this country, too; we got them from Sparta.

Ath. Well now, suppose we join in putting a question to our poet to some such effect as this: 'Tyrtaeus, you inspired poet, we are convinced of your wisdom and merit by the excellence of your eulogies of the eminent in warfare. So Clinias of Cnossus, myself, and our friend here believe ourselves to be decidedly of one mind with you already on the main point, but we should like to be quite certain that we are all speaking of the same persons. Tell us, then, do you agree with us in making a marked distinction between two forms of war, or not?' I fancy it would not require a poet of anything like the eminence of Tyrtaeus to give the true answer that there are two forms. There is what all mankind call faction, and it is, of course, the most dangerous kind of war, as we said a few minutes ago; the other, and much milder form, as I imagine we shall all agree, is that waged when we are at variance with external aliens.

Clin. Just so.

Ath. 'Then to which kind of warriors, or war, do your magnificent eulogies, and your corresponding censures, refer? Presumably to the external. At least, you speak in your verses of your intolerance of men who have not the nerve to "face the carnage, close with the foe and strike him down".' So we might continue thus: 'Your special commendation, Tyrtaeus, is, we gather, meant for those who distinguish themselves in an external war against the stranger'. No doubt he would agree to admit this?

Clin. To be sure.

Ath. But we affirm that good as such men are, those who 630 prove themselves conspicuously best in the gravest kind of war are still better, and immensely better, and we, too, can cite a poet, Theognis of Megara in Sicily, whose words are: 'A loyal man, Cyrnus, is worth his weight in gold and silver in the hour of deadly feuds'. We assert, then, that this type of character proves himself, and proves himself in a deadlier warfare, a far better man than the other in the measure in which justice, self-command,[1] and wisdom, combined together and seconded by valour, are better than mere valour by itself. For a man will never prove himself loyal and sound-hearted in times of faction unless he has all virtue, whereas there are plenty of hired combatants who are ready enough to take a firm stand and fight to the death in the kind of war of which Tyrtaeus has to speak, though most of them prove reckless, unjust, brutal, and superlatively imprudent, but for a very few rare exceptions. Now to what does our argument conclude? What do we mean to establish by urging it? Obviously that your Cretan legislator from the school of Zeus, or any other worth his salt, could have no other object in view in his legislation than the supreme virtue. This supreme virtue is what Theognis speaks of as loyalty in peril, and we may call it complete righteousness. As for the quality specially commended by Tyrtaeus, it is noble enough, and nobly celebrated by the poet; but, to speak with precision, it comes only fourth in order and worth.

Clin. That, sir, is to rank our Cretan legislator very low.

Ath. No, not your legislator, my friend, but ourselves, if we dream that Lycurgus or Minos had warfare primarily in view in all his legislation for Lacedaemon or Crete.

Clin. But what, then, ought we to have said?

Ath. What, I take it, is true and ought to be said in an inquiry into the truth.[2] Their legislation was framed in the interest of virtue as a whole, not of one fragment of it, and that the least considerable. They aimed at devising a classified code,[3] though not on the lines of our present-day framers of such codes. To-day each of them frames any additional paragraph he finds necessary; one a section on estates and their heiresses, another one on assault and battery, others, others of the same kind, in indefinite number. But we contend that the right procedure

---

[1] σωφροσύνη.

[2] θείας in *e* 1 calls for some correction, and I adopt Burnet's suggestion <ἀλη>θείας (explained by his citation of *Phaedr.* 247, *c* 5).

[3] On this difficult passage see England's note.

631 for the framer of a legislation is that with which we have just
made a beginning. I unreservedly approve the intention of
your own remarks about your national jurisprudence. It was
quite right to begin with virtue, and explain that virtue was the
aim your legislator had in view. But when you stated that
the whole of his enactments regard only one fragment of it, and
that the most inconsiderable, I thought you were misappre-
hending. But there is a further distinction I could wish you
to observe in your own discourse and to expect in that of others.
May I explain its nature?

Clin. With all my heart.

Ath. 'Sir,'—so I would have had you say—'it is not without
good cause that the laws of Crete have this exceptionally high
repute with all Hellenes. They serve the right end, that of
effecting the happiness of those who enjoy them. They, in
fact, secure them all good things. But there are two different
kinds of good things, the merely human, and the divine; the
former are consequential on the latter; hence a city [1] which
accepts the greater goods, acquires the lesser along with them,
but one which refuses them, misses both. The lesser are those
among which health holds the first place, comeliness the second,
strength for the race and all other bodily exercises the third,
while the fourth place belongs to a wealth which is not "blind",
but clear-sighted, because attendant on wisdom. Of divine
goods, the first and chiefest is this same wisdom, and next
after it,[2] sobriety of spirit; a third, resultant from the blending
of both these with valour, is righteousness, and valour itself is
fourth. All of these naturally rank before the former class, and,
of course, a lawgiver must observe that order. Next, he should
impress it on his citizens that all his other injunctions have a
view to these ends, and that among the ends, the human look
to the divine, and all the divine to their leader, wisdom. He
should superintend by a right distribution of honour and dishonour, the matrimonial alliances among his citizens, and their
subsequent behaviour in the procreation of offspring, male and
female, and rearing of it, from infancy right on to old age.
He must make a careful and observant study of the pleasures,

---

[1] With the punctuation of Burnet the MS. text in *b* 8, πόλις, κτᾶται will
just translate, and accordingly I have kept it, but it is tempting to adopt
Badham's παρίσταται: 'one who accepts the greater goods, wins the lesser
as well'.

[2] Keeping the μετὰ νοῦν of MSS. at *c* 7. But perhaps νοῦ (found in a
quotation of Eusebius and adopted by Schanz, Burnet, England) is
better: 'sobriety of soul *joined with* insight'.

the pains, the desires, and all the vehement passions aroused in
them by all these social relations, and distribute censure and
praise among them rightly, in the actual text of his laws. So, 632
again, with the passions of anger and fear, with the various
troubles of soul engendered by misfortune, and the reactions
from them in seasons of good fortune, and the emotions which
are incidental to humanity in sickness, in war, in penury, and
their opposites; in all such cases, he should explain and determine how far each human mood is becoming, and how far it is
not. Next, our legislator must watch over the methods by
which his citizens acquire and expend their wealth, and have
an eye to the presence or absence of justice in the various pro-
cedures by which they all contract or dissolve associations with
one another, voluntary or involuntary, assigning marks of
honour to those of them who conform to his laws, and imposing
specific penalties on the disobedient. When he comes at last
to the close of his whole constitution-making, he must decide
in what manner the funeral rites of each class of citizen should
be celebrated, and what marks of respect should be assigned to
them. When the law-maker has completed his discovery he
will set over the whole system a body of guardians endowed
some with wisdom, some with true beliefs, to the end that
intelligence may knit the whole into one, and keep it in subjection to sobriety and justice, not to wealth or self-seeking.'
Those, gentlemen, are the lines on which I should have wished,
and do still wish *you* to explain how all these merits are to be
found in the laws ascribed to Zeus and the Pythian Apollo,
and enacted by Minos and Lycurgus, and how they form a
system, readily discernible by one familiar with law from
scientific study, or even habit of life, though far from manifest
to ordinary persons like myself.

Clin. Then what, sir, should be our next step?

Ath. I think there will need to be a fresh start of the examination, beginning, as before, with the practices by which courage
is developed; then we will examine a second, and then a third
form of virtue, if you are so minded. When once we have
dealt with our first topic, we may try to take it as a model of
procedure, and beguile our journey with further chat on the
same lines. After we have treated of all virtue, we will try,
with God's permission, to show that all the regulations we
were just enumerating, have it for their object.

Meg. Excellent. And suppose you begin by trying your 633
criticism on our friend here, the admirer of Zeus.

Ath. On you and myself, no less than on him; we are all concerned in the argument. Come, then. We may say that your common meals and physical exercises were devised by your legislator with a view to war?

Meg. Yes.

Ath. And thirdly, or fourthly? For in considering this and other virtues, it is possibly well to make such an enumeration of their parts (or whatever else they should be called, so long as a man's meaning is clear).

Meg. Well, thirdly, as I, or any other Lacedaemonian would say, he devised the chase.

Ath. Suppose we try to find a fourthly, or a fifthly, if we can.

Meg. Then I will venture on naming a fourthly, too, the endurance of bodily pain which finds so much scope among us Spartans in our boxing-matches and our system of foraging raids, which regularly involve heavy whippings. Besides, we have what we call a *crypteia*, which is a wonderfully hard discipline in endurance, as well as the practices of going without shoes or bedding in the winter, and wandering all over the country, night and day, without attendants, performing one's menial offices for one's self. Further, again, our Gymnopaediae involve rigid endurance, as the matches are fought in the heat of the summer, and we have a host of other similar tests, in fact, almost too many for particular enumeration.

Ath. You state your case well, my Lacedaemonian friend. But, pray, what are we to make of courage? Is it a conflict with fear and pain, just that and no more? Or does it also include conflict with longings and pleasures and their dangerous seductive blandishments, which melt even the mettle of the would-be precisian like so much wax?

Meg. That, I believe, is the true account; it is a conflict with all of these.

Ath. Now, unless we have forgotten our earlier conversation, our friend from Cnossus spoke of cities, and men too, as defeated by themselves. Did you not?

Clin. To be sure, I did.

Ath. Well, shall we give the name *bad* now to the man who is defeated by pain, or to him who is defeated by pleasure as well?

Clin. I think it belongs more properly to one who is defeated by pleasure. And I imagine all of us are readier to say that one who is mastered by pleasure is shamefully self-defeated than to say it of one who succumbs to pain.

634   *Ath.* Then very surely our pair of legislators instructed by

Zeus and Apollo cannot have canonized a lop-sided courage, which can only stand its ground before a sinister enemy, but proves impotent against the dexterously and ingeniously seductive opponent? Surely they would have her face both?

Clin. Both, I am confident.

Ath. Then I must ask a second question. What practices have your two cities which teach a man the taste of pleasures without any evasion? (Just as pains were not evaded; the man was thrust into the thick of them, but forced, or persuaded by marks of honour, to get the mastery of them.) Where, I say, is the same regulation about pleasure to be found in your laws? I want to know what there is in your institutions to give the same person courage alike against pain and against pleasure, to make him victorious where he ought to be victorious, and secure him from defeat at the hands of his most intimate and mortal enemies.

Meg. Nay, sir, possibly I could not readily allege conspicuous illustrations, on a large scale, in the matter of pleasure, to match the numerous laws I was able to produce as a counterpoise to pain, though I might be more fortunate with minor details.

Clin. I, too, cannot produce an equally obvious illustration from our Cretan laws.

Ath. No, my friends, and it is no matter for surprise. But if any of us should be led, in his desire to discover what is true and best, into censure of some detail in the national laws of any of us, I trust we shall take such treatment from each other gently, without resentment.

Clin. Truly spoken, Athenian; we must do as you say.

Ath. Harshness would, in fact, hardly become our years, Clinias.

Clin. Indeed, it would not.

Ath. Well, how far the reproaches which are brought against the systems of Laconia and Crete may be deserved or undeserved is another matter; in any case, I am probably better qualified than either of you to report the criticisms which are generally current. If your laws are but reasonably good, as they are, we must reckon among the best of them the enactment that no young man shall raise the question which of them all are what they should be and which not, but that all should agree, without a dissonant voice, that they are all god-given and admirable, flatly refusing a hearing to any one who disputes the point, while if an older man has any reflections to make, he must impart them to a magistrate of his own age, when none of the younger men are by.

635   *Clin.* Perfectly true, sir; remote as to-day is from the times of our ancient legislator, I believe you have fairly divined his intentions and are exactly right.

   Ath. Well, we have no younger men with us now, and for ourselves, our years give us the legislator's licence to hold a private conversation on the subject without offence.

   Clin. Just so; accordingly we invite you to criticize our institutions without reserve. One is not insulted by being informed of something amiss, but rather gets an opportunity for amendment, if the information is taken in good part, without resentment.

   Ath. Thank you. But my object for the present is not to criticize your laws, which we have not yet thoroughly examined, so much as to state a difficulty. You are the only communities, Greek or non-Greek, known to us whose lawgiver has enjoined you to leave the intensest pleasures and delights utterly untasted, though, in the matter of pains and fears which we have just been discussing, he held that one who is allowed to flinch from them on system from his boyhood, and then has to face fatigues and fears and pains which are not to be evaded, will flinch from those who have been disciplined in them, and be enslaved by them. Now, surely the legislator, to be consistent, should take the same view of pleasures. He should say to himself, 'if our citizens are to grow up from childhood without experience of the intensest pleasures, if they are to have no training in constancy and refusal to disgrace themselves when assailed by pleasures, susceptibility to pleasure will lead them to the same fate as those who succumb to their fears. They will fall slaves, in a different, but even more dishonourable fashion, to those who can resist the allurements of pleasure, and have the means of producing it at their disposal, though these may sometimes be utterly evil men. Thus, their souls will be half enslaved, half free, and they will not deserve to be called brave men, or free men, without qualification'. I would have you consider whether you find these remarks at all pertinent.

   Clin. Pertinent enough, on such a first hearing. But it might show immaturity and folly to form confident conclusions on such weighty matters on the instant.

   Ath. Then suppose we proceed to the next point of our programme, my friends, and turn from courage to sobriety. Can we discover any point of superiority in these two systems over those of societies organized on no systematic principles, as we did in connection with war? 636

Meg. Not too easily; still, our common meals and physical exercises were presumably well devised to promote both virtues.

Ath. Ah, my friends, how difficult it seems to ensure that the working of an institution shall be as unquestionable as its theory! Presumably it is with states as it is with human bodies; one cannot prescribe one definite treatment for one subject, which involves no physically injurious consequences along with its beneficial effects. For example, these physical exercises and common meals you speak of, though in many ways beneficial to a city, provide dangerous openings for faction, as is shown by the cases of the Milesians, Boeotians, and Thuriotes. And, in particular, this practice is generally held to have corrupted the ancient and natural rule in the matter of sexual indulgence common to mankind with animals at large, and the blame for these corruptions may be charged, in the first instance, on your two cities and such others as are most devoted to physical exercises. Whether these matters are to be regarded as sport, or as earnest, we must not forget that this pleasure is held to have been granted by nature to male and female when conjoined for the work of procreation; the crime of male with male, or female with female, is an outrage on nature and a capital surrender to lust of pleasure. And you know it is our universal accusation against the Cretans that they were the inventors of the tale of Ganymede; they were convinced, we say, that their legislation came from Zeus, so they went on to tell this story against him that they might, if you please, plead his example for their indulgence in this pleasure too. With the tale we have no further concern, but the pleasures and pains of communities and of private lives are as good as the whole subject of a study of jurisprudence. For pain and pleasure are, as it were, nature's twin fountain-heads; whoso draws from the right fount, at due times, and in due measure, be it city, or person, or any living creature, is happy, but he that draws without science, and out of due season, has the clean contrary lot.

Meg. Sure, sir, this is finely said, and I would not deny that we are dumbfounded for an answer to it. Yet, for myself, I hold that our Lacedaemonian lawgiver is right to command avoidance of pleasures (as to the law of Cnossus, its defence shall be made by our friend, if he will accept the task). In Sparta, 637 to my mind, this matter of pleasure is ordered better than in any place on earth. That which, by its keen delightsomeness, most easily entangles men in outrage and all manner of follies is, by our law, banished clean out of our territory. Neither in our country districts, nor in towns which are controlled by Spartans, can you find drinking-parties, with the strong incentives to various pleasures that attend them; there is not a man of us who would not forthwith lay the heaviest penalty on a tipsy reveller, if he fell in with him; the very festival of Dionysus would not serve as an excuse for the offender's discharge.[1] I have seen such revelling before now in your Attica on the 'wagons', and at Tarentum, a settlement of our own, I beheld the whole city in its cups at the feast of Dionysus; but there is no such practice among us.

Ath. Friend from Sparta, any recreation of this kind is commendable, when the power of resistance persists, though mere foolishness when it is relaxed. A countryman of my own might well defend himself by retorting on you the licence of your Spartan women. To be sure, there is a rejoinder which is commonly held to be a sufficient vindication in all such cases at Tarentum, or in my own country, no less than in yours; a native will always meet the stranger's astonishment at an unfamiliar practice with the words: 'There is no call for surprise; this is our established custom in the matter, though yours may perhaps be different'. What you and I are now discussing is not the practice of mankind at large, but the merits or demerits of the legislators who create the customs. So we must take the whole subject of convivial drinking into fuller consideration; it is a practice of grave importance, and calls for the judgment of no mean legislator. The question is not that of the mere drinking of wine or its complete prohibition, but of the convivial drinking of it. Should we follow the fashion of Scythians and Persians (to say nothing of Carthaginians, Celts, Iberians, and Thracians, who are all of them warlike peoples), or that of your own countrymen? They, as you remind me, absolutely reject the practice, whereas the Scythians and Thracians, men and women alike, take their wine neat, and let it run down over their garments, and count this a laudable and glorious practice. The Persians, again, indulge freely in this, as in other luxurious habits which you Spartans prohibit, though with less disorder than the nations I have mentioned.

638   *Meg.* Yes, my dear sir, but do not forget that we make them all run when we have weapons in our hands.

Ath. Nay, sir, you must not urge that plea. A flight or

---

[1] I read in 637 *b* 2, λύσαιτο, with the MSS.

pursuit has so often gone unrecorded, and will in the future; this shows that we cannot regard victory or defeat in the field as more than a very dubious test of the laudability of a practice. For the matter of that, the more populous city may defeat the less populous and reduce it to subjection, as Syracuse has done with Locri, which, you know, has the reputation of enjoying the best laws to be found in that part of the world, or Athens with Ceos; and no doubt many similar instances could be produced. No, we must leave victories and defeats out of court for the present, and discuss the various practices on their own merits, in the hope of convincing ourselves that some are laudable and others the reverse. But first let me make an observation as to the right method of investigating the worth of such practices.

Meg. And what is it you would say?

Ath. When such a practice is under consideration, I hold that it is always highly improper to undertake to condemn or approve it out of hand, on the bare mention of its name. This is as though one who had heard wheat, for instance, commended as a wholesome article of diet should denounce it out of hand, without any inquiry into its effects, or the manner of its administration; I mean, how it is to be administered, and to whom, or with what accompaniments, in what form it is to be served, and to persons in what state of health. Well, that is exactly how I think we all argue our present question. As soon as we hear the mere word 'drinking', one party condemns the practice and another commends it, and both in a very odd fashion. Both sides rest their case on producing evidence to fact or character; the one thinking it decisive that its witnesses are so numerous, the other that we see the abstainers victorious in the field of battle—though there even the fact is open to dispute. Now if we are to go on to deal with established customs in general on these lines, I, for one, shall be left unsatisfied. So I propose to deal with our immediate subject, drinking, by a different method—the right one, I believe—as an attempt to illustrate the proper procedure in treating such questions generally. For there are countless peoples ready to contest the issues at stake in these matters against your two cities.

Meg. Most certainly, if a right way of treating such problems is to be found, we must not refuse it a hearing.

Ath. Then let us treat our question somewhat in this fashion. Suppose that someone should commend goat-keeping, or the goat itself as a valuable animal, and another man, who had seen goats damaging lands under cultivation by grazing on them without a keeper, should denounce the brutes, or find fault with any creature he had seen thus under no control or bad control, can we say that censure of anything coming from such a quarter would have the least validity?

Meg. Of course not.

Ath. And what do you say to this? Is a man a useful commander at sea, so long as he only possesses the science of navigation, whether he happens to be seasick or not?

Meg. Certainly not, if he combines that disorder with his professional knowledge.

Ath. And what of the commander of an army in the field? Is he a competent commander, so long as he has military science, even if he is a coward and falls seasick in peril from the inebriation of terror?

Meg. A thoroughly useless officer, that! A commander for the veriest of women, not for men!

Ath. And what of him who commends or condemns any social activity, be it what it may, which naturally calls for a leader, and is beneficial under his conduct, though he has never seen that activity rightly organized under such leadership, but only discharged with no leaders, or bad ones? Can we possibly imagine that there is any value in the censure or commendation of such concerted action by such observers?

Meg. How can we, on the assumption that they have never witnessed nor taken part in any such association, conducted as it should be?

Ath. Now, stay; I suppose we may reckon a drinking-party and its members as one kind of social activity?

Meg. Surely, surely.

Ath. Then has any one ever seen such a party conducted as it ought to be? Neither of you can hesitate to give the answer, 'Never'; the whole thing is foreign and unfamiliar to you both. And for my own part, though I have been present at many, in different places, and what is more, may even say I have studied them all carefully, I have never seen nor heard of one rightly managed throughout; here and there a few minor details may not have been amiss, but, in the main, I have found universal wrong management.

Clin. You must explain your meaning, sir, rather more precisely. Our inexperience in these matters, as you were saying, is such that, even if we were present at such a gathering, we should very likely not distinguish proper management from 640 improper at first sight.

Ath. No, possibly not. But do your utmost to follow my explanation. No doubt you understand as much as this, that in every assembly or concerted action for any purpose, there should always be someone in control of the parties?

Clin. Beyond a doubt.

Ath. And mark that we were lately saying that in a combat the commander must be a brave man.

Clin. So we were, to be sure.

Ath. Now a brave man is less agitated by alarms than a coward.

Clin. True again.

Ath. And if we could contrive to place an army under a general who was utterly devoid of alarm and agitation, we should by all means do so, should we not?

Clin. Most decidedly.

Ath. But at the present moment we are contemplating a man who is to take command, not in the embattled meeting of foes with foes, but in the peaceful intercourse of friends with friends, for the promotion of common good feeling.

Clin. Exactly.

Ath. Now, as the kind of gathering we have in view is to be attended by drinking, it will not be free from excitement.

Clin. Of course not; very much the contrary, I should presume.

Ath. To begin with then, here, too, a commander is wanted.

Clin. Wanted, indeed; nowhere more.

Ath. And should we secure freedom from excitement in such a commander, if the thing is possible?

Clin. Decidedly.

Ath. And further, I presume, he should be a man of social tact. For his business is to conserve the existing friendly relations between the parties, as well as to ensure that they shall be still further augmented by the gathering.

Clin. True enough.

Ath. So the commander set to control a company of drinkers should be both sober and sagacious, not the reverse. If the drinkers are under the control of a young and indiscreet man who is drinking himself, he may think himself very fortunate if no grave disaster results.

Clin. Indeed, he may.

Ath. Well then, if such parties were conducted among us under the most correct regulations attainable, an unfavourable critic who should attack the institution as such, might perhaps be

right in his disapproval; but when a man inveighs against a
practice because he sees it mismanaged in every possible respect,
he is obviously unaware, in the first place, that the practice in
question is misconducted, and in the second, that any proceeding
whatever will appear mischievous on the understanding that it is
executed without a sober master or commander.   Surely you
can see that a tippling navigator, or commander of any kind,
will wreck anything, vessel, or car, or army, or whatever it may
641 be, for which he sets the course.

Clin. Your last remark, sir, is unquestionably true.   But
pray go on to explain what possible good this custom of drinking-
bouts would do us, if they were rightly conducted.   Take the
case of an army, such as we were just speaking of; if it gets the
right kind of leadership, the result is a victory for the force—
no inconsiderable good; and so with our other examples.   But
what appreciable benefit accrues to individuals, or to the city,
from the proper surveillance of a wine-party?

Ath. Well, and what appreciable benefit could we say accrues
to the city from the proper surveillance of one boy, or one group
of boys?   If the question is to be put in that form, must we not
reply that the city certainly gets but a trifling advantage from
the single case?   But if the question is universally what considerable advantage the city derives from the education of the
educated, the answer is easy.   Education is the way to produce
good men, and, once produced, such men will live nobly, and
vanquish their enemies in the field into the bargain.   So
education brings victory in her train, though victory sometimes
leads to loss of education, since victorious warfare often enough
leads men to pride, and through pride they take the taint of other
vices innumerable.   Moreover, there has never been a 'Cadmean'
education, whereas 'Cadmean' victories have been, and will be,
only too common.

Clin. We may gather, then, that you regard time spent in
companionship over the bottle as contributing much to education, when it is rightly so spent?

Ath. Most assuredly.

Clin. Then can you, in the next place, offer us proof that the
statement is true?

Ath. Why, sir, as to truth, to be positive the thing is so,
when there are so many to dispute it, must be left to a god.
But if I am called on to give my personal opinion, I will state
it frankly, since our present conversation has struck into the
subject of law and politics.

Clin. That is just what we are attempting to do—to discover your own conviction on the matter now in dispute.

Ath. Well then, to our task. You will have to make an effort to follow, and I to elucidate the argument, with such powers as I have. But first let me make one observation. The universal belief of Hellas is that whereas my own city delights in discourse and is copious in it, Lacedaemon is inclined to taciturnity, and Crete to versatility of mind rather than fluency of utterance.[1] So I fear you may get the impression that I am expending too 642 many words on a minor matter, if I deliver[2] myself of a long discourse on so inconsiderable a topic as drinking. But the truth is that a really sound theory on the point cannot be surely and adequately expounded apart from a true theory of music, nor that, again, apart from a theory of education at large, and these are subjects for protracted discussion. How would it be, then, I ask you, if we should drop them for the present, and divert the conversation to some other department of jurisprudence?

Meg. Sir, you may perhaps be unaware that my own family hold the position of *proxeni* for Athens. Now it may well be the universal experience of boys anywhere that when they are told they are *proxeni* for a city, an early kindness for that city promptly finds its way into the boy's heart; we feel that it is a second fatherland, only next to our own. This is certainly what has happened in my own particular case. From the first, if Lacedaemon felt herself aggrieved by Athens, or obliged by her, the boys used to tell me: 'Megillus, your city has done the shabby (or the handsome) thing by us'. Well, by listening to these speeches and constantly replying in your defence against persons who brought reproaches against your city, I contracted a strong affection for her. To this day, I love the sound of your dialect, and am persuaded of the truth of the current saying that when an Athenian is a good man, he is exceptionally good. It is only at Athens that goodness is an unconstrained, spontaneous growth, a genuine 'gift of God' in the full sense of the words. So, as far as I am concerned, you need feel no misgiving in discoursing at any length you please.

Clin. I, too, sir, have a statement to make which will relieve you from diffidence in speaking your full mind. You have presumably heard of Epimenides, an inspired person born in this

---

[1] As Mr. Bury notes, this is a courteously disguised allusion to the reputation of the Cretans as 'artful' liars.

[2] ἀνακαθαιρόμενος, *a* 2, seems to mean 'cleansing the bosom' of its contents, getting them 'off one's chest'. But see England's note *in loc.*

city and connected with my own family, who visited Athens ten
years before the Persian wars at the bidding of the oracle, and
offered certain sacrifices enjoined by the god, besides telling the
citizens, who were alarmed by the Persian preparations, that the
enemy would not come within ten years, and when they did,
would depart again with their purpose uneffected, after receiving
more damage than they inflicted. That was when my family
contracted their friendship with your countrymen, and my
643 ancestors and myself have had a kindness for them ever since.

Ath. I take it, then, that there is full readiness to hear on your
part; on mine, there is readiness enough of intention, but performance is none too easy; still I must do my endeavour. As
the first step in the argument, then, let us define education and
its effect, since we hold that the discussion on which we have
adventured must follow that route to its destination, the
wine-god.

Clin. By all means, since that is your pleasure.

Ath. Good; then I will attempt an account of what true
education is; you must consider whether the account is
acceptable.

Clin. Pray proceed.

Ath. Well, I proceed at once to say that he who is to be good
at anything as a man must practise that thing from early
childhood, in play as well as in earnest, with all the attendant
circumstances of the action. Thus, if a boy is to be a good
farmer, or again, a good builder, he should play, in the one case
at building toy houses, in the other at farming, and both should
be provided by their tutors with miniature tools on the pattern
of real ones. In particular, all necessary preliminary instruction
should be acquired in this way; thus, the carpenter should be
taught by his play to use the rule and plumb-line, and the
soldier to sit a horse, and the like;[1] we should seek to use games
as a means of directing children's tastes and inclinations towards
the station they are themselves to fill when adult. So we may
say, in fact, the sum and substance of education is the right
training which effectually leads the soul of the child at play
on to the love of the calling in which he will have to be perfect,
after its kind, when he is a man. But, as I said, you must
consider whether what has been said has your approval so far.

Clin. Indeed, it has.

Ath. Then let us further guard against leaving our account

---

[1] ποιοῦντα, c 6, is clearly a slip for ποιεῖν, and I translate accordingly.
But the slip is not unlikely to be Plato's own.

of what education is too indeterminate.   When we are to express
approval or censure of a man's training, we currently speak of
one of ourselves as educated and another as uneducated—and
the reference is sometimes to the business of a huckster or a
supercargo—and of other such fellows of mighty fine education.
But our present discourse is in place only on the lips of one who
holds that education is none of these things, but rather that
schooling [1] from boyhood in goodness which inspires the recipient
with passionate and ardent desire to become a perfect citizen,
knowing both how to wield and how to submit to righteous rule. 644
Our argument, I take it, would isolate this training from others
and confine the name education exclusively to it; any training
which has as its end wealth, or perhaps bodily strength, or some
other accomplishment unattended by intelligence and righteousness, it counts vulgar, illiberal, and wholly unworthy to be called
education.   So we must not wrangle over a word, but abide by
the proposition on which we have just agreed, that the rightly
educated prove what we mean by good, and that no aspect of
education is to be disparaged; it is the highest blessing bestowed
on mankind, and it is the best of them on whom it is most fully
bestowed.   When it takes a false turn which permits of correction, we should, one and all, devote the energy of a lifetime to
its amendment.

Clin. True indeed; we admit the point.

Ath. We also agreed some time ago that those who can command themselves are good, and those who cannot, bad.

Clin. Precisely.

Ath. Then let us once more consider rather more exactly just
what our words mean.   Perhaps you will allow me to make the
point clearer, if I can, by a parable.

Clin. We are all attention.

Ath. Well then, we may take it that any human being is
one person?

Clin. Of course.

Ath. But one person who has within himself a pair of unwise
and conflicting counsellors, whose names are pleasure and
pain?

Clin. The fact is as you say.

Ath. He has, besides, anticipations of the future, and these of
two sorts.   The common name for both sorts is *expectation,*

---

[1] παιδειαν in *e* 4 is pretty clearly a slip for παιδαγωγίαν, which C. Ritter
proposed, but again it is highly possible that the oversight came from
Plato, dictating his words.

the special name for anticipation of pain being *fear*, and for anticipation of its opposite, *confidence*. And on the top of all, there is *judgment*, to discern which of these states is better or worse, and when judgment takes the form of a public decision of a city, it has the name of *law*.

Clin. I fear I hardly follow you; yet pray proceed with your statement as though I did.

Meg. I, too, find myself in the same condition.

Ath. Let us look at the whole matter in some such light as this. We may imagine that each of us living creatures is a puppet made by gods, possibly as a plaything, or possibly with some more serious purpose. That, indeed, is more than we can tell, but one thing is certain: these interior states are, so to say, the cords, or strings, by which we are worked; they are opposed to one another, and pull us with opposite tensions in the direction of opposite actions, and therein lies the division of virtue from vice. In fact—so says our argument—a man must always yield to one of these tensions without resistance, but pull against all the other strings,—must yield, that is, to that golden and 645 hallowed drawing of judgment which goes by the name of the public law of the city; the others are hard and iron-like, it soft, as befits gold, whereas they resemble very various substances. So a man must always co-operate with the noble drawing of law; for judgment, though a noble thing, is as gentle and free from violence as noble, whence its drawing needs supporters, if the gold within us is to prevail over the other stuff. In this wise our moral fable of the human puppets will find its fulfilment; it will also become somewhat clearer first, what is meant by self-conquest and self-defeat, and next that the individual's duty is to understand the true doctrine of these tensions and live in obedience to it, the city's to accept this doctrine from a god, or from the human discoverer just mentioned, and make it law for her converse with herself and other societies. This will lead us to a more exact articulation both of vice and of virtue, and the elucidation of the subject will presumably throw further light on education and institutions at large, and more particularly on this business of social drinking—a trifling matter, it might be thought, to waste such a long discussion on, and yet it may well prove to deserve the whole.

Clin. Very true; so let us treat it at whatever length our present business demands.

Ath. Well then, tell me; suppose we ply our puppet with drink, what effect are we producing on it?

Clin. Now why are you recurring to that? What is the purpose of the question?

Ath. I have not yet reached the *why*; what I want to know is generally *how* this puppet is affected by participating in this practice. Let me try to explain my meaning still more exactly. My question amounts to this: the drinking of wine makes our pleasures and pains, our tempers and passions more intense, does it not?

Clin. Much more intense.

Ath. And what of our perceptions, memories, beliefs, knowledge? Are they likewise intensified? or do they desert a man altogether, if he is thoroughly soaked with drinking?

Clin. Why, utterly.

Ath. And so the man is brought back to the mental condition of his remote infancy?

Clin. To be sure.

Ath. Now that is the condition in which his self-command is at its lowest.

Clin. It is.

646

Ath. Such a man, we may say, is at his worst?

Clin. Decidedly.

Ath. Thus the phrase 'second childhood' would seem to be as applicable to inebriation as to old age.

Clin. Admirably put, sir.

Ath. Now can there be an argument daring enough to suggest that we should try the taste of a practice such as this, and not avoid it with all our might?

Clin. It should seem there can; at least you say so, and only just now you offered to produce it.

Ath. An apposite reminder, and I repeat the offer now, since both of you have professed yourselves eager to give me a hearing.

Clin. Of course you must be heard. There is a reason, if there were no other, in the sheer incredibility of your paradox, that it can be right for a man to fling himself voluntarily into a state of sheer degradation.

Ath. Degradation of soul, that is?

Clin. Yes.

Ath. Well, my good sir, and what of a bad habit of body—leanness, disfigurement, feebleness? Would it be a paradox that a man can voluntarily bring himself into those conditions?

Clin. Of course it would.

Ath. Why, sir, when men freely go to the physician for a course of medicaments, must we imagine they do not know they will very soon be, for days together, in such a state of body that, were it to be permanent, they would be sick of life? Again, when men resort to gymnasia, or to heavy bodily exertions, we know their health suffers for the time being,[1] do we not?

Clin. Yes, we know all that.

Ath. As also that they go of their own motion, for the sake of subsequent benefits?

Clin. To be sure.

Ath. And surely we should take the same point of view about other habitual practices too?[2]

Clin. I own we should.

Ath. And therefore also about spending time over the wine-cup, if it is a view which can rightly be taken in this case?

Clin. Naturally.

Ath. Then, if only wine-drinking can be shown to lead to benefits comparable with those to be secured for the body, it certainly has the advantage over physical training in its initial stage; the second begins in pain, the other not so.

Clin. Quite true, but I shall be surprised if we can find any such benefit in the custom.

Ath. That, I take it, is just what we have at last to do our best to make clear. Tell me this: can we not distinguish two kinds of fear?

Clin. And what may they be?

Ath. They are these; in the first place, we are afraid of evil, when we expect it to befall us.

Clin. We are.

Ath. But we are often also afraid for our reputation, when we apprehend we are getting a bad reputation from some unworthy act or speech; it is fear of this sort to which we, and I fancy the
647 rest of the world too, give the name of shame.

Clin. Certainly.

Ath. Well, those are the two fears of which I was speaking, and the second kind opposes itself to our commonest and most passionate pleasures, as much as to pains and to fears other than itself.

Clin. Very true.

Ath. Now does not a lawgiver, or any other man worth his salt, hold this sort of fear in the highest honour? He calls it modesty, and regards the kind of confidence contrary to it,

---

[1] It suffers from the exhaustion which these exertions produce.
[2] viz. that temporary inconvenience is well worth while, when it leads to solid future benefits.

which he calls impudence, as universally one of the gravest evils in private or public life?

Clin. True again.

Ath. And, to say nothing of the many other great advantages this kind of fear secures for us, when you take one thing with another, nothing contributes more effectually to victory and preservation in war itself. In fact, victory has a double source, fearlessness of the enemy, and fear of disgrace in the eyes of one's friends?

Clin. Just so.

Ath. And consequently each of us needs to be at once free from fear and filled with fear, the reason for these contrasted moods being as we have stated?

Clin. Agreed.

Ath. And when we intend to make a man immune from various fears, we achieve our purpose by bringing him into contact with fear, under the direction of law?

Clin. So it would appear.

Ath. But now, suppose our aim is to make him rightly *fearful*, what then? Must we not ensure his victory in the conflict with his own lust for pleasures by pitting him against shamelessness and training him to face it? If a man can only attain mature courage by fighting the cowardice within himself and vanquishing it, whereas without experience and discipline in that contest, no man will ever be half the champion he might be, is it credible he should come to fullness of self-command unless he first fights a winning battle against the numerous pleasures and lusts which allure him to shamelessness and wrong, by the aid of precept, practice, and artifice, alike in his play and in his serious hours? Can he be spared the experience of all this?

Clin. The view, certainly, does not seem plausible.

Ath. Now, tell me, has any god bestowed on mankind a specific to induce fear—a drug whose effect is that the more a man permits himself to imbibe of it, the darker he fancies his fortunes at every draught, present and future alike grow increasingly alarming, and the climax is abject terror in the bravest, though 648 when the subject has recovered from his stupor and shaken off the effects of the potion, he regularly becomes his own man again?

Clin. Nay, sir, where in all the world can we find a liquor like this?

Ath. Why, nowhere. But suppose one could have been found, would the lawgiver have availed himself of it to develop courage?

I mean, it would have been very much to the purpose to discuss it with him to some such effect as this: 'Pray, sir legislator—whether it is for Cretans or for any other society your legislation is intended—in the first place, would you be thankful for a touchstone of the courage or cowardice of your citizens?'

Clin. And he would, no doubt, be sure to say, 'Yes'.

Ath. 'Well then, would you like the touchstone to be safe and applicable without serious risks, or the reverse?'

Clin. There, again, he would be certain to prefer safety.

Ath. 'You would employ it to bring your citizens into such a state of fear and test them under its influence, thus constraining a man to become fearless, by encouragement, precept, and marks of recognition, as well as of disgrace for those who declined to be such as you would have them in all situations? He who shaped himself to this discipline well and manfully would be discharged from the test unscathed, but on him who shaped badly you would lay some penalty? Or would you simply refuse to employ the liquor, supposing you had no fault to find with it on other grounds?'

Clin. Why, of course he would employ it, my dear sir.

Ath. It would, at least, give us an infinitely readier and safer training than our present arrangements, whether for the individual, for small groups, or for groups of any desired numbers. A man would do pretty right to save endless trouble by providing himself with this single specific and training himself in privacy to face his fears, isolating himself, of course, from public view behind his regard for decorum until he had obtained a satisfactory result. And, again, he would do right, when confident that he was already adequately prepared by native endowment and preliminary practice, to prosecute his training in the company of fellow-drinkers, and make public exhibition of the virtue which enables him to transcend and master the effects of the inevitable disturbances due to the potion, without once suffering a serious fall or deterioration; though he would leave off before he reached the final draught from fear of our universal human weakness before the liquor.

Clin. Why yes, sir, even such a man as you speak of would be wise to do that.

649 *Ath.* Then let us resume our conversation with the legislator. 'Very good', we shall say to him; 'as for such a fear-inducing specific, providence has given us none, and we have invented none ourselves (for we need not take quacksalvers into account); but what about fearlessness, excessive confidence, improper

confidence at the wrong moment? Is there a liquor which has these effects, or is there not?'

Clin. He will, of course, say 'Yes', and he will mean wine.

Ath. And are not its effects the very opposite of all we have just mentioned? When a man drinks it, its first immediate effect is to make him merrier than he was, and the more he takes, the more it fills him with optimistic fancies and imaginary capacity. In the very final phase the drinker is swollen with the conceit of his own wisdom to the pitch of complete licence of speech and action, and utter fearlessness; there is nothing he will scruple to say, nothing he will scruple to do. I think this will be universally conceded?

Clin. Of course.

Ath. Then let me remind you of something we said before: there are two qualities to be cultivated in our souls, supreme confidence, and its contrary, supreme fearfulness.

Clin. What you spoke of as modesty, I take it?

Ath. Well recollected. And seeing that the practice of courage and fearlessness has to be learned in the midst of alarms, it has to be considered whether the contrary quality does not demand the contrary conditions for its cultivation.

Clin. The presumption, certainly, is that it does.

Ath. It would seem, then, that the conditions in which we are naturally inclined to be more than usually confident or bold are the very conditions in which we must practise to be least audacious or unashamed, but rather apprehensive of ever presuming to say a shameful word, or submit to a shameful act, or even commit one.

Clin. So it seems.

Ath. Now, are not all the following conditions in which we are in the mood in question—anger, lust, pride, folly, greed [, cowardice [1]]? We may add to the list wealth, beauty, physical vigour, and whatever else drives us frantic with the intoxication of pleasure. And if we want an inexpensive and comparatively harmless pleasure [2] to serve, in the first place, as a test of these conditions, and in the next, as a training for them, what can we find more suitable than the sportive touchstone of the wine-cup, provided only that it is employed with a little precaution? For do but consider: which is the more dangerous course with a

---

[1] δειλία, cowardice, is quite out of place in this enumeration, and I suspect Schanz was right in proposing to omit the word.

[2] The adjectives εὐτελῆ and ἀσινεστέραν in 649 d 7–8 seem to me to qualify neither πεῖραν (so England) nor βάσανον 'understood' (so apparently Bury), but ἡδονήν (e 1), and I render accordingly.

sullen and untamed temper—the source of so many crimes; to
650 test it by entering into a business agreement, with the risk of
its failure, or by association in a Bacchanalian celebration?[1]
Or to put the soul of a slave of sex to the test by entrusting him
with our own daughters, sons, and wives, and discover his
character at the risk to our nearest and dearest?[2]   One might
allege endless such illustrations without exhausting the advantages of a sportive method of inquiry involving no serious
painful cost.   And there is certainly one part of the case[3]
which, I fancy, will not be disputed by Cretans, or any other
body of men: the proposed test of one another is a reasonably
good one, and has the advantage of others in point of inexpen-
siveness, security, and speediness.

Clin. That, at least, is beyond doubt.

Ath Here, then, in the discovery of native disposition and
character, we have something of incomparable service to the
art whose business it is to cultivate them; that is, as I suppose
we may say, to the art of the statesman?

Clin. Just so.

[1] μετὰ τῆς τοῦ Διονύσου θεωρίας, 650 *a* 1–2.   The wine-party is playfully
spoken of as a θεωρία, as though it were one of the great festivals of the god.

[2] I render the sentence as nearly literally as I can.   The meaning is
clear, but the expression would need complete rewriting to be satisfactory.

[3] It is implied that there might be dispute about some further point in
the speaker's case.   What is this still conceivably disputable point?   The
opening sentences of Book II show that it is whether 'the bottle' can be of
any further service to the legislators, beyond being a safe and easy test of
the characters of his citizens.

BOOK II

Ath. Then the question which next arises in discussing these 652 matters, as I think, is this: rightly controlled fellowship over our cups affords a disclosure of our native disposition; but is this its sole recommendation? Or has it some further considerable and serious advantages. Yes or No? Yes, or so our argument should seem to suggest. But if we are to learn just what these advantages are, we must be on our guard against the snares it [1] lays for us.

Clin. Say on, then.

Ath. I am fain, then, for my part, to recall once more our account of right education; 'tis this, or so I seem to divine, for 653 which this institution, under proper management, affords as a safeguard.

Clin. Truly a bold assertion!

Ath. And therefore what I would say is this: a child's first infant consciousness is that of pleasure and pain, this is the domain wherein the soul first acquires virtue or vice. For wisdom and assured true conviction, a man is fortunate if he acquires them even on the verge of old age, and, in every case, he that possesses them with all their attendant blessings has come to the full stature of man. By education, then, I mean goodness in the form in which it is first acquired by a child. In fact, if pleasure and liking, pain and dislike, are formed in the soul on right lines before the age of understanding is reached, and when that age is attained, these feelings are in concord with understanding, thanks to early discipline in appropriate habits [2]— this concord, regarded as a whole, is virtue. But if you consider the one factor in it, the rightly disciplined state of pleasures and pains whereby a man, from his first beginnings on, will abhor what he should abhor and relish what he should relish—

---

[1] 'it' = 'the argument', rather than 'the custom of wine-drinking'.

[2] The translation assumes here a slight departure from Burnet's text, an insertion of $<τῷ>$ before ὀρθῶς εἰθίσθαι in 653 *b* 5. The suggestion comes from Stallbaum. If the MS. text is kept, I think we must take εἰθίσθαι as dependent on the λέγω of *b* 1, and to translate 'and if these feelings are in concord with understanding ... (I say) they have been disciplined rightly'.

if you isolate this factor and call it education, you will be giving it its true name; at least, that is my own conviction.

Clin. Yes indeed, sir; we grant the truth of what you have just said, no less than of your former observations about education.

Ath. Good; but to proceed. Education—this rightly disciplined state of pleasures and pains—is apt to be relaxed and spoiled in many ways in the course of a man's life. But the gods, in their compassion for the hardships incident to our human lot, have appointed the cycle of their festivals [1] to provide relief from this fatigue, besides giving us the Muses, their leader Apollo, and Dionysus to share these festivals with us and keep them right, with all the spiritual sustenance these deities bring to the feast. Wherein we must see whether the argument whereon we are now harping is true to the facts of things or no. What that argument says is this: no young creature whatsoever, as we may fairly assert, can keep its body or its voice still; all are perpetually trying to make movements and noises. They leap and bound, they dance and frolic, as it were with glee, and again, they utter cries of all sorts. Now animals at large have no perception of the order or disorder in these motions, no sense of what we call rhythm or melody. But in our own case, the gods of whom we spoke as given us for companions in our revels have likewise given us the power to perceive and enjoy rhythm and melody. Through this sense they stir us to movements and become our choir-leaders. They string us together on a thread of song and dance, and have named our 'choirs' so after the 'delight' (*chara*) they naturally afford. Now may we begin by taking this point as settled? May we assume that our earliest education comes through the Muses and Apollo, or not?

654

Clin. We may make that assumption.

Ath. So by an uneducated man we shall mean one who has no choric training, and by an educated man one whose choric training has been thorough?

Clin. Exactly.

Ath. And, mark you, the choric art as a whole embraces both dance and song.

Clin. No doubt.

Ath. Thus it follows that a well-educated man can both sing well and dance well.

Clin. So it would seem.

[1] I follow England in regarding τοῖς θεοῖς in 653 *d* 3, as a mistaken gloss on ἀμοιβάς, wrongly taken to mean *requitals*.

Ath. Next let us observe what that statement comes to.

Clin. What statement precisely?

Ath. Why, we say the man 'sings well' and 'dances well'. But should we, or should we not, add the qualification, 'if he sings *good* songs and dances *good* dances'?

Clin. Suppose we take in that qualification.

Ath. Well, suppose he judges the really good to be good and the bad bad, and acts accordingly. Shall we call a man who is in that case better educated in choric and musical art when he can be regularly counted upon for adequate physical and vocal rendering of what he apprehends to be good, though he feels no pleasure in the good, nor dislike of the bad, or rather when, though none too capable of correctness of vocal and physical execution, or of apprehension, he has correct feelings of pleasure and pain, is attracted by the good, and repelled by its opposite?

Clin. Sir, the advantage is vastly on the side of the education you are describing.

Ath. Then if the three of us understand what is good in song and dancing, we likewise know who has been rightly educated and who is not so; whereas, if we do not know this, we shall be equally at a loss to decide whether there is any safeguard for education, and wherein it lies. Do I take you with me?

Clin. Entirely.

Ath. So we must follow up the trail by investigating the goodness of figure, melody, song, and dance; if we let the quarry escape us, all further discourse of right education—Hellenic or non-Hellenic—will be so much waste of breath.

Clin. Just so.

Ath. Well, come now; pray what are we to speak of as *goodness* in a figure, or a melody? For instance, take a manly soul struggling with distress and a cowardly soul in the same or equal straits; do we find they express themselves in similar 655 postures and utterances?

Clin. Why, of course not, not even in similar complexions.

Ath. True, indeed, friend. But though there are figures and tunes in music, as its subject-matter is rhythm and melody, and we may accordingly speak of a tune or a posture as rhythmical or melodious, we cannot properly use the metaphorical expression of the choir-trainers, 'brilliantly-coloured', of either. But coward and brave man have their characteristic postures and strains, and it is very proper to call those of brave men good, those of cowards bad. In fact, to spare ourselves a great deal of verbal repetition in our treatment of the whole subject,

we may take it, once and for all, that universally all postures
and melodies connected with goodness of soul or body—whether
with such goodness itself or with some image of it—are good,
and those connected with badness universally the reverse.

Clin. An excellent proposal, and you may treat it as understood that we have answered you to that effect.

Ath. And now to one further point; does any choric performance give all men the like degree of enjoyment, or is the
state of the case very different?

Clin. Very different? Utterly different.

Ath. Then what shall we say is likely to be the source of this
confusion? Is it that the excellent is not the same thing for
all alike? Or that it is in fact the same, but not believed to
be so? For no one, I take it, would profess that the choric
expressions of vice can in fact be more excellent than those of
virtue, or that he personally enjoys the postures of turpitude,
though other men may prefer the opposite Muse; though, to
be sure, it is commonly *said* that the standard of rightness in
music is its pleasure-giving effect. That, however, is an intolerable sentiment, in fact, 'tis a piece of flat blasphemy.
The cause of our confusion is more probably that I am now
to mention.

Clin. And what is that?

Ath. A choric exhibition is a mimic presentation of manners,
with all variety of action and circumstance, enacted by performers who depend on characterization and impersonation.
Hence, those who, from temperament, or habit, or both at once,
find words, melodies, or other presentation of the choir, to their
taste cannot but enjoy and applaud the performance, and
further pronounce it good, whereas they who find it repugnant
to temperament, taste, or training can neither enjoy nor applaud,
and so call it bad. But where a man's native temperament is
right, and his training wrong, or his training right and his natural
temperament wrong, there enjoyment and approbation are at
656 variance. The performance is, in fact, said to be pleasant,
but bad; the man is ashamed to declare his serious approval by
executing such movements or singing such tunes before others
whom he credits with judgment, but in his own heart he enjoys
the performance.

Clin. Perfectly true.

Ath. Now do you think a man is in any way the worse for
enjoying degrading postures or melodies, or any the better for
getting his pleasure from the opposite quarter?

Clin. Presumably he is.

Ath. Only presumably? Is not his case inevitably the same as that of one who views the evil characters of bad companions in real life not with disgust, but with enjoyment, condemning their actions in a playful fashion, like one not awake to their vileness?[1] In such a case it is, surely, inevitable that a man should grow like whatever he enjoys, whether good or bad, even though he may be ashamed to approve it. The result is absolutely inevitable—and what result could we call more momentous for good or evil?

Clin. None, as I believe.

Ath. Then is it conceivable that anywhere where there are, or may hereafter be, sound laws in force touching this educative-playful function of the Muses, men of poetic gifts should be free to take whatever in the way of rhythm, melody, or diction tickles the composer's fancy in the act of composition and teach it through the choirs to the boys and lads of a law-respecting society, leaving it to chance whether the result prove virtue or vice?

Clin. To be sure, that does not sound rational; decidedly not.

Ath. And yet this is precisely what they are actually left free to do, I may say, in every community with the exception of Egypt.

Clin. And in Egypt itself, now—pray how has the law regulated the matter there?

Ath. The mere report will surprise you. That nation, it would seem, long enough ago recognized the truth we are now affirming, that poses and melodies must be good, if they are to be habitually practised by the youthful generation of citizens. So they drew up the inventory of all the standard types, and consecrated specimens of them in their temples. Painters and practitioners[2] of [all] other arts of design were forbidden to innovate on these models or entertain any but the traditional standards, and the prohibition still persists, both for these arts and for music in all its branches. If you inspect their paintings and reliefs on the spot, you will find that the work of ten

---

[1] At 656 *b* 4 I feel sure we must read, with Λ, ὀνειρώττων αὐτοῦ τὴν μοχθηρίαν. The reading αὑτοῦ adopted by some editors from inferior MSS. would mean 'seeing his own vileness in a dream'. But 'his own vileness' is just what the sort of person Plato is describing does not see at all. The meaning is that the man is not really 'alive' or 'awake' to the badness of the acts which he only censures 'with a smile'.

[2] I think the words of 656 *e* 2, καὶ ὁποῖ' ἄττα, should be deleted as an accidental 'dittography' from the καὶ ὁποῖ' ἄττα of *d* 9. If they are genuine, they must be intended to mean 'of whatever kind'.

thousand years ago—I mean the expression not loosely but in
657 all precision—is neither better nor worse than that of to-day;
both exhibit an identical artistry.

Clin. A most amazing state of things!

Ath. Or rather, one immensely to the credit of their legislators
and statesmen. No doubt one could find grounds for censure
in other Egyptian institutions, but in this matter of music, at
least, it is a fact, and a thought-provoking fact, that it has
actually proved possible, in such a sphere, to canonize melodies
which exhibit an intrinsic rightness permanently by law.[1]
That must have been the doing of a god, or a god-like man
(as, in fact, the local tradition is that the melodies which have
been preserved for so many ages were the work of Isis). So,
as I was saying before, if we can but detect the intrinsically
right in such matters, in whatever degree, we should reduce
them to law and system without misgiving, since the appeal to
feeling which shows itself in the perpetual craving for novel
musical sensation can, after all, do comparatively little to corrupt choric art, once it has been consecrated, by deriding it as
out of fashion. In Egypt, at any rate, its corrupting influence
appears to have been nowise potent, but very much the reverse.

Clin. That seems to be the state of the case from your present
account.

Ath. Then may we say boldly that the right way to employ
music and the recreations of the choric art is on some such
lines as these? When we believe things are going well with us,
we feel delight, and, conversely, when we feel delight we believe
things are well with us. You agree with me?

Clin. Surely, surely.

Ath. And, mark, when we are in that case—I mean, when we
feel delight—we cannot keep still.

Clin. Just so.

Ath. And so our young folk are eager to dance and sing
themselves, while, as for us elders, we think it the becoming
thing to pass the time by looking on at them and enjoying
their play and merriment. We miss the agility which is beginning to fail us at our years, and so we are glad to arrange
competitions for performers who can reawaken the youthfulness
in us by reminiscence.

Clin. Very true.

---

[1] I have omitted the θαρροῦντα of the MSS. in 657 *a* 7, as it creates a
verbal difficulty in the Greek, and may conceivably have got into the
text from *b* 3 below.

Ath. So we can hardly deny that there is much in the current popular judgment about the providers of entertainments. I mean, the judgment that the palm for superior ingenuity should be awarded to the entertainer who gives us most pleasure and enjoyment. Since we are granted the liberty to play on such occasions, so it is argued, of course he who gives the keenest enjoyment to the greatest number is rightly held in the highest esteem, and, as I just put it, carries off the palm. That is the right thing to say, and the right way to act, too, if the occasion 658 arises?

Clin. Yes, perhaps it is.

Ath. Still, my dear sir, let us avoid a hasty pronouncement on such a topic. It would be better to break the subject up into its details for consideration, in some such fashion as this. Suppose a man were to institute a competition without any further qualification, not specifying that it was to be an athletic or a musical contest, or a horse-race: imagine him to collect all his fellow-citizens, offer a prize, and announce that any one may enter as a competitor in simple pleasure-giving; the prize to be awarded [1] to the performer who entertains the spectators most. There are to be no restrictions as to the manner of the entertaining, so long as the man beats his competitors on that one score, and is voted the most pleasing. What should we expect to be the likely result of the announcement?

Clin. What have you in your mind?

Ath. Well, it is likely enough that one performer would produce a recitation of epic poetry, like a Homer, a second a chant to the lyre, a third a tragedy, and a fourth, perhaps, a comedy, and I should not be surprised if one of them actually thought his best chance of the prize was to exhibit a puppet-show. But, now, can we say which of all these competitors, and the host of others who would enter, *deserves* the prize?

Clin. That is a singular question. How could any one answer you, as though he could decide before he had listened and given a personal hearing to each of the different candidates?

Ath. Well, come now, would you like me to give the answer to this singular question for both of you?

Clin. To be sure.

Ath. Then here it is. If the tiny children are to decide, they will, no doubt, give it for the man with the puppet-show.

Clin. Why, of course.

---

[1] ὃς δ' ἂν τέρψῃ, 658 *b* 1.   I follow Dr. England here in regarding the δ' of the MSS. as a mistaken copyist's insertion.

Ath. The bigger boys for the comedian; the cultivated women, youths, and perhaps the absolute majority, for the tragedy.

Clin. Yes, perhaps they would.

Ath. Whereas oldsters like ourselves would be likely to get most pleasure from a reciter who gave a fine rendering of the *Iliad*, or *Odyssey*, or a Hesiodic poem, and put him far and away first. Then, who would be the rightful winner? That is our next question, I presume?

Clin. Yes.

Ath. Clearly you and I cannot avoid saying that rightful winners are those who are preferred by men of our own age. From our point of view that custom¹ is far the best of existing arrangements in all societies everywhere.

Clin. And naturally so.

Ath. So I actually go myself with the current opinion so far as this: the standard by which music should be judged is the pleasure it gives. But not the pleasure given to any and every auditor; we may take it that the finest music is that which delights the best men, the properly educated, that, above all, 659 which pleases the one man who is supreme in goodness and education. And the reason why we say judges in such matters need goodness is that they require to be equipped not only with wisdom, but particularly with courage. A judge who is truly a judge must not learn his verdict from the audience, letting himself be intimidated into it by the clamour of the multitude and his own incompetence, nor yet, out of cowardice and poltroonery, weakly pronounce a judgment which belies his own convictions with the very lips with which he invoked the gods as he entered on his functions. To tell the plain truth, the judge takes his seat not to learn from the audience, but to teach them, and to set himself against performers who give an audience pleasure in wrong and improper ways.² By the ancient and general Hellenic rule, there was none of the freedom of the present custom of Sicily and Italy, which leaves things to the majority of the audience and decides the victory by their

¹ This seems to me the true sense of the rather obscure words of 658 *e* 3–4. The 'custom' (ἔθος) of which the speakers, as themselves old men, inevitably approve, is that of deferring to the tastes of the older part of the audience.

² In 659 *b* 4–5 it would be grammatically *possible* to render 'to set himself against auditors who display their pleasure in wrong and improper ways'. But the remarks which follow seem to indicate that the speaker rather means that the 'judge' has a double duty, to instruct the audience, and to condemn the performer who appeals to the taste of its more uncultivated members.

votes, a practice which has corrupted the poets themselves
(since their standard in composition is the debased taste of their
judges, with the result that it is actually the audience who
educate *them*), and equally corrupted the tastes of the audience.
The repeated exhibition of characters better than their own ought
to produce an improvement in their taste; as things are, the
result is the direct contrary, and it is their own doing.   Once
more, then, what lesson is indicated by the conclusion of our
present argument?   Something, perhaps, to this effect.

Clin. To what effect?

Ath. Why, I believe the argument is bringing us back for the
third or fourth time to our old position, that education is, in
fact, the drawing and leading of children to the rule which has
been pronounced right by the voice of the law, and approved
as truly right by the concordant experience of the best and
oldest men.   That the child's soul, then, may not learn the
habit of feeling pleasure and pain in ways contrary to the law
and those who have listened to its bidding, but keep them
company, taking pleasure and pain in the very same things as
the aged—that, I hold, proves to be the real purpose of what
we call our 'songs'.   They are really spells for souls, directed
in all earnest to the production of the concord of which we have
spoken, but as the souls of young folk cannot bear earnestness,
they are spoken of as 'play' and 'song', and practised as such.
Just so, in the case of the physically invalid and infirm, the practitioner seeks to administer wholesome nutriment in palatable
articles of meat and drink, but unwholesome in unpalatable, 660
to accustom the patient to accept the one and reject the
other, as he should.   In the same fashion a true lawgiver likewise will persuade, or if persuasion fails, will compel, the man
of poetic gifts to compose as he ought, to employ his noble
and fine-filed phrases to represent by their rhythms the bearing,
and by their melodies the strains, of men who are pure, valiant,
and, in a word, good.

Clin. Great God! sir, do you imagine that is how poetry is
actually produced in other cities?   As far as my own observation goes, I know of no such practice as you recommend, except
here at home, or in Lacedaemon; elsewhere I notice endless
innovation in dancing and all branches of music generally,
constant change, inspired not by the laws but by a sort of
unregulated taste which is so far from being fixed and permanent, as is the case in Egypt by your account, that it never
shows any constancy.

Ath. Well observed, Clinias. But if you imagined my remarks to refer to existing practice, the unfortunate impression is probably due to my failure to make my thought clear. I did, perhaps, say things which might give you that impression, but they simply explained what I could wish to see done in the matter of music. For the denunciation of error which is far advanced and without remedy, though sometimes unavoidable, is a decidedly unpleasant duty. But since we are at one about the principle, pray tell me, is it put into practice better among yourselves and our Spartan friends than among the Greeks at large?

Clin. Certainly it is.

Ath. And suppose the rest of us followed the same practice; may we say that this would be an improvement on the existing state of things?

Clin. An extraordinary improvement, I take it, if they would follow the example of Sparta and ourselves, and the precepts which you yourself have just given us.

Ath. Come then, let us have an understanding on the issue before us. In both your communities the teaching conveyed by all education and music is to this effect, is it not? You constrain your poets to teach that a good man, since he is temperate and just, is a fortunate and happy man, no matter whether he be great and mighty or small and feeble, rich or poor. But if a man be unjust, even though he were 'richer than Midas or Cinyras', he is a pitiable creature, and his life a miserable one. To borrow the words—and true words they are—of your own poet: 'I would neither name' a man, nor 'hold him in any account', though he should practise or acquire all that is currently 661 reputed good without justice, not though, being the man he is, 'he should close with the foe and strike him down'; if a man be unjust, I would not have him 'look the bloody carnage in the face unblenched', or 'outstrip the north wind of Thrace', nor enjoy any of the goods currently so reputed. For the things popularly called goods do not really deserve the name. The saying, you know, is that health is the greatest of all goods, beauty ranks second, and wealth third, and there are innumerable other goods, such as keen sight and hearing, and acute sensibility generally; it is good also to be an autocrat and gratify all one's passions, and the very crown of felicity would be that the possessor of all these advantages should forthwith become immune from death. But what you and I maintain is that though all these endowments are great goods to men of justice and religion, one and all of them, from health down, are great evils to the unjust. To be more specific, sight, hearing, sensation, life itself, are superlatively evil, if one could persist for ever without dying in the enjoyment of all these so-called goods unaccompanied by justice and virtue at large, though less evil if he who is in such case survive only for a short while. This is my teaching, and I conceive you will persuade, or constrain, your national poets to teach it too, and likewise to produce correspondent rhythms and scales for the education of your young people. Consider, now; I affirm with confidence that so-called evils are good for the unjust, though evil for the just, and so-called goods, though really good for a good man, evil for a bad one. So, as I was asking, are you and I in accord, or not?

Clin. Partly, I think, in accord, partly decidedly not so.

Ath. Then can the point on which I fail to convince you, by any chance, be this, that if a man enjoys lifelong health, wealth, and absolute power—and I will add, if you like, exceptional strength, and immunity from death, and exemption from all other so-called evils—so long as he but has injustice and arrogance within himself, such a man's life is miserable, not happy?

Clin. Exactly; that is the point.

Ath. Good. Then what should I say next? Granted that a man is brave, strong, handsome, rich, and can satisfy every passion of a lifetime, do you deny that, if he is an unjust and arrogant man, his life must inevitably be dishonourable? Or possibly you would go so far as to concede the dishonour. 662

Clin. Readily.

Ath. And inevitably evil, too? Would you allow that?

Clin. No, that is not to be so readily admitted.

Ath. And, further, unpleasant and inexpedient for himself?

Clin. How can we possibly carry concession to that pitch?

Ath. How? Apparently only by the intervention of a god to produce a concord as complete as our present discordance. For my part, dear Clinias, I find it even more certain that these truths are beyond question than that Crete is an island. Were I a legislator, I would do my best to constrain my poets and all my citizens to proclaim them; I would inflict a penalty little short of the capital on any inhabitant heard to maintain that there are wicked men who have a pleasant life, or that one course may be advantageous and profitable, but a different course more truly rightful—not to mention many other points on which I would try to persuade my citizens to use language very different

from that current, apparently, among Cretans and Lacedae·
monians, and, certainly, among mankind in general. Why,
for the love of Zeus and Apollo, my worthy friends, imagine
we could put the question to the very gods who were the authors
of your own laws: 'Is the justest life also the most pleasant,
or are there two different lives, one which is the most pleasant,
and another which is the most just?' Should they answer that
there are two, we might probably go on to ask, if we knew how
to put the right question: 'And which should be called the
happier men, those who live the more just life, or those who live
the more pleasant?' Should they say, 'those who live the more
pleasant', the statement would come very oddly from *them*.[1]
Yet I could wish not to introduce the names of gods into such
a matter, and should prefer to use those of fathers and legislators. We will, therefore, take my questions as having been
addressed to such a father and lawgiver, and imagine him to
reply that he who lives the pleasantest life is the most blest
of mankind. 'Father', I should next remark, 'did you not mean
me to have the happiest of lives? Yet you were never weary
of enjoining me to lead the justest life.' Thus the father or
legislator, whichever he might be, who should decide in that
sense, would, I fancy, appear strangely wanting in self-consistency. But should he take the other view that the justest
life is happiest, any hearer, I conceive, would ask what good or
663 blessing greater than pleasure that life has in it, that the law
should commend it. What good, in fact, can come to the just
man unattended by pleasure? Good fame, for example, and
commendation from men and gods, are they good and honourable, but unpleasant? And is the reverse true of ill-fame?
Not a bit of it, respected legislator. Or again, neither to inflict
wrong nor to suffer it, is that a course which, though good and
honourable, is unpleasant, or its opposite pleasant, though
dishonourable and evil?

Clin. Surely not.

Ath. And thus the theory which declines to separate the
pleasant from the just, or the good from the honourable, if
it has no other merits, is at least a persuasive to a just and
religious life.[2] Hence from the legislator's point of view any
theory which denies these positions is highly disgraceful and

---

[1] An allusion to the religious associations of the word εὐδαίμων (happy),
'under the favour of heaven'. It is these associations which make it
'odd' to think of a god as calling a man who is wanting in virtue εὐδαίμων.

[2] Or possibly, 'is at least a persuasive to a just and religious life, if to
nothing more'.

dangerous, since no one, if he can help it, will let himself be persuaded into following a course not attended by a surplus of pleasure over pain. It is distance which causes confusion of vision in, I may say, all of us, and particularly in children, unless the lawgiver will effect a reversal of our judgments and dissipate our darkness, persuading us, as best he can, by institutions, eulogies, and arguments that right and wrong are like puzzle-pictures, wrong appearing, in the opposite perspective to right, pleasant when viewed from the standpoint of one who is himself unjust and evil, and right most unpleasant, but everything the precise contrary, on both sides, from the point of view of the righteous.

Clin. So it would seem.

Ath. And which verdict, should we say, has the more valid claim to be true, that of the worse soul, or that of the better?

Clin. Certainly, I should presume, that of the better.

Ath. Then it is consequently certain that an unjust life is not merely more dishonourable and despicable, but actually more truly unpleasant than a just and religious.

Clin. So it should follow from our present argument, my friend.

Ath. And even had it not been so—as our present argument has shown that it is—could a legislator of even moderate merits, supposing him to have ventured on any fiction for the sake of its good effect on the young, have devised a more useful fiction than this, or one more potent to induce us all to practise all justice freely, and without compulsion?

Clin. Why, as to truth, sir, truth is a glorious thing and an enduring thing, but it seems no easy matter to convince men of it.

Ath. Well, and that most improbable fable of the man from Sidon [1]—was it easy to convince any one of that? Now there are many such tales.

Clin. Tales? Of what sort?

Ath. Why, they say teeth were once sown in the ground and armed men sprang up from them. And yet the example is striking proof for a lawgiver that the youthful mind will be persuaded of anything, if one will take the trouble to persuade it. Thus he need only tax his invention to discover what conviction 664 would be most beneficial to a city, and then contrive all manner of devices to ensure that the whole of such a community shall

[1] Cadmus, who killed the dragon from whose teeth, when sown in the ground, sprang the first inhabitants of Thebes.

treat the topic in one single and selfsame lifelong tone, alike
in song, in story, and in discourse. Still, if you incline to a
different opinion, you are perfectly free to controvert my view.

Clin. Nay, neither of us, I conceive, feels equal to disputing
the point.

Ath. Then it becomes my business to proceed to the next
point. I maintain that all our choirs, of which there will be
three, must enchant the souls of our children, while they are still
young and tender, by reciting all the noble doctrines we have so
far rehearsed or may hereafter rehearse, the sum and substance
whereof may be worded thus: if we say that the gods account
the pleasantest and the best life one and the same, our statement will be at once perfectly true, and more convincing to
those whom we have to convince than if we spoke in any
other tones.

Clin. The contention must be admitted.

Ath. In the first place, then, it will be proper that the choir
of boys (which will be sacred to the Muses) should make its
entry first to sing publicly to this effect with all its might before
the whole city. Next the choir of men under thirty should make
its appearance, invoking the God of Healing [1] to bear witness
to the truth of the doctrine uttered, and praying him of his
grace to convince the young of it. And there must, of course,
be still a third song from those who are between the ages of
thirty and sixty. Men of more advanced age, who are naturally
no longer equal to singing,[2] will be left to tell stories about the
same types of character in inspired accents.

Clin. And pray, sir, whom may you mean by this third choir?
My friend and I do not understand what you would say of them
any too clearly.

Ath. And yet they are the very parties we have had in view in
the greater part of our previous conversation.

Clin. We are as much in the dark as ever; would you kindly
make your explanation rather clearer.

Ath. You may recollect that we said, at the opening of our
discussion, that all young creatures are naturally full of fire,
and can keep neither their limbs nor their voices quiet. They
are perpetually breaking into disorderly cries and jumps, but
whereas no other animal develops a sense of order of either
kind, mankind forms a solitary exception. Order in movement
665 is called *rhythm*, order in articulation—the blending of acute

[1] Apollo Paean.
[2] Or perhaps, 'who can naturally no longer contribute a song'.

with grave—*pitch*, and the name for the combination of the two
is *choric art*. We further said that, in their pity for us, the gods
have granted us companions and leaders of our choirs in Apollo
and the Muses, to whom, you may remember, we added Dionysus
as a third.

Clin. Why, of course we recollect this.

Ath. Well, we have already spoken of choirs of Apollo and of
the Muses, so the remaining choir, the third, must be called that
of Dionysus.

Clin. What! pray explain yourself. A choir of old men
sacred to Dionysus! That sounds very oddly on a first hearing,
if you seriously mean that men between thirty, or even fifty,
and sixty are to form his chorus.

Ath. You are quite right. It does call for some argument,
I take it, to show that such an arrangement would be a
reasonable one.

Clin. To be sure it does.

Ath. We are in agreement, then, upon the results reached
so far?

Clin. And what are they?

Ath. That the spell we have described must be recited without
intermission by every one, adult or child, free man or slave, man
or woman; in fact the whole city must repeat it incessantly to
itself in forms to which we must somehow contrive at all costs
to give inexhaustible variety and subtlety, so that the performers' appetite for their own hymnody and enjoyment of it
may persist unabated.

Clin. That is the result to be secured, as every one must agree.

Ath. Now where must this worthiest element in our city—
its combined years and wisdom will give it more authority than
any other class, and the matter of its odes will be the noblest
of all—do its singing, if it is to be most potent for good? Are
we, in pure folly, to leave the body principally responsible for
the noblest and most useful music without directions?

Clin. We certainly must not neglect it, if your argument is
to be trusted.

Ath. What, then, would be the becoming arrangement?
Something of this kind, perhaps?

Clin. Of what kind?

Ath. As a man gets into years, the reluctance to sing grows
upon him. He feels less pleasure in the act, and, if it is forced
on him, the older and more sober-minded he grows, the more
bashful he feels about it. I am right, am I not?

Clin. Decidedly right.

Ath. And of course he will feel still more bashful about standing up and singing in a theatre before an audience of all sorts. And besides, if men of such years and character were made, like competing choirs, to train their voices for the performance by a lowering regimen and abstinence from food, their singing would surely be a thoroughly disagreeable and humiliating task, and consequently their execution would be spiritless.

666   *Clin.* There is no disputing what you say.

Ath. Then how shall we encourage them to sing with spirit? Might we not make a law to the following effect? In the first place, we shall absolutely prohibit the taste of wine to boys under eighteen. We shall tell them they must have too much concern for the passionate temperament of youth to feed the fire of body or soul with a further current of fire [1] before they address themselves to the labours of life. In the next, while we permit a moderate use of wine to men under thirty, we shall absolutely forbid carousing and free potations. But when a man is verging on the forties, we shall tell him, after he has finished banqueting at the general table, to invoke the gods, and more particularly to ask the presence of Dionysus in that sacrament and pastime of advancing years—I mean the wine-cup [2]—which he bestowed on us for a comfortable medicine against the dryness of old age, that we might renew our youth, and our harsher mood be melted to softness by forgetfulness of our heaviness, as iron is melted in the furnace, and so made more tractable. To begin with, in that mood any man would be ready, would he not, to render his song—or, as we have so often called it, his spell—with more spirit and less bashfulness, not perhaps before a numerous audience of strangers, but in a smaller circle of personal friends?

Clin. Emphatically so.

Ath. As a means of inducing them to take their part in our proposed singing, then, the device is not so wholly out of place?

Clin. Out of place? By no means.

Ath. But what manner of strain should they utter? Of course it must be a music in keeping with their persons.

---

[1] Lit. 'to let in a channel of fire upon the fire of soul or body', the metaphor being from the irrigation of a market-garden. (Cf. *Tim.* 77 *c* 7 ff.) 'Fire upon fire' is a proverbial expression of the same import as our 'coals to Newcastle'.

[2] Possibly the words τὸν οἶνον, 666 *b* 6, 'the wine-cup', should be deleted as an explanatory 'adscript'.

Clin. Why, of course.

Ath. And what is the music which befits godlike men? Choric song? [1]

Clin. Why, sir, personally we Spartans and our Cretan friends are quite incapable of any singing but that we learned when we were trained to sing in choirs.

Ath. I am not surprised at it; in plain fact, you have never risen to the noblest kind of song. Your cities are organized like armies, not like societies of town-dwellers; you keep your young men in herds like so many colts at grass in one troop. None of you ever takes his own colt, draws him out of the general herd, for all his restiveness and fuming, and puts him in the charge of a special groom to be stroked and tamed and treated with all the attention required by a training which will make him no mere good soldier, but a man fit to administer a 667 state and its townships—will make him, in fact, the type of man of whom we spoke at first as a better warrior than those of Tyrtaeus, because he will esteem valour, always and everywhere, the fourth, not the first, point of goodness in individuals and in society at large.

Clin. Somehow or other, sir, you are back again at your belittling of our legislators.

Ath. Nay, my dear sir, if I do so at all, it is of no set purpose; but please let us follow where our argument leads. If we can find a music more excellent than that of choirs and public theatres, let us make the attempt to assign it to these men, who, as we are saying, are anxious to take their part in the noblest music, though bashful where the kind just mentioned is concerned.

Clin. By all means.

Ath. Well, to begin with, must it not hold good of all things which have an attendant charm that their chief value lies either in this mere charm itself, in their rightness in some sense, or, finally, in their utility? To give an example, I mean that meat and drink, and articles of nutriment generally, are attended by a charm which we may call flavour; [2] as to rightness and

---

[1] We are now coming to the real point. We shall see that the 'third choir' is not meant literally to sing, but to set the standard for the music of younger performers, and apparently to take part in 'compiling the anthology'. This, I think, explains the use they are to make of 'the bottle'. Their natural tendency would be to make the standard and the anthology too 'elderly'. They are less likely to commit this fault if they come to the work mellowed by a bottle of generous wine.

[2] The word rendered 'flavour', 'gusto' in these passages is ἡδονή, the word for 'pleasure' in general. It is here, however, being used with a conscious echo of its sense in Ionian physics, 'savour', agreeable taste or smell.

utility, it is precisely what we call the wholesomeness of the
various viands which is also their true rightness.

Clin. Exactly.

Ath. Again, the act of learning is attended by a charm, a
gusto,[1] but it is the truth of what is learned which gives it its
rightness and utility, its goodness and nobility.

Clin. Just so.

Ath. And what of the various arts of imitation which work by
producing likenesses? If they are so far successful, I mean if
they give rise to an attendant pleasure, charm, I suppose, would
be just the right name for it?

Clin. Yes.

Ath. Whereas the rightness of such products, speaking generally, depends not on their pleasantness, but on accurate correspondence in quality and magnitude?

Clin. True.

Ath. Thus the only case in which it will be right to make
pleasure our standard of judgment is that of a performance
which provides us with neither utility, nor truth, nor resemblance, though, of course, it must do us no harm either, an
activity practised solely with a view to this concomitant charm,
which is very properly called *pleasure,* unattended by any of
the results just specified?

Clin. You refer only to *harmless* pleasure?

Ath. Yes, and I also use the name *play* for it in cases where it
does neither harm nor good worth taking into serious account.

Clin. Very true.

Ath. Then surely it follows from the argument that a man's
feeling of pleasure, or his erroneous belief, is never a proper
standard by which to judge of any representation, and I will
668 add, any proportionality.[2] Equal is never equal, nor symmetrical symmetrical, because someone believes it to be so,
or because someone feels[3] † no pleasure; no, we should judge
by the standard of truth, never, on any account, by any
other.

Clin. Assuredly.

---

[1] i.e. in this case 'utility' and 'correctness', or 'rightness', coincide.

[2] ἰσότητα, 668 *a* 1, lit. *equality.* But Plato is thinking of 'geometrical'
equality, i.e. proportionality. He does not suggest that a good portrait,
for example, must be life-sized.

[3] ἢ μή τις χαίρει τῳ, 668 *a* 1–2. There is clearly something wrong about
the words, since the negative μή, as it stands, does not suit the context.
But it seems impossible to restore the text intended with certainty. The
mere replacing of the μή by εἰ gives a suitable sense, 'because someone
feels pleasure', but the supposed corruption is not a likely one.

Ath. Now we may say that all music is an art of producing likenesses or representations.

Clin. Of course.

Ath. Consequently, when a man tells us that in music pleasure is the standard of judgment, we must refuse to accept his statement. It is not this type of music, if indeed there could be such a type, which we should make our serious object, but that other which retains its likeness to the model of the noble.[1]

Clin. Just so.

Ath. And these citizens of ours, too, will naturally have to do the same. As they aim at the noblest kind of song, they will also have to aim not at a music which is pleasing, but at one which is *right*. In fact, we explained the rightness of a representation to lie in reproduction of the proportions and quality of the original.

Clin. To be sure.

Ath. Again, it would be universally allowed of music that its productions are all of the nature of representation and portraiture. Composers, performers, audience, all of them would be in complete agreement so far?

Clin. Beyond doubt.

Ath. Hence it should seem that a man who is to make no mistake of judgment about a particular production must, in every case, understand what that production is. If he does not understand what it is, that is, what it is meant for, or of what it is in fact an image, it will be a long time before he will discern the rightness or wrongness in the artist's purpose.

Clin. A long time indeed.

Ath. And if a man does not understand this *rightness*, can he possibly be in a position to discuss the *goodness* or *badness* of the work? My question is not very clearly expressed, but it will perhaps become clearer if I put it thus.

Clin. How, pray?

Ath. There are, as you know, numerous likenesses which are apprehended by the eye.

Clin. Of course.

Ath. Now suppose that, in their case too, a man did not know what the various bodies represented were. Could he possibly judge of the rightness of the artist's work? For example, could he tell whether it shows the members of the body in

---

[1] τῷ τοῦ καλοῦ μιμήματι, 668 *b* 2. I think C. Ritter right in holding that here, and at 669 *e* 4, 796 *b* 3, μίμημα, which usually means the *product* of imitation, is used for the *model* imitated. Cf. our uses of the word *copy*.

their true and natural numbers and real situations, so disposed relatively to one another as to reproduce the natural grouping —to say nothing of colour or shape—or whether all this is confused in the representation? Could a man, think you, possibly decide the question, if he simply did not know what the creature depicted was?

Clin. Naturally he could not.

Ath. Now suppose we are aware that the figure the artist has drawn or modelled is that of a human being, and that he has reproduced all its members, with their colours and outlines; 669 does it follow that one who is alive to this need be competent to judge on the further point whether the work is beautiful, or falls short of beauty in some way?

Clin. Why, sir, at that rate, we should all, without exception, be connoisseurs of an animal's points.

Ath. Quite true. Then must not one who is to be an intelligent judge of any representation, whether in drawing, in music, or in any other branch of art, have three qualifications? He must understand, first, what the object reproduced *is*, next, how *correctly*, third and last, how *well* a given representation has been effected, in point of language, melody, or rhythm.

Clin. So it would appear.

Ath. Now we must not omit the full explanation of the difficulty of music. There is much more talk about musical imagery than about any other kind, and this is the very reason why such imagery demands more cautious scrutiny than any other. It is here that error is at once most dangerous, as it encourages morally bad dispositions, and most difficult to detect, because our poets are not altogether on the level of the Muses themselves. The Muses, we may be assured, would never commit the grave mistake of setting masculine language to an effeminate scale, or tune, or wedding melody, or postures worthy of free men with rhythms only fit for slaves and bondsmen, or taking the pose of a free man and combining it with an air or words of inappropriate rhythm. Not to say that they would never make a pretended presentation of a single theme out of a medley of human voices, animal cries, noises of machinery, and other things. Whereas our mere human poets tend to be only too fond of provoking the contempt of those of us who, in the phrase of Orpheus, are 'ripe for delight', by this kind of senseless and complicated confusion. In fact, not only do we see confusion of this kind, but our poets go still further. They divorce rhythm and figure [1] from melody, by giving metrical form to bare discourse, and melody and rhythm from words, by their employment of cithern and flute without vocal accompaniment, though it is the hardest of tasks to discover what such wordless rhythm and tune signify, or what model worth considering they represent. Nay, we are driven to the conclusion that all this so popular employment of cithern or flute, not subordinated to the control of dance or song, for the display of speed and virtuosity, and the reproduction of the cries of animals, is in the worst of bad taste; the use of either as an independent instrument is 670 no better than unmusical legerdemain. So much for the theory of the thing; but, after all, the question for ourselves is what kind of music our citizens of thirty or more, and again our men of over fifty, are to practise, not what they are to avoid. And I think we may at once infer from what has been said as much as this: those quinquagenarians whose business it will be to sing for us must at least have had an education better than that of a choir. They must, of course, be keenly sensitive to rhythms and melodies and able to judge of them. How, indeed, is a man with little or no familiarity with the Dorian scale to judge of the rightness of the airs, or the rightness or wrongness of the rhythm to which the poet has set his air?

Clin. Plainly he can do nothing of the sort.

Ath. In fact, the general public are simply ridiculous in their belief that men are adequate judges of what is good or otherwise in melody and rhythm, if they have merely been drilled into singing to the flute [2] and marching in step, though it never occurs to them that they do the acts without understanding anything about them. Whereas, of course, any tune is correct if it has the proper constituents, incorrect if it has unsuitable ones.

Clin. Undeniably.

Ath. But what now about a man who does not even know what constituents a piece has? As I was asking, will he be a judge of its correctness in any instance whatever?

Clin. Unquestionably not.

Ath. Thus it seems we are brought back again to our discovery

---

[1] The 'figures' meant are apparently those of the *ballet d'action* which Plato would have combined with the voices and the instrumental accompaniment.

[2] I translate in 670 *b* 10, Badham's palaeographically admirable correction, αὐλῷ (for MSS. αὐτῶν). With the MS. αὐτῶν the sense is, 'the general public are ridiculous in their belief that they are adequate judges, that is, those of them who have been drilled into singing to an accompaniment and marching', etc.

that these singers of ours, whom we are urging and placing
under a kind of voluntary coercion to sing, will need as much
previous education as this: they will all need the ability to
follow the steps of the rhythms and the notes of the airs, to
qualify them to pass the scales and rhythms under review,
select from them those proper to be rendered by men of their
own years and character, and sing them as they should be sung,
a performance which will both give the performers an immediate
innocent pleasure and provide their juniors with a lesson in
proper appreciation of sound character.[1] If they are educated
to this pitch they will have at their disposal a more careful
education than either that which is applicable to the generality,
or that of the poets themselves. For the poet it is not indispensable to be a judge of our third point—whether his representation is a good one or not—though judgment of scale and rhythm
certainly cannot be dispensed with; but the men we have in
view will need all these qualifications to fit them to make the
671 selection of the absolute best and the second-best;[2] otherwise
none of them will effectually charm the young into virtue.
The argument has now done its best to achieve its original
purpose, to show that our defence of the 'choir of Dionysus'
is a good one, and we have to consider its success. Of course,
any such gathering inevitably grows noisy as the drinking goes
further and further, as we began by assuming is bound to happen
in cases like these.

Clin. Yes, inevitably.

Ath. In such a company every one soars above his common
level of lightsomeness and jollity, bubbles over with loquacity,
pays no heed to the talk of his companions, but thinks himself
fully entitled to give the law to himself and all the rest.

Clin. Assuredly.

Ath. As we were saying, then, in this state of affairs the souls
of the drinkers grow softer as they are heated, like heated iron,
and become more juvenile, and consequently more ductile in
the hands of one who has the power and skill to train them and
mould them, much as when they were still youthful, and the

[1] i.e. the old men set the example of a sound taste by their relish for the
best music, which, as we have been told before, is 'imitative' of the tones
and bearing of a manly, noble character.

[2] The 'three points', on one of which the composer himself need not be
a competent judge, are those mentioned already: (1) what the subject of
the work of art is; (2) how correctly it has been represented; (3) whether
the representation, besides being correct, is *good*. The composer need not
be, and usually is not, a judge on this last point; he may leave it to the
authorities who act as 'censors'.

moulding should now, as formerly, be the task of the good legislator. It is for him to lay down laws for the wine-party effectual to induce our reveller, who is growing so sanguine and confident, so unduly relieved of his modesty, and so unwilling to observe order and alternation of silence with speech, drinking with music, to do the contrary of all this of his own accord; effectual also to confront this uncomely confidence, at its first entrance, with a righteous antagonist in that most comely, that divine, fear which has received the name of modesty and the sense of shame.

Clin. Very true.

Ath. And for wardens of these laws and fellow-workers with them, we must set the unperturbed and sober as captains over the unsober, for without them the battle with drink is more hazardous than a battle against an enemy in the field without unperturbed commanders. Moreover, if a man cannot yield willing obedience to them and to Dionysus his officers, that is, the citizens of over sixty, he must be put to as much disgrace as one who disobeys the officers of Ares, or to more.

Clin. Rightly said.

Ath. Then if wine and merriment were used in such fashion, would not the members of such a party be the better for it, and part, not as they do to-day, on terms of enmity, but with an increase of friendship, seeing [1] their intercourse would have been regulated throughout by laws, and they would have followed the path marked out by the sober for the unsober? 672

Clin. True enough, if there could indeed be a party such as you describe.

Ath. Then pray let us have done with the old unqualified censure of the gift of Dionysus as an evil thing, not fit to be tolerated in a city. Indeed, one might be still more copious on the topic, though I feel some reluctance even to mention the principal benefit of the god's gift before the public, as the statement has been misunderstood and misjudged.

Clin. And what benefit is that?

Ath. There is a current of story and pious tradition to the effect that this god was bereft of his intellects by his stepmother Hera, and that this is why he afflicts his victims with Bacchic possession and all its frenzied dancing, by way of revenge; that, and nothing else, was the motive for his gift of wine. For my own part I leave such stories to those who think it safe

[1] In 672 *a* 1 the translation adopts England's change of κατὰ νόμους δέ to κατὰ νόμους δή.

to tell them of deities, but of one thing I am certain: no creature whatsoever is born with that intelligence, or all that intelligence, which characterizes it in its maturity. Hence, so long as a creature has not yet attained its proper level of native sense, it is quite mad, indulging in random cries, and, as soon as it has found its feet, in equally random leaps. And let me remind you that we pronounced these the source of both music and gymnastic.

Clin. Naturally we have not forgotten that.

Ath. You will recollect, too, how we said that in mankind this beginning has preluded to perception of rhythm and melody, and that the gods responsible for that development are Apollo, the Muses, and Dionysus?

Clin. To be sure.

Ath. And as for wine in particular, the general story would seem to hold that it has been bestowed on men in vindictiveness, to drive us frantic, whereas our present version is that the gift was meant, on the contrary, as a medicine, to produce modesty of soul, and health and strength of body.

Clin. An admirable summary of the argument, sir.

Ath. Then we have finished our treatment of one half of the choric art; shall we go on with further consideration of the other half, or should we perhaps dismiss the subject?

Clin. What are the halves you speak of? How do you distinguish the one from the other?

Ath. Why, the choric art as a whole we found to be the same thing as the whole of education, and one half of the art, that which has to do with the voice, consists of rhythms and melodies.

Clin. Just so.

Ath. And the part which deals with bodily movement has rhythm in common with the movements of the voice, but 673 posture and gesticulation are proper to it, just as melody, on the other side, is to vocal movement.

Clin. Precisely so.

Ath. Now the training of the voice to goodness,[1] continued till it reaches the soul, we named, in a sense, music.

Clin. And a very proper name for it, too.

Ath. As for the training of the body—we spoke of it as the dancing of creatures at play—when the process culminates in goodness of body, let us call scientific bodily discipline with that purpose gymnastic.

---

[1] In 673 *a* 4 the translation follows C. Ritter's certain correction of ἀρετῆς παιδείαν to ἀρετὴν παιδείας.

Clin. As we may very properly do.

Ath. As for music—that half of the choric art of which we have just professed to have given a complete review—our statement may be taken as still standing. How shall we proceed next? Shall we discuss the other branch, or what?

Clin. My dear sir, you are conversing with Cretans and Lacedaemonians: what possible answer, then, do you expect from either of us to that question, if we pass over gymnastic, now that we have disposed of music?

Ath. I take that remark as a pretty plain answer to my question; in fact, I recognize that though in form a question, it is actually what I have called it, an answer, and something more—an instruction to complete our treatment of gymnastic.

Clin. You take my meaning correctly, and I entreat you to comply with it.

Ath. Why, so I will, nor will it be particularly difficult, as you are both at home in the subject, having indeed made more experimental acquaintance with this art than with the former.

Clin. There you are very much in the right.

Ath. Well, this art similarly has its origin in the habitual leaping native to all living things, and in mankind, as we have said, the acquisition of a sense of rhythm has generated dancing; since melody suggests and awakens consciousness of rhythm, the two in conjunction have given rise to the play of the choric dance.

Clin. Quite so.

Ath. One branch of the subject, as I have said, we have treated already, and will next do our best to deal with the other.

Clin. With all my heart.

Ath. Then, if you both approve, we may first give the final touch to our account of drinking.

Clin. And how do you propose to do this?

Ath. If a city is to practise the custom now under discussion in a serious spirit, in subjection to the control of law and rule, as a training in self-command, and permits a similar indulgence in other pleasures on the same principle, as a means to mastery of them, all without exception should be treated on the lines we have laid down. But if the practice is treated as mere play, and free licence is to be given to any man to drink whenever he pleases, in what company he pleases, and when engaged on any undertaking he pleases, I could no longer vote for allowing any 674 indulgence in the wine-cup to such a city, or such a man. I would even go further than the practice of Crete and Lacedaemon

and propose an addition to the Carthaginian law which pro-
hibits the very taste of this liquor to all soldiers in the field,
and enforces water-drinking throughout the duration of a campaign. I would absolutely prohibit its taste in civic life to
slaves of both sexes, to magistrates throughout the year of their
office, and equally absolutely to captains of vessels and jurymen
when on duty, and likewise to any member of an important
council when about to attend its meetings. Further, I would
prohibit its use during the day absolutely, except under the
orders of a trainer or a physician, and at night also
to any person of either sex contemplating the procreation of
children, to pass over many other cases in which wine is not to
be drunk by rational men with a sound law. Thus you see that
by our argument no city would need many vineyards; agricultural production and bodily regimen in general would be
matters for regulation, and viticulture in particular would be
kept within very reasonable and narrow bounds. And this,
gentlemen, if it has your approval, may be taken as the finale
of my remarks on the subject of wine.

Clin. It is well said, indeed, and we fully concur.

BOOK III

Ath. Enough, then, on this matter. But what may we take 676 to have been the first beginning of a State? I wonder whether the best and easiest way to treat the problem may not be this?

Clin. What?

Ath. To start from the same point with which we regularly have to begin when we would study the double progressive development of a city in virtue and vice.

Clin. And that point is?

Ath. Why, the interminable length of time, I conceive, and the changes time brings with it.

Clin. Pray explain yourself.

Ath. Well, cities have existed and men have lived in civil society for a long time; do you think you could possibly tell how long?

Clin. Not readily, to say the least of it.

Ath. But you admit at least that it must have been so for an immense and incredible time?

Clin. Oh yes, there is no doubt about that.

Ath. And you will surely grant that thousands and thousands of cities have come into being during this time, and no less a number have ceased to exist? Moreover, every form of constitution has repeatedly appeared in one or other of them; sometimes a small city has grown larger, sometimes a large city smaller; a bad city has sometimes grown better, a good city sometimes worse?

Clin. Indubitably.

Ath. Thus we have, if possible, to discover the cause of these variations; there, I suspect, we may find the key to the primal origin of constitutions and their modification.

Clin. A happy thought, and we must all do our best endeavour, you to expound your thoughts on the subject, and my friend and myself to keep pace with you.

Ath. Then what view do you both take of the ancient legends? 677 Have they any truth behind them?

Clin. Which legends might you mean?

Ath. Those which tell of repeated destructions of mankind by floods, pestilences, and from various other causes, which leave only a handful of survivors.

Clin. Oh, that kind of story must be perfectly credible to any man.

Ath. Very well; let us suppose one of those various exterminations, that which was once effected by the Flood.[1]

Clin. And what is the point you would have us observe about it?

Ath. That the few who then escaped the general destruction must all have been mountain shepherds, mere scanty embers of humanity left unextinguished among their high peaks.

Clin. Why, obviously.

Ath. And of course men like these were bound to be unfamiliar with the crafts at large and, above all, with the tricks of town-dwellers for overreaching and outdistancing one another and the rest of their devices for mutual infliction of mischief.

Clin. The probabilities are certainly on that side.

Ath. Now may we assume that at such a time there is a total destruction of the cities situated in the lowlands and on the sea coast?

Clin. We may, no doubt.

Ath. And we may add that all implements are lost, and that any discoveries of value due to the science of statesmen or other specialists all vanish at such a time? For to be sure, my dear sir, if such inventions could persist permanently in their present excellence, how could there ever be a new discovery of anything?

Clin. As much as to say that we must take the men of those ages to have known nothing of these matters for untold tens of thousands of years; it is only some thousand or two thousand years since they were revealed, partly by Daedalus, partly by Orpheus, partly by Palamedes, music by Marsyas and Olympus, the lyre by Amphion, and various other discoveries by numerous other persons—a mere business, so to say, of yesterday and the day before.

Ath. It is delicate in you, Clinias, to omit your connection, who was in strict fact a man of yesterday.

Clin. You refer to Epimenides, I presume?

Ath. To no other. You know, my friend, his invention left them all in the lurch. True, Hesiod had long before had a

[1] Apparently the speaker means the famous 'Flood' of Greek legend, that of Deucalion, though we are told in the *Timaeus* (22 *b*) and *Critias* (112 *a*) that this was only the most recent of a series.

glimmer of it in theory, but the practical achievement belonged
to the other, by your Cretan story.

Clin. It did, indeed.

Ath. Then I suppose one may say that the state of mankind
at the time of the calamity was this: there was frightful and
widespread depopulation, but a vast territory of unoccupied
land; most of the animals had perished, but there were a few
herds of cattle, and perhaps a surviving stock of goats, and
these provided those who grazed them with a sustenance which
would be scanty enough in the first instance.   678

Clin. No doubt.

Ath. But as for a city, a constitution, a legislation—the
themes of our present conversation—can we imagine that,
to put it broadly, the faintest recollection of them was
preserved?

Clin. Why, surely not.

Ath. Now that is the condition which has given rise to the
whole complex of our actual life, with its cities and constitutions,
its sciences, its laws, its manifold moral evil and equally manifold
moral goodness?

Clin. I do not quite follow you.

Ath. Why, my good sir, can we suppose that the men of that
day, unacquainted as they were alike with the numerous
blessings and the numerous curses of town life, would be mature
either in moral virtue or in vice?

Clin. Well demanded; we appreciate your point.

Ath. Thus it is by progress of time and the multiplication
of the species that life has come to be as we actually
find it?

Clin. Exactly.

Ath. And that, I presume, not all at once, but little by little
in the course of an immense period of time.

Clin. Nothing can be more likely.

Ath. Indeed, they were still haunted, I should presume, by
a terror of coming down from the highlands to the plains.

Clin. Naturally.

Ath. Thus, though the sight of another's face must have been
welcome indeed in those days when men's numbers were so few,
all conveyances for travel by land or water must have been
pretty universally abolished, must they not, with the loss of the
arts? So social intercourse, I conceive, was not easily feasible.
For iron, copper, and metallic deposits in general had been so
obliterated by the inundation that it was a problem to get

them clear again,[1] and they had little opportunity of cutting timber. For what few tools might have survived among their mountains must soon have been used up and disappeared, and they would not be in a condition to replace them until the art of mining reappeared among them.

Clin. Of course not.

Ath. And how many generations must we suppose to pass before that would happen?

Clin. A very considerable number, beyond all doubt.

Ath. Consequently, all arts which require iron, copper, and similar materials had then been lost for this period, or even longer.

Clin. Naturally.

Ath. And therefore both civil conflict and war had equally disappeared all through this period, for more reasons than one.

Clin. And what were those reasons?

Ath. For one thing, men's loneliness made them sociable and friendly; for another, there could be no quarrelling over the 679 means of subsistence. Except perhaps in some instances at the very first, they were not stinted for flocks and herds, the principal support of life in that age; in fact, there was no shortage of milk or meat, and besides, they could supply themselves with plenty of excellent viands by hunting. Again, they were quite well off for clothes, bedding, shelter, or vessels, culinary and other. Iron, as you know, is wholly superfluous for the arts of the potter and the weaver, and these two crafts have, by divine appointment, been empowered to supply all our wants, that our species may still be enabled to germinate and increase when it falls into such straits. Thus they were not extremely poor, for the reason I have assigned, and so were not set at variance by the stress of penury; rich they could never become in the absence of gold and silver which was then their case. Now, a society in which neither riches nor poverty is a member regularly produces sterling characters, as it has no place for violence and wrong, nor yet for rivalry and envy. Thus they were good men, partly for this reason, and partly from their proverbial 'simplicity'; they were so 'simple' that when they heard things called fair or foul, they obediently took the statements for infallible truths. No one was sufficiently subtle to

---

[1] The connection of thought is this. There would be neither carriages nor boats, since timber is required for both, and timber could not be felled for want of the necessary tools until the arts of mining and metallurgy had been recovered.

suspect deception, as men do to-day; what they were told about God or man they believed to be true, and lived by it. Thus they came to be just the kind of men you and I have been describing.

Clin. I agree with the statement, for one, and so does my friend here.

Ath. Then I take it we may say that the many generations of men who led such a life were bound, by comparison with the age before the Deluge or with our own, to be rude and ignorant in the various arts, particularly in those of warfare, as practised to-day by land or water, and again within the city, under the names of litigation and party-faction, with their manifold artful contrivances for the infliction of mutual injury and wrong by word and by deed; they were simpler and manlier, and by consequence more self-controlled and more righteous generally. The reason of this has already been explained.

Clin. Just so.

Ath. Now it must be understood that our purpose in the statement we have made and all the inferences we have based on it, is simply to learn how laws came to be needed in those remote ages and who enacted them.

680

Clin. Yes; excellently put.

Ath. May we not perhaps say, then, that in that age men were in no need of a lawgiver, and that such a thing as a law was as yet unusual? In fact, those whose lives fall in that part of the cycle [1] do not as yet so much as possess an alphabet, but regulate their lives by custom and what is called *traditionary* law.

Clin. That is at least the fair presumption.

Ath. Still, even this is already a form of polity.

Clin. But what form?

Ath. The form of polity in that age was, I believe, what is universally called *dynasty*,[2] a form still to be found in many places among Greeks, as well as among non-Greeks. Homer, for one, apparently speaks of it as the mode of life of the Cyclopes, when he says: 'These have neither gatherings for council nor oracles of law, but they dwell in hollow caves on the crests of

---

[1] The περίοδος or cycle means the complete interval between each great natural convulsion which wrecks human civilization in the fashion just described, and the next.

[2] The ordinary meaning of δυναστεία in Greek is the conduct of government by a number of families of 'notables'. What Plato means here is a 'patriarchal system' in which the word of the 'chief of the clan' is law to his clan, as the quotation from Homer shows.

the high hills, and each one utters the law to his children and his wives, and they reck not one of another'.[1]

Clin. This poet of yours seems indeed to have been quite a pretty fellow. I assure you I have perused other passages from him which are equally neat, though not many, as we Cretans are not much given to cultivating verse of alien origin.

Meg. Now in Sparta we do cultivate it, and regard Homer as the best composer of it, though the life he is always describing is decidedly Ionian rather than Laconian. He certainly seems to give full confirmation to your present theory where he ascribes the primitive manners of the characters in his story to their savage condition.

Ath. Yes, to be sure he does, and we may take him as evidence to show that this type of polity is actually to be found at times.

Clin. Certainly.

Ath. That is, they are found among such men as we are speaking of, who have been dispersed in single homesteads and families as a result of the distress caused by these disasters? In such societies do we not find that the oldest members rule, because their authority has come down to them from father or mother; the rest follow them, and form one flock, like so many birds, and are thus under patriarchal control, the most justifiable of all types of royalty?

Clin. Exactly so.

Ath. The next step is to come together in larger numbers, which will increase the size of the communities, and turn to agriculture. This will be at first practised in the skirts of the 681 hill country; dry fences of a kind will be contrived as walls for defence against savage beasts, and a new and larger single homestead thus erected for the community.

Clin. At least that is the probable succession of events.

Ath. Well, and is there not something else which is no less probable?

Clin. And what may that be?

Ath. As these larger homesteads are in process of growth from the smaller and most primitive, each of the smaller groups will bring along with it its patriarchal ruler and certain private customs of its own; private, I mean, because the groups are isolated from each other, and the several groups have been trained by their different progenitors and fosterers in different habits of conduct towards gods and fellow-men, in more orderly habits where the ancestors have been more orderly, in more

[1] Homer, *Odyssey* I 112–15 (Tr. Butcher and Lang).

valiant where they have been valiant. Thus each group comes accordingly, as I say, into the larger settlement with special laws of its own, and prepared to imprint its own preferences upon its children, and their children after them.

Clin. Why, inevitably so.

Ath. And of course each group unavoidably gives its approval to its own laws, and only in the second place to those of the others.

Clin. Exactly.

Ath. And thus, to all appearance, we find ourselves insensibly embarked on the beginnings of legislation.

Clin. Yes, precisely so.

Ath. At least the next step is bound to be that the coalescing groups choose certain representatives who will, of course, review all the usages, publicly and plainly indicate those which most win their own approval to the chiefs and leaders of the various clans—their kings as we may call them—and propose them for adoption. Hence these representatives will themselves get the name of legislators, and when they have appointed the chiefs as magistrates, and thus made the patriarchal groups into an aristocracy, or possibly a monarchy,[1] they will direct affairs during this transformation of the polity.

Clin. To be sure, this may be presumed to be the next stage in the process.

Ath. Then let us proceed to remark the rise of a third type of polity, under which polities and the societies which exhibit them alike manifest all varieties of form and fortunes.

Clin. And what type is that?

Ath. That which Homer, too, has commemorated as succeeding the second, when he says that the third form originated thus: 'He founded Dardania'—those, I believe, are his words—'for holy Ilios had not yet been builded in the plain, a city for mortal (?) men, but they still dwelt on the slopes of many-fountained Ida'.[2] The lines, like those which speak of the Cyclopes, are as true to nature as they are inspired. Poets, 682 you know, singing as they do under the divine afflatus, are among the inspired and so, by the help of their Graces and Muses, often enough hit upon true historical fact.

Clin. I can fully believe it.

Ath. Well, let us carry the tale which has engaged our

[1] The new 'polity' would be an aristocracy if all or several of the heads of clans were appointed magistrates with equal powers, a monarchy if some one 'chief' were given a predominant position.
[2] *Iliad* Υ 216.

imagination some steps further, as it may very probably suggest some hints which will be much to our purpose. So the procedure will surely be proper?

Clin. Most proper.

Ath. Well, as I say, the foundation of Ilium was due to a descent from the heights to a wide and noble plain; it was built on a hill of low elevation watered by a number of rivers coming down from the higher ground of Ida.

Clin. So the story goes.

Ath. Then we must surely suppose that this happened many ages after the Deluge?

Clin. Many ages later, no doubt.

Ath. The founders, in fact, must have been singularly oblivious of the disaster we are now recalling, to build a city on such a site exposed to a number of rivers flowing from the mountains, with such confidence in hills of inconsiderable height.

Clin. Why, yes, that calamity must obviously have belonged to a very remote part.

Ath. There were also by that time, I conceive, a good many other city-communities, thanks to the multiplication of mankind.

Clin. Yes, of course.

Ath. It was they, you know, who assailed her, and probably enough by sea too, as all mankind had long ago forgotten their dread of the sea.

Clin. So it should seem.

Ath. And there was a delay of some ten years before the Achaeans succeeded in sacking Troy.

Clin. Just so.

Ath. Now during this period of ten years while Ilium was under investment, occurred the various domestic misfortunes of the different besiegers, occasioned by the insurrectionary movements of the younger generation. Moreover, when the warriors returned to their cities and families, the reception they met at the hands of these young men was neither honourable nor equitable, but attended with numerous instances of homicide, massacre, and expulsion: the expelled then returned again under a new name, calling themselves now not Achaeans, but Dorians, after Dorieus, who reassembled the exiles of that time. As to the sequel of the story, it is told, and told fully, in your own Lacedaemonian tradition.

Meg. It is indeed.

Ath. Thus we find ourselves, providentially as it were, brought back to the very point at which we were led into a digression at the outset of our discussion of law by our stumbling upon this topic of music and the wine-cup, and we may now, so to say, close with the argument. For it has come round to the actual 683 settlement of Lacedaemon, a system you both declared sound —as also that of Crete which has closely related laws. And we have certainly gained this much vantage from our desultory argument, with its review of a variety of polities and foundations; we have inspected a first, a second, and a third community succeeding one another in order of foundation through a vast period of time, and now at last we come, in the fourth place, to the foundation of a city—or you may prefer to say, a *nation*—which persists to this day as it was founded. If the whole discussion enables us to understand what has been commendable in such foundations, or the reverse, what types of laws lead to their preservation, where it is achieved, and what, in the opposite case, to their dissolution, and what kind of changes will contribute to the happiness of a community, why then, Megillus and Clinias, we must cover the ground again pretty much from the beginning, unless, indeed, you have some objections to urge against what has been already said.

Meg. Why, sir, if we could have the word of a god for it that on our second attempt to study this matter of legislation we are to hear discourse as good, yes, and as long, as that which has already passed, I would readily make our walk a long one and should think this day short enough, though, if I am rightly informed, it is the day of the summer solstice.

Ath. Then I presume we are to undertake the inquiry.

Meg. With all my heart

Ath. Then, Megillus, let us place ourselves in imagination at the date at which Lacedaemon, Argos, and Messene, with all their domains, had come, to all intents, into the power of your ancestors. Their next step, as the story goes, was the resolution to divide their forces into three, and establish three cities, Argos, Messene, and Lacedaemon.

Meg. Precisely.

Ath. Thus Argos became the kingdom of Temenus, Messene of Cresphontes, Lacedaemon of Procles and Eurysthenes.

Meg. To be sure.

Ath. Whereupon the whole body took an oath to these sovereigns to support them against any attempt to subvert their monarchy.

Meg. Certainly.

Ath. And, in God's name, is a monarchy ever subverted, or

for the matter of that, has any government ever been over-thrown, except by itself? That was our position when we fell a while ago into a discussion of the point, and can we have forgotten it now?

Meg. Oh, surely not.

Ath. Then we may assert the position even more confidently now, as we have met with historical facts which seem to lead to the same conclusion, and shall thus be dealing with realities 684 and facts, not empty fiction. The historical facts, as we know, are these: three reigning houses and the cities over which they reigned swore a mutual oath to one another, as required by the laws they had adopted as definitory of sovereignty and allegiance, the monarchs engaging that the continuance of the crown in the family should lead to no enlargement of prerogative,[1] their subjects that, so long as they respected the compact, they would neither abolish the monarchies from within, nor submit to their subversion from without; the monarchs covenanted to support a populace, no less than a monarch, if its rights should be infringed, and the peoples, in like case, to support a monarch no less than a populace. Those, I believe, are the facts?

Meg. And so they are.

Ath. Well then, have we not here provision made by the legislation of the three cities from the outset for a matter of prime importance to the established constitutions—whether the initiative was due to the monarchs or to others?

Meg. What matter do you mean?

Ath. I mean that in any case of infraction of the law of the constitution, there were always to be two cities leagued against the single defaulter.

Meg. Yes, manifestly.

Ath. Now I may remind you that a legislator is commonly expected to enact only such laws as a populace, or multitude, will accept of its own motion, which is much as though a trainer or physician were expected to make his treatment, or cure, of the body a pleasure to the recipient.

Meg. Exactly.

Ath. Whereas in real fact one has often ground for thankfulness

---

[1] I omit in translation the words τὸν αὐτὸν λόγον, 684 *a* 1, which look, as Badham held, to be an accidental repetition of the same phrase from 683 *e* 10, immediately above. The meaning is, as appears in the sequel, that all three royal houses and all three 'peoples' were united by a common oath that all parties would unite to resist encroachment by any one king, or any one people, on the rights of either people or monarch.

if one can secure bodily health and good condition at the cost
of a moderate amount of pain.

Meg. To be sure.

Ath. The statesmen of that period had moreover a second
initial advantage which would greatly facilitate their legislative
task.

Meg. And what was that?

Ath. They were not exposed, in their attempts to establish
a certain equality of possessions, to the grave charge so persistently levelled, in connection with the passing of laws for
other cities, at one who proposes change in the tenure of land,
or a cancellation of debts, from his perception that equality can
never be properly attained without these measures. When a
legislator attempts a change in these matters, every one meets
him with a cry of 'no meddling with fundamentals', and an
imprecation on the author of redistribution of lands and repudia-
tion of debts, sufficient to reduce any man to despair. Now the
Dorians, you know, from their situation, had this further initial
advantage, which relieved them of unpleasant recriminations:
the land could be divided without controversy, and they had
no burden of accumulated debts.

Meg. True enough.

Ath. Then what, I must ask you, can be the reason that their
foundation and its legislation proved the failure it has been?

Meg. Why, in what respect has it failed, and why this censure 685
of them?

Ath. Because in two of their three settlements there was a
rapid degeneration of constitution and laws, only one of the
three, your own city of Sparta, remaining unperverted.

Meg. Not precisely an easy question to answer.

Ath. All the same, there is the point we have now to envisage
and discuss, if we are to relieve the distress of our journey by
this sober old man's game of jurisprudence, as we called it at
the beginning of our walk.

Meg. No doubt, and so we must do as you say.

Ath. What laws, then, could be a fairer subject of inquiry
than those by which these communities have been regulated?
What greater and more illustrious cities are there, whose foundation we might take for our consideration?

Meg. If we dismiss them, it will be no easy matter to name
any others.

Ath. Well, one thing is plain enough; the founders of that age
meant their creation to be an adequate protection, not merely

for the Peloponnese, but for the Greek world at large, if it should
be wronged by an alien people, as it had already been wronged
by the inhabitants of Ilium, when they provoked the expedition
against Troy in their arrogant confidence in the power of the
Assyrians of Nineveh. For the still surviving prestige of that
empire was considerable; the men of that age had then the same
fear of that united dominion which we feel to-day of the Great
King, as the second capture of Troy, a city which formed part
of the Assyrian empire, was a formidable grievance against them.
It was to meet this situation that the militia of those days was
organized as a single body, distributed over three cities under
monarchs who were brothers, being all sons of Heracles, an
excellent invention and disposition, superior, as was generally believed, to that of the force which had invaded Troy.
For in the first place, commanders for commanders, the Heraclids
were thought better than the Pelopids, and in the second, this
army was held to have the advantage in valour of that which had
assailed Troy, since it was composed of the victorious Dorians,
but the other of the defeated Achaeans.   Such, may we not say,
were the dispositions of that time, and such was their purpose.

Meg. Why, surely.

Ath. So it was presumably expected that their work would
686 prove stable and endure for ages, considering their past association in so many difficulties and dangers, and their subordination
to three royal brothers of the same house; to say nothing of the
fact that they had the sanction of many oracles, in particular of
the Delphic Apollo.

Meg. That, to be sure, was the presumption.

Ath. And yet, as we see, these magnificent anticipations
vanished speedily into air, except, as we were saying, in the
case of the fraction in your territory of Laconia, and it, you
know, has been in incessant warfare with the other two-thirds
to this day.   Though had the original project been carried out,
and a single confederacy formed, its military power would have
been irresistible.

Meg. Yes, quite irresistible.

Ath. Then where was the source of the failure? Surely it is
a question worth examining, what mischance may have been
the undoing of so vast and admirable a formation?

Meg. Yes surely; one who turned his attention from this case
in another direction [1] might look long enough for an example of

---

[1] 686 *b* 8.   Reading with Ast ἄλλο<σε> σκοπῶν for the ἄλλο σκοπῶν of
the MSS.

the laws and institutions which preserve or destroy grandeur and greatness.

Ath. So here, I take it, we find ourselves happily launched on an inquiry of magnitude.

Meg. Very certainly.

Ath. Then I would ask, my dear sir, whether we were not just now unconscious victims of a mistake universal to mankind. Men are perpetually fancying they have discovered some splendid creation which might have worked wonders if only someone had known the proper way (whatever it may be) to use it. Now it is just on this point I suspect you and I may be thinking falsely and unnaturally, like every one else who has the same thought about anything.

Meg. Pray, what do you mean? What is the special point of your observation?

Ath. Why, my friend, I am actually amused by my own recent mood. As I pictured to myself the army of which we were talking, I thought 'What a splendid force, and what a wonderful acquisition it would[1] have proved for the Greeks, if only (as I was saying) the proper use had been made of it at the time!'

Meg. Well, and was not all you said, like our assent to it, the soundest of sense?

Ath. That may be, but what is in my mind is this. When any one sees something big, strong, and powerful, he feels at once that if the owner of such a marvellous thing knew how to use it, he could effect wonders with it, and so achieve felicity.

Meg. Well, and that is equally true, is it not?   687

Ath. Let me beg you to consider the light in which a thing must be viewed to justify this eulogy. Take the case of the armament of which we are now speaking as a first example: If its creators had understood how to construct it properly, they would fairly have attained their aim; but how? I presume, if they had constituted it securely and assured its permanent continuance in being, with the consequences of freedom for themselves, sovereignty over any desired subjects, and, in a word, ability for themselves and their posterity to deal at their pleasure with all mankind, Greeks and non-Greeks alike. These are the grounds on which they might base their eulogy.[2]

---

[1] 686 *d* 9-10. Reading κτῆμ' ἀν παραπεσεῖν for κτῆμα παραπεσεῖν.

[2] 687 *b* 2. Reading with Ast ἐπαινοῖεν for MSS. ἐπιθυμοῖεν.

Meg. Exactly.

Ath. And, again, when a man's notice is attracted to a great fortune, or pre-eminent family distinction, or the like, and he expresses the same commendation, he speaks from the same point of view; his thought is that the advantage will enable its possessor to gratify all his desires, or the most numerous and considerable of them?

Meg. So I should suppose.

Ath. So it follows that there is a certain desire, that indicated by our argument, which is universal in all men, as the argument itself asserts.

Meg. And that is——?

Ath. That events shall fall out in accord with the bidding of a man's own soul, all of them, if possible, but if not, at least those which depend on human agency.

Meg. Of course.

Ath. Now if this is what all of us, from boyhood to age, are wishing all the time, it will necessarily also be our standing prayer.

Meg. Certainly.

Ath. And, again, I suppose, our petition for our dear ones will be that they may receive what they ask for themselves.

Meg. Of course.

Ath. Now a son, who is a boy, is dear to his father, a grown man.

Meg. Certainly.

Ath. And, mark you, there is much a boy prays to befall him, of which his father would beseech Heaven that it may never fall out as the son prays.

Meg. You mean when the petitioner is thoughtless and still young?

Ath. Yes, and what of the case when the father—old, or only too youthful as you please to consider him [1]—has no sense of good and right, and prays from the heart in a passion akin to that conceived by Theseus against his unfortunate victim, Hippolytus, but the son has such a sense? Will the son, think you, second the father's prayer in such a case?

Meg. I see your point. You mean, I apprehend, that the object of a man's prayers and endeavours should not be that the universal course of events should conform to his own wishes,

[1] That is, when the father conjoins grey hairs with passions he ought to have outgrown. The reference is to Theseus, who cursed his innocent son in his fury at accusations which he ought to have seen to be false.

unless his wishes further conform to his sober judgment.[1] It is the possession of intelligence that should be the mark of prayer and aspiration for the community and every individual of us alike.

Ath. Yes, and I am particular to remind myself that it is 688 this which a statesmanlike legislator should always have in view in framing his enactments, as I would also remind you, if we have not forgotten how our conversation began—that whereas you both agreed that a good legislator must devise all his institutions with an eye to war, I, for my part, urged that this is an injunction to legislate with a view to one single virtue out of four; he should keep them all in view, I said, but chiefly and in the first place that virtue which brings all the rest in its train, that is, judgment, intelligence, and right conviction attended by appropriate passionate desire. So our argument has come back again to the old point; I, its mouthpiece, say once more now what I said before, in jest or earnest, as you please to take it. I look on prayer, I say, as a dangerous instrument in the hands of the man without intelligence; it defeats his wishes.[2] If you please to consider me in earnest, pray do so; I have every confidence that if you follow up the story we have just set before ourselves for consideration, you will directly discover that the cause of the ruin of the three kings [3] and their whole design was no cowardice and no military ignorance on the part of commanders or commanded; what ruined them was their abundant vice of other kinds, and, above all, their folly in the supreme concerns of man. That this was the sequence of events on that occasion, is so still to-day in similar cases, and will be the same in the future—that is what, by your leave, I shall try to establish in the fuller development of our argument, and friendship will lead me to make the point as clear to you as I possibly can.

Clin. Verbal applause, sir, might be in doubtful taste, but our conduct will show our emphatic approval; we shall follow your discourse with the keenest attention; that is the way in which a self-respecting man best shows approbation or the reverse.

[1] In 687 *e* 7 I translate the MS. text τὴν βούλησιν δὲ μηδὲν μᾶλλον τῇ ἑαυτοῦ φρονήσει. There is a marginal variant πολὺ for μηδὲν (adopted by Burnet) which gives the sense, 'but much rather that his wishes should conform to his sober judgments'.

[2] Because every man wishes for true happiness, but the things for which the fool prays are conducive to his unhappiness, and his god might take him at his word.

[3] Or, adopting Boeckh's change of βασιλέων in 688 *c* 3–4 to βασιλειῶν, 'the three kingdoms'.

Meg. Well said, Clinias; so we will.

Clin. Certainly, with God's permission. Pray proceed.

Ath. Well then, to follow up the thread of our argument, we say that what then destroyed that mighty power was the greatest folly, and that it inevitably produces the same results to-day. This being so, then, a legislator's aim must be to create all the wisdom he can in a community, and with all his might to eradicate unwisdom.

Clin. Yes, manifestly.

689 *Ath.* Now what type of folly may fairly be called the *greatest*? I should certainly say that I am on the point of describing, but you must consider whether you agree with the observation.

Clin. What type do you mean?

Ath. That of a man who hates, not loves, what his judgment pronounces to be noble or good, while he loves and enjoys what he judges vile and wicked. It is this dissonance between pleasure and pain and reasoned judgment that I call the worst folly, and also the 'greatest', since its seat is the commonalty of the soul; for pain and pleasure are in the soul what the populace or commonalty is in a community. Accordingly, when the soul sets itself at variance with knowledge, judgment, discourse, its natural sovereigns, you have what I describe as unwisdom, alike in a community where the commons rebel against magistrates and laws, and in one individual man when fair discourse is present in the soul, but produces no effect, but rather the very contrary. These are the types of folly I would pronounce the gravest dissonances in community or individual citizen, not the follies of professionals [1]—if you take my meaning.

Clin. Indeed we do, sir, and we grant your point.

Ath. Then let us take it as definitely settled, and proclaim our conviction that no function of government may be entrusted to citizens who are foolish in this sense. They must be reprehended for their folly, though they were the most expert of calculators, and laboriously trained in all curious studies and everything that makes for nimbleness of mind, while those of the contrary sort should be styled wise, even though, as the proverb puts it, they can 'neither read nor swim', and it is to them, as the men of sense, that our magistracies should be given. How, indeed, my friends, can there be the barest particle of

---

[1] δημιουργῶν, *lit.* craftsmen. But Plato means to include all professions under this head. His point is that there is a more ruinous ignorance than the *military* incompetence of the commander of the national army. It was ignorance of the end of life, not of the military art, which ruined the Dorian Confederation.

wisdom where there is no concord? 'Tis a flat impossibility, whereas the fairest and greatest of consonances may very properly be called the greatest wisdom. In this wisdom he who lives by rule has his share, while he who is without it will invariably be found to be a waster of his substance and no saviour of society but the very reverse, all because of his folly in this respect. Well, as I just said, let this stand as our recorded conviction.

Clin. By every means.

Ath. Now in a community, I take it, there must be those who govern and those who are governed.

Clin. Of course there must.

Ath. Very good. Now what recognized titles to government 690 and obedience, and how many, do we find alike in large cities, in small, and in families? Is there not, for one, the claim of father and mother? or speaking generally, would it not be universally recognized that parents have a title to rule their offspring?

Clin. Most assuredly.

Ath. And next by consequence that the well-born have a title to rule the worse-born, and third, by further consequence, that it is for elder men to rule and for younger to submit.

Clin. To be sure.

Ath. And fourth, that it is for slaves to submit and for their owners to rule them.

Clin. Why of course.

Ath. And fifth, I conceive, for the stronger to rule, and for the weaker to submit.

Clin. Ay, there is a title which is not to be disputed.

Ath. Yes, and one which is prevalent all through the animal kingdom—by nature's own appointment, as Pindar of Thebes has said.[1] And sixth we may place the supreme claim of all which prescribes that it is for the ignorant to follow and for the wise men to take the lead and rule. And yet it is just this, this unforced rule of law over willing subjects, my all-accomplished

---

[1] Pindar (Fr. 169), quoted and discussed at *Gorgias*, 484 *b*: νόμος ὁ πάντων βασιλεὺς | θνατῶν τε καὶ ἀθανάτων | ἄγει δικαιῶν τὸ βιαιότατον | ὑπερτάτᾳ χειρί. 'Use that is king of all, men and gods alike, maketh just the most violent deed by might of hand.' In the *Gorgias*, according to the MSS., the words are *misquoted* as ἄγει βιαιῶν τὸ δικαιότατον, 'use . . . doth violence to the fairest right,' and Plato perhaps is here thinking of them in this inaccurate form, which may have been actually current in Athens in his youth. He is also putting the sense 'law' on the word νόμος, by which Pindar means rather 'precedent'.

Pindar, that I cannot pronounce unnatural; I should call it nature's own ordinance.

Clin. And you would be quite right.

Ath. Then there is a seventh kind of rule by the favour of Heaven [1] and fortune, as we say; we bring our men to a casting of lots, and call it the most equitable of arrangements that he who has the chance of the lot should rule, and he who misses it retire into the ranks of subjects.

Clin. True, indeed.

Ath. ' You see, then, my legislator,'—so we might playfully address a man who sets light-heartedly about the enactment of laws—'how many titles there are in this matter of governing, and how conflicting they are. We have just discovered a whole fountain-head of dissensions; it is yours to provide the remedy for them. But suppose you begin by joining in our inquiry about the kings of Argos and Messene. How did they effect their own ruin and that of the Hellenic power which was so superb in their day? What offence did they commit against these principles?' Was not their error that they forgot the solid truth of Hesiod's saying [2] that 'the half is often more than the whole'? He meant that when it is baneful to get the whole, but the half is sufficient, then the modestly sufficient, the better, is more than the disproportionate, the worse.

Clin. He was right, too.

Ath. Now when the ruin sets in, where does it regularly make its first appearance? In kings or in the common people? How say you?

691 *Clin.* Probability and common experience suggest that it is the malady of kings whose luxury leads to pomp.

Ath. Plainly, then, this infection of encroachment on the established laws began, in the old days, with the kings. They did not keep concord with one another, as they were pledged and sworn to do. It was this discord—in our judgment really supreme folly, for all its semblance of wisdom—which ruined the whole system by its shrill and tuneless dissonance.

Clin. Probably enough.

Ath. Well and good. Now what precaution should a legislator have taken at the time against the development of this

---

[1] The primitive view that casting lots, or 'tossing up', is a way of leaving a decision in the hands of God. Cf. the prayer of the Apostles in Acts i, before casting lots for a successor to Judas.

[2] Hesiod, *Works and Days*, 40. 'Poor fools! they do not even know how much more is the half than the whole, nor what wealth there is in mallow and asphodel.'

symptom? God knows it is easy enough to give the answer now and takes no great wisdom to perceive it, but a prophet who could have foreseen it at the time would have been a wiser man than ourselves, would he not?

Meg. And what answer may you mean?

Ath. Why, Megillus, what should have been done then may be discovered and readily stated to-day if we will only look at what was done in your own society.

Meg. You must put it still more plainly.

Ath. Well, what is absolutely plain is just this.

Meg. What?

Ath. If we disregard due proportion by giving anything what is too much for it, too much canvas to a boat, too much nutriment to a body, too much authority to a soul, the consequence is always shipwreck; rankness runs in the one case to disease, in the other to presumption and its issue is crime. What is it we would say? you ask; why, my friends, surely this: No soul of man, while young or accountable to no control, will ever be able to bear the burden of supreme social authority without taking the taint of the worst spiritual disease, folly, and so becoming estranged from its dearest intimates; when this happens, that soul very soon suffers ruin and the loss of all its powers. Hence it calls for a great legislator to forestall this danger by his insight into due proportion. The reasonable inference to-day, then, is that the danger was forestalled, but in very truth it seems there must have been——

Meg. What?

Ath. Some divinity in charge of you with prevision of the future, who gave you a double line of kings instead of a single,[1] and so contracted their power within more proportionate limits. Even after this a human intelligence, with some divine assistance, observed that your rulers were still in their fever-fit, and so blended the temperate authority of age with the peremptory 692 self-will of royal lineage by giving the eight-and-twenty elders an equal voice with the kings in affairs of moment. Then a third deliverer remarked that your governing body was still

[1] The reference is to the traditional explanation of the dual monarchy of Sparta as caused by the death of the Heraclid Aristodemus, leaving twin sons behind him. In what follows, Plato adopts the tradition that the Spartan 'senate' of thirty, in which the kings, who were *ex officio* members, had only an equal vote with the rest, was the creation of Lycurgus. The 'divine assistance' is probably an allusion to the supposed encouragement given to Lycurgus by the Delphic oracle. The mention of a 'third deliverer' shows that Plato agrees with those who regarded the institution of the ephors as belonging to the later epoch of the Messenian wars.

swelling with mettle and introduced the office of the ephorate, an office as good as filled by lot, as a curb. This is how the monarchy of your own Laconian state came to be a mixture of the right ingredients, and acquired due limitation, with the result that it was preserved itself, and has proved the means of our general preservation. For had things been left to Temenus Cresphontes, and the legislators of that age, whoever they may have been, not even the 'portion of Aristodemus' itself would have survived. In fact, they were mere amateurs in legislative work, or they could hardly have fancied an oath a guarantee of moderation in a youthful spirit succeeding to an authority which could be converted into autocracy, but God has shown us by the event how a government should have been constituted then and must be constituted now, if it is to have good prospects of permanence. That you and I should be able to understand this to-day, as I said before, is no proof of wisdom—it is always easy to see by the light of examples from the past—but had there been a man at the time with such foresight, and with the power to limit the sovereignties and make one of three the excellent discoveries of that age would have been retained in their entirety, and contempt of our slender resources would never have launched a Persian, nor any other, armada against Hellas.

Clin. Very true.

Ath. Indeed, Clinias, the repulse of those attacks was no credit to any one. I do not mean, when I say this, that the victories of the time, on land and sea alike, were not honourable to the victors; what I mean by calling the history discreditable is this. Only one of those three states took up arms for the defence of Hellas on the first assault; the other two were so badly corrupted that one[1] of them even tried to hinder the efforts of Lacedaemon by vigorous hostilities against her, while the second, Argos, which had held the primacy in the old days of the first division of the Peloponnese, sent no answer to the

[1] Messene. The historical difficulties of this passage are notorious. The Spartans did nothing before Marathon beyond despatching a belated force which arrived after the battle. There is no evidence that there was any revolt or disorder in Messene at the time. What is said of Argos is true, but it is not mentioned that the city had been temporarily completely crushed by the Spartans themselves. Plato cannot have been ignorant of the facts, as they are all recorded by Herodotus, on whom he has drawn in this very part of the *Laws* for his account of the Persian kings. Possibly the Spartans may have excused their indifference to the danger of Athens by an exaggerated story about the conditions in Messene (their 'Ireland'), which the Athenian allows to pass, as a piece of politeness to Megillus.

appeal for aid against the foreigner, and did nothing at all. And if a man were to tell the story of that war at length, it would amount to an unseemly indictment of Hellas. In fact, Hellas could not truly be said to have made any defence; had not the combined resolution of Athens and Lacedaemon repelled the menace of enslavement, there would long ago have been a 693 complete confusion of Hellenic stocks with one another, of barbarian with Hellenic and Hellenic with barbarian, like the wretched sporadic condition of the present dispersed and confused subjects of the Persian despotism. This, Clinias and Megillus, is the charge I bring against the so-called statesmen and legislators of both past and present, and I bring it in the hope that examination into its causes will disclose the very different course which ought to have been taken. It was in this spirit that I said just now that after all it is wrong to establish over-powerful or unmixed sovereignties, when we consider that a community should be at once free, sane, and at amity with itself, and that these are the ends a legislator must keep in view in his enactments. And I must ask you not to be surprised that we have already more than once proposed certain ends as those to which the legislator must look, and that our proposals have not always appeared to be identical. You must reflect that when we say he must look to sobriety, or again to wisdom, or to amity, these ends are not distinct but identical, and if we find ourselves using a further variety of expressions to the same effect, we must not be confused by that.

Clin. We shall do our best to keep it in mind as we review our discussions. For the present, you might explain your remarks about amity, wisdom, and liberty. What is it you were going to say a legislator should aim at?

Ath. Then let me have your attention. There are two matrices, as we may call them, of constitutions from which all others may truly be said to be derived; the proper name of the one is monarchy, of the other democracy. The first is seen in its perfection among the Persians, the second among my own countrymen. These are the strands, as I have said, of which all other constitutions, generally speaking, are woven. Very well; it is indispensably necessary that there should be both ingredients where there is to be the combination of liberty and amity with wisdom. This is what our argument means to enjoin when it urges that no community which has not those characters can be rightly administered.

Clin. Of course it cannot.

Ath. Well, one of the societies we have mentioned has shown exclusive and inordinate devotion to the principle of monarchy, the other to that of liberty, and thus neither has effected a proper balance between them, whereas yours of Laconia and Crete have succeeded better.   There was a time when this was

694 more or less true of Athens and Persia, but it is less true to-day. Shall we inquire into the causes of this or not?

Clin. By all means, if we mean to complete our investigations.

Ath. Then lend me your ears.   While the Persians steered a middle course between subjection and liberty, in the time of Cyrus, they began by winning their own freedom and went on to make themselves masters of numerous peoples.   As a government they gave these subjects their share of liberty and placed them on equal terms with themselves; their soldiers thus grew attached to their commanders, and showed themselves forward in danger.   Again, if a subject was a man of wisdom and a capable adviser, the king showed no jealousy of him, but permitted free speech and bestowed distinctions on such competent counsellors, so that the gift of wisdom was freely placed at the disposal of the public service.[1]   Hence the combination of liberty with amity and generally diffused intelligence led, for the time, to all-round progress.

Clin. That certainly seems to have been much the course of the history.

Ath. Then what can have brought about the decay under Cambyses and the general recovery under Darius?   Shall we hazard a guess at the reading of the riddle?

Clin. It would at least be a contribution to the study of our original problem.[2]

Ath. Then my own present reading of Cyrus is this.   Though a good general and a true patriot, he had been wholly untouched by right education, and had never given a thought to the discipline of his household.[3]

Clin. What are we to understand by that remark?

[1] The special point is indicated by the reference to *jealousy*.   In the best days, the Persian king did not treat his counsellors, after the usual fashion of an Oriental sultan, as mere tools for the execution of his *personal* projects; he did not assume that the *mind* of the state was concentrated in himself.

[2] Reading with Badham τοῦ for τοῦτο in 694 *c* 4.

[3] A veiled and temperate criticism of writers who had romanced about Cyrus as a 'philosophic prince'.   The allusion is pretty certainly to Xenophon's historical novel, *The Education of Cyrus*, and probably also to the (lost) *Cyrus* of Antisthenes.

Ath. It should seem that he spent his life, from his youth, in perpetual campaigning, and left the training of his sons to the women, who treated them from their childhood as blessed creatures and born favourites of fortune endowed with every advantage. They would allow no one to cross such vastly superior beings in anything, forced every one to commend all their sayings and doings, and so turned them out what you might expect.

Clin. A mighty fine training, by your account of it.

Ath. Why, the training one could look for when the children were left to the women of a royal harem, new to affluence and without a man to help them, thanks to perpetual preoccupation with the wars and their dangers.

Clin. That sounds reasonable, to be sure.

Ath. As for their father, he was busy winning for them flocks and herds and drove after drove of men and other creatures, but he forgot that the successors to whom he was to 695 bequeath this wealth were getting no training in their ancestral Persian calling, an austere one—for the Persians, you know, were shepherds and sons of the barren hills—well fitted to turn out sturdy shepherds, equal to the endurance of exposure and wakefulness, and the hardships of a campaign too, when necessary. He shut his eyes to the way in which his sons had been imbued by women and eunuchs with an education—the Median —corrupted by what is called 'fortune', and so they proved what might have been anticipated from the neglect of correction in their training. At least, when the succession fell to them, at their father's death, they were swollen with pride and indiscipline: Cambyses, the elder, would brook no equal, and began by making away with his brother; then, what with strong drink and want of education, he went out of his own wits, and lost his throne at the hands of the Medes and the famous eunuch,[1] who had conceived a contempt for his folly.

Clin. Certainly that is how the story runs, and it is presumably pretty true to the facts.

Ath. And then, we are told, the throne was recovered for the Persians by Darius and the 'Seven'.

Clin. Exactly.

Ath. Well, let us follow up the train of thought suggested by

---

[1] Plato follows some version of the facts which is no longer extant. The statement that the Magian whom Cambyses was hurrying back from Egypt to suppress when he died was an eunuch is repeated at *Ep.* VII, 332 *a*, but its source is unknown.

our argument. Darius, you know, was no king's son,[1] educated
in pride and pomp; when he came to a kingdom which he had
won with the help of six companions, he divided it into seven
departments, of which some faint traces are still surviving;
he was satisfied to live under laws of his own devising which
introduced a certain equality into the state; he promoted general
amity and public spirit among the Persians by fixing, by his legislation, the tribute Cyrus had promised them and thus won the
hearts of the common people by his liberality and munificence.
Consequently his armies served with loyalty, and won him
fresh territory as extensive as that left by Cyrus. But when
Darius was gone, Xerxes, who had again received the pampering
education of a prince of the blood—! 'Darius, Darius,' so I
think we may righteously protest, 'to think you should never
have found out the fault in Cyrus, and should have trained your
Xerxes in the same ways as he his Cambyses!' Xerxes, as I
say, was a product of the same kind of education, and naturally
the consequence was a career of the same sort. From his time
to ours, speaking broadly, the Persians have never had a real
'great king', who has been more than nominally such. And the
cause of this, on my own theory, is not accidental; it is the evil life
696 commonly led by the sons of autocrats and men of extraordinary
wealth. Such a training will never, never lead to outstanding
goodness in boy, or man, or greybeard. This, I maintain, is
a consideration for legislators and equally for ourselves in our
present discussion. And I would remark in fairness to you
Lacedaemonians as creditable to your community that you
assign no special distinction or special upbringing whatsoever
to poor man or rich man, private citizen or prince of the royal
house, beyond what your original source of inspiration revealed
on divine authority. For assuredly special civic honours ought
not to be assigned to exceptional wealth, any more than to
speed of foot, beauty of form, or strength of limb unaccompanied
by goodness, or even to goodness which does not include
temperance.

Meg. How is that remark to be understood, sir?

Ath. Courage, you will grant, is one part of goodness.

Meg. To be sure it is.

Ath. Good; then listen to my argument and decide the point
for yourself. Would you like a man of great courage who

---

[1] We know now from the inscriptions of Darius himself that he was in
fact a member of the Persian royal house, the Achaemenidae; Herodotus,
like Plato, supposed him to be a private man.

should also be intemperate and profligate as an inmate of your house, or a next-door neighbour?

Meg. Heaven forfend!

Ath. And what do you say to a man of professional skill, and wise in that sense of the word, but unjust?

Meg. I have nothing to say to him.

Ath. And justice, again, does not flourish where temperance is not.

Meg. No, how should it?

Ath. Neither does the sort of wisdom we were lately contemplating, that of the man whose pleasures and pains are accordant with and consequent on his right thinking.

Meg. No, decidedly not.

Ath. Besides, we have still a further point to consider for its bearing on the right or wrong distribution of various civic distinctions.

Meg. And what may it be?

Ath. Suppose temperance to exist in a man's soul all by itself, apart from any further goodness; ought it, or ought it not, to be a rightful title to distinction?

Meg. That is more than I can say.

Ath. A most becoming answer. Had you said either 'yes' or 'no', in either case you would have struck what I take to be a wrong note.

Meg. Then it is as well I replied as I did.

Ath. Just so. A mere adjunct to the true object of honourable distinction, or the reverse, calls for no discussion, and may well be passed over in silence.

Meg. By the adjunct in question, I take it you mean temperance.

Ath. I do. The truly sound procedure would be to assign the first place in honour to that other thing, be it what it may, which, combined with this adjunct, does us the chiefest service, and the second to that which serves us in the next degree. We have only to travel in the same fashion down the whole series for everything to receive its right place in the scale of distinctions.

Meg. I quite agree with you. 697

Ath. Well then, surely it is one part of the legislator's business to construct this scale.

Meg. Most assuredly.

Ath. Then, while leaving it to him to make the construction as a whole, and in all its particulars and details, shall we try to establish a three-fold division, a distinct first, second, and third class, for ourselves, who are also, in a sort, amateurs of legislation?

Meg. With all my heart.

Ath. Then I say that it is clearly an imperative duty for a society, which is minded to survive and enjoy all the felicity men may, to award its marks of honour and dishonour in the right way. And the right way is to put the good qualities of the soul in the first and most honourable rank—its temperance always presupposed as a *sine qua non*—advantages and good qualities of body in the second, and in the third, goods of estate, 'wealth' as we call them. Should any legislator or society transgress these limits by promoting wealth to honour, or giving anything of a lower class the distinctions of a higher, the act is an offence alike against religion and statesmanship. May we take this as our conviction?

Meg. Emphatically and absolutely, yes.

Ath. What led us into this lengthy discussion of the point was our examination of the Persian commonwealth. We find that they degenerated . . . [1] still further. The reason is that excessive curtailment of the liberty of the commons, and improper intensification of autocracy, made an end of their national feeling and public spirit. Since their disappearance, the concern of the authorities is no longer for their subjects, the commonalty, but for their own position; they give over loyal cities and peoples to fire and desolation whenever they think it of the slightest advantage to themselves, and consequently hate and are hated with savage and unrelenting animosity. On the other side, when they need the arms of the common people for their defence, they find no patriotism in them, no loyal readiness to hazard themselves in the field; in theory their forces are reckoned by countless thousands, but all these thousands are worthless for service. Hence they hire mercenaries and aliens, 698 as though they had no troops of their own, and look to them for their salvation. Moreover they are forced to an exhibition of their folly, since their habitual conduct amounts to a proclamation that all that society esteems honourable and of good repute is a toy in comparison with gold and silver.

Meg. Exactly so.

Ath. And with this we may close our proof that the present

---

[1] There is some small corruption at this point (697 *c* 7). The ἐπὶ ἔτι or ἐπὶ ἐπὶ ἔτι of the MSS. is untranslatable, and no really convincing emendation has been made. ἔτι is possibly sound, but I think it impossible to say what ἐπὶ or ἐπὶ ἐπί has extruded from the text, and have accordingly marked a small lacuna.

maladministration of Persia is due to an excess of servitude and autocracy.

Meg. Undoubtedly.

Ath. Next as to the state of Attica; we are similarly to show that unqualified and absolute freedom from all authority is a far worse thing than submission to a magistrate with limited powers. In the old days of the Persian assault on the Greeks—or perhaps I should say on the denizens of Europe at large—my countrymen enjoyed a venerable constitution with magistracies based on a four-fold system of social classes; moreover conscience had a sovereignty among us which disposed us to willing subjection to the laws. Besides, the spectacle of the sheer magnitude of the military and naval armament threw us into helpless consternation, and led us to submit to laws and magistrates with a still stricter obedience; all these causes continued to intensify our loyalty to one another. Some ten years before the naval engagement at Salamis, Datis arrived at the head of the Persian armada, with express orders from Darius against the Athenians and Eretrians; he was to capture and deport them, and had been warned that his own life would be the price of failure. Well, Datis speedily effected the complete capture of the Eretrians by force of numbers, and thus originated the alarming report which reached us in Athens. It was said that not a man of the Eretrians escaped; in fact, the troops of Datis joined hands and so swept the whole territory of Eretria as with a net.[1] True or false, whatever its source, this story appalled the Greeks, and more particularly the Athenians; they sent out appeals for help to every quarter, but were refused by all except the Lacedaemonians. Even they, whether under the pressure of their war with Messene, or from some other impediment—I am not acquainted with any statement on the point—even they, from whatever cause, arrived a day too late for the battle at Marathon. After Marathon there were frequent reports of vast preparations, and repeated menaces reached us from the King, and in course of time it was learned that Darius was dead and had been succeeded by his son, who was persisting 699 in the project with all the heat of youth. The Athenians conceived the whole undertaking to be directed against them-

---

[1] In Herodotus this device is said to have been employed not by Datis at Eretria, but in the island of Samos, and on a different occasion (Hdt. iii, 149). Herodotus also says nothing of any threat that Datis would pay for failure with his life. Plato tells the story with the same details in the *Menexenus*, and it is easy to believe that the reports current at Athens before Marathon were coloured by exaggerations of this kind.

selves in reprisal for Marathon; when they heard of the canalizing of Athos, the bridging of the Hellespont, and the numbers of the enemy's flotilla, they felt that there was no escape for them by land or by sea. No support could be looked for; (they remembered how they had found no supporters or allies in peril before, when the first expedition sailed to deal with Eretria, and naturally supposed that on land events would take the same course again). On the other side, all hope of escape by sea was visibly precluded,[1] since they had a fleet of a thousand vessels and more threatening them. There was just one chance of deliverance conceivable—faint and desperate, indeed, but still their only chance—when they looked at the past and observed how then, too, victory had appeared to emerge from the struggles of desperation. Supported by such hopes, they realized that their only refuge lay in their own right arm, and their gods. These causes combined to inspire them with loyalty to one another—the fear aroused by their present plight, and that other fear instilled by subjection to pre-existing law, which they had learned by subjection to the existing laws—conscience, as we have called it more than once already. This, as we said, is the sovereign to whom we must submit if we are ever to become men of worth; 'tis the dastards who are emancipate from that service and immune to that fear. Had they not been terrified[2] at the time we are speaking of, they could never have rallied for the repulse of the invader and the defence of temples, tombs, country, and all that is nearest and dearest, as in fact they did; we should have been pulverized at such a crisis and scattered severally to all the quarters of heaven.

Meg. The observation sir, is not only perfectly just, but most becoming to yourself and your countrymen.

Ath. No doubt, Megillus; and you, who have inherited the character of your ancestors, are the right person to hear the history of those times. But I would have you and Clinias consider the relevance of my narrative to our legislation; I give

[1] As Dr. England says, the meaning is that the Athenians could not hope to escape by emigration *en masse* to some new home across the water. (Herodotus, viii, 62, represents Themistocles as threatening that if the Peloponnesians withdrew their ships from Salamis, as they had proposed, the Athenians would retire in a body to southern Italy. Plato's point is that nothing of the kind was practicable while the Persians were masters at sea.)

[2] The various 'emendations' of δέος in 699 *c* 6 only obscure the thought. The meaning is that even the 'dastards' who were not held to their duty by reverence for conscience were driven by their very terror to behave like men for the time.

it, not for the sake of the story, but for the reasons I indicate. For do but mark; seeing that our fate has, in a way, been the same as that of the Persians—though they reduced the commonalty to utter subjection, whereas we encouraged the multitude towards unqualified liberty—our foregoing conversation has been, in a way, very pertinent to the question what should be said next and how it should be said.

Meg. Good; but you must try to make the point of the 700 remark a little plainer.

Ath. And so I will. Under our old laws, my friends, our commons were not masters; in a sense they were the willing servants of the laws.

Meg. Of what laws are you thinking in particular?

Ath. In the first instance, if our progress in extravagant liberty of living is to be traced from its origin, of the laws of music as it was in those days. Our music was then divided into several kinds and patterns. One kind of song, which went by the name of a hymn, consisted of prayers to the gods; there was a second and contrasting kind which might well have been called a *lament*; paeans were a third kind, and there was a fourth, the *dithyramb*, as it was called, dealing, if I am not mistaken, with the birth of Dionysus. The actual word *nome* was used as the name of still another kind, though with the qualification 'citharoedic'[1]. Now these and other types were definitely fixed, and it was not permissible to misuse one kind of melody for another. The competence to take cognizance of these rules, to pass verdicts in accord with them, and, in case of need, to penalize their infraction was not left, as it is to-day, to the catcalls and discordant outcries of the crowd, nor yet to the clapping of applauders; the educated made it their rule to hear the performances through in silence, and for the boys, their attendants, and the rabble at large, there was the discipline of the official's rod to enforce order. Thus the bulk of the populace was content to submit to this strict control in such matters without venturing to pronounce judgment by its clamours. Afterwards, in course of time, an unmusical licence set in with the appearance of poets who were men of native genius, but ignorant of what is right and legitimate in the realm of the Muses, possessed by a frantic and unhallowed lust for pleasure. They contaminated laments with hymns

---

[1] The point is that νόμος, besides meaning a *law*, is also the name for a certain type of composition, the 'nome', and that originally the cithern was the instrument appropriated to the nome.

and paeans with dithyrambs, actually imitated the strains of
the flute on the harp, and created a universal confusion of forms.
Thus their folly led them unintentionally to slander their
profession by the assumption that in music there is no such
thing as a right and a wrong, the right standard of judgment
being the pleasure given to the hearer, be he high or low. By
compositions of such a kind and discourse to the same effect,
they naturally inspired the multitude with contempt of musical
law, and a conceit of their own competence as judges. Thus
our once silent audiences have found a voice, in the persuasion
701 that they understand what is good and bad in art; the old
'sovereignty of the best' in that sphere has given way to an evil
'sovereignty of the audience'. If the consequence had been
even a democracy, no great harm would have been done, so
long as the democracy was confined to art, and composed of
free men. But, as things are with us, music has given occasion
to a general conceit of universal knowledge and contempt for
law, and liberty has followed in their train. Fear was cast
out by confidence in supposed knowledge, and the loss of it
gave birth to impudence. For to be unconcerned for the
judgment of one's betters in the assurance which comes of a
reckless excess of liberty is nothing in the world but reprehensible
impudence.

Meg. Very true.

Ath. So the next stage of the journey towards liberty will be
refusal to submit to the magistrates, and on this will follow
emancipation from the authority and correction of parents and
elders; then, as the goal of the race is approached, comes the
effort to escape obedience to the law, and, when that goal is
all but reached, contempt for oaths, for the plighted word, and
all religion; the spectacle of the Titanic [1] nature of which our old
legends speak is re-enacted; man returns to the old condition
of a hell of unending misery. Now, once more, why have we
said all this? I think we should rein in our argument from time
to time. We must not let it run away with us, as though it
had no curb in its mouth, and so, as the proverb says, lose our
seat in the saddle.[2] No, as I was saying, we must be constantly
asking ourselves why we have said what we have.

[1] I take this as an allusion to the Dionysiac myth that mankind are
sprung from the ashes of the Titans who killed and devoured the divine
child Dionysus, and were destroyed by the thunderbolts of Zeus. The
end of the 'rake's progress' to freedom is that men find themselves in
a 'hell on earth'.

[2] The 'proverb' of *d* 1 in the Greek is ἀπ' ὄνου πεσεῖν, 'to come a cropper'
(*lit.* 'to fall from one's donkey').

Meg. To be sure.

Ath. Well then, I said it for its relevance to what had gone before.

Meg. And what was that?

Ath. Why, I said a legislator should have three aims in his enactments; the society for which he makes them must have freedom, must have amity with itself, must have understanding. That, I believe, was our position.

Meg. Exactly.

Ath. This was why we took the examples of the most autocratic of communities and the freest, and are now asking ourselves in which of the two public life is what it should be. We found that when we had a certain due proportionality in either case, in the one of authority, in the other of liberty, there was a maximum of well-being in both societies, whereas when things were pushed to an extreme in either case, an extreme of subjection in the one, and of its opposite in the other, the consequences were unsatisfactory in both societies alike.

Meg. Very true.   702

Ath. It was for the same purpose that we reviewed the settlement of the Dorian invaders, the foundation of Dardanus in the foot-hills, and that of the city on the coast,[1] and even the life of the first survivors of the deluge. Our earlier conversations about music and drinking, and all that preceded them, were equally to the same end. The purport of the whole discourse has been to learn how a society is best administered and how a man will best conduct his personal life. But have we achieved any result? I would ask you both, Megillus and Clinias, what test we can propose to ourselves.

Clin. Why, sir, I believe I can find one. I fancy there has been something providential in the whole course of our argument; in fact, I find myself just now in a position in which it meets my needs well, and both your appearance and that of our friend Megillus are most opportune. So far from hiding my situation from you, I even count your presence a favourable omen. You must know that the largest part of Crete is undertaking the foundation of a colony, and has charged the Cnossians with the management of the business, which has been entrusted by the authorities of Cnossus to myself and nine others. Our instructions are further to frame a legislation from such local Cretan laws as have our approval, or laws from other quarters; we

[1] i.e. the city of Laomedon and Priam, the Troy of the famous war. The topics dwelt on in I–III are being enumerated in an inverted order.

are not to concern ourselves about their foreign origin, so long as we judge them superior. Suppose then we serve my turn and yours at once; let us use a selection from our results for the theoretical construction of a society, which we will imagine we are founding from the very start. The procedure will disclose the object of our search,[1] and, at the same time, I may find our construction useful for the society that is to be.

Ath. No declaration of hostilities that, Clinias! If Megillus has no objections to offer, I, for one, promise compliance to the best of my ability.

Clin. Thank you.

Meg. And so do I for another.

Clin. My best thanks to both of you. Well, let us begin by trying to imagine the foundation of the city.

[1] 'The object of our search' is the test of the soundness of our argument asked for at *b* 2.

BOOK IV

Ath. Good, then; what must we suppose our State is to be?
I do not mean that I am asking what its name is at present,
or by what name it will have to be called hereafter. That
might well come from the circumstances of the foundation or
the locality; or the appellation of some river, or fountain, or
local divinities might confer their own revered title on the city
in its earliest days. What I am more concerned about in my
question is this: is the site maritime or inland?

Clin. Why, sir, the city of which I was just speaking is some
eighty stadia,[1] more or less, from the coast.

Ath. Well, and are there harbours on that side of it, or is it
entirely without a harbour?

Clin. By no means, sir. The coast on that side is as well
furnished with harbours as a coast can be.

Ath. Tut, tut! How distressing! And what about the surrounding territory? Does it yield produce of all sorts, or has
it its deficiencies?

Clin. None to speak of.

Ath. Is there a neighbouring city within easy distance?

Clin. Dear me, no; that is the very reason for the settlement.
There was long ago an emigration from the district which has
left this territory vacant for ages.

Ath. What about plain-land, mountain, and forest? Pray,
how is it furnished in all these respects?

Clin. Much like the rest of Crete in general.

Ath. You mean it is rugged rather than level?

Clin. Decidedly so.

Ath. Then its case, from the point of view of the acquisition
of goodness, is not desperate. Had it to be on the coast, well
furnished with harbours and ill off for many of its necessaries,
not productive of all, we should need a mighty protector and
lawgivers who were more than men to prevent the development
of much refined vice in consequence of such a situation. As it
is, there is comfort in those eighty stadia. Even so, the site is
nearer to the sea than it should be, all the more as you say it is
well provided with a harbour. Still, we ought to be thankful

[1] Roughly about ten miles.

for even so much.   It is agreeable enough to have the sea at
one's door in daily life; but, for all that, it is, in very truth, a
'briny' and bitter 'neighbour'.   It fills a city with wholesale
traffic and retail huckstering, breeds shifty and distrustful
habits of soul, and so makes a society distrustful and unfriendly
within itself as well as towards mankind at large.   In view of
this situation, there is further comfort, however, in the universal
productiveness of our site.   Clearly, since it is so rugged, it
cannot at once produce everything and yield much of anything.
Were that the case, there would be the opportunity for exportation on a large scale, and, once more, our city would abound
with currency in gold and silver.   Now, all things considered,
nothing is a more serious impediment to the development of
noble and righteous character in a society, as you may recollect
that we have already said.[1]

Clin. We well recollect the remark and agree with you now,
as we did before, about its truth.

Ath. Then, as to a further point: how is our territory supplied
with materials for ship-building?

Clin. It has neither fir nor pine to speak of, and not much in
the way of cypress.   As for the kinds of wood which, as you
know, builders regularly require for the interior of boats,
larch [?] and plane, there is a little of them to be found.

Ath. That again is not a bad feature in the topography.

Clin. How so?

Ath. It is just as well that a society should have a difficulty
in copying the practice of its antagonists to its own undoing.

Clin. Now which of our results have you in view when you
say that?

Ath. Why, my dear sir, I would have you watch my procedure
in the light of our opening observations about the single object
of your Cretan institutions.   You both affirmed more precisely
that this object is military, whereas I rejoined that it is right
enough that goodness should be the object of such institutions,
but could not quite concede that their aim should be some part
of goodness short of the whole.   It is now the turn of both of
you to follow me in my proposals, taking care that I enjoin
nothing which does not tend to goodness, or some part of goodness.[2]   I take it as a postulate from the outset that a law is

---

[1] Apparently a reference to 696 *a* above.
[2] Others render 'does not tend to goodness, or tends only to a part of
goodness'.   But the 'only' is not in the Greek, and it is more in keeping
with idiom that, in the absence of such a word, the negative μή should
be taken as extending to both alternatives.

rightly enacted only when its aim is exclusively directed on that 706
object of all others which is steadily and invariably attended by
some worthy result, to the disregard of every other end whatsoever, be it wealth or anything else of the sort, divorced from the
objects I have specified.   And as for the pernicious imitation
of an antagonist to which I referred, this is how it comes about
in the case of a maritime population harassed by an enemy.
Minos, for example—and I tell the story without any vindictive
feeling against your countrymen, Clinias—Minos, in fact, once
laid Attica under a cruel tribute, thanks to his strength at sea.
His victims had as yet no men-of-war such as they have to-day,
nor yet was their territory rich in timber suitable for the facile
construction of a navy.   So they could not imitate his seamen
by turning sailors themselves and promptly repelling the invader
out of hand.   Had the case been so, it would have been better
for them to lose many times 'seven youths'[1] than to convert
themselves from steady infantry-men into marines, with the
marines' tricks of repeated descents followed by a helter-skelter
retreat to the boats, their notion that there is nothing discreditable in shuffling out of dying at one's post when the
enemy attacks, and their plausible and ready excuses for throwing down their arms and betaking themselves to 'flight without
dishonour', as it is called.   Phrases like this are the normal
consequences of employing men-at-arms on ship-board, and
what they call for is not 'infinite commendation', but the very
reverse.   Men should never be trained to evil ways; least of all,
the best element in the community.   That the practice in
question is ignoble might actually have been learned, I take it,
from Homer, whose Odysseus upbraids Agamemnon for directing the ships to be drawn down to the water's edge when the
Achaeans were hard pressed by the Trojans.   What Odysseus
says by way of remonstrance is this:

When thou biddest draw down the fair-benched ships to the
sea while the battle and din encompass us, that the Trojans, fain
as they are, may have their desire yet more fulfilled, and sheer
destruction fall on ourselves.   For when the ships are drawing
seaward the Achaeans will not cleave to the battle, but look askance
from it and flinch from the onset; then will counsel such as thou
givest prove our bane.[2]   707

Thus, you see, Homer was too well aware what a bad thing it

---

[1] The annual tribute of seven noble youths and the same number of
maidens as victims for the Minotaur was a fixed datum of the legend.
Cf. *Phaedo*, 58 *a* 3.
[2] Quoted, with trifling inaccuracies, from *Iliad*, Ξ 96-102.

is for infantry in an engagement to be supported by a line of men-of-war; why, lions would learn to run from deer if trained in habits like these. Not to add that states which owe their power to a navy also bestow the reward for their security [1] on an inferior element of their forces. As they owe the security to the arts of the sea-captain, the lieutenant, the oarsman, and to a miscellaneous and not over-reputable crowd, there is no possibility of awarding honours aright to the various individuals. Yet where this is excluded, how can the state continue unimpaired?

Clin. It is hardly possible it should. And yet, sir, it was the sea-fight at Salamis between Hellenes and non-Hellenes which was the salvation of Hellas—or so, at least, we say here in Crete.

Ath. To be sure that is what mankind at large say, Greeks or otherwise. But we—that is to say, Megillus here and myself—insist that the deliverance of Hellas was begun by one engagement on land, that at Marathon, and completed by another, that at Plataea; moreover these victories made better men of the Hellenes, whereas the others did not, if such language is permissible about actions which contributed to the deliverance of those times. (You see I am ready to throw you in the naval engagement at Artemisium along with the action at Salamis.) The fact is, the object we are keeping in view in our present investigations into topography and legislation is the moral worth of a social system; we do not agree with the multitude that the most precious thing in life is bare preservation in existence; we hold, as I think we have said before, that it is better to become thoroughly good and to remain so as long as existence lasts.

Clin. Surely, surely.

Ath. Then the one and only point we have to consider is whether our treatment of settlements and legal enactments is following the same lines—the best for a society.

Clin. Indeed far the best.

Ath. Then tell me, in the next place, what is the population for which you are to construct a settlement? Is it made up of volunteers from all parts of Crete—the masses in the various

---

[1] Adopting Badham's emendation σωτηρίας for σωτηρίᾳ at 707 *a* 5. The difficulty of which Plato speaks seems to be that of discriminating between the merits of individual contributors to a victory, as it is implied could be done in the case of an infantry engagement. The 'naval honours' have to be *indiscriminately* apportioned among a host of claimants, and thus recognition goes to the wrong man.

communities presumably having grown too great for the local food-supply? For you are not, I take it, collecting applicants from Hellas at large, though I do observe that contingents from Argos, Aegina, and other Hellenic districts have settled in your country. But pray tell me from what quarter you expect the present host of citizens now to be dealt with.

708

Clin. They will most likely come from all over Crete; of other Hellenes, Peloponnesians seem to have had the warmest welcome as settlers. In fact, it is true, as you were just saying, that we have emigrants from Argos among us, and among them the most distinguished of our societies of the present day, that of Gortyn;[1] it is an offshoot from the well-known Gortyn in the Peloponnese.

Ath. Well, it is not such an easy matter for a state to deal with a settlement when it is not formed, like a swarm of bees, by the emigration of a single stock from a single territory, with friendly feeling on both sides, under the stress of insufficient territory, or the pressure of some similar necessity. Sometimes, again, one section of a community may be driven to expatriate itself by the violence of party strife, and there has been the case of a whole society going into exile because it had been utterly crushed by an overwhelming attack. Now in one way the work of settlement and legislation is the easier in all these cases, but in another the harder. The unity of descent, speech, and institutions certainly promotes friendly feeling, since it involves the community in religious ceremonies and the like, but is not readily tolerant of novel laws or a constitution different from that of the home-land, while a group which has, perhaps, been driven into faction by the badness of the laws, yet still clings, from force of habit, to the very practices which had already led to its undoing, proves recalcitrant to the founder and his legislation, and refuses obedience. On the other side, a stock due to a confluence of various elements may perhaps be more willing to submit to novel laws, but it is a difficult business, and takes a long time for it to 'breathe and blow in unison', as the proverbial phrase has it of a pair of horses. No, in very truth to make a legislation or found a society is the perfect consummation of manly excellence.[2]

---

[1] Since the Peloponnesian Gortyn was in Arcadia, the Cretan apparently falls into a momentary oversight in speaking as though its citizens were of Argive descent.

[2] This seems to be the sense of the MSS. text, but it is tempting to adopt Badham's τελεωτάτων for the τελεώτατον of 708 *d* 7, 'to make a legisla tion . . . is work for men of consummate excellence'.

Clin. No doubt, but you might explain the point of the remark a little more clearly.

Ath. Why, my dear man, I suspect my reiterated reflections about legislators will lead me to say something which is partly derogatory; still, if the remark is pertinent, no harm will be done. After all, why should I scruple at it; it is much what might be said about all human concerns.

Clin. What is it you have in your mind?

709   *Ath.* I was on the brink of saying that man never legislates at all; our legislation is always the work of chance and infinitely various circumstance. Constitutions are wrecked and laws revolutionized by the violence of war, or the helplessness of sheer destitution. Again, innovations are often forced on us by disease, in the case of the visitations of pestilence, or of protracted and recurrent periods of insalubrious weather.[1] In view of such facts one might be moved to say, as I have just done, that no law is ever made by a man, and that human history is all an affair of chance. Still, the same thing may be said with apparent plausibility of seafaring, navigation. medicine, or strategy, and yet there is something else which may also be said with no less plausibility of them all.

Clin. And what is that?

Ath. That God is all, while chance and circumstance, under God, set the whole course of life for us, and yet we must allow for the presence of a third and more amenable partner, skill. Thus I should count it no small advantage that the navigator's skill should co-operate with circumstance in a tempest; would not you?

Clin. Naturally.

Ath. Now the same thing will hold good for the other cases, and so we should make the same admission in the case of legislation. Granting the concurrence of the local conditions necessary for a fortunate settlement, such a community necessarily presupposes the appearance of a true legislator.

Clin. Beyond all doubt.

Ath. Thus one who has the skill called for by any of the contingencies we have mentioned will also know well enough what form of fortune to pray for, that he may be dependent on nothing further besides his own skill.

Clin. To be sure.

[1] Either the grammar of the sentence suffers from want of final revision, or we must accept Stallbaum's correction of ἀκαιρίαι (709 *a* 7) to ἀκαιρίας. The two causes of disease contemplated are the introduction of 'plague' from abroad, and the persistence of unhealthy weather at home.

Ath. And any of the other professionals we have mentioned could, no doubt, tell us, if we asked them, what it is they are praying for?

Clin. Of course.

Ath. And presumably, then, a legislator could do so, too.

Clin. Presumably.

Ath. 'Come, then, legislator'—let us so apostrophize him—'what must we give you—I mean what social conditions—if their provision is to make you competent to model your society for the rest by your own efforts?'

Clin. Now I wonder what *is* the right reply.

Ath. You understand we are speaking in the name of the legislator?

Clin. Yes.

Ath. Then here is the answer. 'Give me a society,' he will say, 'which is under an autocrat, but let that autocrat be young, of retentive memory, quick to learn, and temperamentally bold and high-souled. Also, if all these advantages are to be of any service, they must be further attended in the autocrat's soul by something we have already mentioned as an 710 indispensable accompaniment of all the parts of goodness.'

Clin. I think, Megillus, what our friend means by this accompaniment is temperance. Am I right, sir?

Ath. Yes, Clinias, temperance in the popular sense of the word, not in that high and forced sense in which temperance might be said to be the same thing with wisdom. 'Tis a native surface quality which shows in mere children and animals that some of them have no self-restraint in the matter of pleasures, and others have—a quality, as we said, of no great account when divorced from the various other goods. You take me, no doubt?

Clin. Why, certainly.

Ath. Very well; our autocrat must have that endowment as well as all those we have named, if the society is to achieve the constitution which will bring felicity into its life with maximum speed and success. I assure you there neither is, nor can be, any better and more rapid way to the settlement of the constitution.

Clin. Nay, sir, how or by what argument can a man possibly persuade himself of the truth of such a doctrine?

Ath. Why, surely, Clinias, it is easy enough to see how natural it is that it should be so.

Clin. What is the theory, once more? There is to be an

F 275

autocrat, you say, and he must be young, temperate, quick to learn, retentive, bold and high-souled?

Ath. And, you must add, fortunate—fortunate, that is, in the single point that there is a contemporary legislator of distinction with whom chance has brought him in contact; with that one coincidence, God has done his utmost towards his purpose of heaping blessings on a community. The next best thing would be that there should be a pair of such potentates; it would be third best, and so on proportionately more difficult, the more of them there were, and vice versa.

Clin. The best state, as I understand you, might arise out of an autocracy, provided, that is, there were a consummate legislator and an autocrat of disciplined character, and the transition to it would be particularly easy and rapid in that case, less so from an oligarchy—is not that your meaning?—and still less from a democracy.

Ath. By no means; the readiest starting-point would be autocracy, the next best, constitutional monarchy, the next best again, democracy of a kind; oligarchy would come fourth, and only admits of such a development with great difficulty, for there the number of persons of influence is greatest. The occasion for it, mark you, is provided, according to us, when nature produces a real legislator who happens to share power of a kind with the most influential persons in society. Where, 711 as in an autocracy, this latter element is numerically fewest but strongest, you have the normal occasion and opportunity for facile and speedy revolution.

Clin. What? This is more than we can follow.

Ath. Yet the point has been made, unless I am mistaken, more than once already. But perhaps you and your friend have never observed a society under an autocrat.

Clin. And I must say I have no particular desire to do so, either.

Ath. If you did, you would certainly remark the presence of the feature I first spoke of.

Clin. What feature?

Ath. An autocrat who desires to make a change in the tone of public life has no laborious or protracted task: he has only to take in his own person the first steps on the road—be it the path to virtue or to vice—into which he would guide the community; he must first set the copy of his own conduct, awarding credit and distinctions to one course, discredit to another, and disgracing the refractory in the various departments of conduct.

Clin. But why should you suppose that the rest of society will be so quick to follow the example of the wielder of this combined persuasion and coercion?

Ath. O my friends, never let yourselves be persuaded that there is any speedier or easier way to change the laws of a community than the personal guidance of those in authority; there is none to-day, and will be none hereafter. No, it is not there that we shall find the impossibility or difficulty; the true difficulty lies in the occurrence of something which has been uncommon enough in the whole course of history, but never happens without bringing a whole infinity of blessings to the society in which it occurs.

Clin. Now I wonder what this may be.

Ath. The awakening of a heaven-sent passion for ways of temperance and justice in persons of the highest station, monarchs, for example, or men of exceptionally outstanding wealth or family, or, it may be, in one who recalls the qualities of Nestor who is said to have towered above all his contemporaries even more by his temperance than by his eloquence.[1] That happened, we are told, in Trojan times, though it has never been known in our own. Be that as it may, if such a man there has been, or should be hereafter, or is now among us,[2] how blessed is his own life, and how blessed they who hearken to the words which proceed from those virtuous lips! We may say the same of power in all its forms: when supreme power is 712 combined in one person with wisdom and temperance, then, and on no other conditions conceivable, nature gives birth to the best of constitutions with the best of laws. So you may take these oracular remarks [3] as a parable embodying the proof that though in one way it is hard for a society to get good laws, in another, if things only fall out as I say, it would be the quickest and easiest of all developments.

Clin. But why so?

Ath. Suppose we apply the parable to your city and try to

---

[1] The contingency contemplated is that of a democratic leader who is also a man of outstanding moral genius, a greater Pericles.

[2] ἢ νῦν ἡμῶν ἔστιν τις, 711 e 5. As the words stand they can only mean 'if one of us three should be such a man', but the sense requires 'if there should be such a man alive to-day'. This is given by Stallbaum's proposal to insert <ἐφ'> before ἡμῶν, but the slip may be the author's.

[3] The point of comparison with an oracle lies in the structure of the preceding sentence, 'when so-and-so happens, then expect such-and-such consequences'. This is a familiar oracular formula, the 'when' clause usually stating a paradoxical conjunction of circumstances. Thus Plato's point is the extreme rarity and improbability of the conjunction of power and moral greatness in the same person.

model its laws in imagination, like elderly men playing a boys' game.

Clin. En avant, then, and a truce to all delays!

Ath. Of course we must invoke God's presence at our foundation. So may he hear us and come, gracious and debonair, to our help as we construct our city and its laws!

Clin. Amen to that!

Ath. And pray what type of constitution are we proposing to impose on our society?

Clin. But what do you mean by that question? You should put it a little more plainly. You mean, is it to be a democracy, an oligarchy, an aristocracy, or a monarchy? You surely cannot be thinking of an autocracy, or at least my friend and I can hardly credit it.

Ath. Come now, which of those names describes your own constitution? I wonder which of you will be the readier with his answer.

Meg. As I am the elder man, perhaps it would be fairer that I should speak first?

Clin. Yes, I think so.

Meg. Why, sir, when I consider our Lacedaemonian constitution, I really cannot tell you off-hand which would be the proper name for it. It actually seems to have its resemblances to an autocracy (in fact, the power of our ephors is astonishingly autocratic), and yet at times I think it looks like the most democratic of all societies. Again, it would be sheer paradox to deny that it is an aristocracy, while yet again, a feature of it is a life-monarchy, asserted by all mankind, as well as ourselves, to be the very oldest of such institutions. When the question is put to me,[1] like this, on a sudden, as I say, I really cannot tell definitely to which of these types of constitution it belongs.

Clin. I find myself in the same perplexity as you, Megillus. I am quite at a loss to identify our Cnossian constitution confidently with any of them.

713   *Ath.* That, my friends, is because you enjoy real constitutions, whereas the types we have specified are not constitutions, but settlements enslaved to the domination of some component section, each taking its designation from the dominant factor. But if a society must take its name from such a quarter, the proper course is to call it by the name of the god who is the master of rational men.

Clin. And what god is that?

---

[1] Reading with Madvig ἀνερωτηθείς at 712 e 4.

Ath. Perhaps we may need to employ parable a little longer, if I am to answer the question to your full satisfaction.

Clin. Oh, so that is the way we must proceed, is it?

Ath. Certainly. Why, long before the time of the societies whose foundation we have discussed, in the age of Cronus— so they say—there was a much earlier form of settled government, and a very happy one, which is reflected in the best of our present-day communities.

Clin. Then, I should say, we must very decidedly be told about it.

Ath. Certainly, in my own judgment, and that is the very reason why I have brought it into the argument.

Clin. Very properly, too, and, seeing how relevant it is, you will do right to tell the whole story.

Ath. I must do as you propose. Well, according to the received tradition, in that age of bliss, all life needs was provided in abundance and unsought, and the reason, we are told, was this. Cronus was of course aware that, as we have explained, no human being is competent to wield an irresponsible control over mankind without becoming swollen with pride and unrighteousness. Being alive to this he gave our communities as their kings and magistrates, not men but spirits, beings of diviner and superior kind, just as we still do the same with our flocks of sheep and herds of other domesticated animals: we do not set oxen to manage oxen, or goats to manage goats; we, their betters in kind, act as their masters ourselves. Well, the god, in his kindness to man, did the same; he set over us this superior race of spirits who took charge of us with no less ease to themselves than convenience to us, providing us with peace and mercy, sound law and unscanted justice, and endowing the families of mankind with internal concord and happiness. So the story teaches us to-day, and teaches us truly, that when a community is ruled not by God but by man, its members have no refuge from evil and misery; we should do our utmost— this is the moral—to reproduce the life of the 'age of Cronus', and therefore should order our private households and our public 714 societies alike in obedience to the immortal element within us, giving the name of law to the appointment of understanding.[1]

---

[1] We are to regard the word νόμος (law) as derived from νέμειν in the sense of to *divide, apportion*, not in the sense of to *practise* (a custom). I doubt whether it is further meant that there is any linguistic connection between νέμειν and νοῦς (understanding). The thought is that in real life it is 'understanding' within the soul which acts as the vicar of an unseen God.

But when a single person, an oligarchy, or a democracy with a soul set on their pleasures and passions and lusting for their satisfaction—a soul that cannot contain itself, and is in the grip of unending and insatiate disease—when such a one tramples law under his feet and takes command of an individual or society, then, as I was just saying, all hope of deliverance is gone. That is my thesis, Clinias, and we have to consider whether it convinces us or not.

Clin. Convinces us? Of course it does.

Ath. Then are you acquainted with a theory that there are as many types of law as of constitution? And we have just seen how many types of constitution there are in the popular view. And pray believe me that the issue now at stake is no trifle, but of paramount moment. We are back again at the question of the standard of right and wrong. The standard of our laws, it is said, should be neither war nor goodness as a whole; whatever the existing constitution may be, the law should look to its interest, its permanent security against dissolution, and the best way to define real justice would be to say——

Clin. To say what?

Ath. That it is the interest of the sovereign.[1]

Clin. You must explain yourself rather more clearly.

Ath. And so I will. They say, you know, that the laws in a society are always enacted by the dominant section?

Clin. Just so.

Ath. Well then, it is said, can you imagine that when the populace, or some other political party, or an autocrat, if you like, has got the upper hand, the victorious side will, of its own accord, enact laws with any principal aim but its own interest in the permanence of its authority?

Clin. Of course not.

Ath. And if a man contravenes these enactments, their author will punish him for his violation of justice, meaning by justice these same enactments.

Clin. So I should apprehend.

Ath. These enactments, then, will in every case be justice, and for these reasons.

Clin. Yes; according to this account of the matter.

Ath. In fact, this is one of our former principles of sovereignty.

Clin. Principles? What principles?

Ath. Why, the claims to authority which we passed under

---

[1] The same definition which is given by Thrasymachus in *Rep.* I, where it is defended, in the first instance, by the same reasoning.

review. We found parents claiming authority over their
descendants, the older men over the younger, the well-born over
the base-born, and you may remember that there were several
other mutually incompatible claims. This was actually one of 715
the list, and we remarked that Pindar treats the 'high hand of
violence'—to use his own phrase—as natural justice.

Clin. Yes, that is certainly what we said before.

Ath. Now consider to which side[1] we are to entrust our
society. For here is a situation which has recurred over and
over again in public life before now——

Clin. What situation is that?

Ath. After a contest for office, the victorious side engrosses
the conduct of public affairs so completely to itself that no share
whatsoever of office is left to the vanquished, or even to their
descendants; each party watches the other in jealous apprehension of insurrection, due to the attainment of office by
someone with memories of past wrongs. Such societies, we
are now, of course, contending, are no constitutional States,
just as enactments, so far as they are not for the common
interest of the whole community, are no true laws; men who are
for a party, we say, are factionaries, not citizens, and their so-
called rights are empty words. And our reason for saying it
is that you and I have no intention of conferring an office in
your society on any one for his wealth, or his possession of some
similar advantage, such as physical strength, stature, or family.
It is, we hold, the man who is most perfect in obedience to
established law, the man whose victory over his fellow-citizens
takes that form, to whom we should give the function of
ministry to the gods,[2] the highest post to him who stands first,
the second to him who is next in the contest—the remaining
posts being assigned similarly to the succeeding candidates in
order. If I have just styled the so-called 'authorities' *ministers*
of the law, it is not for the sake of a novel phrase, but because
I am persuaded that the preservation or ruin of a society depends
on this more than on anything else. Where the law is overruled or obsolete, I see destruction hanging over the community;
where it is sovereign over the authorities and they its humble

---

[1] προτέροις, 715 *a* 4. The 'sides' are that of parents, elders, nobly born
. . . on the one hand, that of progeny, juniors, the common folk . . .
on the other. The answer to the question is, in effect, that we are not
espousing the claims of either 'side'.

[2] The meaning is, that office, as it should be won by obedience to the
laws, is itself a life of service to the law; the reward for service is higher
service. The speaker, in view of what he has already said of law or the
'voice of God', expresses this thought by calling 'office' the service of God.

servants, I discern the presence of salvation and every blessing Heaven sends on a society.

Clin. Right, sir, right in God's name! You have the long sight of your years.

Ath. Why, yes; a man is always most short-sighted in such matters in youth, and most far-sighted in age.

Clin. Yes, indeed.

Ath. Well, and our next step? May we not assume our settlers to be here in the country and under our eyes, and address the rest of our discourse to them in person?

Clin. By all means.

Ath. 'My friends!'[1]—this is what I would say to them—'God, 716 who, as the old saw has it, holds in his hands beginning, end, and middle of all that is, moves through the cycle of nature, straight to his end, and ever at his side walks Right, the justicer of them that forsake God's law. He that would be happy follows close in her train with lowly and chastened mien, but whoso is lifted up with vanity—with pride of riches or rank or foolish conceit of youthful comeliness—and all on fire within with wantonness, as one that needs neither governor nor guide, but is fitted rather to be himself a guide to others—such a one is left alone, forsaken of God. In his abandonment he takes to him others like himself, and works general confusion by his frantic career. Now to some he seems to be some great one, but after no long while he makes no stinted amend to Right by the sheer ruin of himself, his house, and his State. Now since these things are so, what must the man of judgment do or purpose, and what forbear?'

Clin. So much is plain; every man must purpose to be of the company who follow after the god.

Ath. 'What line of conduct, then, is dear to God and a following of him? There is but one, and it is summed up in one ancient rule, the rule that "like"—when it is a thing of due measure—"loves its like". (For things that have no measure can be loved neither by one another nor by those that have.) Now it is God who is, for you and me, of a truth the "measure of all things", much more truly then, as they say, "man". So he who would be loved by such a being must himself become such to the utmost of his might, and so, by this argument, he that is temperate among us is loved by God, for he is like God,

---

[1] From this point the speaker imagines himself to be delivering to the prospective citizens of the Cretan colony a general preliminary address on the principles of sound social morality, which is to serve as a preamble to the code of laws. The address is broken off at 719 *a* 4 by a digression justifying such preambles, but is resumed again at the opening of the next book (726), and only formally concluded at 734 *e* 2.

whereas he that is not temperate is unlike God and at variance with him; so also it is with the unjust, and the same rule holds in all else. Now from this rule, I would have you note, follows another, of all rules, to my mind, the grandest and truest, which is this: for the good man 'tis most glorious and good and profitable to happiness of life, ay, and most excellently fit, to do sacrifice and be ever in communion with Heaven through prayer and offerings and all manner of worship, but for the evil clean contrary. For the evil man is impure of soul, where the other is pure, and from the polluted neither good men nor God may ever rightly accept a gift; thus all this toil taken with Heaven is 717 but labour thrown away for the impious, though ever seasonable in the pious. Here, then, is the target at which we have to aim, but what shall we call the shafts which make straight for it, and the engine from which they are fired? Well, first, I say, the mark of godliness will be truly hit if the gods of the lower world are held in honour next to the Olympians, and the patron deities of the State, the even, the second-best, and the left-hand being consecrated to them, their superior counterparts to the powers which have just been named. After these gods a man of judgment will do worship to spirits, and after them to heroes, and I would give the next place to each man's images of his household gods, worshipped as the law directs. And now we come to honour to be shown to parents while they are yet in life. Here religion [1] demands the due discharge of this earliest and heaviest debt, the most sacred of all our obligations. It bids a man count all he has and owns at the service of those who gave him birth and breeding, to minister to their needs to his utmost ability, first with his substance, then with his body, and then with his mind, in repayment of a loan of care and painful labour made so long ago on the security of his youth, and now to be made good to his elders in their age and sore necessity. Moreover, all his life through, a man should observe particular reverence of tongue towards his parents, for light and winged speech brings heavy doom; Right has her appointed messenger, Nemesis, to keep watch over the matter. So one should yield to them when they feel anger, and discharge it, in word or deed, and understand that 'tis but natural in a father who thinks himself wronged by his son to be moved to uncommon anger. But when parents are once no more, the most modest burial is the best; a man should not exceed the customary pomps, nor yet come short of those wherewith his forefathers were wont to

---

[1] 717 b 6. I would, with Hermann and England (and probably Ficinus), read οἷς (for ὡς) θέμις.

entomb their own sires; he should keep also to the same rule in paying the decent annual rites of tendance to the departed. Above all, he should honour the deceased at all times by keeping 718 the memory of them green, while he expends on them what is proportionate to the means fortune permits him. If we act thus and frame our lives to this model, we shall, one and all, always reap the due reward from Heaven and the higher powers, and our days, for the main of life, will be passed with bright hopes.' As regards duties to children and kinsmen, friends and fellow citizens, as well as works of pious service to strangers, and our relations with them all, by discharge whereof, as the law enjoins, a man should adorn and illustrate his life—in all this the actual recital of the laws will, with Heaven's consent, ensure our society bliss and well-being, in part by persuasion, and in part by enforced and legal correction of characters not amenable to persuasion'. There are other things, too, which should be said and must be said by a legislator like-minded with myself, and yet cannot be fittingly said in the form of a statute; as to these I would advise him,[1] when he has finished the rest of his discourse to the best of his power, to propound a sample to himself and those for whom he is to legislate before he enters on his actual enactments. In what form, then, is such matter best couched? To confine it all within the bounds of a single outline, as I might call it, is none too easy; still, we may be able to reach a definite result if we look at the matter in some such way as this.

Clin. And what result may that be?

Ath. I should wish the subjects to give a ready audience to persuasions to virtue, and plainly this is the effect at which our legislator will aim throughout his legislation.

Clin. Of course.

Ath. Well, it struck me that what we have said might do some service—if our words have not been an appeal to utterly brutal souls—towards gaining a civil and friendly hearing. So, as I say,[2] if it makes an auditor a little, even if ever so little, more friendly, and so readier to be instructed, we have every reason to be thankful. Men earnestly bent on becoming thoroughly good and that with all speed are not easily to be found, nor in large numbers, and Hesiod is commonly pronounced a wise man for his saying that 'the path to vice is smooth', and, being

---

[1] Inserting δεῖν, with Apelt, after δεῖγμα at 718 b 7.
[2] Reading with Vermehren φημὶ for the φησὶν of the MSS., Burnet and others.

so short, can be travelled without sweat, whereas 'before virtue
the immortal gods have set sweat, and the road thither is long 719
and uphill and rough at the outset, though when the summit
is reached, the going is easy, for all its hardness'.[1]

Clin. And a fine saying it is, too.

Ath. Yes, no doubt. But I should like to propose to your
common consideration the effect our foregoing argument has
produced on myself.

Clin. Then let us hear it.

Ath. Well, let us address our remarks to the legislator, thus:
'Tell us one thing, legislator. If you knew what we ought
to do and say, you would tell us what it is. Surely that is
manifest?'

Clin. Of course it is.

Ath. 'Well, but did we not hear you not so long ago pronouncing that a legislator must not permit poets to compose
whatever they please. For they are not likely to know where
they may contradict the law to the detriment of the society.'

Clin. I must admit that it is the fact.

Ath. Then suppose we put the case for the poets to him;
I wonder whether it might fairly be stated thus?

Clin. How?

Ath. As follows: ''Tis an old story, legislator, which we
poets are always telling with the universal approval of the rest
of the world, that when a poet takes his seat on the Muse's
tripod, his judgment takes leave of him. He is like a fountain
which gives free course to the rush of its waters, and since
representation is of the essence of his art, must often contradict
his own utterances in his presentations of contrasted characters,
without knowing whether the truth is on the side of this speaker
or of that. Now it is not the legislator's business in his law to
make two such statements about one and the same topic; he
has regularly to deliver himself of one pronouncement on one
matter. Take, as an example, one of the very topics on which
you have just delivered yourself. A funeral may be extravagant, it may be mean, it may be decently modest. You select
one and only one of those types, the intermediate type, for
universal imposition and unrestricted commendation. But, in
my case, if my poem dealt with an opulent woman and her
instructions for her own funeral, I should commend extrava-
gance, whereas a frugal poor man would be for parsimony, and
a man of moderate estate and modest personality would have

[1] Hesiod, *Works and Days*, 287 ff.

the same preference as yourself.[1] But in your position it is
not enough to use the word "moderate", as you did just now;
you must tell us what and how much is "moderate", or else
confess that your statement is not yet a law.'

Clin. Truly said, indeed.

Ath. Then is our appointed law-maker to set no such prefatory
statement in front of his code? Is he just to tell us curtly what
we are to do or not to do, add the threat of a penalty, and then
turn to the next enactment, without one word of exhortation
720 or advice to the recipients? Just as one type of physician
treats us, when we call him in, in one way, and a second in
another—but let us remind ourselves of the difference between
the two methods, and then we shall have a request to make of
our legislator, as children might beg their physician to give them
the gentlest treatment. You would like an illustration? Well,
there are physicians, and again there are physicians' assistants,
whom we also speak of as physicians.

Clin. Just so.

Ath. All bear the name, whether freemen or slaves who gain
their professional knowledge by watching their masters and
obeying their directions in empiric fashion, not in the scientific
way in which freemen learn their art and teach it to their pupils.
You agree that there are those two types of so-called physicians?

Clin. Certainly I do.

Ath. Now have you further observed that, as there are slaves
as well as freemen among the patients of our communities, the
slaves, to speak generally, are treated by slaves, who pay them
a hurried visit, or receive them in dispensaries? A physician of
this kind never gives a servant any account of his complaint,
nor asks him for any; he gives him some empiric injunction with
an air of finished knowledge, in the brusque fashion of a dictator,
and then is off in hot haste to the next ailing servant; that is
how he lightens his master's medical labours for him. The
free practitioner, who, for the most part, attends free men,
treats their diseases by going into things thoroughly from the
beginning in a scientific way, and takes the patient and his
family into his confidence. Thus he learns something from the
sufferers, and at the same time instructs the invalid to the best
of his powers. He does not give his prescriptions until he has

---

[1] ἐπαινέσοι of the MSS. is grammatically impossible at 719 e 3. If,
like Burnet, we adopt Bekker's ἐπαινέσαι I think the sense will probably
be 'would commend a funeral like himself' (i.e. one neither mean nor
gorgeous). I adopt Badham's ἐπαινοίη σοι (but suspect Plato wrote it
ἐπαινοῖ σοι).

won the patient's support, and when he has done so, he steadily
aims at producing complete restoration to health by persuading
the sufferer into compliance. Now which of the two methods
is that of the better physician or director of bodily regimen?
That which effects the same result by a twofold process or that
which employs a single process, the worse of the two, and
exasperates its subject?

Clin. Nay, sir, the double process is vastly superior.

Ath. Then would you like us to consider the two methods,
the double and the single, in their application to legislation itself?

Clin. To be sure I should.

Ath. Then, I ask you, what will be the first law our legislator
will enact? Is not his natural course to begin with an ordinance
regulating the first stage in the creation of a society?   721

Clin. Why, of course.

Ath. And the first stage in the creation of any society is
surely conjugal conjunction and association?

Clin. Certainly.

Ath. Presumably, then, if the legislation of any society is to
be sound and right it must start with a marriage-law.

Clin. I quite agree.

Ath. Then let us state that law in the simple form first; it
might run to some such effect as this:

ITEM: A man to marry when he has reached the age of thirty
and before he comes to that of thirty-five[1]; neglect to do so to
be penalized by fine and loss of status; the fine to be of such and
such an amount, and the loss of status to take such and such
form.

That may be taken as the simple form of our law of marriage;
its double form we may word thus:

ITEM: *A man to marry when he has reached the age of thirty and
before he comes to that of thirty-five,* bethinking him that there is
a sense in which mankind naturally partakes of immortality,
a prize our nature makes desirable to all of us in its every form;
for to win renown and not lie in our graves without a name is
a desire of this. Thus the race of man is Time's equal twin and
companion, bound up with him in a union never to be broken,
and the manner of their immortality is in this wise: by succession of generations the race abides one and the same, so

---

[1] Thirty is also mentioned as the age at which a man should begin to
think of marrying at 785 *b*; at 772 *e* twenty-five is given as the 'under
limit' of the period during which a man should marry. This is one of
a number of small inconsistencies which confirm the tradition that the
text of the *Laws* received no final revision.

partaking in immortality through procreation. Whence piety flatly forbids a man to deprive himself of the boon by his own act, as he wilfully deprives himself who takes no thought of children and wife. So him who will obey the law we will hold scatheless, but as for him who disobeys and comes to five-and-thirty unwed, let him be yearly *mulcted in such and such a sum*, that he may not take his solitary state for a source of profit or ease, and *let him have no part in the public honours* paid from time to time by the younger folk to their elders.

You have heard this law set by the side of that, and are now in case to judge universally whether our laws, thus joining persuasion to menace, should be, at the very least, of double length, or should confine themselves to menace and so be of half the length.

Meg. To prefer the concise, sir, is ever our Laconian way; yet were I bidden to decide which of these statutes of yours I would rather see in force in our city, my vote would be for the more prolix. Indeed, my choice would be the same about any law whatsoever after this model, if both alternatives were possible. But we must not forget that our present proposals need the approval of our friend Clinias, too, since it is his city which is now proposing to adopt such laws as we may enact.

Clin. My thanks for your words, Megillus.

Ath. Why, to raise debate about a number of syllables more or less were, indeed, futile—it is quality, I take it, not length or brevity we should prize; 'tis the matter of the one kind of law just mentioned that is of more than double excellence in use, by comparison with the other. As I said but now, our illustration of the two types of physicians was exactly apposite. Yet, in despite of us, none of our legislators would seem ever to have remarked that they rely wholly on one instrument in their work, whereas there are two available, so far as the mass's lack of education will permit, persuasion and compulsion. Authority [1] is never tempered in their law-making with persuasion; they work by compulsion unalloyed. Ay, and by Heaven, to my mind, there is yet a third requisite of a law [2] which is universally disregarded in fact.

Clin. And pray what may it be?

---

[1] πειθοῖ κεραννύντες τὴν μάχην (722 c). μάχην, the reading of all MSS., is corrupt. For purposes of translation I adopt Stallbaum's suggestion, ἀρχήν, which seems to me palaeographically superior to Ast's ἀνάγκην.
[2] The third requisite is that suggested by the language of 722 d, 'system', 'method'. 'Before making a law, we must be clear about the principle on which it is to be made' (England).

Ath. Why, it has been providentially disclosed by our own conversation to-day. Since we began our talk of law, daybreak has given place to noonday, and we have reached this delightful arbour, and all our conversation has been exclusively of laws; yet I fancy we are only now beginning to talk laws; all we have said hitherto has been but preambles to laws. Now why do I say this? Because I would observe that discourse and vocal utterance of every kind have their preludes, their preliminaries, as I might say, preliminaries which furnish a useful methodical introduction to the coming performance. High-wrought and elaborate preludes are prefixed, for example, to the so-called 'nomes' for the harp, and to musical compositions in general, whereas in the case of what we regard as the real 'nomes', the laws of the community, no one has ever uttered the name, nor constructed or published anything of the kind; it is taken for granted that such a thing does not exist. Yet our present conversation, I believe, suggests that it does; the deliverances which impressed me just now as laws of double length are not, I think, just precisely that; they contain two things at once, a law and the prelude to it. The 'dictatorial prescription' in tones which we compared with the prescriptions of our unfree 723 physician is unqualified law, while all that preceded—persuasive, as Megillus called it—is, in fact, such a persuasive, but has the rhetorical character of a preamble. For I find I framed the whole of this discourse, uttered by its speaker in the tones of persuasion, to prepare the auditor of the legislator's enactments to receive his prescription, that is to say, his law, in a spirit of friendliness and consequent docility, and for that very reason, it should, in my opinion, properly be called by no other name; it is not the text of the law but its preamble. You will ask me, then, how I propose to follow up the observation. Thus: I would have a legislator take constant care to leave neither his code as a whole nor its various divisions unprovided with introductory preludes. This will make as great a difference as in the two examples we were just considering.

Clin. I, too, would urge a legislator who understands his business to do the work in this fashion and no other.

Ath. I thoroughly agree with you, Clinias, as far as this. All laws have their preambles, and any one who is beginning the work of legislation should prefix to each section the preamble appropriate to the whole subject; the pronouncement he is about to make is no trifle, and it will make a great difference whether it can be distinctly remembered or not. Yet we should be wrong if we insisted on the presence of a preamble alike for minor laws, as they are called, and major. In fact, one must not treat every song or every speech in that fashion. It is true that there are appropriate preludes in all cases, but we are not to make invariable use of them; we must leave it to the individual speaker, or singer, or legislator to use his own judgment in each case.

Clin. I fully agree with you. But, pray, sir, let us waste no more time in delay. Let us go back to our argument and make a start, if you please, with what you said a while ago, though not as an avowed preamble. Let us begin it all over again, as they say in games, with a better 'second shot', on the understanding that we are no longer constructing a casual argument, but a preamble; let us begin, I say, with the admission that we are making our preamble. As for the worship of the gods and the service of our progenitors, what has been already said is adequate enough, but we must try to pursue the theme further until you feel that our whole prelude is sufficiently complete; then, and not before, you shall rehearse the actual statutes.

724 *Ath.* Good, then; our preamble, as we are now agreed, has already dealt adequately with gods, subordinate powers, and ancestors living and dead. As I understand you, you want me to throw some light on such parts of the subject as we have not yet touched.

Clin. Precisely.

Ath. Why, in the next place, it is proper and to their common highest interest that speaker and hearers should do their utmost to achieve their own education by meditation on their duties of effort and remission in all that concerns mind, body, and substance. Whence these, and no others, are doubtless the matters of which we must next speak and hear.

Clin. Very true.

BOOK V

Ath. Listen then, all ye who but now gave ear to our dis- ⁷²⁶course of gods and well-beloved sires. Of all a man has—after his gods—the divinest thing, and the most truly his own, is his soul. Now things which pertain to any man are ever of two sorts,[1] a superior and better sort to be sovereign, an inferior and worse to be subject. So a man should ever prefer those that are sovereign in honour before those that are subject. Therefore, when I bid men honour their own souls next to the ⁷²⁷gods, our sovereign lords, and the powers under them, the counsel I give is right   Yet not a man of us, I may say, honours his soul aright, though he dreams he does. Honour, I take it, is a thing divinely good, and can be conferred by nothing that is evil; he who deems he is advancing his soul by speech, gifts, or compliances, and all the while makes it no better than it was before, may dream that he shows it honour, but in truth does it none. Barely, for example, has a man come to boyhood before he counts himself fit to pronounce on all things, honours his soul, as he fancies, by this flattery, and gives it ready licence to act whatever it will. Now our present declaration is that by these courses he does it hurt, not honour, whereas we bid him honour it next to Heaven. So again, when a man lays the blame for his several misdeeds and the greater and graver part of his mischances not on himself but on others, ever accounting himself clear of fault, by way of reverence—or so he fancies—for his soul; that is no honour done the soul—far from it—but hurt. Again, when he courts pleasures in defiance of the legislator's admonition and approval, he does his soul no honour, but rather dishonour, by thus defiling it with misery and remorse. Again, in a different way, when a man will not harden himself to endure commended hardships, fears, pains, sufferings, but makes submission, the surrender brings no honour, for all such courses bring disgrace on the soul. Again, when a man counts it good to live at all costs, that also is dishonour to the soul; 'tis surrender to that within him which accounts the unseen world merely evil, whereas a man should

[1] In 726 l. 4 I follow a suggestion, made in Dr. England's notes, to replace the full stop after πᾶσιν by a comma.

make head against his fancy with cogent proof that he knows not even whether our chiefest good may not be in the gift of the gods of that land. Again, when a man prefers comeliness before goodness, this also is no other than real and utmost dishonour to the soul. For this estimate pronounces body more honourable than soul, and that most falsely; nothing born of earth is more honourable than the heavenly, and he that conceits himself otherwise of the soul than this knows not the preciousness of this possession he despises. Again, when a man lusts after wealth basely won, or has no disrelish for the 728 winning, he does no real honour to his soul by such offerings— far, far from it! He sells its goodly treasure for a parcel of coin, but all the gold on earth or under earth is no equal exchange for goodness. To say all in one word: whosoever will not at all hazards keep himself from all the legislator lists in his count of things base and bad, and exercise himself with all his might in all that is in the contrary table of things good and lovely, knows not that by all such ways a man ever heaps foul dishonour and deformity on the divinest thing he has, his soul. In fact, none of us, or few, reckon with the sorest 'judgment'—as the phrase is—on evil-doing, which judgment is that a man grows like those who already are evil, and, as the likeness grows, avoids good men and good converse, and cuts himself off from them, but follows after the other sort and cleaves to them in intimate fellowship, and he who clings to such men cannot but do and have done to him what men of that sort naturally do and say. This state then is not *judgment*—for judgment is, like justice, a good—but vengeance, the painful consequence of iniquity. He that meets it and he that misses it are alike unhappy, the one because he gets no healing for his disease, the other in that he is cut off for the salvation of many another. But honour, we hold, is, in sum, to follow after what is better, and for what is worse but may be amended, e'en to make it good as best may be.

There is nothing, then, of all a man owns so natively quick as the soul to shun the evil but follow on the trail of the chief good, win it, and spend the rest of a lifetime at home with it. Whence we have given the soul the second place in honour. The third, and so much must be plain to any vision, belongs to due honour to the body. But next it must be asked, what various honours there are, which of them ring true, which are counterfeit? and here is a task for our legislator. He will suggest, I think, that they are these and the like: the body to be honoured is not the

comely, nor the strong, nor swift, no, nor the healthy, though
so many might be of that mind—nor yet that of the contrary
sort; the body which displays all these qualities in intermediate
degree is by far the most sober, and soundest as well; for the one
sort make men's souls vain and overbearing, the other tame and
abject. 'Tis the same with ownership of wealth and property,
and they must be rated by the same scale. Excess of all such
things, as a rule, breeds public and private feuds and factions, 729
defect, subjection. Let no man covet wealth for his children's
sake, that he may leave them in opulence; 'tis not for their own
good nor for the State's. For the young an estate that tempts
no sycophants and yet has no lack of things needful is of all
others best and most consonant; it works general concord and
concert and banishes pains from our lives. We should leave
our children rich, not in gold but in reverence. Now we fancy
we shall assure that inheritance if we rebuke the young when
they forget their modesty, but in truth the thing is not to be
done by giving the young such admonition as they receive
to-day when they are told that 'youth must respect all men'.
A legislator of judgment will be more likely to charge older men
to respect their juniors and, of all things, to take heed that no
young man ever see or hear one of themselves doing act or
speaking word of shame, since when the old forget their modesty,
the young, too, cannot but be most graceless. Far the best
way to educate our young men and ourselves along with them
is not by admonition, but by life-long visible practice of all
to which a man would admonish others. If a man pays honour
and respect to kindred and all fellowship of common blood in
worship of the gods of the kin, he may reasonably expect the
favour of the gods of birth for the propagation of his own
children. As to friends and comrades in the several affairs of
life, a man will gain their good-will if he counts their services
to him greater and ampler than they do, but rates his own
kindnesses to friend and companion lower than they themselves.
In all that concerns city and fellow-citizens, the best man, and
the best by far, is he who would prize before an Olympian
victory or any triumph in war or peace, the credit of victory
in service to the laws of his home, as one who has all his life
been their true servant above all men. Then, as regards the
alien, we must remember that compacts have a peculiar sanctity;
indeed, offences by alien against alien, we may say, compared
with sins against fellow-citizens, more directly draw down the
vengeance of God. For the alien, being without friends or

kinsmen, has the greater claim on pity, human and divine. Whence he that is able to exact the vengeance is all the readier to come to his help, and none is so able as the god or spirit who 730 protects the alien as minister of Zeus Xenios.[1] What anxious care, then, should a man of any foresight take to come to the end of life's journey guiltless of offence towards aliens! Moreover, the gravest of offences, whether against landsmen or aliens, is always that done to a suppliant, for the god in whose name the suppliant made his appeal when he obtained a promise keeps jealous watch over the sufferer, and thus he will never suffer his wrongs unavenged.

We have now fairly reviewed a man's relations to parents, to himself, his possessions, his city, his friends, his kindred, to aliens and to countrymen, and must next in order consider what manner of man he must himself be to pass through life with full credit; we come to speak now, of the effects not of law, but of education through commendation and reproach in making men more amenable and well-disposed towards the laws we are hereafter to enact. Now of all things good, truth holds the first place among gods and men alike; for him who is to know felicity and happiness, my prayer is that he may be endowed with it from the first, that he may live all the longer a true man. For such a man is trusty, whereas he that loves voluntary deception is untrustworthy, and he that loves involuntary, a fool, and neither lot is to be envied. For, sure, the traitor or the fool is a man of no friends; course of time discovers him and he prepares for himself utter loneliness in the trials of age at the end of his days, so living equally destitute of companions and children, whether they survive or not. Honour is due to him who himself does no wrong, but he that will not so much as suffer another to do it merits twofold and more than twofold honour; the first has the worth of one man, the second, who reveals the wrong-doing of others to the authorities, the worth of many.[2] But he that further does his endeavour to second

[1] One's engagements with the 'foreigner' are not sustained by the law of one's own State, and international law did not exist in the fourth century B.C. Since an engagement is therefore regularly placed under a 'religious sanction', the particular deities invoked to be witnesses to its good faith will vary with circumstances, but they are all to be regarded as agents of the supreme God as the power who ultimately expects loyalty to the word once passed, Zeus in his capacity of 'protector of aliens'.

[2] This is not to be understood as an encouragement to the professional informer. It is meant that a man does not do the whole of his duty by abstaining from personal infractions of other men's rights. It is also a good citizen's business to 'expose' injustice and to second the authorities in their attempts to suppress it.

the authorities in their work of repression, he is the great and
perfect citizen, and the palm of virtue shall be declared to be his.
We must make this same grading in our recognition of temperance and judgment and all good qualities which a man imparts
to others as well as enjoys in his own person. To him who
communicates them we should give the supreme degree of
honour; he that cannot impart them, yet would fain do so, must
be left in the second rank. As for him who engrosses good things
to himself and will never, if he can help it, share them with
a friend, we should censure his person, but with no depreciation 731
of the quality on the possessor's account; rather we must do all
we can to make it our own. In this contest for virtue we will
have all men competitors, but there must be no jealousies.
For a man such as we would have him promotes a State, since
he runs in the race himself without hampering others by evil
reports, whereas the jealous man, who fancies slander of others
the right means to his own advancement, strains less to reach
real virtue himself, and causes his rivals to be discouraged by
unmerited censure; thus he cripples the whole society for the
race for virtue, and does what lies in him to lower its good
repute. High-spirited every man should be, but likewise
gentle in eminent degree. For cruel and almost or wholly
irreparable wrongs at the hands of others are only to be escaped
in one way, by victorious encounter and repulse, and stern
correction, and such action is impossible for the soul without
generous passion. But as concerns the transgressions of those
who commit wrong, but reparable wrong, we must first of all
rest assured that no wrong-doer is so of deliberation. For no
man will ever deliberately admit supreme evil, and least of
all in his most precious possessions. But every man's most
precious possession, as we said, is his soul; no man, then, we
may be sure, will of set purpose receive the supreme evil into
this most precious thing and live with it there all his life through.
And yet, though a wrong-doer or a man in evil case is always
a pitiable creature, it is with him whose disease is curable that
there is scope for pity; with him one may curb and tame one's
passion, and not scold like a vixen; but against the unqualified
and incorrigible offender, the utterly corrupt, we must give the
rein to wrath. This is why we say it is meet for a good man to
be high-spirited and gentle, as occasion requires.

But of all faults of soul the gravest is one which is inborn in
most men, one which all excuse in themselves and none therefore
attempts to avoid, that conveyed in the maxim that 'every

one is naturally his own friend', and that it is only right and proper that he should be so; whereas, in truth, this same violent attachment to self is the constant source of all manner of misdeeds in every one of us. The eye of love is blind where the beloved is concerned, and so a man proves a bad judge of right, 732 good, honour, in the conceit that more regard is due to his personality than to the real fact, whereas a man who means to be great must care neither for self nor for its belongings, but for justice, whether exhibited in his own conduct, or rather in that of another. From this same fault springs also that universal conviction that one's own folly is wisdom, with its consequences that we fancy we know everything when we know as good as nothing, refuse to allow others to manage business we do not understand, and fall into inevitable errors in transacting it for ourselves. Every man, then, must shun extreme self-love and follow ever in the steps of his better, undeterred by any shame for his case.

There are also minor and often formulated, but no less salutary, rules which must be kept in mind by repetition. For where waters, as we may say, are wasted by emission there must always be a balancing immission, and recall is the immission which makes waste of wisdom good. This is why there must be restraint of unseasonable laughter and tears and each of us must urge his fellow to consult decorum by utter concealment of all excess of joy or grief, whether the breeze of fortune is set fair, or, by a shift of circumstance, the fortunes of an enterprise are confronted by a mountain of difficulty. It should be our constant hope that God, by the blessings He bestows, will lighten the troubles that come upon us, and change our present state for the better, while, with Heaven's favour, the very reverse will always be true of our blessings. These are the hopes, and these and the like the meditations, in which each of us should live, sparing no pains, alike in work and in play, to bring them to his neighbour's confident recollection and to his own.

We have now dealt pretty completely with what divinity has to say of the institutions which ought to be established, and the personal character to which all should aspire; on purely human considerations we have not touched, and yet we must; it is to men, not to gods, we are speaking. Nothing is so native to men as pleasure, pain, and desire; they are, so to say, the very wires or strings from which any mortal nature is inevitably and absolutely dependent. We have therefore to commend the

noble life, not only as superior in comeliness of repute, but 733
further as superior, if a man will but taste it and not decline it
in the days of his youth, in that on which we are all set, life-long
predominance of pleasures over pains.   That this will certainly
be so, if only the tasting is done in the right way, will easily
be made abundantly apparent.   But what is the right way?
This is what we must now learn from our argument to see:
the following are the lines along which we must discover, by
comparison of the relative pleasantness and painfulness of
lives, whether one is naturally conformable to our constitution
and another unconformable.   We wish for pleasure; pain we
neither choose nor wish for; a neutral state, though not desired
as an alternative to pleasure, is desired as a relief from pain.
Less of pain with more of pleasure is desired; less of pleasure
with more of pain is not desired; as for an equal balance of both,
we can give no certain reason for desiring it.   And all these
objects affect our several choices or leave them unaffected, in
virtue of their frequency, their magnitude, their intensity, their
equality, and the conditions which are the opposites of these
in their influence on desire.   All this, then, being inevitably
ordered so, a life which contains numerous, extensive, and
intense feelings of both kinds is desired, if there is an excess
of pleasures, not desired if the excess is on the other side; again,
a life where both kinds of feeling are few, inconsiderable, and
of low intensity is not desired if the pains predominate, but is
desired in the opposite case.   As for a life in which the balance
is even, we must stand to our earlier pronouncement; we desire
it so far as it contains a predominance of what attracts us, and
yet do not desire it so far as it is predominant in what repels.
So we must regard our lives as confined within these limits
and must consider what kind of life it is natural to desire.   But
if we ever speak of ourselves as desiring an object other than
those aforesaid, the statement is due to ignorance and defective
experience of actual lives.

What lives, then, are there, and how many, from which, on
a review of the desirable and undesirable, a selection must be
made and erected into a self-imposed law, if the choice of the
course which is pleasant and attractive as well as virtuous and
noble may lead to an existence of supreme human felicity?
We shall, of course, name the life of temperance as one, and
may count that of wisdom as another, that of courage as another,
and that of health as another, thus making four in all, against
which we may set four other types, the lives of folly, cowardice,

profligacy, disease. Now the verdict of one acquainted with the facts will be that the life of temperance is uniformly gentle; 734 the pains and pleasures it offers are alike unexciting, its desires and passions never furious, but mild; whereas that of profligacy is uniformly rash; the pains and pleasures it offers are alike violent, its intense desires and frantic passions maddening in the extreme. But in the temperate life the pains are surpassed by the pleasures, in the profligate the pleasures are surpassed by the pains, in respect of magnitude, number, and condensation. Hence it follows naturally and inevitably that the former is the more pleasurable life, the latter the more painful, and a man who desires a pleasant life is no longer free to choose a career of profligacy. Nay, it is at once patent, if our present reasoning is sound, that the profligate must always be what he is against his own will; the reason why the great mass of men live without temperance is always either ignorance, or lack of self-control, or both at once. We must say the same thing of the lives of disease and of health; there are pleasures and pains in both, but pleasure predominates over pain in health, in disease pain over pleasure. Now the object of our choice between lives is not to secure preponderance of pain; the life we have pronounced the pleasanter is one in which the preponderance is on the other side. The temperate life, then, we shall maintain exhibits both sorts of feeling in lesser number, smaller magnitude, and looser concentration than the profligate, the wise than the foolish, and the life of courage than that of cowardice; but since in each case the first-named has the superiority in pleasure over its rival, which has a superiority in pain, the life of courage is triumphant over that of cowardice, that of wisdom over that of folly, with the consequence that, lives for lives, the temperate, courageous, wise, and wholesome are pleasanter than the cowardly, foolish, licentious, and diseased, and, in sum, the life of bodily or mental excellence pleasanter than that of depravity, to say nothing of its further superiority on the score of comeliness, rightness, virtue, and fair fame; whence it results that such a life renders its possessor's existence absolutely and unreservedly happier than that of his rival.

Here our discourse by way of prelude to our legislation may come to its end; after the prelude, of course, must come the composition itself,[1] or, as it would be truer to say, an outline of a civic code. Now just as in the case of a web or other piece of woven work, woof and warp cannot be fashioned of the same

[1] A play on the two senses of νομος, 'musical composition' and 'law'.

threads, but the material of the warp must be of superior quality—it must be tough, you know, and have a certain tenacity of character, whereas the woof may be softer and display a proper pliancy; well, the illustration shows that there must be some similar distinction made between citizens who are to fill magistracies, and those who have been but lightly tested by education, this distinction being drawn appropriately to the various cases. For you must know that there are two things which go to the making of a constitution; the conferring of office on individuals is one, the other is the providing of the officials with a code of laws. 735

But before we come to any of these subjects, the following observations should be made. A man who takes in hand a herd of animals, a shepherd, neatherd, horse-breeder, or the like, will never dream of trying to tend that herd without first submitting the group to the purgation proper to it; he will separate the sound animals from the sickly, the thoroughbreds from the mongrels, removing the latter to other herds, and exercising his tendance on the former, since he is well aware that, unless he thus purges his stock, he will have endless and fruitless trouble with bodies and minds already degenerate by nature or ill management, which will further communicate a taint to the sound and unimpaired in body and disposition in the various herds. With the lower animals this does not so much matter— they only call for mention by way of an illustration—but in the case of man it is of the first concern to the legislator to discover and explain the method of procedure appropriate to various cases, in this matter of purgation as well as in all his other dealings with them. For instance, in the business of social purgation, the case stands thus: there are many ways of effecting a purgation, some of them milder, some sharper; some—the sharpest and best of all—will be at the disposal of one who is at once autocrat and legislator, but a legislator who establishes a new society and new laws with less than autocratic power will be well satisfied if he can so much as reach his end of purgation by the mildest of methods. The best method of all, like the most potent medicines, is painful; it is that which effects correction by the combination of justice with vengeance, and carries its vengeance, in the last instance, to the point of death or exile, usually with the result of clearing society of its most dangerous members, great and incurable offenders. The milder method of purgation we may describe much as follows: persons who, from want of the means of subsistence, show themselves

ready to follow their leaders in an attack of the Have-nots on the
736 Haves are treated by the legislator as a deep-seated disease in
the body of the State, and, with all possible good feeling, sent
abroad as a 'measure of relief', to use the euphemistic phrase;
the name given to the procedure is 'colonization'.[1] Now every
legislator has to act more or less in this way at the outset, but
our own situation, at the present juncture, is still less irksome;
we need contrive neither a colonization, nor any other method
of selecting our purgation. We have, so to say, a conflux into
the reservoir of waters from many sources, some springs, some
mountain becks, and need only take careful pains to secure
maximum purity in the accumulating water by drawing off the
supply from one quarter and diverting it into a different course
in another. True, there is naturally some trouble and risk
about any political undertaking; still, as we are concerned at
the moment with theory, not with practical execution, we may
take our recruitment of citizens to have been completed, and
its purity ensured to our wish; we shall, in fact, submit the
bad among those who propose to come into our proposed State
as members to the test of manifold exhortation and adequate
time, and prevent their arrival; the good we shall welcome with
all benevolence and complaisance.

Do not forget that we enjoy the same good fortune on which
we congratulated the foundation of the Heraclids, escape from
cruel and dangerous controversy about confiscating of estates,
cancellation of debts, and redistribution of property. In an
old-established society, when legislation of this kind has become
inevitable, innovation and refusal to innovate prove, in a way,
alike impossible; room is left for little more than pious wishes
and insensible and cautious modification by slow and gradual
advances in the following direction. Among the innovators
there should always be a section with extensive property in
land and numerous debtors, who are not indisposed to share
their advantages in a liberal spirit with the distressed by a
remission of debts and redistribution of estates, thus evincing
a certain regard for moderation, and showing their conviction
that poverty consists not so much in the diminution of one's
property as in the intensification of one's cupidity. This conviction is the surest of all sources of social security, a firm
foundation for the subsequent erection of any political super-

---

[1] The 'euphemism' does not lie in calling the 'relief measure' a 'colonization', but in using the word 'relief' itself about a proceeding which we
might call a 'good riddance of bad rubbish'.

structure in keeping with such conditions; where these initial
conditions are unsound,[1] a statesman's subsequent action will 737
always be beset with difficulties. The danger, as I say, is one
from which we are exempt; still, it is the better course to explain
how we might have escaped it even without this exemption.
Let us say, then, once for all, that escape must be sought in the
combination of justice with freedom from avarice; there is no
road to deliverance, broad or narrow, on other lines, and we
must take the principle as a buttress of our society. In fact,
properties must be fixed by some system which excludes recriminations among their owners; otherwise, any man of any
intelligence will refuse to go further, if he can help it, with a
social system for a population among whom there are long-
standing mutual jealousies. In persons who have, like ourselves
at this moment, the providential opportunity to found a new
society where there are as yet no internal hostilities, to introduce
such hostilities by the distribution of land and houses would be
a combination of sheer depravity with superhuman folly.

What, then, would be the right method of distribution?
First we must fix the total number of the citizens at the
suitable figure; next we must come to an agreement about their
distribution, the number and size of the sections into which they
should be subdivided; the land and houses should be partitioned
among these sections as equally as may be. What would be a
satisfactory total for the population is more than can be rightly
said without consideration of the territory and the neighbouring
communities. The territory should be large enough for the
adequate maintenance of a certain number of [2] men of modest
ambitions, and no larger; the population should be sufficient
to defend themselves against wrongs from societies on their
borders, and to assist their neighbours when wronged to some purpose. These points we will settle, practically and theoretically,
by an inspection of the territory and its neighbours, but for the
present our argument may proceed to the completion of our
code of laws, in outline and as a general sketch.

Let us assume—to take a convenient number—that we have
five thousand and forty landholders, who can be armed to
fight for their holdings, and that the territory and houses are
likewise divided among the same number, so that there will be

[1] In 736 e 7, I follow England, and depart from Burnet's text, in regarding τῆς μεταβάσεως as a mistaken gloss intended to explain the preceding
ταύτης.

[2] At 737 d 1 I would read ποσούς with Ficinus, Stephanus, and England,
or the πόσους of the MSS. retained by Burnet.

one man to one holding. Let this total be divided first by two, and then by three; in fact it will permit of division by four, five, and the successive integers up to ten. Of course any one who is acting as a legislator must be at least familiar enough 738 with figures to understand what number, or kind of number, will prove most useful in a given State. Accordingly we will select that which has the greatest number of immediately successive divisions. The whole integer-series, of course, admits division by any number and with any quotient, while our 5,040 can be divided, for purposes of war, or to suit the engagements and combinations of peace, in the matter of taxes to be levied and public distributions to be made, into fifty-nine quotients and no more, ten of them, from unity onwards, being successive.

These facts of number, then, must be thoroughly mastered at leisure by those whose business the law will make it to understand them—they will find them exactly as I have stated them —and they must be mentioned by the founder of a city, for the reason I shall now give. Whether a new foundation is to be created from the outset or an old one restored, in the matter of gods and their sanctuaries—what temples must be founded in a given community, and to what gods or spirits they should be dedicated—no man of sense will presume to disturb convictions inspired from Delphi, Dodona, the oracle of Ammon, or by old traditions of any kind of divine appearances or reported divine revelations, when those convictions have led to the establishment of sacrifice and ritual (whether original and indigenous, or borrowed from Etruria, Cyprus, or elsewhere), the consequent consecration by the tradition of oracles, statues, altars, and shrines, and the provision for each of these of its sacred precinct. A legislator should avoid the slightest interference with all such matters; he should assign every district its patron god, or spirit, or hero,[1] as the case may be, and his first step in the subdivision of a territory should be to assign to each of them his special precinct with all appertaining dues. His purpose in this will be that the convocations of the various sections at stated periods may provide opportunities for the satisfaction of their various needs, and that the festivities may give occasion for mutual friendliness, familiarity, and acquaintance. There is indeed no such boon for a society as this familiar knowledge of citizen by citizen. For where men have no light on each other's characters, but are in the dark on the sub-

---

[1] The 'hero' is a 'deceased human or semi-human ancestor who receives worship'.

ject, no one will ever reach the rank or office he deserves, or get the justice which is his proper due.   Hence in every society it should always be the endeavour of every citizen, before anything else, to prove himself to all his neighbours no counterfeit, but a man of sterling sincerity, and not to be imposed on by any counterfeiting in others.

Our next move in this business of legislation must be—like 739 the moving of a man on the board from the 'sacred line'—so singular that it may well surprise you on a first hearing.[1] Yet reflection and practical experience will make it clear that a society is likely to enjoy but a second-best constitution.   Some of us may be dissatisfied with such a society from their unfamiliarity with the situation of a legislator who does not possess autocratic power, but the procedure of strict exactitude is to discriminate a best constitution, a second-best, and a third-best, and then to leave the choice between them to the party responsible for the foundation.   Accordingly I propose that we should adopt this method in our present proceedings.   We will describe the best, second-best, and third-best constitutions, and leave the choice between them to Clinias in the present case, or to any one else who may at any time come to the task of selection with a desire to incorporate what he values in his own native institutions to suit his own taste.

The first-best society, then, that with the best constitution and code of law, is one where the old saying is most universally true of the whole society.   I mean the saying that 'friends' property is indeed common property'.   If there is now on earth, or ever should be, such a society—a community in women-folk,

---

[1] In the game of πεσσοί the line down the middle of the board was called the 'sacred line', and a piece was only moved from it in case of absolute necessity, when no other move was open.   The general meaning is that persons who do not reflect on the limitations imposed on a legislator by circumstance will be surprised that Plato does not simply propose to enact every arrangement which he regards as ideal, and does establish many which he owns to be far from ideal.   A man who really understands the position of a legislator will see that these are cases of a 'forced move'. The distinction between the 'second-' and 'third-best' societies seems to be this: In any actual society the 'inevitable imperfections of human nature' will make it necessary to be content with something short of the ideal.   A society in which there are no further drawbacks to be reckoned with is 'second-best'.   But there will often be circumstances, not to be avoided by the practical legislator, which will call for still further compromise.   One such circumstance is indicated in the text.   In the Cnossian colony, where so large a proportion of the settlers are Cretans, and the legislative commission Cretan also, one must allow for a certain 'patriotic' attachment to Cretan institutions as well as for the more general imperfections of humanity.   This is what is meant by the references to a 'third-best'.

in children, in all possessions whatsoever, if all means have been taken to eliminate everything we mean by the word *ownership* from life; if all possible means have been taken to make even what nature has made our *own* in some sense common property, I mean, if our eyes, ears, and hands seem to see, hear, act, in the common service; if, moreover, we all approve and condemn in perfect unison and derive pleasure and pain from the same sources—in a word, when the institutions of a society make it most utterly one, that is a criterion of their excellence than which no truer or better will ever be found.   If there is anywhere such a city, with a number of gods, or sons of gods, for its inhabitants, they dwell there thus in all joyousness of life.   Whence for the pattern of a constitution we should look to no other quarter, but cleave to this and strive to come as near it as may be in our State.   That we have now in hand, were it once brought to the birth, would be in its fashion the nearest approach to immobility and . . .; [1] of the third, under Heaven's favour, we will treat hereafter, for the present, what, in any case, is this system we speak of, and how may it come to be what it is?

First, then, let them make a division of lands and houses
740 among themselves, and not till the soil in common, for that were a project beyond their birth, breeding, and education. But let the division be made with some such thought as this, that he to whom a lot falls is yet bound to count his portion the common property of the whole society, and, since the territory is his fatherland, to tend it with care passing that of son for mother, the more that the land is the divine mistress of her mortal children; and to think likewise of all the gods and spirits of the locality.   That this temper may persist for all time to come, we must practise this further contrivance: the number of hearth-fires established by our present division must remain for ever unchanged, without increase or deviation whatsoever. Now the way to ensure this in any city will be as follows: Let him who has a lot assigned him ever leave after him one son, of his own preference, to be his heir in that household and

---

[1] I have left the last words of 739 *e* 4, καὶ ἡ μία δευτέρως, untranslated. They have been supposed to mean 'and truly one in a secondary degree' (i.e. only less of a perfect unity than the ideal already described). But it seems more doubtful whether such a sense, can be got out of the words.   The proposal καὶ τιμία δευτέρως (Apelt, Bury) is palaeographically excellent, and gives the right general sense 'and is honourable in the second degree'.   But I do not feel sure that ἡ μία is not a simple error for ἡμῖν, and that a word like μακαριστή has not been accidentally omitted after δευτέρως ('and deserves our felicitation in the second degree').

successor in the worship of the gods of clan and city, living or already previously deceased; as for other children, when a man has more than the one, let him give the females in marriage as a law yet to be enjoined shall direct; the males let him distribute among citizens who have a lack of offspring, to be their sons, and that preferably by friendly agreement. If a man have no friendly connections, or if there be families too numerous in issue, female or male, as in the contrary case, when there is a paucity of issue due to childlessness, in all these cases the highest and most august of the magistracies we shall create must consider what should be done to meet the excess or defect, and contrive the best device they may to keep the number of households always at our five thousand and forty and no more. Now there are several such devices; there are shifts for checking propagation when its course is too facile, and, on the other side, there are ways of fostering and encouraging numerous births which affect the young by marks of honour and dishonour and admonition conveyed in warning speeches of their seniors, and these will do our business. Besides, in the final extremity, if all means fail us to keep the number of five thousand and forty households constant, if mated love should cause an excessive glut of population, and we find ourselves at a loss, we have ready to our hand the old contrivance we have more than once spoken of—we can send out colonies of such persons as we deem convenient with love and friendship on both parts. Or in the contrary event, if our citizens are visited by a flood-tide, as we may call it, of disease, or by destruction in battle, and so **741** reduced far below the appointed number by untimely deaths, why, then, though we should never, if we can help it, foist in citizens whose education has been base, with necessity, as the proverb says, not even a god can cope.

Let us fancy, then, that we hear our present argument exhorting us in tones like these: Worthiest of men, see to it that you grow not slack in rendering the honour nature bids render to congruity and equality, identity and conformity, alike of number and of all that can produce fair and good effects. In especial you are herewith charged first, to keep fixed thoughout life the numbers prescribed you, and next to do no despite by mutual purchase and sale to the bulk and measure of substance assigned you at the first as your fitting portion; therein you will have against you the lot by which the division was made—and it is a god—and the lawgiver to boot. For first of all, our present law, with its warning that a man must take the lot, if so he pleases, on those terms or let it alone, contains this furthe1 enactment, that whereas the soil is consecrate to all hallows, and whereas moreover priests of either sex shall offer prayers with sacrifice to that intent, once and twice and thrice, he who shall vend house or land assigned him, or purchase the same, shall suffer the fitting penalties for his act, written records inscribed on tables of cypress-wood being laid up in the temples as a memorial to times to come. Moreover, surveillance over the execution of this statute shall be made the charge of the magistracy which shall be deemed most keen-sighted, that contraventions of it, when they occur, may not go unremarked, but the offence at once against the law and against God receive its chastisement. What a wealth of blessing the regulation now enjoined brings to any society which complies with it, if it be but conjoined with an organization to match, no evil man will ever know, but only, to speak with the old proverb, one who has made trial of it and is formed to ways of virtue. For such an organization leaves no great room for the making of fortunes; 'tis a consequence of it that none has either need or licence to make them in any sordid calling—as even the sound of the reproach 'base mechanical' repels the man of free soul—and none will ever stoop to amass wealth by such devices.

742   With these injunctions goes also a further law by which no possession of gold or silver is permitted to any private man, but only a currency for the purpose of daily exchange, such as is hardly to be avoided by craftsmen or any whose business it is to pay wages in such a kind to wage-earners, whether slaves or alien settlers; whence we shall lay it down that they must have an (internal) currency of value at home but worthless abroad. As for a common Hellenic currency, to meet the needs of campaigns and foreign expeditions, such as embassies or other necessary missions of State on which a man may be dispatched, to serve these various purposes the State must possess current Hellenic money. If a private man should ever be forced to travel in foreign parts, let him get leave of the magistrates before he departs, and if on his return he have coin from any foreign quarter left, let him deposit it with the State, receiving the equivalent in local currency; if he be found to be secreting it, let it be confiscated to the Treasury, and let any who is privy to the act and conceals it be liable equally with the importer to curse and reproach, and in addition to a fine of amount not less than the amount of foreign currency imported. Let there be no dowry whatsoever, given or received, in marrying or giving in

marriage, no depositing of money with one who is not trusted, and no lending on usury, the law permitting the borrower to withhold both interest and capital. That these practices are best for a society will be rightly discerned by the inquirer who considers them in the following light, with constant reference to their principle and intention. The intention of a sane statesman, mark you, is not what the many suppose; the good legislator, they would say, must intend the city for which he legislates in his wisdom to be as great as may be, and as wealthy, to possess mines of gold and silver, and to have a multitude of subjects by land and sea. They would further add that if he is a legislator of the right kind he must intend his city to be as good and as happy as possible. Now some of these objects are possibilities, others not so; hence the State-builder will intend the possible; the impossible he will neither make the object of a futile intention nor attempt it. In fact, speaking generally, happiness necessarily waits on goodness, so that combination he would intend. But to be at once exceedingly wealthy and good is impossible, if we mean by the wealthy those who are accounted so by the vulgar, that is, the exceptional few who own property of great pecuniary value—the very thing a bad man would be likely to own. Now since this is so, I can never 743 concede to them that a rich man is truly happy unless he is also a good man; but that one who is exceptionally good should be exceptionally wealthy too is a mere impossibility. 'But why so?' someone may ask. Why, I answer, because the profits of righteousness and iniquity together are more than double those from righteousness alone, while the expenditure of one who will spend neither honourably nor discreditably is less by half than that of one who is ready to lay out money honourably on honourable objects. Hence he who acts in the contrary fashion can never become wealthier than the man whose gains are double his own, and his expenditure but half his. Now of the two men, the one is good; the other, when he is frugal, not bad—though on occasion he can be utterly bad too—but good, as I have just said, he never is. In fact, the man who will get by honest and dishonest means alike, and will spend neither righteously nor unrighteously, if he is only frugal to boot, grows wealthy, though the utterly bad man, being as a general rule a prodigal, is very poor, whereas a man who will spend on honourable objects and only make gains from honest sources, will not find it easy to become either remarkably wealthy or exceedingly poor. Thus our thesis that the immensely rich are not good men is sound, and if they are not good, neither are they happy.

The object our laws had in view was that our people should be supremely happy and devotedly attached to one another, but citizens will never be thus attached where there are many suits at law between them, and numerous wrongs committed, but where both are rarest and of least consequence. Our society, we pronounce, must have neither gold nor silver, nor yet much making of profits from mechanic crafts, or usury, or raising of sordid beasts,[1] but only such as husbandry yields or permits, and of it only so much as will not force a man in his profit-gathering to forget the ends for which possessions exist, that is to say, soul and body, which will never be of any account without bodily training and education at large. Wherefore we have said, and said more than once, that concern for possessions should take the lowest place in our esteem; for whereas the objects of universal interest to man are in all three, interest in possessions, rightly pursued, holds the third and lowest rank, the interest of the body is second, of the soul first. And so also with the polity now under consideration, if it prescribes its honours on these principles, its laws have been rightly made; but should any law there to be imposed be found to put health
744 before sobriety in point of public esteem, or wealth before health and sober-mindedness, it will stand detected as wrongly imposed. Hence a legislator should time and time again ask himself the plain questions, 'What is my intent?' 'Do I hit the mark in this, or do I miss it?' Thus perhaps, but in no other way whatsoever, will he finish his work of legislation and relieve others of the task.

Let him who has obtained a lot, then, as we say, hold it on the conditions here stated. It had indeed been well that all settlers should further enter our colony with equal means of every kind. But since this cannot be, but one arrival will bring more property and another less, there must be classes of unequal census, and that on many grounds, and in particular because of the equal opportunities our society affords,[2] that so

[1] What Plato means by this expression we can only guess. C. Ritter's guess (followed by Bury in his translation) that the objection is to the raising of fatted animals of all kinds for the table, and perhaps especially to the practice of castration for this object, is plausible, but of course conjectural.

[2] The meaning is obscure, but seems to be rightly explained by C. Ritter. The conditions of life in Plato's city make it fairly certain that superior wealth will be the fruit of a man's own industry and thrift. The poorer citizens have an 'equal chance', if they like to use it, to improve their condition.

in election to office and assessment of payments to and receipts from the exchequer regard may be had to a man's due qualifications, not only of personal and ancestral virtue, or of bodily strength and comeliness, but of enjoyment of means or lack of them, honours and offices apportioned fairly by a rule of proportional, though unequal, distribution, and dissensions avoided. On these grounds we must arrange our citizens in four classes according to the amount of their property, a first, a second, a third, and a fourth—or they may be called by some other names —whether the members remain in the same class, or shift, as they pass from poverty to wealth, or wealth to poverty, each to the class appropriate to him.

As a further consequence of what has preceded I would enact another law of the following type. In a society which is to be immune from the most fatal of disorders which might more properly be called distraction than faction, there must be no place for penury in any section of the population, nor yet for opulence, as both breed either consequence. Accordingly the legislator must now specify the limit in either direction. So let the limit on the side of penury be the value of an allotment; this must remain constant, and no magistrate, and no other person who is ambitious of a repute for goodness must connive, in any case, at its diminution. The legislator will take it as a measure, and permit the acquisition of twice, thrice, and as much as four times its value.[1] If a man acquires further possessions, from treasure-trove, donation, or business, or by 745 any other similar chance makes acquisitions in excess of this measure, he may retain his good name and escape all proceedings by consigning the surplus to the State and its gods. If there is any disobedience to this law, it shall be open to any one who pleases[2] to lay an information and claim half the property, the convicted offender also paying a fine to the same amount out of his own possessions; the other half shall go to the gods. The whole property of every citizen, other than his allotment, must previously be inscribed in a public record under the custody of magistrates appointed by law for the purpose with a view to

[1] Aristotle (*Politics*, 1265 *b* 23) understood this to mean that the whole property of the citizens of the richest class, including the patrimonial 'allotment', may amount at most to five times the value of the 'allotment'; the maximum property of a citizen of the poorest class to twice that value.
[2] The explanation of the frequent permission given in the *Laws* to lay information against offenders is that no Greek legal system knew anything of the office of 'public prosecutor'. The initiative in bringing a criminal to justice was left to the individual citizen. Under such a system the laying of information became part of the duty of a public-spirited man.

making suits at law affecting any question of property capable
of easy and most assured determination.

Next, the founder must see that his city is placed as nearly
as possible at the centre of the territory, after selecting a site
possessed of the other favourable conditions for his purpose;
(it will not be difficult to discover or to state them). Then he
must divide his city into twelve parts; but first he should establish and enclose a sanctuary of Hestia, Zeus, and Athena—which
he will call the citadel—from which he will draw his twelve
divisions of the city and its whole territory. Equality of the
twelve regions should be secured by making those of good soil
small and those of worse soil larger. He should then make a
division into five thousand and forty allotments. Each of these,
again, sho ld be bisected and two half-sections, a nearer and a
remoter [1] paired together to form an allotment, one which is
contiguous to the city with one on the border, one in the next
degree of proximity to the city with one next most nearly on the
border, and so on in all cases. We should further practise in
these half-sections the already mentioned contrivance relative
to the poverty or excellence of the soil,[2] and effect an equaliza-
tion by the greater or less size of the divisions. Of course, the
legislator must also divide [3] the population into twelve sections,
constructing these sections so as to be as nearly as possible on
an equality in respect of their other property, of the whole of
which he will have made a careful record. Next he will be at
pains to assign the twelve divisions to twelve gods, naming each
section after the god to whom it has been allotted and consecrated, and calling it a 'tribe'. Further, the twelve segments
of the city must be made on the same lines as the division of the
territory in general, and each citizen must have two houses,
one nearer the centre of the state and the other nearer the border.
And this shall complete the business of settlement.

But here is a consideration on which we must be careful to
reflect. All the arrangements we have just proposed are never

[1] The precise text and rendering are a little uncertain, though the
meaning is clear. I take the words of 745 c 6, τοῦ τε ἐγγὺς καὶ τοῦ πόρρω
μετέχοντα ἑκάτερον, 'either [half-section] partaking of the nearer and
remoter', to mean simply being at a lesser or greater distance from the
central town of the territory. In c 7 I omit the words εἰς κλῆρος (after
Peipers) as probably a marginal annotation, since they will not construe.

[2] φαυλότητός τε καὶ ἀρετῆς χώρας, 745 d 3, seems to me absolutely to
require the insertion of a <πέρι> to give a construction, and I think
with Bury that the most likely place for the insertion is after the τε.

[3] Unless, as is possible, Plato has made a slip here in dictation, the
νείμασθαι of 745 d 5 should probably be emended, with England, to νεῖμαι.

likely to find just such conditions that the whole programme will be completely executed. The conditions suppose a popula- 746 tion with no disrelish for such social regulations, who will tolerate life-long fixed limitation of property, restrictions such as those we have proposed on procreation, and deprivation of gold and other things which it is certain, from what has been said already, that the legislator will prohibit; they presuppose further the central position of the capital, and the distribution of the dwelling-houses over the territory, as he has prescribed, almost as though he were telling his dreams or fashioning a city and its inhabitants out of waxwork. To be sure, the scheme does not sound amiss,[1] but its author needs to give it his reconsideration to the following effect. So our legislator gives us once more the ensuing admonition: 'Do not imagine, my friends, that I am less alive than yourselves to a certain truth in what you urge in your present discourse. But the fact is that I take it to be always the most equitable course in dealing with a plan for the future that he who exhibits the model on which an undertaking should be fashioned should abate nothing of perfect excellence and absolute truth, while one who finds it impossible to compass some point of this perfection should decline to put it into practice, and contrive the realization of the remaining possibility which approximates most nearly to what ought to be done and is most akin to it in character. But he should allow the legislator to perfect the delineation of his heart's desire; only when that has been done, should he begin to discuss with him which of his legislative proposals are expedient and which involve difficulties. For self-consistency, you know, must be aimed at in everything, even by the artificer of the paltriest object, if he is to be of any account.'

Our immediate concern, now that we have resolved on the division into twelve parts, must be precisely to see in what conspicuous fashion these twelve parts, admitting, as they do, such a multitude of further [2] divisions, with the subsequent groups which arise from them,[3] down to the five thousand and forty individuals—this will give us our brotherhoods, wards, and parishes, as well as our divisions of battle and

---

[1] ἔχει δὴ τὰ τοιαῦτα οὐ κακῶς τινα τρόπον εἰρημένα, 746 a 8. Others suppose that what 'does not sound amiss' is the criticism of the scheme just suggested.
[2] I adopt Stallbaum's suggestion αὖ for αὐτοῦ at 746 d 5.
[3] In 746 d 6 I suspect that a <τὰ> has fallen out between καὶ and ἐκ. This would give the sense 'with the subsequent groupings and those to which they give rise'.

columns of route, not to mention our currency and measures of capacity, dry and liquid and of weight—to see, I say, how all these details must be legally determined so as to fit in and harmonize with each other. There is a further fear we must dismiss, apprehension of a possible reputation for finicking pedantry if the law enacts that no utensil whatever in the possession of a citizen shall be of other than the standard size.

747 The legislator must take it as a general principle that there is a universal usefulness in the subdivisions and complications of numbers, whether these complications are exhibited in pure numbers, in lengths and depths, or again in musical notes and motions, whether of rectilinear ascent and descent or of revolution. All must be kept in view by the legislator in his injunction to all citizens, never, so far as they can help it, to rest short of this numerical standardization. For alike in domestic and public life and in all the arts and crafts there is no other single branch of education which has the same potent efficacy as the theory of numbers; but its greatest recommendation is that it rouses the naturally drowsy and dull, and makes him quick, retentive, and shrewd—a miraculous improvement of cultivation upon his native parts. So all these branches of study will be found fair and becoming, if only by further laws and institutions you expel illiberality and commercialism from the souls of those who are to pursue them thoroughly to their profit; otherwise you will be surprised to find that you have produced not a philosopher but a regular knave—an effect already produced, as we can see, in the case of Egyptians, Phoenicians, and many other races, by the illiberality of their other pursuits and of their opulence, whether the result may have been due to the defects of their legislator, to incidental misfortune, or possibly to some other natural circumstance of such a tendency. In fact, Megillus and Clinias, there is a further consideration we must not ignore; some localities have a more marked tendency than others to produce better or worse men, and we are not to legislate in the face of the facts. Some, I conceive, owe their propitious or ill-omened character to variations in winds and sunshine, others to their waters, and yet others to the products of the soil, which not only provide the body with better or worse sustenance, but equally affect the mind for good or bad. Most markedly conspicuous of all, again, will be localities which are the homes of some supernatural influence, or the haunts of spirits who give a gracious or ungracious reception to successive bodies of settlers. A sagacious legislator will give these facts

all consideration a man can, and do his best to adapt his legislation to them.   So you, too, Clinias, must of course do the same: as the intending colonizer of a district you must give your first attention to such points.

Clin. Admirably said, sir.   I must certainly do as you recommend.

BOOK VI

751   *Ath.* Well, now, your next business, after all that has now been dealt with, will presumably be to constitute the magistracies in your society.

Clin. Why, of course it will.

Ath. There are really two branches of social organization implied here: first there is the creation of offices and the appointment of the persons who are to fill them, the determination of the proper number of such posts and the proper manner of appointing to them; then, when this has been done, comes the assignment of the laws to the several offices, the decision which laws, how many, and of what type it is proper for each magistracy to administer. But before we make our election, we may pause a little while to lay down a principle of some relevance to the occasion.

Clin. And what may this principle be?

Ath. Why, it is this. Any one may surely see that, while legislation is a great achievement, if a well-equipped State gives its excellent laws into the charge of unqualified officials, not merely does no good come of all their excellence, and not only does the State become a general laughing-stock, but such societies are pretty sure to find their laws a source of the gravest detriment and mischief.

Clin. Yes, surely.

Ath. Why then, my friend, we must note the presence of this danger in the case of the society you are now contemplating, and its constitution. You see, no doubt, how necessary it is first that men who are to be rightly advanced to posts of power should, in every case, have been thoroughly put to the proof, themselves and their families, from earliest boyhood to the time of their election, and next that those who are to elect them should have been well trained by a schooling in law-abiding habits for the work of selecting with right approval, and rejecting with proper disapprobation, candidates who deserve either fate. But in this case how can men who have but recently come together and are unfamiliar with one another, and devoid of education into the bargain, be expected to choose their magistrates in an irreproachable fashion?

132

Clin. Indeed, 'tis hardly possible.

Ath. Still, when you are once in the ring, as they say, the time for excuses is past, and that is the case just now with you, and with me too. You with your nine colleagues, as I understand, have pledged yourselves to the Cretan people to throw your souls into the work of the foundation, and I, on my side, am pledged to help you with our present fanciful tale. And, to be sure, since I am telling a tale, I should not like to leave it without its head; it would look monstrous ugly if it roamed at large in that condition. 752

Clin. Very true, sir.

Ath. Yes, and besides, I mean to do my best for you.

Clin. Then, with all my heart, let us do as we say.

Ath. So we will, with God's permission, if we can get the better of our years so far.

Clin. We may fairly count on God's permission.

Ath. To be sure we may. So with His help, let us make a further point.

Clin. What point is that?

Ath. What a spirited adventure our present experiment in founding a State will prove.

Clin. Of what are you thinking in that remark, and why in particular do you make it?

Ath. Of the light-hearted temerity with which we are legislating for the inexperienced in the hope that they will end by accepting our proposed enactments. Yet this much must be reasonably clear, Clinias, even to the not specially discerning, that no body of men will accept them readily from the first, but only if we could contrive to wait until those who have been given a taste of them in their boyhood, grown up under them, and become thoroughly at home with them come to play their part in choosing the whole body of public officials. But, mark you, this point once compassed, supposing there is any plan or device by which it can be truly secured, I believe a society so schooled would have an assured guarantee of survival well beyond that interval.

Clin. That sounds reasonable enough.

Ath. Well then, let us consider whether some such measure as this would be sufficient for our purpose. What I maintain, Clinias, is that it is the duty of you Cnossians, before all other Cretans, not merely to treat the soil you are now settling with all religious care, but to give unflagging attention to the

*G 275

appointment[1] of the original officials by the surest and best method possible. In general, this will be a comparatively light task, but it is indispensably necessary that we should begin by taking the utmost pains with the selection of Curators of the Laws.

Clin. Well, what measure or plan have we in contemplation for this?

Ath. I will tell you. Sons of Crete, I declare it the Cnossians' duty, in view of their leading position among your numerous cities, to join with the new arrivals in your settlement to elect a body of thirty-seven men in all from both sections, nineteen from 753 the new arrivals and the rest from Cnossus itself. This body the Cnossians should present to your city, including yourself as a citizen of the colony and one of the eighteen, either with their free consent or by a modest measure of compulsion.

Clin. But pray, sir, why have you not proposed a share in our citizenship for yourself and Megillus as well?

Ath. Why, Clinias, Athens is a proud State and so is Sparta, and both are far away, but you have every proper qualification, as have also your fellow-founders. What has just been said about you is equally applicable to them. So much, then, for the most satisfactory procedure in our present circumstances; in course of time, if the constitution has survived, let the board be appointed by some such process as this. All shall have a voice in the election of these magistrates who bear arms in the cavalry or infantry and have served in the field as long as their age permitted. The election shall be held in the sanctuary regarded as most venerable by the State. Each voter shall deposit on the altar a tablet inscribed with the name of his nominee, his father, his tribe, and the ward to which he belongs, and subscribe his own name with the same particulars. Any one who pleases shall be permitted to remove any voting-tablet to the contents of which he has an objection and expose it in the market-place within not less than thirty days. The names found to head the poll, to the number of three hundred, shall then be exhibited by the authorities to the view of the whole community, and every citizen shall again vote for any of them he pleases, the officials once more publishing the hundred names which stand first. On the third occasion any one who pleases is to vote for any name he pleases of the hundred, passing between sacrificial victims; the seven-and-thirty who receive most

---

[1] In 752 *d* 7 I would, with England and others, keep the στῶσιν of the MSS. against Hermann's ἱστῶσιν, adopted by Burnet.

votes shall be submitted to a scrutiny[1] and appointed to the magistracy by the officials.

Who, then, Megillus and Clinias, are to institute all these regulations in our State about official posts and the scrutiny for them? We can see, I suppose, that there must be such persons in a society which is just beginning to 'get under way', but who they can be before there are any magistrates is a problem.[2] Have them we must, by hook or crook, and they must be no common fellows either, but men of the highest parts. For, as the adage runs, 'Well begun is half done', and we all commend a fair beginning of anything; though the beginning is, in my own opinion, more than half the work, and a fair beginning has never 754 yet been commended to its full merits.

Clin. Very true.

Ath. Then as we are agreed on the point we must not pass it over in silence without making clear to ourselves how it should be set about. Though, for my own part, I am ready with no more than one observation which is needful and salutary at this juncture.

Clin. And what is that?

Ath. That the city we are about to found has, as I may say, neither father nor mother, other than the society which is founding it. Not that I forget that plenty of such foundations have often enough been, and will herafter be, at variance with their founders. But as things stand at present, it is as it is with a child; even if he is some day to have his differences with his parents, yet while the helplessness of childhood lasts, he is attached to them and they to him; he is always running to his family and finds his only allies among his own relatives. Now I say the same connection is to be found all ready to our purpose between the Cnossians and our new State—thanks to their care for it—and between it and Cnossus. So I maintain, as I have already maintained—a sound thought is not spoiled by repetition—that the Cnossians must join in taking charge of all this business: they should co-opt not less than a hundred of the newly-

---

[1] The object of this scrutiny, like that of the δοκιμασία of magistrates at Athens, is to ensure that every candidate who has survived the final stage shall really have the qualifications required for the office.

[2] I do not see how to translate the uniform reading of the MSS., kept by Burnet, at 753 e 4, πρὸς πασῶν τῶν ἀρχῶν γεγονότες, so as to obtain a suitable sense. As a makeshift, I have translated Cornarius's πρὸ πασῶν τῶν ἀρχῶν γεγονότες, though I find it hard to believe that this is what Plato wrote, since πρὸ is hardly likely to have been corrupted to πρὸς in so straightforward a phrase. But for the fact that πάρος is an exclusively poetical word, I should be tempted to suggest π<ά>ρος <πρό>.

arrived colonists, selecting the most aged and best men they can, and there should be another hundred from Cnossus itself. These latter, as I say, must come to our new city and take their share in providing for the lawful appointment of officials and the scrutiny following on appointment. When this business has been done, the Cnossians should keep themselves to Cnossus, and the new State should be left to preserve itself and prosper by its own endeavours. To proceed: Let those who belong to the thirty-seven, now and for all time to come, be taken to be appointed for the purposes under stated. They are to be curators in the first place of the laws, and in the next of the records in which every citizen has made his return to the officials of the amount of his property, with the exception of four minae for those of the highest assessment, three for the second, two for the third, and one for the lowest. If any one is detected in possession of anything further in excess of the returns, let the whole of such sum be forfeited to the public, and let it further be open to any one who will to pursue him on a charge that is neither creditable nor of comely name, but infamous for him who is convicted of contemning law for gain. Let him who will, that is, lay an indictment for *infamous gain* and

755 prosecute the case before the Curators in person. If the defendant lose the case, he shall have no share in the 'common good', and in any distribution from the public funds, he shall go without his part, except for his allotment; his conviction shall also be recorded, for his life-time, in a place where it may be read by all who will. No curator shall hold office for more than twenty years, or be elected to his office at an age earlier than fifty; if he is sixty at the time of appointment he shall hold office no longer than ten years, and conformably to this rule, when a man's life is prolonged beyond seventy, he must in no case expect to hold office on this important board.

As to the Curators of the Laws, then, let us take it that they are charged with these three duties: each fresh statute, as legislation proceeds, will lay on them such further duties as they should undertake beyond those now specified. For the present we may turn to the appointment of the rest of our officials in order. We must next, of course, choose generals of the forces, and their military assistants, as we may call them, hipparchs and phylarchs, as well as divisional commanders of the tribal infantry, whom we may very conviently designate by that very title, taxiarchs; it is, in fact, the name commonly given them. As to these posts, there shall be a first nomination of generals, taken solely from among our citizens, by the Curators of the Laws, and a selection from the nominees by all who have borne arms at the proper age, or are actually bearing them on the occasion. Should any one, however, judge a person whose name has not been included a better candidate than one of the nominees, he shall name his man, as well as the person in whose place he proposes him, take an oath to that effect, and put him forward as a rival candidate; whichever of the two shall be approved by show of hands shall then be placed on the select list. The three who receive most votes shall be appointed generals and controllers of military affairs, after passing the same scrutiny as the Curators of Laws. The generals so elected shall make their own preliminary nomination of taxiarchs to the number of twelve, one for each tribe; the procedure as to counter-nomination, voting, and final scrutiny shall be for taxiarchs the same as for generals. This assembly shall for the present—as neither council nor prytanes have been appointed—be convoked by the Curators in the holiest and most spacious area available, the full-armed infantry and the cavalry occupying distinct stations, and all who rank after them in the forces forming a third group. Generals and hipparchs shall be chosen by a vote of the whole body, taxiarchs by a vote of all the infantry, and their phylarchs by a vote of all the cavalry. The generals must appoint their 756 own commanders of light-armed troops, archers, or other divisions of the forces. Thus it only remains to arrange for the appointment of hipparchs. Accordingly, the preliminary nomination in their case shall be made by the same authority which nominates in the case of generals, and the selection and counter-nomination shall proceed as in the case of generals. The cavalry shall give its vote in the presence of the infantry, and the two candidates who receive most votes shall be commanders-in-chief of the whole mounted force. There may be two challenges of the vote; if it is challenged a third time, those whose business it was to deal with the several returns shall put the issue to a vote among themselves.[1]

There shall be a Council of thirty dozen—three hundred and sixty will be a convenient number for our subdivisions—and this whole number shall be divided into four groups of ninety, ninety councillors being elected from each property-class.[2]

[1] The meaning is apparently that the *tellers* shall, in this case, vote among themselves, and their decision shall be final (England).

[2] The statement is clearly meant as a preliminary account of the final result of the protracted proceedings to be described. Ultimately, at the close of the election, each of the four classes is to be represented on the Council by ninety members.

First there shall be a vote compulsory upon all citizens for representatives of the highest property class, abstention being visited with a fine prescribed by law. When the voting is over, the names shall be duly recorded, and representatives of the second class voted for on the following day with the same procedure as before. On the third day representatives of the third class shall be chosen by a vote open to all citizens, but compulsory on those of the three first classes, the fourth and lowest class being exempt from fine in the case of abstention from the voting. On the fourth day representatives of this lowest fourth class shall be chosen by a vote of all, but there shall be no penalty for members of the third and fourth classes who may choose to abstain, whereas members of the second and first classes who decline to vote shall be fined, a member of the second class thrice and a member of the first four times the amount of the previous fine. On the fifth day, the authorities shall exhibit the names already recorded to public view, and there shall be a selection from them in which every citizen shall once more vote, or else pay a fine to the original amount. A hundred and eighty names shall thus be selected from each class; half of them shall be taken by lot and submitted to their scrutiny, and these shall form the Council for the year.

Conducted in this way, the election will strike a mean between monarchy and democracy, as a constitutional system always
757 should. There can never be friendship between the slave and his owner, nor between the base and the noble when equal honours are bestowed on both; indeed, equal treatment of the unequal ends in inequality when not qualified by due proportion; it is these two conditions, in fact, which are the fertile sources of civil discord. It is an old saying, and as true as old, that equality gives birth to friendship; that maxim is most sound and admirable. But 'tis none too clear what sort of equality it is has these effects, and the ambiguity makes havoc with us. There are, in fact, two equalities under one name, but, for the most part, with contrary results. The one equality, that of number, weight, and measure, any society and any legislator can readily secure in the award of distinctions, by simply regulating their distribution by the lot; but the true and best equality is hardly so patent to every vision. 'Tis the very award of Zeus; limited as is its scope in human life, wherever it has scope, in public affairs or private, it works nothing but blessings. For it assigns more to the greater and less to the lesser, adapting its gifts to the real character of either. In this matter

of honours, in particular, it deals proportionately with either party, ever awarding a greater share to those of greater worth, and to their opposites in trained goodness such share as is fit. For we shall in truth find that this sheer justice is always also the statesmanlike policy. It is this, Clinias, at which we must aim, this equality on which we must fix our gaze, in the establishment of our nascent city. And if others would found other such societies, they should shape their legislation with a view to the same end—not to the interest of a handful of dictators or a single dictator, or the predominance of a populace, but always to justice, the justice we explained to be a true and real equality, meted out to various unequals. And yet, after all, a society as a whole will also have to apply these standards with some qualification, if it is to escape dissensions somewhere among its constituent parts; equity and indulgence, you know, are always infractions of the strict rule of absolute and perfect justice—which is, in fact, the reason why we must introduce some use of the equality of the lot to avoid disaffection among the masses; though when men do so they should breathe a prayer to God and good luck to direct even the fall of the lot to the justest issue. So you see that while we cannot help availing ourselves of both sorts of equality, we should make the most sparing use 758 we can of one of them, that which appeals to luck.

Such, my friends, must be the conduct of a society which means to survive, for the reasons we have given. Now, just as a ship at sea must have a perpetual watch set, day and night, so also a State, tossed, as it is, on the billows of inter-state affairs and in peril of being trapped by plots of every sort. Magistrate must therefore follow magistrate in steady sequence from day to night and night to day, sentinel make over to and take over from sentinel in unbroken succession. No large body will ever be able to discharge these tasks with dispatch; no, we must perforce leave the most part of the councillors for most of the time to stay at home and administer their local business, appointing a twelfth part of them for each of the twelve months of the year to serve as guardians who will give prompt audience to all comers, from abroad or from our citizens themselves, with reports to make or questions to put about matters in which it concerns a State to reply to other States or receive their replies to its own inquiries, and will, before all things, see to it in view of the frequent internal innovations of all kinds which so commonly occur, that, if possible, no such incidents arise, or, if they do, that the State may be quick to

perceive and repair the mischief.   For all these reasons the power
of convoking and dissolving all meetings of the citizen-body,
ordinary and stated, or extraordinary and occasional, must lie
with this presidential board.   The twelfth part of the council,
then, will take order for all these functions, and will be relieved
of them for eleven months of the year, but a twelfth part of that
body must be perpetually associated with our other officials in
maintaining this watch over the State.

This, then, will be a reasonable way of ordering matters within
the city.   But what of the general superintendence and regulation of the territory at large?   Now that our city and territory
as wholes have both been divided into twelve sections, must
we not designate superintendents of the city streets, of buildings, private and public, of harbours, of the market, of springs,
and not least, of consecrated precincts, sanctuaries, and the
like?

Clin. To be sure we must.

759   *Ath.* So we may say that there will have to be sacristans,
priests, priestesses, for the sanctuaries.   For streets and buildings and the maintenance of proper order in them, for human
beings—to avoid infringement of rights—for lower animals—
to secure decent civil conditions within the city walls and in
the suburbs—we shall have to appoint officials of three kinds,
of whom we may call those who are concerned with the matters
just specified 'city commissioners', and those who have the
control of the market, ''commissioners of the market'.[1]   As to
priests of either sex for the sanctuaries, any whose dignity is
hereditary must be left undisturbed; but if—as may well be the
case in such matters in a first settlement—few or none are so
provided, priests of either sex should be instituted, where they
are not already instituted, to act as sacristans for the gods.
In all these appointments use should be made partly of election,
partly of the lot; in each urban and rural district we must effect
a friendly combination of the popular element with the non-
popular element in the way which will make for fullest concord.
As far as priesthoods are concerned, then, we must allow God
to effect his own good pleasure by just leaving appointments
to the inspired decision of the lot, but every man on whom the
lot may fall must be subjected to a scrutiny, first as to his
freedom from blemishes and legitimate birth, next as to his

---

[1] If the text is sound — as is not quite certain — the 'priests' and
'sacristans' just spoken of must be taken to constitute the third of the
three types of official.

provenance from houses pure of all pollution, and the cleanness of his own life, and likewise of those of his father and mother from blood-guiltiness and all such offences against religion. Religious law universally should be fetched from Delphi,[1] and this must be adhered to, official exponents[2] of it being first appointed. Each priesthood should be tenable for a year and no longer; the man who is to celebrate worship in accord with our sacred law should be of the age of not less than sixty; the same regulations shall apply to priests of the other sex. As for the exponents, groups of four tribes are thrice to elect four persons, one from each of themselves; when they have held the scrutiny on the three who obtain most votes, they must send the nine to Delphi for the oracle to nominate one from each three; the rules for the scrutiny and age on appointment to be the same as for priests. The election to a vacancy shall be made by the group of four tribes in which the vacancy occurs. As concerns treasurers of the sacred funds and precincts of the various sanctuaries and controllers of their produce and rents, three persons shall be appointed from the highest property-class for 760 the largest sanctuaries, two for those of medium size, and one for the smallest; the procedure in their election and scrutiny to be the same as in that of the generals. Thus much, then, for the regulation of religion.

Nothing, if we can help it, shall be left unguarded. As for the city, guard shall be kept over it thus: it shall be the concern of generals, taxiarchs, hipparchs, phylarchs, and prytanes as well as of the commissioners of city and market, when once we have them duly elected and instituted. Watch shall be kept over all the rest of our territory in the following manner. As our territory as a whole has been divided into twelve nearly equal districts, one tribe shall be annually assigned by lot to each district and shall provide five 'rural commissioners and captains of the watch', as we may style them; it shall be the business of each of the five to select from their own tribe twelve of the younger men, who must be twenty-five years of age or over, but not over thirty. The territorial districts shall be assigned to these groups in rotation by lot, each for a month of the year,

---

[1] The deference to Delphi has nothing to do with the theology of the State which is prescribed by Plato himself in Book X. What is borrowed from Delphi is merely 'canon law' regulating the cultus.

[2] The 'exponents' of what we may call 'religious' or 'canon' law were recognized officials at Athens, and it is said that their number was three. Presumably the part played by Delphi in Plato's scheme is also a reflection of Athenian practice, though we possess no detailed knowledge on the point. (See Burnet's note on *Euthyphro*, 4 c 8.)

to ensure personal experience and knowledge of the whole
territory on the part of every member. These guards and their
commanders shall hold their respective posts for a term of two
years. From the position, or district, originally determined by
the lot they shall be regularly conducted by the captains of
the watch, at monthly intervals, to the next in order clockwise,[1] 'clockwise' being deemed to be in the sense from W. to E.
On the expiry of the first year of service, to familiarize as many
of the guards as possible, not merely with the state of the
country at one single season of the year, but with the course of
the seasons in all districts, they shall be conducted by the
officers then in command through the successive districts in
the reverse order—counter-clockwise [2]—until the expiry of their
second year. For the following year there must be a fresh
election of rural commissioners and captains of watch [the five
superintendents of twelves].[3] Their functions while on duty in
the various stations shall be these: First, they must provide for
the most effectual blocking of the territory against an enemy by
the construction of all necessary dykes and trenches, and the
erection of fortifications as a check on any would-be despoilers
of territory or cattle. For these purposes they may employ
the draught-animals and household servants of the various
districts, who shall act as their instruments and be under their
orders, though they should do their best to avoid requisitioning
761 them in their own busy seasons. In a word, they are to do their
utmost to make the whole country inaccessible to an enemy and
easily accessible to friends, whether human beings, beasts of
burden, or cattle; it shall be their charge to make all the roads
as comfortable as possible, and to ensure that the flow of rain-
water from the highlands into the hollow valleys between the
hills does good rather than harm to the countryside by regulating its discharge by dams and trenches, so that as the valleys

---

[1] *Lit.* 'towards the right hand', i.e. moving always from left to right.
It depends on an arbitrary convention whether this shall mean movement
'with the sun' or movement 'widdershins'. Plato needs to specify the
convention he is following, since in the *Timaeus* (36 *a* 6) 'to the right' had
been taken to mean from E. to W.

[2] *Lit.* 'to the left', i.e. from E. to W.

[3] The words in brackets, deleted by Schanz and others, though retained
by Burnet, have a suspicious look of being a (correct) marginal explanation
of the preceding. Unless they are omitted, must we not at least emend
τῶν δώδεκα (760 *e* 2) to τῶν δωδεκά<δων>? The general scheme is that each
tribe has a 'rural guard' of sixty men with five officers. These groups are
posted by sortition each in one of the twelve territorial districts, and move
in the course of the year through all the twelve, so that at any moment
there is a total force of sixty-five in each district. The details have not
been completely thought out.

receive or absorb the rainfall, they may supply all the lower-lying farms and localities with water-courses and springs, and furnish even the driest localities with an abundance of excellent water. Spring-waters, whether rivers or fountains, they are to adorn and beautify by plantations and buildings; they shall secure a copious supply by collecting their streams in hewn water-courses; if there is any consecrated grove or precinct in the vicinity they shall enhance its charm by making conduits which convey their waters at all seasons into the very sanctuaries. In all such places our young men should construct exercising-grounds for themselves and their seniors,[1] furnished with [warm] baths for the service of the latter and supplied with plenty of [dry] seasoned fuel; here they shall provide a friendly home for the treatment of invalids and persons worn with the labours of husbandry—a treatment much more profitable than a poorly qualified physician.

Work of this and similar kinds will be both useful and ornamental to a district and will also afford charming recreation; the serious duties of the office shall be as follows. Each group of sixty shall protect its district, not merely against enemies, but against professed friends. If a wrong is done to neighbour or fellow-citizen by any person, bond or free, the case shall come for trial before the five commanders, who shall act alone in petty cases, and in more serious cases of complaint, where the sum involved is one not exceeding three minae, in concert with the twelves.[2] No judge shall try a case, and no official shall discharge an office, without liability to an audit, except those who, like monarchs, pronounce a final decision. In the case of our rural commissioners in particular, if they oppress those who are under their care, by imposing unfair burdens, by attempts to requisition any of their farm-stock without their consent, by reception of presents intended to purchase their good graces, or finally by unjust distributions,[3] they shall be branded with public disgrace for their yielding to corruption; for all further wrong to the inhabitants of a district, where the value involved is one mina or less, they shall submit to a voluntary trial before the villagers and neighbours. If they decline to do so in any

762

---

[1] I have here departed from Burnet's punctuation by putting (with England) a comma after γέρουσι in 761 c 6, since I think it certain that Plato does not mean to confine all 'exercising' to the young.

[2] Like England and Bury, I follow Hug in rejecting the words τοὺς ἑπτακαίδεκα (761 e 3) as a mistaken marginal comment.

[3] I have followed England in omitting the word δίκας (762 a 3), though I see no reason to reject the immediately preceding καί; (may not δίκας have arisen from a misreading of ἢ καί ?).

case of a major or even a minor charge, in the hope that their constant monthly migration to a fresh district will prove a sufficient defence against the prosecution, the complainant in such a case shall take proceedings in the public courts; if he gains the case, he shall exact a double penalty from the absconder who has declined to submit himself to a voluntary judgment. The daily course of life of the commanders and rural commission during their two years of office shall be as follows: In the first place, there shall be in each district a public mess at which all shall take their meals together. If a man absent himself from mess for a single day, or sleep out of bounds for a single night, except at the command of his officers or from some sudden and absolute necessity, provided the Five report the case and post him in the market-place as a deserter from his watch, he shall suffer disgrace as a traitor to his duty to his country, and be subject to chastisement by stripes, for which there shall be no redress, at the hands of any who meet him and care to inflict it. Should one of the five commanders themselves act in the same way on his own authority, it shall be a matter for the attention of the whole sixty, and any of them who may observe the fact or be informed of it without taking action shall fall under the provisions of the same laws and be penalized more severely than the younger men; he shall be deemed disqualified for holding any post of authority over his juniors. The Curators of the Law shall exercise an exact inquisition into such cases, with a view to their complete prevention, or failing that to the imposition of a merited punishment. It must be strictly binding on all to believe that no man whatsoever will prove a creditable master until he has first been a servant, and that less pride should be taken in successful ruling than in loyal service—service, in the first place, of the laws—since to serve them is to serve Heaven—and after the laws, of a young man's honourably distinguished seniors. In the next place, a member of our rural police must have partaken through his two years' service of the mean and meagre daily rations. In fact, immediately after their selection, the twelves shall come together with their five commanders and resolve that, like the servants they are, they shall have no 763 further servants, or slaves of their own, nor yet apply to farmers and villagers at large, and use their servants to minister to their own private requirements, but only upon public employments. In other matters they shall make up their minds to a life of personal exertion in which they shall be their own employers and attendants. They shall further carry out a thorough exploration of the whole country under arms, both summer and winter, with a view to complete familiarity with its topography, as well as to its defence, since such universally diffused and exact acquaintance with their own country may be presumed to be as important a study as they can have. Hence they should practise coursing and other forms of hunting while they are in their prime, quite as much for this reason as for the combined pleasure and benefit which commonly attends such exercises. The men and their profession, then, may be known by any name one likes, 'scouts'[1], or 'rural commission', or another, but the calling must be followed with might and main by any man who is minded to be a competent defender of his native city.

The next step in our selection of officials will be concerned with the appointment of commissioners for the market and the city. To our sixty rural commissioners will correspond three commissioners for the city. These shall divide the twelve urban districts into three regions, and, like the former board, have charge of the roads—the streets of the town itself, and the several highways leading from the country to the capital—as well as of the conformity of all the buildings erected with the legal regulations. In particular, they must take care that the water-supply, which the rural police shall transmit and deliver to them in proper condition, shall reach the reservoirs in due plenty and purity, and so serve the ends of beauty no less than of utility. Hence they must be men at once of capacity and of leisure for public affairs. Accordingly, any citizen may propose for the office any name he pleases from the highest property-class; when the names have been put to the vote and reduced to the six who receive the most numerous suffrages, the officer charged with that function shall select three by lot; these, when they have passed their scrutiny, shall hold the office under the regulations made for them.

There shall next be a selection of five commissioners of the market, to be taken from the first and second property-classes. The procedure in this case shall be in general the same as for the urban commissioners; of the ten who receive most votes,[2] they shall take five by lot and, on their passing their scrutiny,

---

[1] κρυπτοὺς (763 b 7), lit. 'hidden men', an allusion to the Spartan κρυπτεία (cf. 633 b 9, supra). But we can hardly say 'secret service-men', since there is nothing secret about the personnel or the function of Plato's militia.

[2] It seems to me that England is right in holding that the δέκα ἦ τῶν of A²LO (763 e 6), and the words of the Latin version of Ficinus, point to a reading δέκα τῶν ἄλλων <προ>χειροτονηθέντων, which I therefore adopt in translating. (So Bury, except that he, wrongly I think, omits the <προ>.)

proclaim them appointed. In every case, every elector shall cast
764 his vote; any who declines shall, if his conduct is brought to the
cognizance of the authorities, be fined fifty drachmas, and in
addition be declared a bad citizen. Attendance at the assembly,
or public convention, shall be open to any citizen, and compulsory on a member of the first or second property class, under
a fine of ten drachmas if detected in absenting himself from these
gatherings. For the third and fourth classes, there shall be
no compulsion, and their members may escape the penalty,
except in the case of a notification by authority that all are to
attend for some urgent cause. The commissioners, then, shall
superintend the orderly conduct of the market in conformity
with legal regulations, and be charged with the prevention of
injury to sanctuaries and fountains in its precincts; in the case
of such injury they shall punish the offender, if a slave or an
alien, by whipping or imprisonment. If the author of such
disorders is a citizen, they shall be competent to fine the offender
up to one hundred drachmas on their own sole authority—or to
double the sum when acting in conjunction with the urban commissioners. The urban commissioners shall have the same power
of fine and chastisement in their own department; they may
impose a fine of a mina on their own authority, or of two, when
they act with the commissioners of the market.

It will next be in place to create authorities in music and
physical training, in either case two sets, to have charge respectively of education and of competitions. By officers of education the law understands superintendents of gymnasia and
schools in charge of their seemly maintenance as well as of the
education given and the connected supervision of attendances
and accommodation for children of both sexes. By officers for
competitions it understands judges of performers contending
in both musical and athletic competitions, and of these there
should, once more, be two sorts, the one for music and the other
for athletics. In athletics it will be proper to have the same
officials as judges of both men and horses, but in music to have
one set of judges for solo performances—e.g. those of reciters,
harpists, flautists, and the like—and a second and different set
for choral singing. So we should, I take it, begin by selecting
our authority for the play of our choirs of children, men, and
maids as exhibited [1] in the dance and the whole system of the
musician's art. One such authority will be sufficient for them,

---

[1] At 764 e 5 it seems necessary to read with England γιγνομένην for the
γιγνομένῃ of MSS. and earlier editions.

who must be not under the age of forty years. One official of 765
not less than thirty years of age will also be sufficient for the
soloists, to enter the performers and pronounce a competent
decision between competitors. The actual president or con-
troller of the choirs should be appointed in the following way.
All amateurs of such pursuits must attend the assembly on pain
of a fine if they absent themselves—a matter which shall come
under the jurisdiction of the Curators of the Laws—but attendance shall not be compulsory on others against their will.
Then an elector must take the name he proposes from the list
of experts, and the only point that shall count for inclusion or
rejection at the scrutiny shall be the candidate's competence or,
on the other side, incompetence in the subject. Of the ten
candidates who head the poll, he who wins the lot shall, after
scrutiny, preside over the choirs for the year as the law requires.
In precisely the same way the candidate who wins the lot shall
preside for the year over competitors who have entered for the
solos and concerted pieces, the winner of the lot thus submitting
to the decision of the judges. Next we have to appoint from the
third and second of our property classes directors of the athletic
competitions for horses and human beings; it shall be compulsory
on the first three classes to attend this election, but the meanest
class shall not be penalized for their absence. The successful
candidates shall be those who shall be taken by lot from twenty
elected by a previous vote and must also be approved by the
suffrage of the scrutinizing body. In appointing to or selection
for any office whatsoever, if any names are rejected on scrutiny,
others shall be substituted by the same methods and submitted
to scrutiny by the same procedure.

There is still one office to be filled in the department under our
consideration, that of the supervisor of education, male and female,
as a whole. Accordingly, the law will require this post also to
be held by a single official who must be a man of not less than
fifty years, and the father of a legitimate family, preferably of
both sexes, but failing that, of one or the other sex, and nominee
and nominator alike must bear in mind that the post is far the
most important of the highest offices in the State. For in all
growing creatures alike—trees, beasts gentle or savage, human-
kind—the first sprouts and shootings, if but fair, are most
potent to effect the happy consummation of goodness according
to kind. Now man we call a gentle creature, but in truth, 766
though he is wont to prove more godlike and gentle than any if
he have but the right native endowments and the right schooling;

let him be trained insufficiently or amiss, and he will show himself more savage than anything on the face of the earth. Wherefore the legislator must make the training of children no secondary or subordinate task; since 'tis a first and primary need that their director shall be well chosen, he must do all that in him lies to appoint to the charge of their direction him who is in all points best of all the citizens. Accordingly, all officials, with the exception of the council and its committees,[1] shall repair to the temple of Apollo, where each of them shall give his vote by secret ballot for one of the Curators of the Laws, whomsoever he judges fittest to control education. He that shall receive most votes shall pass a scrutiny before all hitherto appointed officers other than the Curators themselves [2] and thereafter hold his post for five years; in the sixth, there shall be a fresh appointment to this charge by the same procedure. If a public official die before his term of office be expired, and there be still more than thirty days to run, a substitute shall be appointed in the same manner by the body already duly charged with the election. If an overseer of orphans decease, their resident relatives on both sides down to children of first cousins [3] shall appoint a successor within ten days, or, in default, each such person shall incur a fine of one drachma *per diem* until the appointment of such guardian have been made. A society, as we know, will soon become no society at all, without duly appointed courts of justice. But a judge who may not make his voice heard, and, like an arbitrator, has no more to say in the preliminary proceedings [4] than the contending parties, will in no

[1] πλὴν βουλῆς καὶ πρυτάνεων. The πρυτάνεις are the twelve subdivisions of the 'common council', each of which is to act as an executive committee for one month of the year 756 b 7 ff).

[2] The reason for the provision is obvious; the minister is to be taken from among the thirty-seven Curators, and it would be improper that they should have the last word in the selection.

[3] That is, all those who have a grandparent in common with the orphan, excluding any who may be out of the State's territory at the time. The exception is necessary not only in justice to the orphan, but (in view of the sanction to be imposed) in justice to the absent relative himself.

[4] Plato's judicial arrangements are intended to modify current Attic procedure so as to meet certain serious deficiencies. Two small defects are specified at once. The ἀνάκρισις, or preliminary proceedings before an Attic trial, were almost wholly formal, their main object being to ensure only that the suit had been regularly instituted and all documents to be used at the hearing specified and inventoried. The actual issue was submitted to a jury of citizens, who were judges at once of the law and the fact, as well as of the relevance of the evidence tendered, without any direction from an expert like our British judge. But the jury being a large one and having no function beyond that of giving a silent vote by simple majority on the one side or the other, full justice was unlikely to be done in a complicated case, or one which aroused strong public feel-

case be a sufficient judge of disputed rights, and therefore a good court cannot well be either numerous or small and of poor capacity. It should be clear in every case what the contending claim of either party is, and time and slow and repeated preliminary inquiry conduce to this elucidation of the issues at stake. Hence the challenging parties should first appear before neighbours and friends who are best acquainted with the matters in dispute. If, when all is done, a man cannot get a 767 satisfactory decision from this body, he shall proceed to another court. If the two courts fail to settle the matter, the judgment of a third shall be final in the case.

In a certain sense the appointment of these courts is also an election of magistrates. In fact, any magistrate is bound also to be a judge in some questions, while a judge,[1] though not actually a magistrate, becomes a magistrate, and one of considerable moment, for the day on which he finally decides a case. Thus we may include the judges among our magistrates and proceed to say who will be suited for the function, with what matters they shall deal, and what their number should be in various cases. The truest court, then, will be that which the various litigants appoint themselves for their own cases by an agreed choice. But for all other cases there shall be two tribunals, one when one private person complains of wrong received from another, and desires to bring him before a court for its decision between them, a second when a citizen believes the public wronged by some other and desires to support the State. And we must explain[2] what and who their members are to be. First of all, we must institute a common court of justice for all private persons whose controversies reach the third hearing, and it shall be constituted thus. On the day before that on which a new year opens with the month following the summer solstice,[3] all magistrates, whether their office be

ing. Hence Plato's anxiety that there shall be real material preparation of a case before it comes into court, and that the jury which decides it shall be neither incompetent nor unduly large.

[1] Literally a 'juror' (δικαστής). But we may say 'judge', since the Attic δικαστής, as explained, formed his own judgment on the law of the case and the relevance of the evidence. [With this sentence compare Macaulay's description of the British jury as invested with a temporary magistracy. (*History*, c. 22).]

[2] It seems to me necessary here with most editors (though not Burnet) to follow the emendation of the corrector of O, λεκτέον δ´ for λεκτέον, in 767 *c* 1, since in what follows Plato is still speaking of 'private suits'.

[3] Plato's official year is thus, like that of Athens, to begin at midsummer. Since, however, it is later specified that the year is to have 365 days, its opening will not regularly coincide with a new (or full) moon (as England seems to assume).

annual or of longer duration, shall assemble in the same temple;
then, after an oath sworn in the name of the god, they shall
set apart, as a choice offering, if I may say so, one judge from
each board of magistrates, viz. the member they judge to have
filled his magistracy best and to be likely to decide the cases of
his fellow-citizens best and most religiously for the ensuing year.
When the selection has been made, there shall be a scrutiny by
this electing body itself, and if any name be rejected, another
shall be chosen in like manner; those who pass this scrutiny shall
act as judges for parties who have declined other jurisdiction,
and their suffrages shall be open.[1] Presence as eye-witnesses
and auditors of these trials shall be compulsory on the members
of Council and other officials who appointed the judges, permis-
sive to others who may wish to attend. A person who charges
any judge with deliberate wrongful decision in a case shall go
before the Curators of the Laws with his accusation; the judge
convicted on such a count shall be liable to make good half [2]
the damage to the party who has incurred it; if the case be
deemed to call for a graver penalty, the judges who deal with
the suit shall specify the further punishment to be inflicted or
fine to be paid to the public and the institutor of the prosecution.
As to charges of crime against the public, it will be necessary,
in the first place, to give the commonalty a voice in the hearing
768 —when the State is wronged all are sufferers, and all would have
a just grievance if deprived of a part in such decisions—but
while the initial and final stages in such a case should be assigned
to the populace, the investigation should take place before three
of the highest magistrates, agreed upon by defendant and plaintiff; if the two cannot come to an agreement for themselves,
the Council shall revise the choice of each party. As far as
possible, too, all citizens should take their part in the private
cases, since a man who has no share in the right to sit in judgment on others feels himself to be no real part of the community. Hence there must, of course, be courts for the several
tribes with judges appointed by lot, as occasion arises, to give
their verdicts uninfluenced by personal appeals, but the final
determination in all such suits must be with this court which
we claim to have constituted with the utmost freedom from
corruptibility possible to human power for the service of those

[1] Again an intentional improvement on the Attic procedure, in which
care was taken to keep it a secret how a particular dicast had cast his vote.
[2] From comparison with 846 *b* 3 *infra*, 'half the damage' appears to be
here a slip of Plato or of the scribes for 'twice the damage'.

who can reach no settlement either before their neighbours or in the tribal judicatures.

This matter of courts of justice, then (as I say, it is equally hard to give them the name of magistracies as to refuse it without qualification), this matter has partly now been dealt with in what I may call its outlines, partly left unfinished; in fact, far the best place for a more exact regulation of judicial procedure and classification of actions at law will be found towards the end of our legislation. So we may tell the subject to wait till we come to the end of our work, but the method of appointment to other magistracies has received fairly full regulation. But a full and exact treatment of every single point of civil and political administration cannot be confidently given until our survey has covered the whole ground from start to finish in detail in the natural order. Still you will see that the stage it has now reached with these arrangements for the election of our officials forms a sufficient conclusion of preliminaries and starting-point for legislation without further delay or hesitation.

Clin. Your treatment of the preliminaries, sir, has been wholly to my mind, and the way in which you have just linked up the beginning of what is still to come with the conclusion of what has gone before pleases me even better.

Ath. Then so far, we may say, our grave game for the aged 769 has been finely played.

Clin. What you really mean to call fine, I fancy, is the hard work of active men.

Ath. Possibly; but ask yourself whether you agree with me on a further point.

Clin. What is it, and to what does it relate?

Ath. Why you know how the painter's brush never seems to have finished its work on a figure; it seems as though it could go on with endless embellishments of colouring or relief— or whatever may be the professional name for the process— without ever reaching a point at which the picture admits no further enhancement of beauty or vivacity.

Clin. I think I have heard enough about such matters to follow your description, though I have no personal familiarity with these arts.

Ath. And no loss either! Still there is a point which we may use this chance reference to them to illustrate. Suppose it were an artist's intention to paint a figure of great beauty which should moreover be steadily enhanced, not deteriorated, by the lapse of years,[1] you are aware that since the painter is not immortal, either he must leave behind him a successor capable [2] of repairing any damage done to the figure by time, as well as of embellishing it by improving on defects due to the artist's imperfect craftsmanship, or his immense labour have very transitory results?

Clin. To be sure.

Ath. Well now, and the legislator, has he not a similar intention? He wants first of all to frame his laws with the closest approach to absolute perfection he can compass; then, as time goes on and he puts his scheme to the test of practice, will any legislator, think you, be thoughtless enough to forget that they must be full of such lacunae which some successor will have to correct, to ensure that the constitution and system of the society he has founded may steadily improve, not deteriorate?

Clin. That is the presumable intention of every lawgiver; of course it must be.

Ath. So if a man found some means of effecting this—found out a method of teaching another by example or precept how to understand, better or worse, the way to conserve laws and improve them, he would never tire of explaining that method, I conceive, until he achieved success.[3]

770   *Clin.* Of course not.

Ath. Well, must not I myself and both of you do the same thing now?

Clin. Do just what, do you mean?

Ath. Why since we are about to form a code of law and have appointed curators of it, and those young men by comparison with ourselves, whose sun is setting, we must, as I say, not merely legislate, but at the same time do all we can to make them also legislators as well as curators of law.

Clin. By all means, if only we are equal to it.

Ath. Well, we must at least make the attempt and do our best.

Clin. Certainly.

Ath. So let this be our language to them: Friends and pre-

---

[1] In 769 *c* 2–3 some verb of motion is absolutely necessary. I have adopted England's addition of <ἰέναι> after ἀεὶ in l. 3.

[2] There is again a complete breakdown of grammar in 769 *c* 4, which can be remedied if we follow Hermann in substituting ὃς for τοῦ before ἐπανορθοῦν. Since the general sense thus obtained is certainly that of the passage as a whole, I translate accordingly.

[3] The last words are intentionally ambiguous like the πρὶν ἐπὶ τέλος ἐλθεῖν of the Greek. I agree with England that the meaning is probably 'until he *succeeded* (in making the method understood)'.

servers of law, there will be a host of omissions in the different departments of our present legislation; that simply is not to be helped. Not but what we shall do all we can to sketch the outlines of the more considerable departments as well as of the whole system. But you will have to fill up this outline and must be told what your aim in doing so is to be. Megillus, Clinias, and myself have repeatedly stated it to one another, and are agreed that we stated it well, but we are anxious that you should be our sympathetic disciples, that your aim should be that which we one and all hold should be kept in mind by both curators and authors of law. Our unanimous pronouncement was, in sum, this: that, whatever the way which promises to make a member of our citizen-body—male or female, young or old—truly excellent in the virtues of soul proper to human character—be they results of some occupation, some native disposition, some possession, or passion, or conviction, or course of study—that and no other shall be the end, as I say, towards which every nerve shall be strained so long as life endures, and that not a single soul shall be found to prefer aught which hampers these pursuits; in the last event, should there be no choice but to be driven from the State itself before she deigns to crouch under the servile yoke of rule by the base, or to leave her for exile, any such fate must be borne rather than the change to a polity which will breed baser men.[1] This was *our* concurrent judgment before you; *you*, in your turn, are now to set both ends before you in your commendation or censure of our laws, to censure such as cannot serve the purpose, accept 771 those that can with cordial good-will, and make them the rule of your lives. All other pursuits, which lead to some different so-called good, you must dismiss.'

We may open the legislation which is now to follow in some such way as this, with religion as our starting-point. We must first return to our number of 5040 and the various convenient subdivisions we find both in this total and in the constituent tribe, which was, you will remember, by assumption one-twelfth of the whole, and is thus the exact product of one-and-twenty by twenty. Now our total number permits of division by twelve, and so likewise does that of the tribe, so each such division must be thought of as a sacred thing, a gift of Heaven corresponding with the months of the year and the revolution

---

[1] The text and construction of the words from τελευτῶν δὲ (770 e 1) to ποιεῖν (e 6) are notoriously uncertain. It seems to me that in any case Stallbaum's correction of ὑπομείνασα in e 2 to ὑπομείνασαν should be accepted. In the translation I have followed his punctuation.

of the universe. This, in fact, is why all communities are under the sway of an instinct which consecrates them, though some authorities perhaps have made a truer division than others, and been more fortunate in the result of the consecration. For our own part, our present point is that we were justified in our preference for the number 5040, as it is divisible by every integer from 1 to 12 with the exception of 11, and that can be very readily put right,[1] since one way of mending it is to set two hearths on one side. That the fact is so could be proved in a very few words if we had the leisure. So we may trust in our present task to the traditional belief in question and make this division.[2] Each section will be called by the name of a god or a child of the gods and provided with altars and their furniture, where we shall convoke two sacrificial assemblies per month— twelve for the divisions into tribes, and twelve for the corresponding sections of the town itself; their first purpose will be to ensure the divine favour and to promote religion,[3] and their second, from our point of view, to encourage mutual intimate acquaintance and social intercourse of all kinds. For it is particularly necessary in view of the contraction of marriages and the connections to which they give rise to do away with our ignorance of the quarter from which a bride is taken, the bride herself, and the family she is entering; the utmost possible care should be taken to prevent any mistakes in such matters. To ensure that grave result, even the sports of our lads and lasses should take the form of dances of both sexes, which will inciden-
772 tally give them the opportunity, within reason and at an age which affords a colourable justification, of seeing and being seen in undress, so far as sober modesty in all the parties will permit. The superintendence and control of all such matters should be in the hands of our directors of choirs, who should also, in con-junction with the Curators of Laws, legislate on any points we may omit in our regulations. As I said, in all such cases of multifarious minor details, it is inevitable that the legislator

---

[1] αὕτη δ᾽ ἔχει σμικρότατον ἴαμα, 771 c 4. Strictly it is the divisor 11 of which Plato speaks as having something wrong with it for which a trifling remedy will suffice. He means that if we leave only two households of the 5040 out of account, the remaining 5038 are 11×458.

[2] νείμωμέν τε ταύτην, if correct, presumably means νειμώμεν (τὴν πόλιν) ταύτην τὴν διανομήν, but I think Mr. Bury very possibly right in reading ταύτῃ, 'let us make the division in this way'.

[3] θεῶν μὲν δὴ πρῶτον χάριτος ἕνεκα καὶ τῶν περὶ θεούς, 771 d 5–6. I take χάριτος here to mean 'favour', and the following τῶν περὶ θεούς to depend directly not on ἕνεκα but on χάριτος, and also the τῶν περὶ θεούς to be neuter, so that the sense is 'to get the blessing of heaven and to further religion'.

should make omissions for which those who have regular yearly experience of them should learn by practice to provide by regulations and annual amendments until a sufficient rule for such observances and customs is felt to have been reached. So a moderate but a definite time to allow for the experiment to cover each and all of the details would be a ten years' cycle of sacrifices and festal dances, within which the various magistracies—acting in concert with the original legislator, if he is still alive, or alone if he has deceased—may report omissions in their several departments to the Curators of Laws, and attempt amendments until the various regulations are felt to have been brought to perfection; they should then declare them incapable of modification and thereafter enforce them with the rest of the laws originally established by the legislator's imposition. On these statutes they must in no case make any wilful innovation, but if they should ever judge themselves under the stress of absolute necessity, they are to consult the advice of all magistrates, the whole popular assembly, and all the oracles, and make such modifications as are approved by all these authorities, but no other changes whatever; the law will require that the *non-contents* shall always prevail.[1]

Whensoever, then, a man of five-and-twenty or upwards,[2] on inspection made and submitted to, is satisfied that he has found in any quarter a congenial and suitable match for the common procreation of children, he shall in all cases marry before he comes to five-and-thirty. But let him first be informed of the right manner of seeking for the suitable and fitting, for, as Clinias says,[3] each law must be introduced by its own preamble.

Clin. Thank you, sir, for the allusion; you have taken what I find to be a most appropriate occasion for its introduction.

Ath. You are most kind. This, then, is what we shall say to 773 the son of a worthy stock: 'My lad, the match to be made is that which will find favour with men of sense, and their counsel to you will be not to set your heart overmuch on avoidance of

---

[1] i.e. after ten years of preliminary experiment a change in the regulations shall only be possible if it is desired by the body of magistrates, the popular assembly, and the representatives of the oracular shrines unanimously. The dissent of any one of these authorities shall be fatal to an innovation.

[2] At 721 *b* 1 and again at 785 *b* 4, the age within which a man must marry is fixed as that of *thirty* to thirty-five. We need not trouble to explain away the discrepancy, which is only one of the proofs of the unrevised state of the text of the *Laws*.

[3] At 723 *d* 5 ff.

a poor match, or pursuit of a wealthy, but rather, when other things are equal, always to enter the bond with a preference for the humbler party. This will, in truth, be to the benefit of both society at large and the contracting houses, for balance and due proportion are out of all comparison more excellent than an unqualified extreme. And he who knows himself over-hot of temper and over-hasty to act in all he does should connect himself by preference with a quiet family, while he of the contrary bent should look for connections of the contrary kind. And we may lay down one sole rule for all matches; a man should 'court the tie' that is for the city's good, not that which most takes his own fancy. Yet there is a native instinct by which each of us is ever drawn to his own nearest like, and this brings inequalities of manner and moral temper into society at large; these lead by unfailing consequence in most States to effects which we would not have in ours. To make express and formal statutes, indeed, to such effect—to forbid the rich man to marry into a wealthy house, or the capable into a capable, to force the hasty-tempered to seek partners in matrimony among the phlegmatic and the placid among the hasty—would be ridiculous, and would, moreover, rouse general resentment. It is none too easy to see that a State should be like a well-compounded bowl where the wine when poured in is hot to madness, but when corrected by another and a soberer divinity and fairly mated furnishes us a healthful and modest draught. I say no man, or hardly any, has the wit to discern that it is even so with the blending of offspring. And this is why we are driven to let the matter alone in our law and do our endeavour to charm the individual man to set an inward equipose among his offspring above that equality of condition in wedlock that thirsts so insatiably after riches, and to direct him who is bent upon a wealthy match by reproaches without the compulsion of written enactment.

This, then—as well, of course, as what we said before[1]—shall be our exhortation to wedlock and the duty of man to cleave to everlastingness by ever leaving children and children's children 774 after him to serve God in his room. All this, and still more, might be said in a proper preamble on the obligation to matrimony. But should there be any who refuses willing obedience, but keeps himself apart and unfellowed in the city, and so comes to five-and-thirty unwedded, he shall pay a yearly fine of a hundred drachmas if he belong to the wealthiest class, of seventy

[1] See 721 b–e.

if to the second, of sixty for the third, and thirty for the fourth,
and this fine shall be dedicate to Hera. He that defaults in his
yearly payment shall be indebted in ten times the amount.
Payment shall be enforced by the treasurer of that goddess,
who shall be liable himself to the debt in case of non-exaction,
and all shall be bound to render account of such matters at the
audits.[1] This shall be the pecuniary penalty of refusal to marry.
As to marks of honour from his juniors, the offender shall receive none, and no junior, if he can help it, shall show him any
deference whatsoever. If he presume to chastise any of them,
all shall come to the support and defence of the injured party,
and any person present who fails in this shall be legally pro-
claimed both a dastard and a traitor.

With dowries we have already dealt,[2] but may say once more
that there is every reasonable presumption that the poor will
reach old age when neither he that takes a wife nor he who
gives her is straitened in means; for in our society all citizens
are assured of the necessaries of life; moreover, there will be
less of arrogance on the wife's side, and of mean sordid slavery
to her money-bags on the husband's. So he that obeys us will
have one good deed to his score; he that disobeys, whether by
accepting or by offering more than the worth of fifty drachmas
towards the bride's apparelling—or of one mina, or half as much
again, or in the case of the wealthiest class, twice so much—
shall be liable in an equal sum to the public exchequer, and the
surplus offered or received shall be sacred to Hera and Zeus.[3]
Payment shall be enforced by the treasurers of these deities
precisely as we directed its enforcement against celibates by the
treasurers of Hera, or in case of non-enforcement, they shall
discharge the fine from their own private purses.

The right of valid betrothal shall belong in the first instance
to the father, failing him to the grandfather, in default of both
to brothers on the father's side; if there are no such kinsmen,
it shall pass in like manner to the kindred on the mother's side,[4]

---

[1] The 'audits'—an institution taken from Attic practice—are the solemn
examination incumbent on all magistrates at the end of their term of office
of their whole administration. I believe England right in taking the last
clause to mean that at such an audit every *citizen* shall be liable to be
questioned about his own compliance with the law.

[2] The reference is to 742 *c*.

[3] Zeus, as well as Hera, is a patron of lawful matrimony, since the 'holy
marriage' of Zeus and Hera is the type and example of all earthly
marriages.

[4] i.e. the order is father, paternal grandfather, brothers by the same
father, mother, maternal grandfather, brothers by the same mother.
In the rare cases where none of these relatives are to be found, the matter

should a case of exceptional destitution arise, the nearest kinsmen, whoever they may be, shall have the right to act in
conjunction with the guardians.

775   Concerning the ceremonies introductory to wedlock and any
other holy rites it may be proper to fulfil before, during, or after
the nuptials, the citizen should make inquiry of the exponents of
religious law, and be satisfied that all is well and truly done if
he follows their instructions.

In the matter of the marriage-feast, the persons to be bidden
to it should be not more than five male or female friends of
either family, with the same number of kinsmen and connections
of either, and in no case shall the expenditure be disproportionate
to the means of the giver—one mina for a person of the wealthiest
class, half that sum for one of the second, and thus in proportion
as the means of the party diminish. Obedience to the law
should receive commendation from all; the disobedient shall
be punished by the Curators of the Laws as a boor with tastes
untrained in the strains of the hymeneal Muses. As for drinking to excess, 'tis everywhere unseemly, except at a feast of
the divine giver of the grape—and dangerous as well—above all,
in one whose mind is seriously set on wedlock; then, if ever, 'tis
meet for bride and bridegroom to be in their sober senses, seeing
they are come to so grave a turning on life's road, and must take
all care, moreover, that that which is at any moment begetting
shall be the work of sober parents; for 'tis quite unknown what
night or day shall—under God—give it its being. Besides all
this, the work of kind must never be left to bodies dissolved by
revelry; the growing life must be fashioned with all due order,
surely, firmly, in quiet. But a man in his cups does but sprawl
and fumble all ways at once; his body is as crazy as his mind:
by consequence the drinker is an awkward, bungling sower of
his seed, and 'tis no wonder he commonly begets shambling,
shifty creatures with souls as twisted as their bodies. Wherefore a man should the rather be wary all the year long, and
all his life through, and more particularly while he is procreating
offspring, to forbear, so far as he may, from all action that
prejudices health or is touched with wrong or violence—he cannot
but imprint its colour and impress on the souls and bodies of
the unborn and become sire to a sorely degenerate brood—
above all, to keep himself clear of such things all that day and

is to be in the hands of the nearest living relatives, if any, in conjunction
with the guardians who, as we learn from 926 e, will be provided for
orphans by the νομοφύλακες.

night. For in all the affairs of man's life the first step holds
the place of God himself and makes all the rest right, if but
approached with proper reverence by all concerned.

He that has marriage in mind must think of one of the two 776
homesteads on his own actual lot as a nest and nursery for his
chicks; must leave father and mother and hold his nuptials
there, and there keep house and home for himself and his
children. For in all the kind affections of life the presence of
some dash of unfulfilled longing rivets hearts and knits them
in one, while unbroken companionship, when there is none of
this longing bred of absence, causes them to drift apart from
utter satiety. This is why our young pair should leave mother,
father, bride's kindred, to their old abodes, and live like settlers
in a colony; they will pay visits to the old home and receive
visits from it, beget children and bring them up, and thus hand
the torch of life on from one generation to another and perpetuate
that service of God which our laws demand.

Next for goods and chattels: Which of them should a man
possess if proprietorship is to give him true satisfaction? The
more part of such goods are as easy to name as to acquire, but
there are difficulties of every kind about servants. Why is
this? Because the things we say about them are partly false,
partly true; our very language about slaves contradicts our
experience of them and confirms it at once.

Meg. But pray how are we to take your words? As yet, sir,
my friend and I are at a loss for your meaning.

Ath. And not to be wondered at, Megillus. The status of the
Helots of Laconia—the controversy as to its merits or demerits—
is probably the most puzzling problem of Hellenic life. There
may be a similar, though less acute, controversy about the
system of slavery under which the Mariandyni are held down
at Heraclea,[1] and the position of the serfs of Thessaly. When
we take these instances and others like them into account, how
shall we set about proprietorship in servants? The point on
which I touched in the course of my argument, when you very
naturally asked what I had in mind, is simply this. Of course,
we are aware that we should all say a man should have the
best and most trusty slaves who are to be had. Why, slaves
have often enough before now shown themselves far better
men in every way than brothers or sons; they have often been
the preservation of their masters' persons, property, and whole

[1] Heraclea Pontica in Bithynia, where the surrounding native population had been reduced to vassalage.

family. No doubt you know that such language about slaves is common.

Meg. So it is, to be sure.

Ath. And equally common the rival theory that slaves are rotten at heart, and no man of sense should ever put any trust in the whole tribe of them. Nay, the greatest genius among our poets, in speaking of Zeus, makes the explicit declaration that he

777 'fixed it certain that whatever day
Makes man a slave, takes half his worth away.'[1]

So a man takes one or other side in the dispute for himself; some distrust the whole class and make their servants threefold—nay, a hundredfold—slaves at heart by the scourge and the lash, as though they were dealing with so many wild beasts; others take the very opposite course.

Meg. Very true.

Clin. Well, then, sir, where there is such utter disagreement, how should we act about this territory of ours? How shall we deal with the right to own and to discipline slaves?

Ath. Why, Clinias, the human animal is a kittle beast, and so, clearly, is not likely to be, or become, readily amenable to the indispensable distinction between real slave and real free man and master, and so this form of property presents a difficulty. The facts of the common and repeated risings in Messenia and the experience of communities where there are great numbers of serfs all speaking the same dialect provide accumulated proof of the evils of the system—not to mention the multifarious depredations and adventures of the corsairs of Italy. When we face all this evidence we may well feel perplexed to know how to treat the whole problem. Indeed I see only two courses left open to us—the one that slaves who are to submit to their condition quietly should neither be all of one stock, nor, as far as possible, of one speech, the other that we should treat them properly and show them consideration, for their own sake indeed, but still more for ours. And proper treatment of men in that position is to use no violence towards a servant, but to wrong him—if such a thing could be—with even more reluctance than an equal. For it is his dealings with those whom he can easily wrong which reveal a man's genuine unfeigned reverence for right and real abhorrence of wrong. Hence the man whose character and conduct are unsullied with wickedness and wrong in his relations with slaves is, beyond all others,

[2] *Odyssey*, ρ 322. (The English version is Pope's.)

sowing the seed for a harvest of goodness, and we may truthfully
say the same of every master, or autocrat, or wielder of any kind
of power in his relations with a weaker party. Not, of course,
but what we should chastise our slaves when they deserve it,
not spoil them by such mere admonition as we should use to
free men. Our language to a servant should commonly be that
of simple command, and there should be no familiar jesting 778
with servants of either sex, though many masters show great
unwisdom in this way in their behaviour to their slaves, spoiling
them in a fashion which makes life hard at once for the servant
who is to obey, and the master who is to command him.

Clin. Very rightly said.

Ath. Well, now that we have done our best to provide the
citizen with a sufficient number of servants qualified to assist
him in his various tasks, I suppose our next step should be to
produce a plan of our houses?

Clin. Yes, of course.

Ath. In fact, as our city is a new foundation, without any
earlier habitations, it will have to give its attention to the whole
subject of its architecture in all its details, not forgetting those
of the temples and city-walls. This, Clinias, is a subject which
properly comes before that of marriage; but as our whole construction is imaginary, the present will be an excellent opportunity to dispose of it. When our scheme takes actual shape,
we shall, God willing, deal with domestic architecture first and
make our marriage-law the crown and completion of our work
in this kind. For the present we shall attempt no more than
a brief outline.

Clin. Just so.

Ath. The temples, then, should be built all round the market-
square, and in fact round the whole city, on elevated sites,
with a view at once to security and cleanliness. In their
vicinity should be the offices of the magistrates and courts of
law, where, as on holy ground, judgment will be received and
given, partly because the business itself is so solemn, partly
because these are the seats of awful deities [and among them
courts of law where cases of murder and other crimes worthy
of death may fitly be heard].[1] As for walls, Megillus, I am of

---

[1] Presumably the words 'on high ground' are applicable only to the outer
circle of temples at the outskirts of the city. The market-place would
naturally be on a more or less level site. The text as it stands here cannot
represent Plato's intention. But I believe it possible that it is an editor's
combination of two versions of a sentence between which the author
himself had not made his final choice, and I have indicated this by the
square brackets in the translation.

the same mind as your own Sparta[1]; I would leave them to
slumber peacefully in the earth without waking them, and here
are my reasons. As the oft-quoted line of the poet happily
words it, a city's walls should be of bronze and iron, not of stone,
and we in particular shall cover ourselves with well-merited
ridicule, after taking our young men in annual procession
to the open country to block an enemy's path by ditches,
entrenchments, and actual buildings of various kinds—all, if
you please, with the notion of keeping the foe well outside our
borders—if we shut ourselves in behind a wall. A wall is, in the
first place, far from conducive to the health of town-life and,
what is more, commonly breeds a certain softness of soul in the
townsmen; it invites inhabitants to seek shelter within it and
779 leave the enemy unrepulsed, tempts them to neglect effecting
their deliverance by unrelaxing nightly and daily watching,
and to fancy they will find a way to real safety by locking
themselves in and going to sleep behind ramparts and bars as
though they had been born to shirk toil, and did not know that
the true ease must come from it, whereas dishonourable ease and
sloth will bring forth toil and trouble, or I am much mistaken.
No; if men must have a wall of sorts, they should construct
their own dwellings from the outset in such a fashion that the
whole town forms one unbroken wall, every dwelling-house
being rendered readily defensible by the uniformity and regularity with which all face the streets; such a town, with its
resemblance to one great house, would be no unpleasing spectacle,
and the ease with which it could be guarded would give it an
unqualified advantage over any other in point of security.
The preservation of the original buildings will properly be, in
the first instance, the business of the occupiers, while the Urban
Commissioners will be charged with the task of superintendence,
to the extent of compulsion by fines in the case of neglect, as
well as of making general provision for sanitation within the city
boundary, and of prohibiting all interference with the plan of the
city by buildings or excavations on the part of private persons.
They should also be responsible for the proper carrying-off
of rain-water and any other desirable regulations of housing
within or without the city. For these and any other matters
of detail which have been omitted in our law from inability
to deal with them, the Curators shall issue supplementary

[1] Sparta, unlike other Greek cities, was unfortified, consisting of a
number of unwalled quarters defended by the strength of their position
in the rocky Eurotas valley, and the courage of their citizens.

ordinances, in the light of their practical experience. And now that these buildings and those of the market-place, the gymnasia, schools, theatres, are all ready and waiting—the schools for their pupils, the theatres for their audiences—we may proceed, in the proper legislative order, to what follows upon matrimony.

Clin. By all means.

Ath. Well, then, Clinias, let us suppose the marriage ceremonies over. On them will follow, before the birth of children, an interval of not less than a year. How bride and bridegroom in a society which is to be so far above the common level, should spend their time—for that is what I meant by 'what follows in the proper order'—is not the easiest of questions. We have had not a few such awkward problems already, but none so unpalatable to the great mass of mankind. Still, I suppose, Clinias, what we really believe to be right and true must be said at all costs.

Clin. Of course it must.

Ath. If a man proposes to give a society laws for the conduct of 780 public and communal life, and yet imagines that law is superfluous when it comes to compulsion in private affairs, that it is improper to submit everything to regulation and that the individual should be left free to spend the day just as he pleases—if he leaves personal conduct exempt from legal control and yet flatters himself that his citizens will be ready to guide their communal and public action by law—he is seriously mistaken. Why do I say this? Because I am going to insist that our newly-married men shall frequent the public tables neither more nor less than they did in the years before marriage. That institution aroused surprise when it made its first appearance in your countries, at the dictation, as I presume, of a war or some situation equally urgent for a small population in a desperate extremity; but when you had tried the experiment and been driven to avail yourselves of these public messes, the practice was pronounced to be highly conducive to security. That is fact in the way in which the public table became one of your institutions.

Clin. In all probability it is.

Ath. Well, here is the point: though there were once persons who found the practice singular, and its imposition dangerous, a legislator who should wish to enjoin it would have no such difficulty to-day. But it has a natural consequence, at present adopted nowhere, though its adoption offers every prospect of success, which all but drives a legislator to 'card his wool into the fire', as the saying is, and waste his labour in a host of other

such ways,[1] and this consequence is no light one either to propose
or to put into effect.

Clin. And pray, sir, what is this point you are apparently so
reluctant to explain?

Ath. To avoid long and useless discourse on the subject, let
me have your attention. Wherever due order and law are
found in the life of a society, their fruits are blessings, but
neglect of regulation or mis-regulation more often than not
undoes the work of sound regulation in other directions. And
this is just where our present argument comes to a halt. In
fact, my friends, your public table for men is an admirable
institution, miraculously originated, as I was saying, by a truly
providential necessity; but it is a grave error in your law that
781 the position of women has been left unregulated, and that no
vestige of this same institution of the common table is to be
seen in their case; no, the very half of the race which is generally
predisposed by its weakness to undue secrecy and craft—the
female sex—has been left to its disorders by the mistaken
concession of the legislator. Through negligence of the sex you
have then allowed many things to get out of hand which might
be far better ordered than they are if only they had come under
the laws. Woman—left without chastening restraint—is not,
as you might fancy, merely half the problem; nay, she is a two-
fold and more than a twofold problem, in proportion as her
native disposition is inferior to man's.[2] Hence it would be better
from the point of view of the good of the State, to submit this
matter to revision and correction and devise a set of institutions
for both sexes alike; as things are, mankind are unhappily so
far from such a consummation that it is impossible for a prudent
man so much as to mention the proposal in other territories or
societies, where the very existence of the public table as a
recognized institution of society is unknown. So how is the

---

[1] In this sentence I assume Ast's πονοῦντα (at 780 *c* 9) as an all but certain
correction of the ποιοῦντα of the MSS. (and Burnet). There is something
also to be said for Badham's removal of the comma after the second
γιγνόμενον of *c* 7 and his omission of the τε before ποιοῦν in *c* 8. This
gives the rendering 'there is a natural consequence, with every prospect of
success if adopted, though the universal failure to adopt it at the present
day all but drives a legislator', etc.

[2] i.e. you might be disposed to think that *half* the mischief in the world
is due to the undisciplined tempers and passions of women and half to
those of men—'that it is six of one and half a dozen of the other'; but,
in fact, owing to the greater inherent weakness of the feminine soul—women
do more than *twice* as much mischief as men—if should rather be said,
'four of one and eight of the other', and then the estimate would be still
within the mark.

actual attempt to compel women to take their meat and drink in public to escape derision? There is nothing about which a sex so accustomed to the life of the shady corner would make more difficulties; try to force a woman out into the daylight and she will offer a furious resistance far too powerful for the legislator. As I was saying, in other societies the sex will not so much as suffer the right rule to be named without a storm of outcries, though perhaps in our own they might. So if you desire our discussion of politics at large to attain its ends[1]— so far as theory goes—I am ready to defend my proposal as sound and becoming, provided you would both like to hear my arguments; otherwise we may let the subject drop.

Clin. Sir, I assure you, we are both singularly in favour of hearing you.

Ath. Why, then, so you shall. But you must not be surprised if you find me going a fair way back for my starting-point. You know we have plenty of time on our hands, and there is no pressing business to keep us from examining our subject, law, on all its sides.

Clin. Quite true.

Ath. Good, then, let us revert to the position we began with. Any man, indeed, should be perfectly aware of one thing: either the human race never had a beginning at all, any more than it 782 will ever have an end, but always was and always will be, or else the time which has elapsed since its beginning must have covered immeasurable ages.[2]

Clin. No doubt.

Ath. Very well, then; can we suppose there have not been, all over the world, all manner of risings and fallings of States, all kinds of institutions, orderly and disorderly, as well as every sort of taste in meat and drink,[3] and multifarious climatic revolutions which presumably lead to many modifications of living organisms?

Clin. No, of course not.

Ath. Why, we believe, do we not, that there was once a time

---

[1] Or, as the words may equally well be construed, 'if you judge that our discussion of politics at large has not—so far as theory goes—missed its end.'

[2] ἢ μῆκός τι τῆς ἀρχῆς ἀφ' οὗ γέγονεν ἀμήχανον ἂν χρόνον ὅσον γεγονὸς ἂν εἴη, 782 a 2–3. It seems to me that we are here once more probably dealing with two variants of a phrase, both of which come from the unrevised text of the writer, ἢ μῆκός τι τῆς ἀρχῆς ἀφ' οὗ γέγονεν ἀμήχανον ἂν εἴη and ἢ ἀμήχανον ἂν χρόνον ὅσον γεγονὸς εἴη.

[3] I follow Ast in omitting the καὶ βρώσεως of the text (782 a 6), of which I think nothing can really be made.

when the vine made its first appearance, and that the same is true of the olive and the gifts of Demeter and the Virgin,[1] and that Triptolemus, or someone, was the instrument in the change? So we must suppose, must we not, that before the existence of these supplies, animals had recourse, as they have to-day, to feeding upon one another?

Clin. No doubt.

Ath. Besides, we remark the persistence of human sacrifice to this day in many quarters, while it is reported, on the other hand, of other peoples that they shrank from tasting even the flesh of oxen, and offered no animals in sacrifice; they honoured their gods with cakes and meal soaked in honey and other such 'pure' sacrifices,[2] but abstained from flesh, counting it criminal to eat it, or to pollute the altars of the gods with blood; man's life in those days conformed to the rule known as Orphic, universal insistence on vegetarianism, and entire abstention from all that is animal.

Clin. 'Tis the widely current and highly credible tradition.

Ath. Well, I may of course be asked the question, 'what is your point in mentioning all this just now?'

Clin. That, sir, is a well-founded apprehension.

Ath. And so, Clinias, I will try, if I can, to expound the thought to which these considerations give rise.

Clin. Pray proceed.

Ath. I observe that mankind are universally impelled by needs or desires, of three kinds, and that this impulsion results in virtue if men are well trained, in its contrary if they are ill trained. Their needs are, in the first place, food and drink, from the hour of their birth. All creatures have the instinctive appetite for gratification in that kind and are furiously defiant of the voice which says that one has any duty except to sate one's craving for pleasures from that source, and to avoid all discomfort of any kind; our third and most imperious need and fiercest passion arises later, but most of all fires men to all manner of frenzies—I mean lust of procreation with its blaze of wanton 783 appetite. These three unwholesome appetites, then, we must divert from the so-called pleasant towards the good; we must try to check them by the three supreme sanctions—fear, law, true

[1] The 'Virgin' is Persephone, and the gifts are the 'cereals'. Triptolemus, according to the Attic legend, was the recipient.

[2] The allusion is to the abstinence from animal food and sacrifices enjoined by the Orphic religion and perhaps also to the story that Pythagoras refused to offer any but vegetarian sacrifices at Delos.

discourse—not without the aid of the Muses and the gods of games, and so to quench their growth and onrush.

Thus we may make the procreation of children follow on our regulations of marriages, and on their procreation, their nurture, and education. As our discourse proceeds on these lines, our several laws may possibly reach their completion, †as[1] in the former instance when we had reached the subject of a common table—(whether, after all, women should be admitted to share the institution, or it should be kept exclusively for men, we shall perhaps see more clearly when we view it at close quarters)— we shall reduce the necessary preliminaries, for which we have as yet given no regulations to order and shelter ourselves behind them; thus, as I was just saying, we shall get a more precise view of these preliminaries themselves, besides being more likely to fit them with appropriate and becoming legislation.[2]

Clin. Very true.

Ath. Then let us keep the points just referred to well before our memory, as we shall probably have to refer to them all.

Clin. But exactly what are the points you would have us remember?

Ath. Those which we made in our three clauses; we spoke, you may recollect, of meat, then of drink, and thirdly, of the excitements of sex.

Clin. Why, sir, I take it we shall be sure to remember what you are now impressing on us.

Ath. Well and good. So let us proceed to our regulations for the wedded pair, with the object of instructing them how and in what fashion they should set about procreation, or, if they should prove disobedient, appealing to the menace of law.

Clin. In what manner?

Ath. Bride and bridegroom should make it their purpose to present the city with the best and finest progeny they may. Now whenever you have human beings conjoined in any action, when the parties give their minds to themselves and what they are doing, the results of their work are every way fair and good, but clean contrary if they have no mind or apply it not to their

---

[1] I agree with England that the text given by our best MSS. cannot be translated as it stands, and that the source of the trouble is the words εἰς τοὐμπροσθεν of 783 *b* 5. As a minimum alteration I adopt from him ὡς for εἰς in this phrase, without being at all confident that the resulting sense represents precisely what Plato intended.

[2] The ambiguities of the English are meant to reproduce those of the Greek, which depend on the impossibility of being sure of the precise reference of the various pronominal words αὐτῶν *b* 8, αὐτὰ *c* 1, αὐτὰ *c* 2, αὐτοῖς *c* 3.

work. So let a bridegroom give his mind to his bride and his work of procreation—and the same with the bride—and most of all while children have not yet been born to them. The mother shall be under the surveillance of the women we have 784 appointed [1]—their number to be more or fewer and the time of their election to be determined as the magistrates shall see fit to ordain—who shall assemble daily for not less than the third part of an hour [2] at the temple of Ilithyia; at these assemblies each member shall report to the board any person, male or female, among the procreants, whom she sees to be paying regard to aught else than the injunctions imposed amid the sacrifices and rites of matrimony. This period of procreation and supervision of procreants shall last ten years and no longer, in cases of plentiful issue; if a pair are without progeny at the end of the period [3] they shall, in consultation with their kinsmen and the official board of women, arrange terms of separation with a view to the interest of both parties. If there should be any dispute as to what is seemly or advantageous to either party, they shall choose ten of the Curators of the Laws, and be bound by this selection of arbitrators and their decisions. The ladies are to have entrance to the households of the young people, and are to stay them from their sinful folly, partly by admonition, partly by threats; if they fail they shall appear before the Curators with their report, and the Curators shall prevent the offence. If their action, too, proves unavailing, they shall bring the matter before the public, posting the offender's name with a sworn declaration of their 'failure to reform the herein designated'. A man so posted—except in the case of his successful prosecution of the authors of the notification before a court of law—shall be subject to the following disabilities: he shall be excluded from both weddings and birthday feasts, or, if he shows himself there, any one who pleases may inflict a beating on him with impunity. The same law shall extend to the case of a female offender; if posted for

---

[1] As a fact nothing has been said of this board of matrons, or the higher authority which determines their number and the method of their election. The passage is a particularly clear proof that the text of the *Laws* is an unrevised draft.

[2] μέχρι τρίτου μέρους ὥρας (784 a 4–5). Presumably the meaning is that the daily meeting may not be terminated at the earliest until some twenty minutes have passed.

[3] Thus the sense is that after ten years of marriage which has been sufficiently fertile, the supervision ceases, the parties being now left to their own discretion; if the marriage has been barren, it is to be dissolved, but the relatives of both spouses are to have a voice in the terms of separation.

similar disorders and unsuccessful in her action at law, she shall
be excluded from the women's processions and honourable
distinctions, and forbidden to attend weddings and children's
birthday parties.   When they have once produced their children
as the law requires, a man who has dealings in this kind with a
woman not his wife, or a woman who has to do with a man not
her husband, shall, if the other party be still among the procreants, incur the same penalties which have been prescribed
for those who are still producing offspring.   Outside this limit
he or she that is continent in the matter shall be held in all
esteem, he that is of the other sort in the contrary repute, or
rather disrepute.   While the more part show reasonable moderation in such things, the law will be silent on the topic, and leave 785
it alone, but if there are disorders, regulations must be put in
force as aforesaid, in accord with the laws but now prescribed.
A man's first year is the opening of his whole life; it should be
registered with that title—'beginning of life'—in the shrines of
the kindred.   There must also be, for each boy or girl in every
phratry, a further record on a whitened wall bearing the number
of the magistrates after whom dates are reckoned; in the vicinity
there must be a record of such members of the phratry as are
alive at each date, the names of those who decease being ex-
punged.[1]   For a girl the limiting age for marriage—the longest
period specified—shall be from sixteen to twenty, and for a male
from thirty to thirty-five.   That for official appointments shall
be forty for a woman, thirty for a man.   For military service
the term, in the case of a man, shall be from the age of twenty
to that of sixty; for a woman—whatever military employments
it may be thought right to impose on women—after she has
borne her children, what it is possible and fit to enact in such
cases, up to the age of fifty.

[1] Thus, Plato would introduce what did not exist at Athens, an official
and easily accessible register of births and deaths.

BOOK VII

788   *Ath.* Now that we have our boys and girls born, the proper course will naturally be to deal with their nurture and education; this subject cannot possibly be passed over in silence, but our treatment will wear the guise rather of instruction and admonition than of legal enactment. The privacy of home life screens from the general observation many little incidents, too readily occasioned by a child's pains, pleasures, and passions, which are not in keeping with a legislator's recommendations, and tend to bring a medley of incongruities into the characters of our citizens. Now this is an evil for the public as a whole, for while the frequency and triviality of such faults makes it both improper and undignified to penalize them by law, they are a real danger to such law as we do impose, since the habit of transgression is learned from repetition of these petty misdeeds. Hence, though we are at a loss to legislate on such points, silence about them is also impossible. But I must try to illuminate my meaning by the production of what I may call samples; at present my remarks must seem something of a riddle.

Clin. You are quite right there.

Ath. Well, now, I suppose we may take this much as truly said: the right system of nurture must be that which can be shown to produce the highest possible perfection and excellence of body and soul.

Clin. Certainly.

Ath. And perfection of the children's bodies, I conceive, means—to put it at the simplest—that they must grow straight from their earliest days.

Clin. Why, of course.

Ath. And further, is it not a fact of observation that in all living things growth is most conspicuous and rapid in its initial sproutings; so much so, indeed, that many have contended that the stature reached by a human being in its first five years is not doubled by the increment due to the following twenty?

Clin. Surely.

Ath. Well, then, when a body is subjected to vast augmenta- 789
tion of bulk without a counterbalancing abundance of appropriate forms of exercise, the consequences are disastrous in all
sorts of ways. That, I think, is a known fact?

Clin. Indeed it is.

Ath. And so the period when the body is receiving its principal
increment from nutrition is also the period when it demands the
maximum of exercise.

Clin. What, sir? Are we actually to impose the maximum of
exercise on infants and new-born babies?

Ath. Not precisely that; we must impose it at a still earlier
stage while the child is being nursed in its mother's womb.

Clin. What, my dear sir! On the embryo? You cannot
mean that!

Ath. Indeed I do, though I am not surprised you should be
unaware of the proper regimen for the case. 'Tis a singular
one, but I could wish to expound it for you.

Clin. By all means do so.

Ath. Well, the point would be more readily understood by
my own countrymen, thanks to the undue devotion of some of
them to sport; among us, in fact, children, and some who are
no longer children too, are in the habit of rearing young
birds for the purpose of cock-fighting. Now they are very
far from thinking the performances in which they train these
animals by pitting them against one another adequate discipline
for such creatures; over and above all this, every one keeps
birds somewhere on his person—the smaller ones in the hand,
the bigger within his cloak, under the elbow—and takes walks
of many furlongs, with an eye not to his own physique but to
that of his beasties—a practice which at least indicates to the
intelligent observer that all bodies are beneficially braced by
every sort of shaking and stirring, whether due to their own
movements, to the oscillations of a conveyance or a boat, the
trot of a horse, or however the motion of the body may be
caused; the frame is thus enabled to cope with its nutriment,
solid or liquid, and presents a spectacle of health and beauty,
to say nothing of robustness. Now in view of these facts, how,
let me ask, shall we proceed to act? Would you have us raise
a laugh by express statutes directing the pregnant mother to
take constitutionals, to mould her infant, when she has borne it,
like so much wax while it is still plastic, and to keep it swaddled
for its first two years? And what of the nurse? Shall we
compel her under legal penalties to be incessantly carrying her

charges to the country, the public temples, the homes of their relatives, until they are strong enough to stand on their own feet, and even later to persist in carrying a child about until it has completed its third year, for fear the limbs may be distorted in infancy if too much weight is thrown upon them? Shall we enact that our nurses must be the most robust we can get, and that there must be more than one for each infant, and crown 730 our work by prescribing a penalty for the offender in case of neglect of any of these various directions? Surely not; it would be to lay ourselves open to more than enough of the consequences I have mentioned.

Clin. What consequences?

Ath. Why the ridicule we should be sure to incur. Not to add that our nurses will have the minds of women, and slave-women at that, and be none too ready to obey.

Clin. Then, pray, why have we thought it needful to give all these instructions?

Ath. I will tell you why. Because the minds of our masters and free citizens may probably be led by hearing them to recognize the truth that while the right regulation of the private households within a society is neglected, it is idle to expect the foundations of public law to be secure. A citizen who understands this will be likely to regard the directions we are now giving as so many laws for his own conduct, and, so regarding them, to be happy in his administration alike of his own household and of his city.

Clin. I believe there is much truth in what you say.

Ath. Consequently, we are not to suppose that we have done with this sort of legislation until we have given a full account of the training of the infant's mind on the same lines as those with which we began our remarks about its body.

Clin. Very true.

Ath. We may take it then as the A B C of the matter in both cases that it is universally beneficial for infants, particularly very young infants, to have the process of bodily and mental nursing continued without intermission, all day and all night long. If it were only possible, it would be desirable for them to spend all their time, so to say, at sea, and as it is, we should come as near that ideal as we can with the new-born baby. We may learn the same lesson from the following facts: the truth and utility of our principles has been learned from experience by children's nurses, and the female healers of 'Corybantic' troubles.[1] You know, when mothers want to put fractious babies to sleep, the remedy they exhibit is not stillness, but its very opposite, movement—they regularly rock the infants in their arms—and not silence, but a tune of some kind; in fact they, so to say, put a spell on their babies just as the priestess does on the distracted in the Bacchic treatment, by this combination of the movements of dance and song.

Clin. And pray, sir, what explanation are we to give of these facts?

Ath. Why, the explanation is not far to seek.

Clin. But what is it?

Ath. Both disturbances are forms of fright, and fright is due to some morbid condition of soul. Hence, when such disorders are treated by rocking movement the external motion thus exhibited dominates the internal, which is the source of the 791 fright or frenzy; by its domination it produces a mental sense of calm and relief from the preceding distressing agitation of the heart, and thus effects a welcome result in both cases, the induction of sleep in the one, in the other—that of patients who are made to dance to the flute in the ritual of the deities to whom sacrifice is done on these occasions—the substitution of sanity for their temporary state of distraction. This, though a brief and summary, is a plausible account of the matter.

Clin. Indeed, most plausible.

Ath. That these methods have such effects should lead us to recognize that a mind subjected from its early days to such frights will be all the more likely to contract a habit of fearfulness; now every one will admit that this is tantamount to a training not in courage, but in timidity.

Clin. Surely.

Ath. Whereas it will be granted that the contrary course, that of mastering our frights and alarms as they arise, is a life-long discipline in courage.

Clin. Very true.

Ath. Why then, here, we may say, is one important element in virtue of soul to which this exercising of infants by movement is contributory.

---

[1] From other allusions (cp. the passages collected in Stallbaum's note on these words) it appears that the reference is to nervous and mental disturbances, like the 'tarantism' of the Middle Ages, believed popularly to be caused by the 'mother of the gods' and to resemble the excitement shown by the priests of her orgiastic worship (the Corybantes). These disorders were treated 'homoeopathically' by working up the sufferer into a frenzied dance and so throwing him into an exhaustion from which he woke up cured.

Clin. Yes, certainly.

Ath. Furthermore, the encouragement of placidity of temper will play a prominent part in the development of moral excellence, and that of a fretful temper in that of vice.

Clin. Unquestionably.

Ath. So we must try to explain the way by which either may be induced in the new-born child at pleasure, so far as the means of effecting such results lie in our power.

Clin. To be sure we must.

Ath. Then—to state the conviction which I share[1]—while spoiling of children makes their tempers fretful, peevish, and easily upset by mere trifles, the contrary treatment, the severe and unqualified tyranny which makes its victims spiritless, servile, and sullen, renders them unfit for the intercourse of domestic and civic life.

Clin. But pray how should the authority of the State be brought to bear on the nurture of creatures who as yet cannot understand human speech, and are wholly incapable of education.

Ath. Why, much in this fashion I believe: new-born creatures, especially new-born human beings, have from the very first a way of screaming, and the human infant in particular is given not only to screaming but to tears.

Clin. Very true.

Ath. So when the nurse would discover its desires she guesses
792 from these indications what to offer it; if the child is quiet when something is offered it, she thinks she has found the right thing, but the wrong if it cries and screams. Thus, you see, the baby's likes and dislikes are disclosed by these ominous signals, its tears and screams; this holds good for a period of no less than three years, no inconsiderable part of one's life to be spent ill or well.

Clin. Just so.

Ath. Now a man of peevish and melancholy temper will be given to self-pity and commonly more prone to complaining than a good man should be.   I take it you will both admit this?

Clin. I certainly shall.

Ath. Well, then, if we employ all our ingenuity to keep our growing child all through these three years from the experience of distress, alarms, and, so far as possible, pain itself, the growing soul is all this time being rendered more cheerful and gracious. Do you not think so?

---

[1] τὸ παρ' ἡμῖν δόγμα, 791 *d* 5.

Clin. Not a doubt of it, sir—above all, if we provide it with plenty of pleasures.

Ath. My dear sir! That is just where Clinias and I must part. The course you propose to us is the most mischievous we could possibly take, because the mischief is systematically introduced at the starting-point of the process of growth. Let us see whether I am not right.

Clin. Pray unfold your meaning.

Ath. Why, I mean that the point now at issue between you and me is of no light consequence. So you must consider it too, Megillus, and help us to a decision. My own contention is that the right road in life is neither pursuit of pleasure nor yet unqualified avoidance of pain, but that contentment with the intermediate condition to which I have just given the name of *graciousness*—a state which we all, on the strength of an oracular saying, plausibly assign to God himself.[1] It is this habit of mind, I maintain, which must likewise be pursued by the man who would be like God; he must not fling himself headlong into the quest for pleasures, or forget that he, too, will have his share of pains, nor yet must we let him suffer such behaviour in another, man or woman, old or young, and least of all, so far as he can help it, in the newly-born, for that is the age at which it is most strictly true that character is made by habit. Why, if I did not apprehend I should be taken to be jesting, I would go still further; I would enjoin that special watch should be kept over our pregnant women during the year of their pregnancy to guard the expectant mother against the experience of frequent and violent pleasures—or pains either—and ensure her cultivation of a gracious, bright, and serene spirit.

Clin. You need not, sir, put it to Megillus which of us has more of the truth on his side; frankly and freely I make the admission that all of us must avoid a life of untempered pain or pleasure, and steer a middle course in everything. Here is the proper answer to your very proper speech. 793

Ath. And an admirably true one, Clinias. Then let us, all three, turn our thoughts to a further point.

Clin. Which is—?

Ath. That all we are now discussing is nothing other than what mankind at large call the 'unwritten law'; it is the whole body of such regulations, and nothing else, to which they give the

[1] I take the reference to be to the famous maxim 'nothing too much' (μηδὲν ἄγαν), which was one of the two famous inscriptions in the temple at Delphi (Pausanias x, 24, 1).

name 'law of our forefathers'. Further, we were quite right in the conviction borne in on us by our recent talk that such traditions should neither be designated laws nor left unformulated. They are the mortises of a constitution, the connecting links between all the enactments already reduced to writing, and preserved by it, and those yet to be recorded, a true *corpus* of ancestral and primitive tradition which, rightly instituted and duly followed in practice, will serve as a sure shield for all the statutes hitherto committed to writing, while if they once swerve from the right bounds, it is as when a builder's supports give and subside under his edifice; the result is a general collapse of one part upon another, substructure and all that has been so admirably built upon it alike, when once the original supports have fallen. We must keep this in mind, Clinias, and do all we can to rivet your city together, while it is still in its inception, with no avoidable omission, major or minor, of anything that may be called law, custom, or usage; all are the rivets of society, and the one sort[1] will not be permanent without the other. Thus we must not be surprised if the bulk of our legislation should be somewhat swelled by a torrent of numerous and—supposedly—petty traditional practices and customs.

Clin. To be sure you are right, and we will not forget the caution.

Ath. Then until the age of three has been reached by boy or girl, scrupulous and unperfunctory obedience to the instructions just given will be of the first advantage to our infantile charges. At the stage reached by the age of three, and the after ages of four, five, six, play will be necessary, and we must relax our coddling and inflict punishments—though not such as are degrading; as we were saying in the case of slaves that we should neither inflame the culprit by brutal punishments nor spoil a servant by leaving him uncorrected, so we must adopt the same course 794 with the free-born. And for their play, there are games which nature herself suggests at that age; children readily invent these for themselves when left in one another's company. All children of the specified age, that of three to six, should first be collected at the local sanctuary—all the children of each village being thus assembled at the same place. Further, the nurses are to have an eye to the decorum or indecorum of their behaviour; as for that of the nurses themselves and the whole group, it must be subjected, in each case, for the year to the control of

[1] The two 'sorts' of 'rivets' are the actual written statute-law, on one side, and the body of unwritten traditions and customs on the other.

one of the already mentioned matrons[1] to be assigned by the
Curators of the Laws. These matrons are to be elected, one for
each tribe, by the ladies charged with the supervision of marriages, and must be of the same age with them. It will be the
official duty of a person so appointed to pay a daily visit to the
sanctuary, and to chastise any offender; if a slave or alien of
either sex, by the hand of some public menial; if a citizen who
disputes the justice of the correction, she shall bring him before
the court of the Urban Commissioners, but where there is no
dispute, she shall punish even a citizen on her own authority.
When the age of six has been passed by either sex, there shall
henceforth be a separation of the sexes—boys now being made
to associate with boys, and girls with girls—and it shall be time
for both to turn to their lessons, the boys being sent to instructors in riding, archery, the management of the dart and sling—
the girls may share in the instruction if they please—but,
above all, in the use of spear and shield. To be sure, the
prevalent notion about these matters rests on an all but universal
misunderstanding.

Clin. What notion?

Ath. The belief that there is a real and natural difference in
the serviceability of either hand for various actions, though, in
fact, where the feet and lower limbs are concerned, there is no
such difference in capacity to be detected; it is only the folly
of nurses and mothers to which we owe it that we are all, so to
say, lame of one hand. Nature, in fact, makes the members on
both sides broadly correspondent; we have introduced the
difference between them for ourselves by our improper habits.
No doubt in actions of no particular importance the practice is
immaterial—as for example, that the player should hold his
lyre in the left hand and his plectrum in the right, and the
like; but to make these cases, without any necessity, precedents for others, is fairly foolish. This is illustrated by the
practice of the Scythians, who do not confine the left hand 795
to the drawing back of the bow and the right to the stringing of
the arrow, but employ both alike for both purposes, and there
are many other examples from the driving of chariots and other
sources which may teach us how unnatural are the devices by
which it is contrived to make a man's left weaker than his right.

[1] I do not believe that any other sense can be got from the words of the
MSS. text, though there is the difficulty that these twelve matrons have
never been 'already mentioned'. But I cannot feel sure that Plato himself
—who never lived to revise the book—may not have fallen into a mistake of
supposing that this board of lady overseers had been already described.

Now, as I said, this is no great matter when one is concerned with a plectrum of horn, or some similar implement, but it makes all the difference when one comes to deal with the iron implements of warfare, bows and arrows, javelins, and the rest, and most of all when spear and shield must be plied against shield and spear. And there is all the difference in the world between one who has learned his lesson, and one who has not, one who is well trained, and one who is not trained at all. A man who has practised the pancratium, or boxing, or wrestling to perfection does not find himself incapable of fighting with his left, he does not halt or make ungainly lunges if his opponent drives him to shift his position and bring that side of his body into play; well, I take it, it should similarly be expected as the proper thing in sword-play and all other cases, that a man who has two sets of members for defence and attack should leave neither set unpractised or untaught, so far as he can help it. Why, if a man should be born with the physique of a Geryones, or a Briareus, if you like, he ought to be able to throw a dart with every one of his hundred hands. All this must be the care of officers of both sexes, the women undertaking the superintendence of the games and meals, the men being responsible for the instruction, so that all our boys and girls may grow up ambicrural and ambidextral, their native endowments suffering no preventable distortion through acquired habit.

Their instruction may be said to fall, for practical purposes, under two heads, *physical culture*, which is concerned with the body, and *music*, which aims at mental excellence. *Physical culture*, again, has two branches, *dancing* and *wrestling*. One department of dancing is the presentation of works of poetical inspiration with a care for the preservation of dignity and decorum; the other, which aims at physical fitness, nobility, and beauty,[1] ensures an appropriate flexure and tension in the actual bodily limbs and members, and endows them all with a grace of movement which is incidentally extended to every form of the dance and pervades all intimately. To come to *wrestling*—
796 the devices introduced into their systems by Antaeus or Cercyon——or again into boxing by Epeus or Amycus—from mere idle vain-glory, are useless in encounters in the field and unworthy of celebration.[2] But anything which comes under 'stand-up

---

[1] This second department of dancing is what we might call callisthenics (England appositely refers to 'Swedish drill').

[2] Antaeus is the African wrestler vanquished by Heracles, whose special trick was falling on his back and wrestling on the ground; Cercyon, one of the nuisances extirpated by Theseus, is credited with introducing the use

wrestling', exercises in the disengaging of neck, arms, and ribs which can be practised with spirit and gallant bearing to the benefit of strength and health, is serviceable for all occasions and may not be neglected. When we come to the appropriate place in our code we shall make it an injunction to our pupils and their prospective teachers alike that all such knowledge shall be generously imparted on the one side and gratefully received on the other. Nor again, must we neglect the presentation of appropriate choric action, the armoured sports sacred in this island to the Curetes and at Lacedaemon to the Heavenly Twins. The Virgin Queen of my own country, too, I may re- mark, who delights in this choric pastime, deemed it wrong to disport herself with empty hands, and right to perform her dance in all the splendour of full battle array. It will certainly be most proper that our boys and girls should copy these models in courting the favour of the goddess, both for their usefulness in war and for the embellishment of our festivals. Moreover, it will be obligatory on the boys, from the very first [1] until they reach the age of liability to service in the field, to be equipped with arms and horses in every festal procession with which they honour a god; their litanies to gods and sons of gods shall always be accompanied by a march or dance, quick or slow. Besides, their matches and practices for matches must have the same objects and no others. Such competitions,[2] in fact, are, in war and in peace-time, beneficial alike to the community and the individual household, whereas other physical exercises, playful or serious, are not for free-born men.

I have now fairly described such a course of physical training as I said at first we should have to examine; the entire scheme is now before you. If either of you can propose a better, it is for you to lay it before us.

Clin. Nay, sir, if we reject these proposals, it will be hard to devise a better plan of physical training and athletic contests.

---

of the legs into the sport. Epeus is the winner of the boxing match at the funeral of Patroclus in *Iliad* Ψ; Amycus, vanquished by Polydeuces (Pollux), was the traditional inventor of the 'boxing-glove' (Theocritus, xxii). Plato playfully uses language which suggests that they all wrote 'manuals' of sports. He is for stand-up wrestling against anything like *ju-jitsu*, and for the 'naked *morleys*' against the 'gloves'.

[1] i.e. from the age at which these 'lessons' begin until that of twenty, when they become liable to field-service.

[2] 'The τούτων 796 *d* 2 is neuter; the following οὗτοι means, I think, οὗτοι οἱ ἀγῶνες. All the 'sports' must be organized with a view to the ends already mentioned ('war' and 'festivals'); sports thus organized, and no others, are proper for free men.

Ath. As for the subject which naturally comes next, the gifts of Apollo and the Muses, we thought at first that we had said all there is to be said, and had only the treatment of bodily training still left on our hands, but now it is plain both what must be said of it to every one, and that these things should be said to them before anything else.

Clin. Ay, to be sure they should.

797 *Ath.* Then I will ask you to give me your attention. It is true you have done so once already; still, speaker and hearer alike are called on to show the greatest caution in dealing with a startling paradox, above all in the present case. I feel some misgivings in advancing the thesis I shall lay before you; still, I will take heart as best I may not to flinch from it.

Clin. And what is your thesis, sir?

Ath. Why, as to this matter of children's games I maintain that our communities are sunk in a universal ignorance; it is not seen that they have a decisive influence on the permanence or impermanence of a legislation once enacted. Where there is prescription on this point, where it is ensured that the same children shall always play the same games in one and the same way, and get their pleasure from the same playthings, the regulations in more serious matters too are free to remain undisturbed; but where there is change and innovation in the former,[1] incessant variation of all sorts and perpetual fluctuation in the children's tastes; where they have no fixed and settled standard of what is pretty or the reverse in their own bearing and movements, or in the pattern of their toys; where the inventor and introducer of an innovation in pattern, colour, or the like is always held in particular esteem—how truly may we say society can suffer from no worse pest. Such a man is constantly changing the young folks' character behind your back; he teaches them to despise the old-fashioned and worship novelty. Once more I say, there can be no graver danger to any society than such language and such notions. Pray let me explain how serious this evil is.

Clin. You mean the evil of public dissatisfaction with the ancient fashions?

Ath. That and nothing else.

Clin. Why, we of all men are least likely to turn a deaf ear to that plea; we shall listen in the most friendly spirit.

---

[1] Perhaps ταῦτα (England) is a more correct punctuation of the text in 797 *b* 4 than the τὰ αὐτὰ of our existing MSS. kept by Burnet and other editors, but the sense is the same, however we divide the letters.

Ath. So I should anticipate.

Clin. Speak on, then.

Ath. Come, then, let us rise above ourselves, as listeners or speakers, as we plead the case thus. Change—except when it is change from what is bad—is always, we shall find, highly perilous, whether it be change of seasons, of prevailing winds, of bodily regimen, of mental habit, or, in a word, change of anything whatever without exception, except in the case I have just mentioned, change from bad. Thus, if we consider our body and the way it can familiarize itself with any kind of food or drink or exertion; how, though they may upset it at first, in time their very use leads to the formation of flesh akin to them- 798 selves, and so the body is reconciled to its scheme of regimen, grows familiar and at home with it, and enjoys a life of pleasure and health; how, if it should be compelled to change again to some approved regimen, the man is at first upset by disorders and only recovers slowly as he once more becomes familiarized with his diet—why, we can but suppose the same thing takes place with men's understandings and souls. When men have been brought up under any system of laws and that system has, by some happy Providence, persisted unchanged for long ages, so that no one remembers or has ever heard of a time when things were otherwise than as they are, the whole soul is filled with reverence and afraid to make any innovation on what was once established. A lawgiver, then, must contrive one device or another to secure this advantage for his community; and here is my own suggestion towards the discovery. They all suppose, as we were saying, that innovation in children's play is itself a piece of play and nothing more, not, as it is in fact, a source of most serious and grievous harm; hence they make no attempt to avert such changes, but compliantly fall in with them; they never reflect that these boys who introduce innovations into their games must inevitably grow to be men of a different stamp from the boys of an earlier time, that the change in themselves leads to the quest for a different manner of life, and this to a craving for different institutions and laws, and thus none of them is apprehensive of the imminent consequence, of which we just spoke as the worst misfortune for a community. A change in other respects, in mere external forms, would, of course, do less mischief, but frequent modifications of moral approbation and disapprobation are of all changes the gravest and need to be most anxiously guarded against.

Clin. Yes, of course.

Ath. Well, then, are we, or are we not, still of the same mind as before, when we said [1] that rhythms and music generally are a reproduction expressing the moods of better and worse men?

Clin. Our conviction on the point remains exactly what it was.

Ath. Every means, then, shall we say, must be employed to keep our children from the desire to reproduce different models in dance or song, as well as to prevent a possible tempter from offering them the inducement of a variety of delights.

Clin. Perfectly true.

799   *Ath.* Well, can any of us find a better device for this purpose than that employed in Egypt?

Clin. And what is that?

Ath. Why, the plan is to consecrate all our dances and all our tunes. First, the festivals must be fixed by compiling an annual calendar to show what feasts are to be celebrated, at what dates, and in honour of what deities, sons of deities, or spirits respectively; next, certain authorities must determine what hymn is to be sung on the feast of each divinity, and by what dances the ceremony of the day is to be graced; when this has been determined, the whole citizen body must do public sacrifice to the Destinies and the entire Pantheon at large, and consecrate each hymn to its respective god or other patron by solemn libation. If any man tries to introduce hymn or dance into the worship of any deity in contravention of these canons, the priests of either sex, acting in conjunction with the Curators of Law, shall have the warrant both of religion and law in excluding him from the festival; if the excluded party declines to submit to this excommunication, he shall for life be liable to indictment for impiety at the instance of any who cares to institute proceedings.

Clin. And rightly so.

Ath. Then, now we are upon this subject, we must be careful to act as becomes us.[2]

Clin. What have you in mind?

Ath. When a young man—not to say an elderly man—has seen or heard something out of the common and quite unfamiliar, he will not be likely to rush on a solution of the puzzle all in a moment; he is more likely to stop short, as a man, travelling alone or in company, who has come to a cross-road and is none too sure of his way, will stop and question himself or his companions about his difficulty, and refuse to take a step

---

[1] Viz. at 655 *d* ff.

[2] i.e. with the caution proper to old men (Bury).

farther until he has formed a pretty definite opinion whither the road is leading. Now that is exactly what we should do at this point. The point of jurisprudence which has now arisen is a singular one, and we are bound, of course, to investigate it thoroughly; men of our years must not lightly insist that we can off-hand make a confident pronouncement about it.

Clin. Very true.

Ath. So we will take our time over the question, and only decide it after searching investigation. Still, we do not wish the completion of the regulations which belong to our legislation on the topic before us to be interrupted to no good purpose, and so we will go on with them to the end. Perhaps, indeed, by the kindness of Providence, when the complete recital reaches its end, it will incidentally provide the answer to our present problem.[1]

Clin. A good suggestion, sir; let us act on it.

Ath. Well, then, let us, I say, take the paradox as granted; our songs have become *canons*,[2] as the men of earlier times seem to have given some such name to melodies for the harp— thus perhaps they too were not altogether strangers to the 800 idea; someone presumably divined the truth in his dreams, or possibly in a vision of waking life—in fine, let us assume a clause on the subject to the following effect: No man shall contravene the public standards of song, ritual, or choric performance of the young at large, whether by vocal utterance or by movement in the dance, any more than he would any other of our canons. Conformity shall be clear of the law, nonconformity shall be visited with penalties by Curators of Law and priests of either sex as before enjoined. May we now take this point as settled?

Clin. We may.

Ath. Then what sort of legal rules can a man lay down on such matters without exposing himself to sheer derision? Here is a further point it will be relevant to consider. Our safest course will be to begin by imagining a few typical cases, and as one such case I propose the following. Suppose sacrifice has been offered and the victims burned as law directs, when some worshipper—a son or a brother—in the immediate presence of

---

[1] The 'present problem' is how to make matters of musical taste matter for legislation, and the suggestion is that its solution will emerge from the consideration of the kind of regulations we should lay down in our legislation on the assumption that the thing is practicable.

[2] Once more a play on the double use of the word νόμος as a name both for 'laws' and for a certain type of musical composition (not, of course, the type *we* call 'canon').

the altar and the offering upon it, breaks out into downright
blasphemy; the utterance, may we not say, will fill his father
and the rest of the group of kinsmen with dismay, forebodings,
and gloomy apprehensions?

Clin. To be sure it will.

Ath. Now that is precisely what happens in pretty nearly all
societies in our own world. A magistrate has just offered sacrifice in the name of the public when a choir, or rather a number
of choirs, turn up, plant themselves not at a remote distance
from the altar, but, often enough, in actual contact with it,
and drown the solemn ceremony with sheer blasphemy, harrowing the feelings of their audience with their language, rhythms
and lugubrious strains, and the choir which is most successful
in plunging the city which has just offered sacrifice into sudden
tears is adjudged the victor. Surely our vote will be cast
against such a practice.[1] If there is really any need for our
citizens to listen to such doleful strains on some day which
stands accursed in the calendar, surely it would be more proper
that a hired set of performers should be imported from abroad
for the occasion to render them, like the hired minstrels who
escort funerals with Carian music? The arrangement, I take
it, would be equally in place in performances of the sort we are
discussing, and I may add—to dismiss the topic as briefly as
may be—that the appropriate costume for these dirges would
not be garlands and cloth of gold, but the very opposite. The
only question I want us to ask ourselves once more is whether
we are satisfied that our first typical rule for hymnody should
be——

Clin. Should be what?

801 *Ath.* That of auspiciousness of language; indeed, may we lay
it down that our hymnody must be wholly auspicious in every
particular? Or perhaps I need not repeat the question, but
may simply impose the rule?

Clin. Out of doubt, you may do so; the proposal is carried by
a unanimous vote.

Ath. Then what shall our second regulation be? That there
must always be a prayer to the gods to whom sacrifice is being
done?

---

[1] The significance of the illustration is that it is meant to strike at the
whole institution of the dithyrambic and tragic chorus. Both dithyramb
and tragedy are part of what is professedly a religious celebration, but
their melodramatic and harrowing themes are utterly out of keeping with
the spirit of serenity, joy, and trust which ought to pervade the wor-
shippers. The attack is not merely on *bad* melodrama and vulgarly
sensational music.

Clin. Obviously.

Ath. And a third, I take it, must be that our poets must understand that a prayer is a request made to a god, and should therefore be scrupulously careful not inadvertently to ask for a curse in mistake for a blessing. To offer such a petition, you know, would be a ridiculous proceeding.

Clin. Of course.

Ath. Now we satisfied ourselves, I believe, a little while ago that wealth of silver or gold must have neither sanctuary nor abode in our city?

Clin. To be sure we did.

Ath. Now what principle, we may ask, did that statement illustrate? Was not the implication that poets are not quite the most competent judges of good and evil? Hence a poet who goes wrong in language or melody on this point—that of praying for the wrong thing—will of course lead our citizens to transgress our regulations in their prayers for things of supreme moment, though, as we just said, it would be hard to find a more serious error. Shall we then add another typical regulation about music to this effect?

Clin. But to what effect? We should be glad of a clearer statement.

Ath. No poet shall compose anything in contravention of the public standards of law and right, honour and good, nor shall he be at liberty to display any composition to any private citizen whatsoever until he has first submitted it to the appointed censors of such matters and the Curators of Law, and obtained their approval. (These censors we have to all intents appointed by our election of legislators for music and a superintendent of education.) Well then—to repeat the question—shall this be taken as our third example of a typical regulation, or what do you say?

Clin. Why, of course it shall.

Ath. This matter once determined, the gods may be properly addressed in hymns and strains of mingled praise and petition; under them, spirits and heroes may similarly receive the prayers and praises appropriate to them.

Clin. Certainly.

Ath. And next, we may now proceed straight away, without any occasion for scruples, to the following regulation: such citizens as have brought to an end a life of honourable and arduous physical or mental achievements and obedience to law shall be deemed fitting recipients for our praises.

Clin. Why, of course.

802   *Ath.* As for the still living, it is perilous to award the honour of praises and hymns until the whole course of life has been crowned by a glorious end. All these distinctions shall be awarded alike to persons of either sex who have been illustrious for their goodness. The regulations for the songs and dances should be determined in the following way. The music of earlier times is rich in fine old poems, and similarly also in dances for the body, from which we shall be perfectly free to select whatever is appropriate and suitable for the society we are instituting. The selection should be made by appointing a number of triers of not less than fifty years of age; old poems pronounced satisfactory shall be accepted, while any that are judged to be defective, or wholly unsuitable, shall in the one case be simply rejected, in the other, revised and corrected, with the aid of advice from experts in poetry and music. While we shall make full use of the poetical gifts of these experts we shall not, except in a very few cases, trust to their tastes or preferences, but make ourselves interpreters of the legislator's intentions, and construct the whole scheme of dance, song, and choric activity in the closest conformity to their purport. Any unregulated pursuit of music is infinitely improved by being subjected to system, even without any addition of musical sweetmeats; delight is something which can be provided by all styles alike. If a man has from childhood to the age of sobriety and discretion been familiar with austere, classical music, he is repelled by the sound of the opposite kind and pronounces it unmanly; if brought up on music of the popular, cloying kind, he finds its opposite frigid and displeasing. Thus, as I was saying, neither type has any advantage or disadvantage over the other in respect of pleasing or displeasing, and there is the additional consideration that the one regularly makes those who are brought up on it better men, the other worse.

Clin. Perfectly true.

Ath. It will further be necessary to make a rough general distinction between two types of songs, those suited for females and those suited for males, and so we shall have to provide both with their appropriate scales and rhythms; it would be a dreadful thing that the whole tune or rhythm of a composition should be out of place, as it will be if our various songs are inappropriately treated in these respects. So we shall further have to legislate on these points, at any rate in general outline. Now it is perfectly possible to make the necessary regulations for both kinds of songs in both respects, but what music should be assigned to females is indicated by the actual natural distinction of sex, which should therefore be our basis for discrimination.[1] Accordingly, we shall pronounce the majestic and whatever tends to valour masculine, while it will be the tradition of our law and our theory alike that what makes rather for order and purity is peculiarly feminine. So much, then, for our regulations; we must next deal with the imparting of instruction in 803 these subjects, how the teaching in the various departments is to be given, to whom, and at what times. The shipwright, you know, begins his work by laying down the keel of the vessel and indicating her outlines, and I feel myself to be doing the same thing in my attempt to present you with outlines of human lives answering to types of character; I am really laying the keels of the vessels by due consideration[2] of the question by what means or manner of life we shall make our voyage over the sea of time to best purpose. To be sure, man's life is a business which does not deserve to be taken too seriously; yet we cannot help being in earnest with it, and there's the pity. Still, as we are here in this world, no doubt, for us the becoming thing is to show this earnestness in a suitable way. But I may probably be met—and very properly met—here by the question: 'What on earth do you mean?'

Clin. You certainly may.

Ath. Why, I mean we should keep our seriousness for serious things, and not waste it on trifles, and that, while God is the real goal of all beneficent serious endeavour, man, as we said before,[3] has been constructed as a toy for God, and this is, in fact, the finest thing about him. All of us, then, men and women alike, must fall in with our rôle and spend life in making our *play* as perfect as possible—to the complete inversion of current theory.

Clin. Inversion; in what way?

Ath. It is the current fancy that our serious work should be done for the sake of our play; thus it is held that war is serious work which ought to be well discharged for the sake of peace. But the truth is that in war we do not find, and we never shall

---

[1] In the difficult sentence, ἔστιν δὲ ... διασαφεῖν (802 *e* 5-8) I take it as certain that ἀνάγκη, which Burnet records as the reading of A in *e* 6, is right against the vulgate ἀνάγκῃ, of which, indeed, I can make no sense. In *e* 7 some change of the MSS. text which Burnet prints is unavoidable. In my own translation I have ventured to assume a change of one letter (διαφέροντα for διαφέροντι).

[2] I depart here from the MSS. (and Burnet's text) by adopting Peiper's σκοπῶν for σκοπεῖν at 803 *b* 3.

[3] Cf. *supra* 644 *d*.

find, either any real play or any real education worth the name, and *these* are the things I count supremely serious for such creatures as ourselves. Hence it is peace in which each of us should spend most of his life and spend it best. What, then, is our right course? We should pass our lives in the playing of games—*certain* games, that is, sacrifice, song, and dance—with the result of ability to gain Heaven's grace, and to repel and vanquish an enemy when we have to fight him. What sort of song and dance will effect both results has partly been stated in outline; the path has, so to say, been cut for us, and we should walk in it, in assurance that the poet was right when he said:

804

> Search, for some thoughts, thy own suggesting mind;
> And others, dictated by heavenly power,
> Shall rise spontaneous in the needful hour.
> For naught unprosperous shall thy ways attend,
> Born with good omens, and with heaven thy friend.[1]

Our nurslings, too, must be of the poet's mind; they must believe that what we have said has been sufficient for its purpose, and that, for the rest, they will be visited by promptings, superhuman and divine, as to their sacrifices and dances, suggestions as to the several gods in whose honour, and the several times at which, they are to play their play, win Heaven's favour for it, and so live out their lives as what they really are, puppets in the main, though with some touch of reality about them, too.[2]

Meg. I must say, sir, you have but a poor estimate of our race.

Ath. Do not be amazed by that, Megillus; bear with me. I had God before my mind's eye, and felt myself to be what I have just said. However, if you will have it so, man shall be something not so insignificant but more serious.

To proceed with our subject: we have already arranged for [3] three public schools with attached training-grounds within the city, and three training-grounds and ample exercising-grounds outside it for horses, suitably equipped for the use of the bow and other long-range weapons, where our young people may

---

[1] Homer, *Odyssey*, γ 26–8.

[2] An alternative interpretation of this last clause (σμικρὰ δὲ ἀληθείας ἄττα μετέχοντες) is that followed by Dr. England and others, 'we are in the main puppets (and so our thinking does not amount to much), but we have our gleams of truth too'.

[3] This is an oversight, as Plato himself makes haste to admit, unless, indeed, the pretended allusion to something which has not, in fact, been yet said, is intentional, and meant to reproduce the style of an actual conversation, where such a slip might readily occur.

both learn and practise these accomplishments; or if adequate
arrangements have not been already made they must be introduced into our theory and the corresponding code at this point.
They shall all be adequately staffed with paid resident and
salaried masters in the various subjects, who must be non-
citizens, and must give a complete course of instruction alike
in the arts of war and in that of music to the boys who attend
their classes; a boy is not to attend if his father so desires, but
otherwise to be exempted from this education; education is,
if possible, to be, as the phrase goes, compulsory for every
mother's son, on the ground that the child is even more the
property of the State than of his parents.[1]   And, mind you,
my law will apply in all respects to girls as much as to boys;
the girls must be trained exactly like the boys.   And in stating
my doctrine I intend no reservation on any point of horsemanship or physical training, as appropriate for men but not for
women.   In fact, I give full credit to the tales I have heard of
ancient times, and I actually know that at the present day
there are untold thousands, one may fairly say, of women
living round the Black Sea—Sarmatian women, they are
called—on whom not horsemanship only but familiarity with 805
bows and other weapons is enjoined no less than it is on their
husbands, and by whom it is equally cultivated.   Besides, here
is a consideration I would submit to you: if such results are
feasible, then I say the present practice in our own part of the
world is the merest folly; it is pure folly that men and women
do not unite to follow the same pursuits with all their energies;
in fact, almost every one of our cities on our present system, is,
and finds itself to be, only the half of what it might be at the
same cost in expenditure and trouble.   And yet, what an amazing
oversight in a legislator!

   Clin. Why, so it would seem, sir, though a good many of our
present proposals are at variance with our customary systems.
However, your proposal to let the argument take its course,
and not to decide on our verdict until it has reached its end,
was most apposite—and in view of it, I feel self-condemned for
my present observation.   So pray go on with your exposition
according to your own mind.

   Ath. Well, Clinias, my mind, as I have already said, is that

───────────

[1] The importance of the passage, as Burnet has pointed out, is that the
proposal to have a permanently organized, paid body of teachers of all
the different 'subjects' of education resident together in a properly
equipped institution is made here for the first time.

if the feasibility of our proposals had not been sufficiently established by actual facts, there might have been some ground for disputing the theory; as it is, an opponent who refuses our proposal a hearing must surely take a different line; such tactics will not deter us from insisting on our principle that there must be the completest association of the female sex with the male in education as in everything else. In fact, we may treat the matter from some such standpoint as this. If women are not to take their part along with men in all the business of life, we are bound, are we not, to propose some different scheme for them?

Clin. To be sure we are.

Ath. And which of the various systems now recognized can we prefer to the comradeship we are just imposing on them? The system followed by the Thracians and many other peoples, that the women till the fields, look after the flocks and herds, and perform menial offices, exactly like slaves? or the practice universal in our own part of the world? You know what our own customs in this matter are; we 'pack' all our belongings, as the phrase goes, 'into one' house, and make over to our women the control of the store-closet and the superintendence of the spinning and wool-work at large. Or should we perhaps 806 vote for the *via media*, which you take, Megillus, in Laconia? Your women are expected in their girlhood to take their share in physical training and music; when they have grown up, they have no wool-work to occupy them, but you expect them to contrive a composite sort of life, one that calls for training and is far from being unworthy or frivolous, and to go half-way with the work of medicine-chest,[1] store-chamber, and nursery, but to take no share in the business of war; the consequence is that if circumstances should ever force them to a fight for their city and their children, they would prove quite unequal to playing an expert's part with the bow, like Amazons, or any other missile weapon; they could not, could they, even copy our goddess by taking up spear and shield with the mien of doughty protectors of a harried motherland, and so strike an invader with alarm, if with nothing more, by their appearance in martial formation? As for the Sarmatian women, yours, while

---

[1] θεραπείας (806 *a* 4) might mean 'domestic tendance' generally, but since, as we see from Xenophon's *Oeconomicus*, looking after sick servants ranked at Athens along with keeping the stores and minding the children as part of the wife's duty, I think Plato means to mention this here as one of the tasks in which the Spartan women, as compared with the Athenian, 'go half-way'.

they lead the life they do, would never venture on imitating
them at all; by comparison with women like yours, theirs would
pass for men.[1] Let him who will applaud your legislators in
this matter; I can only speak as I think. A legislator should
be thorough, not half-hearted; he must not, after making
regulations for the male sex, leave the other to the enjoyment
of an existence of uncontrolled luxury and expense, and so
endow his society with a mere half of a thoroughly felicitous life
in place of the whole.

Meg. What are we to do, Clinias? Must we suffer our visitor
to run Sparta down in our hearing like this?

Clin. Indeed we must; we allowed him full liberty of speech,
and so we must let him alone until our review of our legislation
has fairly reached its completion.

Meg. I own you are right.

Ath. Then it is for me to proceed once more with my exposition.

Clin. Yes, certainly.

Ath. What, then, should life be like with men whose necessities
have been moderately provided for, their trades and crafts put
into other hands, their lands let out to villeins who render from
the produce such rent as is sufficient for sober livers; men, moreover, furnished with common dining-halls, some for themselves,
others near at hand for the members of their families—their
daughters and their daughters' mothers—under presidents of
either sex, whose appointed function is daily to dismiss the
tables after review and inspection of the conduct of the com- 807
pany, and thereafter, libation first duly made by the president
and the company to the gods to whom that night and day
stands consecrate, so to betake themselves home to bed? When
they have been so provided is there no necessary and wholly
proper work left them to do? Is each man of them to pass his
time fattening himself like a stalled ox? No, I say: it were
neither right nor seemly nor yet possible that he who lives
so should miss his proper destiny, that of an idle, sluggish,
fattened beast—which is commonly to be the prey of some other
beast, one worn to bitter leanness by risks and exertions. Now
if we are going to look for an exact realization of our scheme
[as we have styled it][2] it will perhaps never be found, so long as

---

[1] As editors observe, the passage is meant as a censure on the panicky
behaviour of the Spartan women, in spite of their famous training, when
Epaminondas was in the valley of the Eurotas after the battle of Leuctra,
and threatened an assault on the town of Sparta.

[2] As the use of the square brackets is meant to show, I am here trying to represent what I take to be the original sense of a corrupt clause. The MSS.
text kept by Burnet in 807 *b* 4, ὡς καὶ νῦν, εἰ ζητοῖμεν ἄν, can hardly be trans-

there are private wives, children, and houses, and each of us has his private belongings of all sorts. Still, if we can secure the second-best conditions, which we are now describing, we shall indeed come off well enough. But there is, I maintain, a work left for men who lead this life, and that none of the most trivial or meanest; righteous law has appointed them to the gravest work of all. The life of the aspirant to victory at Olympia or Pytho leaves no leisure for any other tasks whatever, and there is a double, or more than double, glut of occupation in the life we have rightly described as concerned with the practice of every virtue of body and mind. No other business can be allowed to come in as a by-end and hinder the provision of needful exercises and regimen for the body, nor of necessary studies and habitual discipline for the mind; the whole day and night is verily not long enough for one who is engaged on this sole work of getting the full and perfect benefit from these pursuits. Now, since this is so, every free citizen will need an ordered disposition of all his hours; he must begin with it at daybreak, and follow it without any intermission until the succeeding dawn and sunrise. A legislator, to be sure, will show lack of dignity if he stoops to a multitude of little trivial directions about household arrangements, and among them to the restrictions on sleep proper in a population which will have to keep perpetual and diligent watch over its whole city. In fact, that any citizen whatsoever should spend the whole of any night in unbroken sleep, and not let all his servants see him always awake and astir before any one else in the house, 808 must be unanimously pronounced a disgrace and an act unworthy of a free man, whether such a regulation should be regarded as law or as custom. In particular, that the mistress of a house should be called by her maids in the morning, and not get up first herself and wake them, and the whole building itself, if only that were possible, that is what every servant, man, woman, or boy, must cry shame on. Much of the business of public and household life should certainly[1] be done in the night hours saved from sleep[2] by the State officials and by the masters

lated as it stands, and I am not quite satisfied by Badham's ὡς καὶ νυνὶ ζητοῦμεν' ἄν. The difficulty, to my mind, is less with the εἰ ζητοῖμεν ἄν (though I do not feel too confident about this) than with the ὡς καὶ νῦν. I *suspect* Plato wrote ὡς καὶ νῦν <εἴρηται> ζητούμενα (or ζητοῦμεν' ἄν).

[1] I think the πάντως of the quotation of this passage in Stobaeus an improvement on the MSS. πάντας in 808 *a* 7 and translate in that sense.

[2] Plato is thinking throughout not so much of what we should call doing business 'late at night'—a thing not very possible under ancient conditions —as of starting it in the early hours before 'sun-up'.

and mistresses at home.   Overmuch sleep, indeed, is naturally
as unsuitable to us in body and mind as it is incongruous with
business of all these kinds.   In fact, a man asleep is of no more
account than a corpse; he who sets most store on vital and
mental activity keeps awake all the hours he can, only reserving
for sleep what his health requires, and this is not much, when
the habit has been well established.   And public officials who
are awake betimes by night are no less a source of fear to evil-
doers, whether enemies or citizens, and of awe and reverence in
the righteous and virtuous than of benefit to themselves and their
whole community.

So much, then, for night; and we may add to what we have
said that to spend it in this fashion will further promote the
spirit of courage in the souls of citizens of all sorts.   With the
return of day and dawn, the boys should betake themselves to
school.   And just as sheep, or any other creatures, cannot be
allowed to live unshepherded, so neither must boys be left
without the care of attendants, nor slaves without that of a
master.   Now of all wild young things a boy is the most difficult
to handle; just because he more than any other has a fount of
intelligence in him which has not yet 'run clear', he is the
craftiest, most mischievous, and unruliest of brutes.   So the
creature must be held in check, as we may say, by more than
one bridle; in the first place, when once he is out of the mother's
and nurse's hands, by attendants to care for his childish helplessness, and then, further, by all the masters who teach him
anything, and, as befits a free-born man, by the teaching he gets;
but further chastisement, as befits a slave, shall be inflicted on
the boy and his attendant and teacher [1] as well, by any free
person in whose presence he commits any of these faults.   If
such a person omits to inflict the due correction, he shall, in
the first place, be held to have disgraced himself most deeply;
also the Curator of Law appointed to take control of boys [2] shall 809
take cognizance of the party who is present at an offence of
the sort we are dealing with without imposing the necessary
correction; this magistrate must be a man of keen vision,
thoroughly devoted to his work of supervising the training of
the boys, who will guide their native dispositions into right ways,
always directing them to the good and lawful.   But, now, as
to this Minister himself, how is he to be sufficiently instructed

[1] The thought is that the teacher is to be held responsible for the good
behaviour of the boys who attend his class.
[2] i.e. the Minister of Education, spoken of before at 765 *d*, who is the
most important person in the whole community.

by the lips of our law? For so far, its utterances have been neither clear nor full, but only partial, though where he is concerned, the law must make no omission it can help, but impart its whole doctrine to him, that he may so prove interpreter and foster-father to others. Now we have dealt already with the choric art—song and dance, that is; we have said what types of these should be selected or corrected, and consecrated; but as for writings without metre [1] which of them may be put in the hands of your charges and on what terms, that, most worthy Director of Education, you have not been told. You have indeed been informed what their military lessons and exercises must be. But what must they know, first of letters, and next of the lyre and of ciphering, of which we said [2] all must master what is needful for war, domestic business, or civil administration, as well as such knowledge of the courses of the heavenly bodies—sun, moon, planets—as is useful for these same ends, in so far as any city is bound to deal with the matter? (What matter, you say? The grouping of days into monthly periods, and months into the year in such fashion that the seasons with their sacrifices and feasts may fit into the true natural order and receive there several proper celebrations,[3] and the city be thus kept alive and alert, its gods enjoying their rightful honours and its men advancing in intelligence of these matters.) These, my friend, are questions to which the legislator has as yet given you no full and sufficient answer. Give diligent heed, then, to what is now to be said.

Your instructions, we have said, are deficient, in the first place, as to reading and writing. Now what is the defect of which we complain? It is that you have so far not been told whether the lad who would be a decent citizen must attain to finished mastery of the study, or must leave it wholly alone, and the same is true of the lyre. Well, we tell you now that these studies must not be left alone. For reading and writing three years or so, from the age of ten, is a fair allowance of a boy's time, and if the handling of the lyre is begun at thirteen, the 810 three following years are long enough to spend on it. No boy and no parent shall be permitted to extend or curtail this period

---

[1] That is 'prose literature'.

[2] At 747 *b*.

[3] The problem is that of adjusting the religious calendar to the actual movements of the sun, by a proper device for holding the year and month together. Without such a device the months will gradually travel round the year, so that, e.g., a festival appropriate to harvest-time will, sooner or later, come to be celebrated in the middle of winter.

from fondness or distaste for the subjects; to spend either more
or less time upon them shall be an infraction of the law, and the
disobedience shall be visited by exclusion from the school
distinctions we shall shortly describe. But what more specifi-
cally is to be learned by the children and taught by their masters
during these years? That is the very question to which you
are first to hear our answer. They must, of course, carry their
study of letters to the point of capacity to read and write, but
perfection of rapid and accomplished execution should not be
insisted on in cases where the natural progress within the prescribed term of years has been slower. As to the study of
written compositions without musical accompaniment, whether
written in metre or without rhythmical subdivisions—in fact,
compositions in simple prose with no embellishments of rhythm
or melody—difficult problems are raised by some of the works
bequeathed to us by our numerous authors in this kind. How
then will you deal with them, reverend Curators of Law? Or
what would be the right injunction for the legislator to lay
upon you as to their treatment? I can conceive they will
cause him no little perplexity.

Clin. Pray, sir, what is the difficulty, for it is plain you speak
with a real sense of a personal difficulty?

Ath. I do, indeed, Clinias; you are right there. But you and
your friend are my colleagues in this juristic discussion, and so
I am bound to tell you frankly where I see difficulties and where
I see none.

Clin. Well, and why do you mention the point just now?
What is the feeling which leads you to do so?

Ath. Why, here it is: 'tis no light matter to speak against so
many thousands of voices.

Clin. But, bless me, do you imagine what we have already
said about jurisprudence only contradicts popular opinion in
a few trifles!

Ath. Yes, that is true enough. You tell me, I conceive, that
though this legislative path of ours is repellent to so many—
perhaps those who find it attractive may be as numerous, or
if fewer, at least not inferior—you tell me, I say, to join this
latter party and follow the path our present discussions have
laid down for us with a stout courage and a good heart, not
to flinch.

Clin. I do, indeed.

Ath. Then there shall be no flinching. Now mark my words.
We have a great number of poets, in hexameter verse, in iambic

trimeter, in a word in all the recognized metres, some grave and some gay; on them, so those many thousands of voices proclaim, young people who are being rightly educated should be fed, in them they should be steeped; their reading lessons must give them a wide acquaintance with their works and an 811 extensive scholarship in them; whole poets must be learned by heart. There are others who compile anthologies of the poets and make collections of whole passages, which they say must be committed to memory and learned by heart if our protégé's wide familiarity with literature and extensive learning is to make a good and wise man of him. What you are now calling on me to do is to tell those persons without any reserve where they are right and where they are wrong?

Clin. To be sure.

Ath. Well, what adequate verdict can I conceivably give about them all in a single sentence? Perhaps something like this—and it is a statement in which I suppose every one will concur—in every poet there is much that is admirably said and also much that is not. But if so, this extensive learning, I must tell you, has its dangers for our young people.

Clin. Then how would you advise our Curator of Law? [1]

Ath. Advise him? On what point?

Clin. On the choice of a standard by reference to which he will permit all the young folk to learn one piece and forbid their learning another. Tell us your mind without any diffidence.

Ath. There, my dear Clinias, I venture to think I am in a way fortunate.

Clin. Fortunate in what?

Ath. In not being altogether at a loss for a standard. As I look back on the discourse you and I have been holding ever since day-break until this moment—and I really believe there has been some divine guiding about the matter—well, be that as it may, our converse has been, to my mind, just like a kind of poem. I dare say there is nothing surprising in my having felt this keen pleasure in reviewing this compact formation, as I may call it, of discourse of my own composition; the fact is that of all the many compositions I have met with or listened to, in verse or in plain prose, I find it the most satisfactory and the most suitable for the ears of the young. So I really think I could not direct our Curator of Law and Minister of Education to a better standard, or bid him do better than instruct his schoolmasters to teach it to their pupils, and also

[1] i.e. the Minister of Education.

if in his researches he should light upon connected and similar matter in the verse of our poets, in our prose literature, or even in the form of simple unwritten discourse of the same type as the present, by no means to neglect it, but get it put into writing.[1] He should begin by making it compulsory on the teachers themselves to learn this material and appreciate it; teachers who are dissatisfied with it he must not employ as colleagues, those who concur with his own appreciation he should employ, and to them he should entrust the young for 812 their instruction and education. And with this what I have to say about reading and writing and the teachers of the subject may come to an end.

Clin. If one is to judge by reference to our professed intentions, sir, I believe we have kept the discussion on the lines originally laid down for it; whether our whole attitude is the right one or not it might be harder to pronounce.[2]

Ath. That, Clinias—to repeat what I have said more than once already—will presumably become clearer of itself when we have reached the end of our review of our legislation.

Clin. True.

Ath. Then we may leave the teacher of letters, may we not, and direct our discourse to the instructor in the cithern?

Clin. By all means.

Ath. Well, as for the teachers of that instrument, I fancy we shall be making a proper assignment of their functions as instructors, and more generally as trainers, in that branch of education, if we call to mind our earlier pronouncements.

Clin. And, pray, what were they?

Ath. Why, I believe we said the sexagenarians of the 'chorus of Dionysus' would need to be exceptionally sensitive to rhythmic and melodic structure to ensure their competence to distinguish a good musical imitation of a soul under the stress of its emotions from a bad, competence, that is, to distinguish the counterfeit presentments of a good soul from those of an evil, to reject the second but produce the first publicly in their hymnody, and thus to put a charm on the youthful mind, challenging one and

[1] The suitable passages from existing literature would, of course, be already in writing. But presumably Plato means that the Minister of Education is to see that they are all put into the officially authorized 'reading-books' of his State schools.

[2] The meaning is apparently that the conclusions now reached are strictly consequences of the principles laid down as postulates (ὑποθέσεις) at the opening of the discussion. It still remains, however, possible that our postulates might prove to be mistakes.

all to join them in pursuit of virtue by means of these same imitations.

Clin. Truly said, indeed.

Ath. That is the purpose, then, for which teacher and pupil must employ the notes of the lyre; they must do so to get the benefit of the emphasis given by its strings, and so must make their tones accordant with those of the voice. As for diversification and complication of the instrumental part—the strings giving out one tone and the composer of the melody another—and, in fact, for correspondence [within or without the octave] [1] of lesser interval with greater, quicker note with longer, lower tones with higher, and equally for all sorts of complication of the rhythm by instrumental accompaniment, no such devices are to be employed with pupils who are to acquire the benefits of their musical studies in the brief space of three years. Such a clash of opposites makes learning a slow business, and it is imperative that our young people should learn their lessons with ease; the compulsory subjects we have imposed on them are neither few nor light, as the progress of our discourse will disclose in due time. All these matters, then, are for our Minister of Education to supervise on the lines laid down. As for the actual tunes and words which the trainers of our choirs are to

813 teach, and the character of them, that too has already been fully discussed. [2] As you remember, we said they must be consecrated and assigned each to its appropriate festival to provide a society with a pleasure that is in very deed fortunate.

Clin. Here, again, what you say is true.

Ath. Ay, absolutely true. So our chosen Director of Music shall have the matter put under his care for supervision, and the blessings of Fortune go with him! Our business shall be to add further specifications to what we have already said on the subject of the dance and the training of physique in general; we supplemented our treatment of music by adding directions for the teacher, and we will do the same for physical culture. Both the boys and the girls will, of course, have to dance and practice bodily exercises, will they not?

Clin. Yes.

---

[1] If the words καὶ ἀντίφωνον are sound at 812 e 1, ἀντίφωνον must have its usual sense of 'answering at the interval of an octave' to the main note, or distinguished from σύμφωνον, 'consonant within the octave'. I feel inclined to agree with England that the two words have been wrongly added here by someone who meant ἀντίφωνον to stand for 'dissonant'.

[2] See *supra*, 798 d 7–802 d 6.

Ath. So the convenient arrangement for these exercises will be that there should be dancing-masters for boys and mistresses for girls.

Clin. I don't dispute it.

Ath. Then once more we must call in the busiest of our functionaries, the Director of Education; his supervision of music and physical training will keep his hands pretty full.

Clin. How then, at his advanced age, will he be equal to the supervision of such varied business?

Ath. Oh, easily enough. The law will permit him, as it has already done, to associate with himself in this work any citizens he may choose of either sex; he will know who are the right persons and have no wish to go wrong in such matters, as he will have a prudent respect for his office and an understanding of its importance, and a life-long conviction that so long as the young generation is, and continues to be, well brought up, our ship of State will have a fair voyage, while in the contrary case the consequences are better left unspoken, and we will leave them so in the case of a city which we are founding for the first time, from regard for the anxious observers of omens. On this subject, too—dancing and the motions of physical training in general—we ourselves have already [1] said much. We are instituting gymnasia and all kinds of military exercises—exercises in archery, the throwing of various sorts of missiles, light skirmishing, infantry-fighting in its different departments, tactical manœuvres, field-marches of all kinds, encampment, and any studies which go to form a cavalryman. In fact, there must be public teachers in all these branches, receiving a stipend from the State, and they must have for their scholars not merely boys and men, but the girls and women, who must get a knowledge of all this. While they are still in their girlhood they must practice dancing and fighting in armour thoroughly, and as women they must take their share in the manœuvring, company-drill, and grounding and shouldering of arms, for this reason if 814 for no other; [2] if circumstances should ever require our whole force to take the field *en masse* outside the city, there will be a defence for the children and the city at large equal to its immediate purpose; on the other hand, if—and the possibility cannot be excluded—there should be a foreign invasion of a large and powerful force of Greeks or others, which might compel

---

[1] 795 *d* ff.

[2] In 814 *a* 2, I think Bury probably right in inserting <ἄλλου> between ἕνεκα and ἀλλά.

a pitched battle for the actual safety of the city, it would be a
sad disgrace to the community if it had trained its women so
ill that they had not even the courage of the hen-bird, who will
face the most dangerous beast in defence of her chicks at the
risk of death or any other peril—if they rushed straight to the
temples, beset all the altars and shrines, and bespattered mankind with the opprobrium of being the most abject creature
alive.

Clin. Why, no sir, such a performance would be no credit
to any city in which it might occur—to say nothing of the
mischief it would do.

Ath. Then we may impose the law that, up to the point
indicated, our women are not to neglect the arts of war;
they must be practised by all citizens, male and female
alike?

Clin. You have one supporter at any rate in me.

Ath. Now as to *wrestling*; we have dealt with it already,
but we said nothing of what is to my mind the most important
point, though one not easy to explain in the absence of an actual
physical demonstration. So we will leave the decision of that
issue until theory and practice combined have cleared up the
whole subject and made it plain that the kind of wrestling we
have in mind is far more closely connected with military combat
than any other sort of movement, and also that it is to be
cultivated with a view to this latter, not the latter with a
view to it.

Clin. That last point is well taken.

Ath. So much, then, at present for what we have to say of
the value of wrestling. As for other movement of the body as
a whole—in the main it may properly be called dancing—we
must bear in mind that it has two species, one reproducing
motions of comely bodies with a dignified effect, the other
those of uncomely bodies with a ludicrous, and that further,
the comic and the serious kinds have each two sub-species.
One species of the serious sort represents the movements of the
comely body and its valiant soul in battle and in the toils of
enforced endurance, the other the bearing of the continent soul
in a state of prosperity and duly measured pleasure; an appropriate name for this latter would be the *dance of peace*. The
815 war-dance has a different character, and may properly be called
the *Pyrrhic*; it depicts the motions of eluding blows and shots
of every kind by various devices of swerving, yielding ground,
leaping from the ground or crouching, as well as the contrary

motions which lead to a posture of attack, and aim at the reproduction of the shooting of arrows, casting of darts, and dealing of all kinds of blows.[1] In these dances the upright, well-braced posture which represents the good body and good mind, and in which the bodily members are in the main kept straight, is the kind of attitude we pronounce right, that which depicts their contrary, wrong. In the case of the dance of peace, the question to be raised in every case is whether the performer succeeds or fails in maintaining throughout his performance a graceful style of dancing in a way becoming to the law-abiding man. So we have, in the first place, to draw a distinction between questionable dances and those which are above question. What then is the distinction, and where should the line be drawn? As for dances of Bacchanals and their likes, which present what is called a 'mimic' exhibition of persons in liquor, under the designations of Nymphs, Pans, Sileni, or Satyrs, and are performed as a part of certain rituals and initiations, it is hard to pronounce that whole style of dance either warlike or pacific, or to determine what possible purpose it has. The most correct course, I think, will be to discriminate it alike from the dances of war and of peace, declare it unfit for a citizen, and leave it so on one side, returning once more to the war-dance and peace-dance as matters which unquestionably concern us. The non-martial arts of worship of gods and their progeny in dances will all form a single *genre* expressive of a sense of well-being, and may be divided into two branches: one expressive of escape from hardships and perils to good fortune, in which the pleasure conveyed is keener, and one of retention and augmentation of good already enjoyed, in which this pleasure is more sedate. Now, as we know, any man in such conditions executes movements of the body, more vigorous when his pleasure is more intense, less vigorous when it is less so. Again, the more sober the man and the more schooled to fortitude, the less violent these motions; the more fearful the 816 man and the less disciplined in continence, the more violent and vehement these movements. But to speak generally, no man who is using his vocal organs whether for song or for speech,

---

[1] There is, as the commentators say, a strange confusion here. Strictly speaking, the war-dance 'reproduces' or 'imitates' the movements of the fighting-man, not motions which *reproduce* these movements. But whether the confusion is due to transcribers, and to be remedied by the correction of ἐπιχειροῦσας (815 *a* 7) to ἐπιχειροῦσαν (Badham, Paton) or comes from Plato himself (and is only one more sign of the unrevised condition of the *Laws*) it is perhaps impossible to say.

can keep his body perfectly still. Hence it is from this representation of things spoken by means of posture and gesture that the whole art of the dance has been elaborated. And in all such cases, one man's motions keep time and tune with his utterance, another's do not. Hence, in fact, the well-merited praise which may be given to many of our traditional names for their excellence and truth to fact, one of which is that bestowed on the dances of prosperous men who preserve measure in their pleasures. We should give credit to the inventor—whoever he may have been—for the truth and musical taste of the names, and the philosophical insight shown by designating fine dancing as a whole *emmeliae* and proceeding to distinguish two kinds— each with its fitting and proper name—the war-dance or *Pyrrhic*, and the *emmelia* or dance of peace. The legislator must deal with these matters in general outline, and the Curator[1] make them an object of study. His investigations should result in the combination of dancing with the rest of music, the assignment to each sacrificial feast of the appropriate measures, and the consecration of the whole arrangement in due course. Thenceforth there must be no innovation in anything which has to do either with dance or with song. No, our citizens and their city must preserve their identity by a uniform life of unvarying pleasures, where all are as utterly alike as may be in all happiness and bliss.

This concludes our treatment of the employment of comely body and noble mind in choric performances such as we have said these displays should be. As for the play of uncomely body and mind and the artistes of ludicrous burlesque in diction, song, dance, and all the caricaturistic effects of the three, we cannot avoid taking notice of this and passing it under review; a man who means to form his judgment can no more understand earnest apart from burlesque than any other contrary apart from its contrary; but, on the other side, a man who means to have any part in goodness, were it never so little, cannot possibly produce both; the very reason why he must get to know such a thing is that he may never be betrayed by ignorance into doing or saying a ludicrous thing when it is out of place. We shall enjoin that such representations be left to slaves or hired aliens, and that they receive no serious consideration whatsoever; no free person, whether woman or man, shall be found taking lessons in them, and there must always be some

[1] i.e. the Minister of Education. It will be left to him to work out all details.

novelty in a performance of the kind.[1] The sportive entertainment to which the name *comedy* is universally given may be 817
taken as dipsosed of on these lines by our law with its accompanying explanation. For our tragic poets and their so-called serious
compositions, we may conceive some of them to approach us with
a question couched in these words or the like: 'May we pay your
city and its territory a visit, sirs, or may we not? And may
we bring our poetry along with us, or what decision have you
reached on the point?' What would be the right answer to
give to such men of genius? Why this, I believe: 'Respected
visitors, we are ourselves authors of a tragedy, and that the
finest and best we know how to make. In fact,[2] our whole
polity has been constructed as a dramatization of a noble and
perfect life; that is what *we* hold to be in truth the most real of
tragedies. Thus you are poets, and we also are poets in the
same style, rival artists and rival actors, and that in the finest
of all dramas, one which indeed can be produced only by a code
of true law—or at least that is our faith. So you must not
expect that we shall light-heartedly permit you to pitch your
booths in our market-square with a troupe of actors whose
melodious voices will drown our own, and let you deliver your
public tirades before our boys and women and the populace
at large—let you address them on the same issues as ourselves,
not to the same effect, but commonly and for the most part to
the very contrary. Why, we should be stark mad to do so, and
so would the whole community, if you could find one which
would let you do as you are now proposing, until its magistrates
had decided whether your compositions are fit to be uttered and
edifying to be heard by the public or not. Go to, then, ye scions
of the softer Muses; first exhibit your minstrelsy to the magistrates for comparison with our own; then, if your sentiments
prove to be the same as ours, or even better, we will grant you
a chorus, but if not, I fear, my friends, we never can.'

Such, then—subject to your approval—shall be our legislation,
and such our conjoined practice in the whole matter of the choric
art and the instruction in it—slaves and their masters to receive
separate treatment.

Clin. Well, of course, we approve—at any rate, for the
moment.

----

[1] i.e. no such piece is to have a 'long run', for fear familiarity might
'give it a hold' on the public taste (England). The linguistically possible
rendering 'and a performance of this kind must always be felt to be the something unusual' does not suit the context so well.
[2] Accepting Bywater's necessary γοῦν for οὖν at 817 *b* 3.

Ath. Then there are, of course, three subjects for the free-born still to study. Ciphering and arithmetic make one subject; mensuration, linear, superficial, and solid, taken as one single study, forms a second; the third is the true relations of
818 the planetary orbits to one another.[1] The elaborate prosecution of all these studies into their minute details is not for the masses but for a select few—who these should be shall be indicated later [2] as our argument draws to its conclusion, where the indication will be in place—for the multitude it will be proper to learn so much of the matter as is indispensable, and as it may truly be said to be a disgrace to the common man not to know, though it would be hard, or actually impossible, to pursue the research into minute detail.[3] We simply cannot dispense with its character of *necessity*; [4] in fact, it is this which the author of the proverb [5] presumably had in view when he said that 'even God is never to be seen contending against necessity. 'No doubt he meant the necessity which is *divine*, for if you understand the words of mere human necessities, like those to which men in general apply such sayings, they are far and away the silliest of speeches.[6]

Clin. Yes, sir, but where in these studies do the other sort of necessities, the divine, come in?

[1] Cf. *Tim.* 39 *c–e* on the general ignorance of mankind on this subject.

[2] The reference is apparently to the closing pages of Book XII (961 *c* ff.) which deal with the composition of the 'Nocturnal Council,' whose members are required to have advanced mathematical knowledge.

[3] The translation follows Burnet's punctuation. A very possible alternative rendering is that of Ritter who places a comma after λέγεται (818 *a* 5), 'for the common folk it is a disgrace that the multitude should not know so much of the matter as is in a certain sense very properly called indispensable.'

[4] There is an intentional shift here from the sense of the word ἀναγκαῖα 'indispensable', 'that without which men cannot make shift to get on,' to the sense, '*necessarily* true'. The 'necessary truth' of a mathematical conclusion is what Plato means here by a divine 'necessity' as contrasted with the merely human 'necessity' of means *indispensable* to the attaining of some end (which perhaps *ought* never to be attained at all).

[5] The reference is to the words of Simonides in the poem quoted in the *Protogoras* (345 *d*) ἀνάγκη δ' οὐδὲ θεοὶ μάχονται, 'not even gods contend against necessity'. Presumably Simonides is quoting an already existing popular 'saw', and 'the author of the proverb' means the unknown originator of the saying.

[6] A direct allusion to the poem of Simonides. From the quotations in the *Protogoras* it is plain that Simonides is there excusing some one on whose reputation there was the stain of some shocking act by 'the tyrant's plea, necessity'. Plato's comment is in the spirit of the retort to the offender who urges that *il faut vivre*, 'Mais Monsieur, je n'en vois pas la nécessité'.

Ath. Why, I presume they are those in neglect[1] or sheer ignorance of which no being could possibly play the part of a god or superior spirit towards us, nor yet of a hero capable of serious supervision of humanity. How far would he be below the level of even inspired humanity who could not tell three from two, or even odd from even, in fact, could not so much as count, or could not even tell off night and day, or had no acquaintance with the orbits of moon, sun, and the rest of the planets! So the mere thought that all this information is not indispensable to any one who means to *know* anything whatsoever of the noblest of all sciences is the idlest folly. What branches of them are to be studied, to what extent, and at what times, which must be taken in conjunction with another and which pursued by itself, and how they are all to be blended into a whole—these are the questions which we must first settle correctly; we may then proceed under the guidance of these sciences to the study of all the rest. It is the natural order, and it has that necessity with which, as we say, no god contends or ever will contend.

Clin. Yes, sir, the views you have just expressed sound true and natural, as you expound them.

Ath. Indeed, they are so, Clinias, though it is difficult to legislate on the subject by anticipation as we are now doing. The more precise details of legislation, with your consent, we may postpone to another occasion.

Clin. You are apprehensive, I take it, sir, of the common unfamiliarity of our countrymen with such topics, but your concern is unwarranted; pray do your best to state your views without any reservation on that score.

Ath. I certainly feel the apprehension you speak of, but am 819 still more alarmed by students who have actually taken up these sciences, but taken them up in the wrong way. Complete unacquaintance with a subject is never a dangerous or formidable obstacle, nor is it the worst of evils; much graver harm is done by wide acquaintance with a subject and extensive learning in it, when they are conjoined with bad training.

Clin. Truly observed.

[1] ἃς μή τις πράξας μηδὲ αὖ μαθὼν (818 *b* 9). The expression πράττειν ἀνάγκας is singular, and it is hard to be sure of its precise meaning, except that the antithesis with μαθὼν seems to show that the general sense is 'acting upon'. Ritter, who has a long and valuable note on 'divine necessity,' proposes to take the word to mean 'creating'. The general sense is plainly that the necessity of mathematical truth has its source in the nature of God himself. Cf. the later story which attributes to Plato the saying, ἀεὶ ὁ θεὸς γεωμετρεῖ, 'God is always at his geometry'.

Ath. Well then, I maintain that free-born men should learn of these various subjects as much as in Egypt is taught to vast numbers of children along with their letters. To begin with, lessons have been devised there in ciphering for the veriest children which they can learn with a good deal of fun and amusement, problems about the distribution of a fixed total number of apples or garlands among larger and smaller groups, and the arranging of a successive series of 'byes' and 'pairs' between boxers and wrestlers as the nature of such contests requires. More than this, the teachers have a game in which they distribute mixed sets of saucers of gold, silver, copper, and similar materials or, in other cases, whole sets of one material; in this way, they, as I was saying, incorporate the elementary application of arithmetic in the children's play, give the pupils a useful preparation for the dispositions, formations, and movements of military life as well as for domestic management, and make them more alert and more serviceable to themselves in every way. Then they go on to exercises in measurements of length, surface, cubical content, by which they dispel the native and general, but ludicrous and shameful, ignorance of mankind about the whole subject.

Clin. And in what may this native ignorance consist?

Ath. My dear Clinias, when I was told, rather belatedly, of our condition in this matter, like you, I was utterly astounded; such ignorance seemed to me more worthy of a stupid beast like the hog than of a human being, and I blushed not for myself alone, but for our whole Hellenic world.[1]

Clin. But what was the reason for your blushes? Let us have your account of it, sir.

Ath. Why, so I will. Or rather I will make it plain by a question. Pray tell me one little thing; you know what is meant by *line*?

Clin. Of course I do.

Ath. And by *surface*?

Clin. Certainly.

---

[1] The words are usually understood as meaning that Plato himself had only realized the existence of 'incommensurables' late in life, or comparatively late. To me this is incredible. 'Incommensurables' are frequently mentioned in the Platonic dialogues from the *Hippias Major*— a certainly very early dialogue—onward. The thing which Plato only 'heard of' late in life may be not the existence of incommensurables, but the wide prevalence of the error of denying their existence. 'I only learned lately what the universal delusion among Hellenics is, and I was amazed to learn of it.' This might well be a discovery which Plato would only make after a long experience as a teacher.

Ath. And you know that they are two distinct things, and that *volume* is another and a third?

Clin. Just so.

Ath. Now you hold, do you not, that all three are commensurable with one another?

Clin. Yes.

Ath. That is, that *line* is in its very nature measurable by line, *surface* by surface, and similarly with *volume*?   820

Clin. Most assuredly.

Ath. But suppose this cannot be said of some of them, neither with more assurance nor with less, but is true in some cases, but not in others, and you believe it true universally; what do you think of your state of mind on the matter?

Clin. That it is unsatisfactory, to be sure.

Ath. And what of the relations of line and surface to volume, or of line and surface to one another?[1] Is it not the fact that we Hellenes all imagine they are commensurable in some way or other?

Clin. Why certainly that is the fact.

Ath. Then if this is another entire impossibility, though we Hellenes, as I said, all fancy it possible, are we not bound to blush for them all as we tell them: 'Worthy Hellenes, here is one of the things of which we said that ignorance is a disgrace and knowledge on a point so necessary, no great accomplishment'?

Clin. We are, indeed.

Ath. There are, besides, other closely related points which frequently give rise to errors akin to those just mentioned.

Clin. Such for example as—?

Ath. The real relation of commensurability and incommensurability to one another.[2] A man must be able to distinguish them on examination, or else must be a very poor

---

[1] The meaning can hardly be that the Greeks commonly imagine that area or cubic capacity can be stated in linear measures. Most probably the mistake meant is to assume that the areas of figures whose sides, or the volume of figures whose edges are commensurable, must themselves be commensurable, and again that if the volumes and the areas are commensurable, the edges or sides of the figures must be commensurable also.

[2] That is, behind the more special problems of the commensurability of specific areas and volumes there lies the problem of constructing a general 'theory of incommensurables.' The *Epinomis* tells us a little more on this point (990 *b*–991 *b*). The common view, even among mathematicians, was that though in geometry there are incommensurable magnitudes, there are no incommensurable numbers, *all* numbers are, as we should say, 'rational'. Against this view, the *Epinomis* insists that the studies popularly called geometry and stereometry are really concerned with *numbers* which, though not themselves commensurable, have commensurable second or third powers.

creature. We should frequently propound such problems to each other—a much more elegant pastime for the elderly than draughts—and give our passion for victory an outlet in amusements worthy of us.

Clin. I dare say, after all, the game of draughts and these studies are not so widely different.

Ath. Accordingly, Clinias, I hold that these are subjects which our young people must learn. Indeed there is neither danger nor difficulty in them, and if they are learned through the medium of play, they will do our city no harm, but rather good.

Clin. Just so.

Ath. Still, while we must clearly include them in our scheme, if our case for this proves to be made out, equally clearly we shall reject them if it is not made out.

Clin. Oh, plainly, plainly.

Ath. Well then, for the present, sir, let them be set down among the requisite studies, to leave no gap in the body of our laws, but set down as detachable from the rest of our polity—like so many redeemable pledges—should they prove unacceptable to us who have deposited them, or you who have received them.

Clin. The terms of proposal are fair enough.

Ath. Next you must consider astronomy; are we to adopt the recommendation that our young folk should study it, or are we not?

Clin. Well, say on.

Ath. Now here, mark you, I find a strange, indeed, a wholly intolerable paradox.

821 *Clin.* And of what kind?

Ath. It is currently said that it is wrong—indeed, positively blasphemous—to prosecute inquiry or busy ourselves with the quest for explanation where the supreme God and the universe as a whole are concerned—though the very opposite should seem to be our right course.

Clin. What!

Ath. What I am trying to say, I know, is startling, and might be thought unbecoming in a man of our years; but the plain truth is that a man who knows of a study which he believes sublime, true, beneficial to society, and perfectly acceptable to God, simply cannot refrain from calling attention to it.

Clin. Presumably not; but what astronomical study shall we find answering to this description?

Ath. Why, my friends, at this moment, all our Hellenic world, as I may fairly say, habitually charges high gods, Sun and Moon, falsely.

Clin. And what may this false charge be?

Ath. We say that they, and certain heavenly bodies associated with them, never keep to the same path, which is why we call them 'planets'.[1]

Clin. Egad, sir, and that is true enough. Why, in my own life-time I myself have often seen the morning and evening stars and some others never keeping to the same track, but divagating in all directions; as for sun and moon, of course, I have seen them behave as we all know they regularly do behave.[2]

Ath. Well then, Megillus and Clinias, that is just the reason why I am now insisting that *our* citizens and their young people must learn enough of all the facts about the divinities of the sky to prevent blasphemy of them, and to ensure a reverent piety in the language of all our sacrifices and prayers.

Clin. That is right, provided, of course, that, in the first place, the knowledge of which you speak is possible; on that assumption, if there are errors in our present language on such matters which study will correct, I, too, confess that a subject of such scope and quality must be taught. Do your best, then, with the demonstration that the facts are as you say, as we will do our best to follow your instruction.

Ath. Why, the lesson I have in mind, to be sure, is not an easy one—and yet it is not so hopelessly difficult either, and takes no very great time to learn, as this one fact is enough to prove; I was not a young man when I heard of the truth myself, and it was no long time ago, and yet I may possibly make it clear to both of you now at no great expense of time. Were the point a really hard one, a man of my age would never be able to explain it to men of yours.

Clin. Quite true. But pray what may this knowledge be—this doctrine, as you maintain, so surprising, yet so proper for 822

---

[1] A playful allusion to the literal meaning of the word, *stellae errabundae*, '*tramps* of the sky', a name given to the sun and his satellites because, by contrast with the 'fixed' stars, they seem to have no permanent 'domicile'. The apparent lawlessness of their movements explains why the pre-Platonic men of science took no interest in these bodies.

[2] The irregularities meant are: (1) that the sun, moon, and planets have no fixed position relative to the other heavenly bodies, but go the round of the Zodiac; (2) that what we call the true planets do not even keep steadily on their path through the Zodiac, but appear from time to time to stand still, go back in their tracks, or make excursions north and south in latitude; (3) that the sun's 'tropics' and 'soltices' do not divide the year equally; the seasons are of unequal length.

the young to learn, and so unsuspected by us? You must try
to explain so much of the subject with all possible clarity.

Ath. I will do my best. The fact is, my friends, that the
belief that sun, moon, and other heavenly bodies are 'wandering
stars' of any sort is not true; the very reverse is the truth—
each of these bodies always revolves in the same orbit and in
one orbit, not many, for all that it looks to be moving in several;[1]

[1] Unfortunately in this important astronomical pronouncement, Plato,
as he says, is merely giving a summary indication of his views without
the necessary explanations. Consequently, interpreters have differed
greatly about his meaning. The astronomers Schiaparelli and Wolf,
of whose views Ritter gives an excellent account in his note on the
passage, actually find in it a complete anticipation of the heliocentric
astronomy taught in the third century B.C. by Aristarchus of Samos,
and revived eighteen hundred years later by Copernicus, and in Burnet's
posthumous Sather lectures on *Platonism* the same interpretation is
repeated. Others have seen no more in the passage than a mere assertion
that the orbit of a planet is *uniform*, and have supposed Plato to be here
enunciating as a recent important discovery the theory that this orbit is
compounded of two circular movements, one from east to west with a
period of twenty-four hours, common to all the heavenly bodies, in the
plane of the sidereal equator, and another, with a period special to each
planet, in the plane of the ecliptic from west to east. (So Burnet at one
time in the second edition of his *Early Greek Philosophy*.) To me both
these views seem inconsistent with the plain words of the text. Plato
cannot be meaning to teach the 'double motion' view just mentioned, for
two reasons: (1) he distinctly implies that his present doctrine is a
recent novelty, whereas the theory of the 'double motion' is taken
for granted throughout the myth of Er in *Republic* X—a work long
anterior to the *Laws*—as a matter of course; (2) the emphasis laid
in our passage on the point that in spite of all appearances, each planet
has only *one* motion is only intelligible if we suppose that the 'double
motion' is the very thing Plato intends now to deny (as Burnet admitted
in the third edition of *Early Greek Philosophy*, p. 110 *b* 2). On the other
hand, it should be plain that there is no intention of teaching a *heliocentric*
theory. The sun is still mentioned as one of the 'planets' whose movements we have to explain by the theory—whatever it is—which Plato has
in his mind. I can therefore see only one interpretation of our passage
which does justice to all the facts. It clearly means to assert that each
'planet' moves in one uniform closed curve, all appearances of 'anomalies'
notwithstanding. To make this view possible at all, clearly what we need
to do is to eliminate the apparent *diurnal* motion of the 'planet' as only
apparent, leaving it only its 'year'. This means transferring the apparent
diurnal motion to the earth, and this, I believe, is what Plato is hinting
at here. The thought is that the 'irregularities' in the observed movements of the 'planets' are really due to the fact that we make our observations from a moving earth. I take it, then, that Plato's final view, as
hinted at in the *Laws*, is like that ascribed by the doxographers (probably
wrongly) to the Pythagorean Philolaus. Earth, true planets, sun, are all
thought of as revolving—in the case of the innermost of all, the earth,
with a period of twenty-four hours—round a centre invisible to ourselves.
This fits in both with the indications of the *Epinomis*, and with the well-
known testimony of Theophrastus, reproduced by Plutarch (*Quaestiones
Platonicae*, VIII, 1006 *c*), that 'Plato in his later years repented of having
placed the earth in the centre of the universe, a place not proper for it',
without adding anything which the statement of Theophrastus does not

and again the actually swiftest of them is wrongly believed to be the slowest and the slowest the swiftest.[1] Well now, suppose these are the real facts, but we hold a discrepant view about them: if we had fancies of this kind about the competing horses or long-distance runners at Olympia, and so were to call the quickest runner slowest and the slowest quickest, and to compose triumphal odes in which we celebrated the vanquished as victor, why, I conceive our bestowal of our praises would neither be correct nor to the liking of the runners, who, after all, are but men. But when we actually make the same mistake to-day about our deities, must we not think that an error which was risible in the other case and on the race course, is now, when transferred to this context, no laughing matter, and no very godly opinion either, since it means reiterated mendacity about divine beings?

Clin. Nothing can be truer—if the facts are really as you say.

Ath. Then, if we can show that they are so, all these matters must be studied—within the limits we have proposed; if not, we must let them alone. May we take it that our agreement extends so far?

Clin. With all my heart.

Ath. Then we may say that our regulations for the studies to be included in our education are now complete. As to the *chase*, we should recur to the thought which has guided us in other cases of the same kind. It should seem that a legislator's task extends to something more than the mere imposing of a law and so dismissing a topic; there is something else he must do besides laying down the law, something which verges at once on admonition and on legislation, as our argument has led us to remark more than once already. A case in point is our treatment of the regimen of infants; as we say, we must not leave our

warrant. For a fuller discussion I would refer the reader to both Ritter's excursus on our present passage, and to my own treatment of the question in my *Commentary on Plato's Timaeus*, pp. 226–39.

[1] If the 'diurnal revolution' is discounted as only apparent, each planet will have only one motion, its 'proper motion' through the signs of the Zodiac. As the moon completes this in a month, while Saturn takes some thirty years to do the same thing, we shall say that the moon gets over the ground quickest, Saturn slowest. But if we regard the diurnal motion as a real motion of the heavenly bodies, it becomes *possible* to take the opposite view. We *may* think of the 'planets'—as Anximander must have done—as really revolving in the same sense with the 'outermost heaven', from east to west, but being 'left behind' in the race. On that view the moon, which is 'left behind' roughly twelve degrees a day, will be the slowest of them, Saturn, which falls behind only about one degree a month, the quickest. This is the confusion of which Plato is speaking. Cf. *Tim.* 39 *a* where we are told in the same way that the planets which appear to be 'caught up' by others are really the catchers.

demands unformulated, and yet when we formulate them it is perfect folly to imagine we are laying them down as law. So when the legal code, and the whole system of the constitution has been reduced to written form, it is not a final encomium on the pre-eminently virtuous citizen to say that he is the good citizen who has shown himself the best servant of the laws and gives them the fullest obedience; there would be more finality in the statement that he is the best who has spent his life without qualification in obedience to all the legislator has written, 823 whether by way of enactment, of approbation, or of reprobation. This is the truest eulogy which can be bestowed on a citizen, and a real legislator should not confine himself to the composition of statutes; he should further entwine with the text of his laws an exposition of all he accounts laudable or the reverse, and the citizen of eminent goodness must feel himself no less bound by such directions than by those enforced with a legal sanction. We may make our meaning plainer if we call the subject of our present remarks, so to say, in evidence. The chase, in fact, is a pursuit with very various departments, all currently comprehended under that single name. There are many ways of taking the denizens of the water, and again of fowling, and especially there are numerous devices for the capture of land-animals; I mean not of brutes merely, but of the noteworthy hunting of men to be seen in warfare, as well as in the various forms under which that quarry is pursued in the way of kindness, some laudable and others the reverse; the kidnappings of brigands and forces in the field are also forms of the chase. Now the legislator framing his statutes of venery can neither omit to explain this, nor yet can he impose a set of legal regulations with directions for all cases and threatened penalties for their breach. What course is he, then, to take in such a case? He must—I mean the legislator must—commend some forms of the chase and condemn others, always with an eye on the exercises and sports of the younger men; the younger man, in his turn, must obey this advice; neither hope of pleasure nor dread of hardship must interfere with his obedience, and he must treat the legislator's various commendations with still deeper respect and more dutiful compliance than his penalty-sanctioned ordinances.

These preliminary remarks may naturally be succeeded by judicious commendation and reprobation of divers forms of the chase, commendation of such as tend to improve the young man's soul, reprobation of those which have the contrary tendency. So we will now, without more delay, direct our address to the young people, couching it in the language of pious wish: 'Our prayer, beloved, is that you may never be smitten with the lust or passion for sea-fishery, for angling or any taking of the creatures of the waters, or for the use of weels, by which the slothful hunter's work is done for him equally whether he wakes or sleeps. May you never be visited by hankerings for the pirate's trade—the chasing of men on the high seas—to make you cruel and lawless hunters! As for petty poaching in town or country, may the bare thought never so much as enter your minds! And may no young soul be haunted by the seductive itch for fowling—hardly a taste for the free-born man! Thus we have left our athletes only the 824 chase and taking of land-creatures; one form of this again, that practised by parties who take it in turns to sleep—night-trapping, as it is called—is for sluggards and deserves no commendation; the intervals of inaction fill as much time as the exercise, and the strength and violence of the quarry is overpowered not by the triumph of an energetic soul, but by nets and snares. Thus the only variety left free to all, and the best variety, is the chase of a four-footed quarry in reliance upon one's horse, one's dogs, and one's own limbs, where the hunters—those, that is, who cultivate godlike courage—all hunt in their own persons and achieve all their success by running, striking, and shooting'.

The discourse we have just rehearsed may serve the end of general commendation and censure in the matter; the actual law may run to this effect: Such hunters are truly 'sacred', and none shall hinder them from following the game with their hounds when and as they please; the night-trapper who trusts to his nets and springes no one shall permit to pursue his game at any time or place; the fowler is not to be disturbed on un-cultivated ground or in the mountains, but shall be turned off tilled fields or untilled consecrated demesnes by any who may find him there: the fisherman shall be free to take his fish anywhere save in harbours and consecrated rivers, marshes, or lakes, with the sole proviso that he may not foul the waters with stupefying juices.[1]

And with this we may say our regulation of education is at last completed.

Clin. And well completed, too.

---

[1] i.e. the poisoning of the fish by preparations which paralyse them and so cause them to rise to the top is prohibited.

BOOK VIII

828   *Ath.* The next task awaiting us is, with the help of oracles from Delphi, to construct the calendar of festivals and give it the authority of law—to determine what sacrifices it will be 'to the welfare and profit' of the State to celebrate, and to what deities they should be offered.   The question of their dates and their number will be—to some extent—one for our own decision.

Clin. That of their number will no doubt be so.

Ath. Then let me deal with the question of number first. This shall be not less than three hundred and sixty-five,[1] to ensure that sacrifice shall be done by at least one magistracy to some god or spirit on behalf of the State, its members, and their chattels without any interruption.   Canonists,[2] priests of both sexes, and prophets are to meet in committee with the Curators of Law and prescribe any details which the legislator has unavoidably omitted; the same committee shall further decide how the omissions aforesaid are to be supplied.   The provision of the actual law will be, in fact, that there shall be twelve festivals of the twelve gods after whom the different tribes are named, to be kept by the doing of monthly sacrifice to each of these deities, with the adjuncts of such choirs and contests, both musical and athletic, as are suitable to the character of the deity and the season of the festival, and the demarcation of celebrations for women from which men must be excluded from those in which this regulation is not necessary. Further, there must be no confusion between the cults of the gods of the underworld with their accessories and those of the celestial powers, as we should call them; the law will keep the two distinct, and put the former in the month sacred to Pluto, the twelfth of the year; true warriors must cherish no repugnancy for such a deity of Death, but venerate him as the constant benefactor of mankind, for union of soul with body, as I would assure you in all earnest, is in no way better than dissolution. Furthermore, an authority which is to make these arrangements

---

[1] See *supra* 771 *d* ff.   It is an important point that Plato's official civil year is to be one of 365 days—a true, solar year.

[2] ἐξηγηταί, official exponents of the *religious* law.

to our satisfaction must be possessed with the convictions that the like of this society of ours is not to be found in the world for ample leisure and abundant provision of all necessaries, that its business, like that of an individual man, is to live well, 829 and that the indispensable precondition of a happy life is that we commit no sin against ourselves and suffer no wrongs from others. Now there is no great difficulty about the first condition, but grave difficulty in compassing a power to protect oneself from *suffering* wrongs; 'tis, indeed, only to be fully got in one way, by becoming fully good. Now the case will be the same with a society; if it become good, its life will be one of peace, if evil, of warfare without and within. And since this is so, its members must train themselves for warfare, not in actual time of war, but during the life of peace. Hence the wise State will be under arms not less than one day in each month, and as many more as its magistrates may think good, without regard to stress of weather, cold or hot; men, women, children, will take the field, in one body when the magistrates so ordain, at other times in sections. They must also devise a round of noble sports, with their accompanying sacrifices, so as to provide festal combats which shall reproduce real warfare with all possible truth to life. On these occasions there should always be a distribution of prizes and rewards for merit, and the citizens should compose panegyrics and censures upon one another according to a man's performance in these contests and in life at large, the honour of the panegyric going to him who proves himself of perfect worth, and the censure to him who fails. The composition of such verses shall not be for every one; the author must, in the first place, have reached the age of not less than fifty; moreover he must not be one of those who have within them a sufficient vein of literature and music but have never achieved one noble and illustrious deed. But the verse of composers who are in their own persons men of worth, held in public honour as authors of noble deeds, may be sung, even though it have no real musical quality. The selection of composers shall be in the hands of the Minister of Education, and his colleagues the Curators of Law, who are to allow them this special privilege: their music, and theirs only, shall be free and uncensored, whereas this liberty shall be granted to no one else, and no other citizen shall presume, without the Curator's licence, to sing an unauthorized air, were its notes more ravishing than those of Thamyras or Orpheus themselves, but only such verse as has been duly consecrated to the gods and such compositions

by men of true worth as have been pronounced to convey
laudation or reproof with due propriety. These directions as
to manœuvres and freedom to compose uncensored verse are
to be taken as applying equally to both sexes; the legislator
must put the case to himself thus in his meditations: Go to,
now; what manner of men am I training by the whole scheme of
830 my institutions? Are they not men who are to be competitors
in the most momentous of all contests, where they will find
countless opponents pitted against them? 'Why, certainly',
will be the ready and the right answer. Well then, suppose our
training were meant for boxers, or pugilists,[1] or athletes in some
similar competition, should we be for going straight into the
actual contest without any previous daily combat with an
opponent? Surely, were we boxers, for days together before
the actual event we should be learning how to fight and working
ourselves hard; we should rehearse all the movements we
expected to make in the actual match, when the time for it
should come, and we should come as near as we could to the
reality; we should fit our hands with practice-gloves in place of
match-gloves,[2] to make sure that we were getting the best
training we could; if we were exceptionally put to it to find
partners to practise with, would fear of the laughter of fools
frighten us from hanging up an inanimate dummy to practise
on? If we were actually without any opponent living or lifeless,
and had no partners whatsoever, should we not have gone the
length of quite literally sparring 'at our own shadows'? What
other name could you give to the training in 'using one's
morleys'?

Clin. Why, sir, I can think of none but the name you have
just employed.

Ath. Very well, then. And is the fighting force of our society
to be worse prepared than such combatants as these when it
ventures itself, as the occasion arises, in the gravest of all
contests, in which the stake is the very existence of self, children,
possessions, nay, of the whole community? Is this precious
fear that our practice on one another may provoke some laughter

---

[1] παγκρατιαστὰς (830 *a* 3) has no precise English equivalent. The
pancratium was a rough and dangerous combination of boxing with
wrestling.

[2] ἀντὶ ἱμάντων σφαίρας ἂν περιεδούμεθα (830 *b* 3-4), 'should have
balls round our wrists instead of *himantes*'. The *himantes* were leather
thongs used in the actual boxing-match to make the blows more severe
(the Roman *cæstus*). The 'balls' will be a lighter leather substitute.
The object (England) is to make sure that the boxer's training will accustom
him to give and take real 'punishment'.

to keep the legislator from his work? Should he not require
drill on the small scale, not involving the use of heavy arms, to
be performed, if possible, daily, directing all physical training,
whether in combined groups or otherwise, to that end, and
exercises of another kind, major and minor, to be held at least
once a month, in which the citizens throughout our territories
will contend with one another in the occupation of military
positions and the laying of ambushes, and imitate all branches
of warfare by very real fighting with gloves and missiles closely
modelled on the genuine articles? These weapons should be
comparatively dangerous, that the sport may not be wholly
without its perils, but give occasion for alarms, and thus serve,
in its way, to discriminate a man of courage from a coward.
Thus it will enable the legislator to train the whole community
to lifelong efficient service in the real conflict, by a right
apportionment of marks of distinction and discredit, and if a 831
life should happen to be lost in this fashion, the homicide will
be regarded as involuntary, and its author pronounced clear
of the innocent blood, when he has undergone ritual cleansing
as the law directs. The legislator's view will be that if a few
men come to their end, others as good will be born to take their
place, whereas, if fear of dangers comes to its end, if I may so
express myself, he can find no touchstone of better and worse
in situations of the kind, and this is a much graver misfortune
for his society than the other.

Clin. My friend and I, sir, agree with you that this is what
the law should enjoin and the whole community practise.

Ath. Now I wonder whether all of us understand the reason
why such contests between opposing teams are nowhere to be
found in our existing societies, except perhaps on the smallest
scale. Should we lay the blame on the ignorance of the
generality of mankind and their legislators?

Clin. Very likely we should.

Ath. My dear Clinias! Not in the least! The true causes
are two, both very powerful.

Clin. And what are they?

Ath. One arises from the passion for wealth which leaves a
man not a moment of leisure to attend to anything beyond his
personal fortunes. So long as a citizen's whole soul is wrapped
up in these, he cannot give a thought to anything but the
day's takings; any study or pursuit which tends to that result
every one sets himself eagerly to learn and practise; all others
are laughed to scorn. Here, then, we may say, is one reason

in particular why society declines to take this or any other
wholly admirable pursuit seriously, though every one in it is
ready enough, in his furious thirst for gold and silver, to stoop
to any trade and any shift, honourable or dishonourable, which
holds out a prospect of wealth, ready to scruple at no act whatsoever—innocent, sinful, or utterly shameful—so long as it
promises to sate him—like some brute beast—with a perfect
glut of eating, drinking, and sexual sport.

Clin. Too true.

Ath. Well then, this, as I say, may be set down for one reason
which tends to keep societies from efficient cultivation of noble
activities, military and otherwise; it turns the naturally quiet
and decent man into a tradesman, skipper, or mere menial, and
832 makes the more adventurous pirates, burglars, temple-thieves,
swashbucklers, and bullies, though often enough they are not
so much vicious as unfortunate.

Clin. Unfortunate; why so?

Ath. Why, what epithet but 'most unfortunate' can I find
for men who are forced to go through the world with an incessant
hunger gnawing at their own souls?

Clin. Well, that is one of your causes, sir; but what do you
mean by the other?

Ath. Thank you for the reminder.

Clin. One cause, as I understand you, is this life-long insatiate
quest which leaves none of us an hour's leisure, and so keeps
us all from practising the arts of war as we should.   Good; but
let us hear something of the other reason.

Ath. I fancy you think my reason for being so slow to name it
is that I cannot.

Clin. Not so; but what one must call your abhorrence of the
character just described is leading you, as we think, into an
invective irrelevant to our present argument.

Ath. I stand properly rebuked, gentlemen. You wish me,
it appears, to proceed.

Clin. You have only to do so.

Ath. Then I say the reason is to be found in those 'no-con-
stitutions'[1] we have so often touched on already, democracy,
oligarchy, autocracy. Not one of them is a true constitution;
the proper name for all would rather be 'party ascendancies'.

---

[1] See 712 *e*, 713 *e*, and especially 715 *b* where it was said that the subjects
of these 'governments by a party' should properly be called not πολῖται,
but στασιῶται. στασιωτεία is, of course, a word coined for the nonce as an
antithesis to πολιτεία, almost as we might say 'not *con*stitutions, but
dis-stitutions'.

In none do we find a willing sovereign with willing subjects; in all a willing sovereign is controlling reluctant subjects by violence of some sort. But a sovereign who goes in fear of his subject will never, if he can help it, permit that subject to become noble, wealthy, powerful, valiant, nor so much as a good fighting-man. Here, then, we have the main sources of almost all mischief—certainly the main sources of the mischief we are treating of now. Both are avoided in the constitution we are now engaged in framing.[1] It provides more ample leisure than any other, its citizens are free from one another's dictation, our laws, I take it, are very unlikely to make them greedy of riches; hence it is but natural and reasonable to believe that a society so constituted, and only such a society of all others, would have a place for the warrior's education described above, which is also his sport, as duly set forth in our discussion.

Clin. Quite true.

Ath. Then I suppose we may next make a general observation about all athletic contests; those which provide a training for war should be encouraged and prizes instituted for success in them; those which do not may be dismissed. Which these are it will be better to make matter for explicit statement and legislation from the very first. To begin with, I apprehend there should be such institution of prizes for fleetness of foot and rapidity of movement in general?

Clin. There should.

Ath. To be sure, bodily agility—quickness of hand as well as of foot—is a first-rate point in the soldier's equipment; fleetness of foot has its use in flight and pursuit, and readiness 833 of hand in the close stand-up fighting which calls for so much stocky strength.

Clin. Of course.

Ath. And again, neither yields its best service without the aid of weapons.

Clin. Naturally not.

Ath. So our herald will follow the existing custom and announce the furlong race as the first event of our sports; the competitor shall make his entry in full armour, we shall give no prize for an unarmed competitor. No, the order of entry

---

[1] In 832 *c* 9 – *d* 1 I translate the MSS. (and vulgate) text, πολιτείας, ἣν νομοθετούμενοι λέγομεν. But probably we should read, with Badham, ἣν νομοθετοῦμεν <ἃ> λέγομεν, 'the city-constitution we are imposing has avoided both the evils of which we are speaking'.

will be *first* the runner for the furlong, in full equipment, *second* for the two furlongs, *third* for the 'chariot-course', *fourth* for the 'long distance', *fifth* there will be an entrant whom we shall call the 'hoplite', and set in the first place to run, in full armour of heavy weight, over a smooth course of sixty furlongs, to a temple of Ares and back, and his rival, an archer in complete archer's equipment, who must run against him over a course of a hundred furlongs, through hilly and varied ground, to a temple of Apollo and Artemis. In arranging the events, we shall wait for their return, and prizes will be given to the victors in each event.

Clin. A good arrangement.

Ath. Now let us make three classes in these athletic events, one for boys, one for lads, and one for men. We will fix the length of the course for lads at two-thirds, and that for boys at one-half the length of the full course, whether they enter as 'hoplites' or as 'archers'. In the case of females, we shall have races of one and two furlongs, a 'chariot-course', and a long-distance event, in which girls below the age of puberty must actually compete stripped, while girls who have passed thirteen and are still awaiting marriage—to ensue at latest at twenty and at earliest at eighteen—must be clad in the proper accoutrement when they enter into these competitions. So much then for races for both males and females. As for competitions of strength, in place of wrestling and the like, the 'heavy events' of current practice, we shall institute fights in armour, single combats, or combats between pairs, or contests between any number of combatants up to ten a side. In determining what points will disqualify for victory or count towards it, we shall follow the precedent set by existing authorities on wrestling in their rules for the proper conduct of that sport: we shall, in like manner call in experts in fencing under arms and invite their help in regulating the faults which must be avoided, and hits which must be scored, to qualify for a victory in these 834 contests, and the code which shall determine defeat. The same regulations shall equally apply to females under the age of marriage. For the element of boxing in the *pancratium* we shall substitute a general combat of peltasts in which the contest will be waged with bow and arrow and light target, darts, stones thrown by the hand, and slings, and in this case too we shall have to draw up the rules and award the prizes of victory to those who best fulfil the demands of our regulations. We should naturally proceed now to make rules for the horse-

race. But in a district like Crete there will be no great use for
horses and few horses to use; hence there will, of course, be less
interest in breeding them and matching them against one another.
As for chariots, to be sure, there will be no one to keep them,[1]
and probably no one to cherish any particular aspirations in
that direction; hence if we instituted anything so contrary to
native custom as a chariot-race,[2] we should look like the fools
we should in fact be. But if we offer prizes for races with
ridden horses—young and half-grown colts as well as full-
grown beasts—we shall be cultivating a form of the sport well
in keeping with the nature of our territory. So the law will
provide for competitive matches between these classes of
sportsmen and no others, and appoint the phylarchs and hipparchs as public judges both of the course and of the competitors
entering—who must be in their armour; here, as in the case of
the athletic sports, it would be a mistake for the law to institute
contests for the unarmed. A Cretan, again, can do useful service as a mounted bowman or javelin-man, and so we should
further have matches between rivals in these lines for our
amusement.[3] As to women, it is really not worth our while to
force them to take part in these competitions by legal enactments, but if their earlier training has led to the growth of such
habits that they are physically equal, in their girlhood or later
maidenhood, to take part without unwelcome results, they
should be allowed to do so unreproved.

We have at last come to the end of this subject of athletic
contests, and the teaching of physical culture, with all the work
it entails both in the competitions and in the daily routine of
school. We have similarly completed our main treatment of
music; rules for rhapsodes [4] and their likes and for the competitions between choirs requisite at our festivals shall be drawn up
later, when months, days, and years have first been assigned to
the various gods and lesser objects of worship—e.g. regulations
deciding whether these festivals should be kept at intervals of

---

[1] Because of the paucity of horses in Crete. In such a district no one
is likely to want to drive 'four-in-hand', or to have a stud for the purpose,
even if the nature of the ground were less unfavourable.

[2] The language in 834 *b* 7–8 is unusual, but the meaning is clear. If
any change is to be made, I think I would suggest merely writing ἀγωνίσματ
for ἀγωνιστὰς in *b* 7.

[3] Possibly, as C. Ritter holds, παιδιᾶς, (sport) in 834 *d* 3 should be
παιδείας, 'education'; the words are constantly confused in MSS. The
thought would then be, 'since it is useful to have mounted archers etc.,
we must, of course, *educate* them for the work'.

[4] 'Rhapsodes', i.e. professional reciters of poems which have received
the State's *imprimatur*.

two years, or of four, or in any other order we may be inspired
835 to think of. On these occasions, further, we must expect that the
musical competitions shall be held, each in its proper turn, as directed by the Presidents of the Sports, the Minister of Education,
and the Curators of Law, who are to act in concert as a special
committee for the purpose, and must make their own legislation
for all choirs and dancers as to the dates at which competitions
shall be held, the persons who may compete, and the company
in which they may do so. The original legislator has explained
more than once what the various compositions must be like, in
words spoken or sung and in mingled melody, rhythm, and dance-
movement; his later successors [1] must follow his lead in their
regulations, assigning the several competitions to appropriate
sacrifices at suitable times, and so providing our city with feasts
for her observance. There is no difficulty in discovering how
to reduce these details and others of the kind to a legitimate
order, nor again will a different arrangement of them cause
much benefit or detriment to society. But there is a matter
of vast moment, as to which it is truly hard to inspire conviction; the task, indeed, is one for God himself, were it actually
possible to receive orders from him; as things are, it will probably need a bold man, a man who puts plain speaking before
everything, to declare his real belief about the true interest of
State and citizens, and make the regulations the whole social
system requires and demands in a corrupt age; a man who will
oppose the passions at their strongest, and stand alone in his
loyalty to the voice of truth without one creature on earth to
second him.

Clin. Pray, sir, where may our argument be getting to now?
As yet we do not see its drift.

Ath. I am not surprised you do not. But come! I must try
to put the matter more plainly still. When our conversation
brought us to this theme of education, there rose before me a
vision of young people of both sexes living in affectionate
intimacy: as you may imagine, I was moved to uneasy apprehensions when I asked myself how one is to manage such a
society; a society where the young of both sexes are in the pink
of condition, exempt from the severe menial labour which does
more than anything else to damp the fires of wantonness, and
all make sacrifices, feasts, and choric song the concern of their
lives. How, indeed, in such a society, are they to be kept free

---

[1] i.e. the committee which has just been named, and is to make all the
particular regulations on its own authority.

from the passions which bring such multitudes to their undoing, the passions from which wisdom, striving to convert itself into law, bids us abstain? To be sure, it would be nothing surprising that our regulations as already enacted should get the better of most of these passions. Our prohibition of excessive opulence, 836 conducive as it is to temperance, is no trivial boon, and the whole course of the training is likewise under sound regulations of the same tendency; besides, the magistrate's eye, drilled as it is to keep its object, and the young generation itself, constantly in view without a moment's diversion, provides a curb for most passions, so far as any device of men can. But what of the passion of love in the young of either sex, or love of grown woman or man for the other? We know its untold effects in the life of private persons and whole societies, but what precautions should we take against it? Whence are you to cull the specific that shall protect all and sundry from its perils? There, Clinias, we have a difficulty indeed. In fact, Crete as a whole and Lacedaemon, which lend weighty and deserved support to a great deal of our proposed legislation where it is counter to common sentiment, are dead against us—I may say it between ourselves—in this business of sex. Were one to follow the guidance of nature and adopt the law of the old days before Laius [1]—I mean, to pronounce it wrong that male should have to do carnally with youthful male as with female, and to fetch his evidence from the life of the animals, pointing out that male does not touch male in this way because the action is unnatural, his contention would surely be a telling one, yet [2] it would be quite at variance with the practice of your societies. Moreover, the very end we require the legislator to keep in constant view is ill-suited with your practices. You know the question we are repeatedly raising is what enactments foster goodness and what do not. Very well, then; suppose our present legislation pronounces this practice laudable, or free from discredit, how will it promote goodness? Will it lead to the growth of the temper of valour in the soul of the seduced? Or the growth of a temperate character in his seducer? That is surely more than any man can believe. Surely, the very opposite is the truth; every one must censure the unmanliness of the one party, who surrenders to his lusts because he is too

[1] Laius was, according to legend, the inventor of *masculi amores*.
[2] In 836 *c* 6–7, if, with Burnet, we keep the MS. text πιθανῷ λόγῳ, καὶ the sense will be as I have given it, but we shall have to force on the καὶ the meaning 'and yet'. This seems to me very hard, and I should prefer, with Hermann, to add a <εἰ> before the καί.

weak to offer resistance, and reproach the other—the impersonator of the female—with his likeness to his model. Who in the world, then, will give legislative countenance to a practice of such a tendency? No one, I say, who has any notion of what a true law is. You ask how I prove my point? We shall have
837 to examine the real nature of affection and its attendant desire and of love so-called, if we are to think rightly of this matter; there are, in fact, two different things, as well as a third compounded of them both, covered here by one single name, and it is this which causes so much confusion and obscurity.

Clin. How so?

Ath. Why, we speak, you know, of the attachment between those who are alike in goodness, or between equals, and again of that between the indigent and the rich, where the one party is the opposite of the other, and when either feeling is intense we call it 'love'.

Clin. We do.

Ath. Now this attachment between opposites is fierce and furious, and we do not often find it reciprocated, whereas that founded on similarity is equable and permanently reciprocal; where both factors are present at once, for one thing it is hard to perceive what the subject of this 'love' is really seeking, and for another, he is distracted and baffled by rival impulses, one inviting him to enjoy the charms of the object, the other forbidding the enjoyment. The man whose love is a physical passion, a hunger for another's charms, like that for ripe fruit, tells himself to take his fill and gives not a thought to his minion's state of soul. But he that treats carnal appetite as out of the question, that puts contemplation before passion, he whose desire is veritably that of soul for soul, looks on enjoyment of flesh by flesh as wanton shame; as one that reverences, ay and worships, chastity and manhood, greatness and wisdom, he will aspire to live with his love in constant purity on both parts. The sort of love in which both factors are involved is that we have now reckoned the third.[1] Now since loves are of

---

[1] The MSS. text at *d* 1-2, ὁ δὲ μειχθεὶς ἐξ ἀμφοῖν τρίτος ἔρως οὗτός ἐσθ' ὃν νῦν διεληλύθαμεν ὡς τρίτον, cannot represent what Plato meant to stand, either τρίτος or ὡς τρίτον is superfluous. The redundancy would be removed if, with England, we adopted Dr. H. Jackson's γ' for τρίτος (Γ for γ̄). But ἐξ ἀμφοῖν τρίτος sounds exactly right and looks like a verbal echo of *a* 3 above; hence the error of transcription, if there is one, is probably rather in ὡς τρίτον. I half suspect that here, as in some other passages, the redundancy may be due to indecision on the author's part between two equivalent wordings of his thought, of which his transcriber has preserved both.

so many kinds, should the presence of all kinds be excluded from our midst by legal prohibition? Is it not obvious rather that we shall wish to find in our city the sort that has goodness for its object, the desire to make a youth as good as he can possibly be, but prohibit the other two, if only we can? Megillus, my friend, what would you have us say?

Meg. All you have even now said of this same matter, sir, is perfectly well.

Ath. I expected I should find you in accord with myself, friend, and it seems I was right. What your Spartan law thinks about such matters is a question I need not raise; I need only welcome your assent to our doctrine. As for Clinias, I must do my best to charm him into acceptance of our view on some later occasion. But enough of your common concession; by all means let us return to our legislating.

Meg. Rightly proposed.

Ath. Well now, and about a device to make the establishment of our law secure? I have one actually ready to my hand, 838 easy enough in one way, though in another of the utmost possible difficulty.

Meg. You mean to say—?

Ath. Even to-day, as you know, lawless as most men are, they are very effectually deterred from cohabitation with the fair, and not against their own will either, but with their full and entire consent.

Meg. Of what cases are you thinking?

Ath. Of persons who have a fair sister or brother. The same law, though unwritten, proves a complete safeguard of son and daughter; so much so that no one lies with them, openly or covertly, or approaches them with any familiarities of that sort; nay the very wish for such congress never so much as enters the mind of the ordinary person.

Meg. True enough.

Ath. Well then, you see how all such lusts are extinguished by a mere phrase.

Meg. Phrase? What phrase?

Ath. The saying that they are all unhallowed, abominations to God, deeds of black shame. The explanation must surely be that no one holds a different language about them; all of us, from our very cradles, are constantly hearing the same report of them from all quarters; we hear it alike from the lips of the buffoon, and again delivered with all the so-called solemnity of tragedy,[1] on those many occasions when the stage presents us with a Thyestes, an Oedipus, or a Macareus, some character who acts the stealthy paramour to a sister and freely sentences himself to death for his crime on discovery.

Meg. You are perfectly right on one point; common fame is indeed a wonderfully potent force, provided only no single soul dares to entertain a sentiment contrary to the established usage.

Ath. So you see how right I was to say that if only the legislator has a mind to subjugate one of the passions which keep humanity in the hardest bondage, it is easy enough for him to find out the way to get a hold on it; he has merely to get the sanction of a common fame which is universal—embraces bond and free, women and children, and every section of society alike—and he will without more ado have secured the best of guarantees for his law.

Meg. No doubt; but, then, how a whole community is ever to be brought to this voluntary unanimity of language on such a point——

Ath. A pertinent rejoinder. That was exactly my own meaning when I said I knew of a device for establishing this law of restricting procreative intercourse to its natural function by abstention from congress with our own sex, with its deliberate murder of the race [2] and its wasting of the seed of life on a stony 839 and rocky soil, where it will never take root and bear its natural fruit, and equal abstention from any 'female field' whence you would desire no harvest. Once suppose this law perpetual and effective—let it be, as it ought to be, no less effective in the remaining cases than it actually is against incest with parents—and the result will be untold good. It is dictated, to begin with, by nature's own voice, leads to the suppression of the mad frenzy of sex, as well as marriage-breach of all kinds, and all manner of excess in meats and drinks, and wins men to affection for their wedded wives; there are also numerous other blessings which will follow, if one can only compass the establishment of such a law. Yet should some young and lusty bystander of exuberant virility overhear us as we propose it, he might probably denounce our enactments as impracticable

---

[1] I render the λεγομένη of the MSS. at 838 *c* 4, since it gives a good sense and is not demonstrably wrong. But one cannot but suspect that Orelli's correction λεγόμενα may be sound, 'and again uttered with all the solemnity of tragedy.'

[2] A reference (*inter alia*) to a consideration important to the legislator that the vice in question is not only 'foul sin', as we have already been told, but menacing to the perpetuation of a society. ;

folly and make the air ring with his clamour. This was what led me to say, as I did, in so many words, that the device I knew for establishing such a law in perpetuity, though easy enough in one way, was most difficult in another. To see that the thing can be done, and how it can be done is perfectly easy; as I say, if once the regulation receives adequate sanction, the minds of all will be subjugated and there will be a universal dread of the established law and conformity to it. But the fact is, things have come to such a pass to-day that no such result is thought possible, even in the case I have supposed. It is just as with the system of the common meal, a practice which it is thought beyond the bounds of possibility for a whole city to adopt throughout its daily life; the institution is proved as a fact to exist in your own societies, yet it is thought its extension to women would be outside the bounds of nature, even in them. It was in that sense, in view of this dead weight of incredulity, that I spoke of the great difficulty of establishing either practice as a permanent law.

Meg. And there was truth in what you said.

Ath. Still, would you like me to do what I can to urge an argument, and a telling one to show that the proposal is feasible, not out of the range of human possibility?

Clin. Most certainly.

Ath. Then tell me, in which case would a man find it an easier task to abstain from sexual gratifications and obey orders on the matter readily, as a decent man should—if his physique were in good condition—in training, in fact—or if it were in poor form?

Clin. If he were in training, of course; most decidedly so.

Ath. Well, we have all heard, have we not, how Iccus of Tarentum is said to have acted for the sake of distinction at 840 Olympia and elsewhere? Such was his passion for victory, his pride in his calling, the combined fortitude and self-command of his character that, as the story goes, he never once came near a woman, or a boy either, all the time he was in training. And you know the same is said of Criso, Astylus, Diopompus, and not a few others. And, after all, Clinias, they had much worse cultivated minds than the citizens for whom you and I are providing, and much more rebellious bodies.

Clin. You are perfectly right when you say that tradition asserts this emphatically as actual fact about these athletes.

Ath. Why then, they made no hardship of denying themselves this 'heaven of bliss', as the vulgar account it, for the sake of

winning a victory in the ring, or the race-course, or the like;
and are our pupils to fail in endurance for the sake of a far
nobler victory—one whose supreme nobility we shall extol in
their hearing, from their earliest years, by story, speech and
song—it is to be hoped with the result of bringing them under
the spell?

Clin. And what victory is that?

Ath. The conquest of their lusts: if they achieve it,[1] we shall
tell them, their life will be bliss; if they fail, the very reverse.
And besides, are we to think the dread of so utterly unhallowed
a deed will be so wholly powerless to compass a mastery which
has been attained before by other men, and worse men?

Clin. We can hardly suppose so.

Ath. Then if this is how we stand in the matter of this law—
if it is the general viciousness which has brought us to a stand-
still—I say it is the law's simple duty to go straight on its way
and tell our citizens that it is not for them to behave worse
than birds and many other creatures which flock together in
large bodies. Until the age for procreation these creatures live
in continence and unspotted virginity; when they have reached
that age, they pair together, the male with the female and the
female with the male their preference dictates, and they live
thereafter in piety and justice, steadfastly true to their contract
of first love. 'Surely you,' we shall say, 'ought to be better
than the beasts.' But if, alas! they should be corrupted by
the example of the great mass of other Greeks and of non-Greeks,
as they learn from their eyes and ears how all-powerful so-called
'free' love is among them all, and should so fail to win the
victory, I would have our Curators of Law turn legislators and
contrive a second law to meet their case.

841   *Clin.* And what law do you advise them to enact, if the one
we are now proposing slips through their fingers?

Ath. Why, of course, Clinias, the next best to it.

Clin. And what is that?

Ath. There was a way of effectively checking the development
of the full violence of these lusts, that of directing the rising
current into some other physical channel by hard work. Now
this result may be attained if sexual indulgence is attended by
a sense of shame; this feeling will make indulgence infrequent,
and the infrequency of the indulgence will moderate the tyranny
of the appetite. So it must be the ordinance of custom and

---

[1] I think England probably right in suggesting that νίκης <ἧς> should
be read for νίκης at 840 *c* 5.

unwritten usage that secrecy in such matters is a point of
honour, and the discovery of the act, though not necessarily
its mere commission, discreditable. The establishment of such
a tradition would give us a second-best standard of honour and
dishonour with its own inferior rightness; the morally corrupt
class whom we speak of as 'slaves to their vices' would be
circumvented and constrained to compliance with the law by
no less than three influences.

Clin. And what are the three?

Ath. Fear of God, desire of honourable distinction, and the
development of the passion for a beauty which is spiritual, not
physical. It may be that my present proposals are no more
than the aspirations of a pious imagination, though I assure
you any society would find their realization a supreme blessing.
However, by God's help, we might not impossibly enforce one
or other of two rules for sexual love. One would be that no
free-born citizen should dare to touch any but his own wedded
wife, and that there should be no sowing of unhallowed and
bastard seed with concubines, and no sterile and unnatural
intercourse with males. Failing this, we may suppress such
relations with males utterly, and as for women, if a man should
have to do with any—whether acquired by purchase or in any
way whatsoever—save those who have entered the house with
the sanction of heaven and holy matrimony, and his act become
known to man or woman, we shall probably be pronounced to
do well by enacting that he be deprived of the honours of a
citizen, as one that proves himself an alien indeed. So whether
this be taken as one single statute, or should rather be called
two, let it stand as our law in the matter of sex and the whole
business of love, our rule of right and wrong in all relations
inspired by those passions.   842

Meg. Indeed sir, I for one shall welcome this law with all my
heart; Clinias, of course, must declare his mind on the matter
for himself.

Clin. And so I shall, Megillus, when I think I have fitting
occasion; for the moment, however, suppose we permit our
friend to proceed with his legislation.

Meg. Well and good.

Ath. Observe then; our progress has now brought us to a
point at which we may well take the public meals to have been
instituted. (As I say, there would be difficulties about this
anywhere else; but in Crete no one is likely to recommend
any other arrangement.) But on what system they should be
*K 275

conducted, that of this country, that of Lacedaemon,[1] or whether some third type of public meal would be better than either, is, I think, not a problem of great difficulty, nor does its solution promise any considerable advantage; in fact I believe the arrangements we have already made quite sufficient.

The question which arises next in natural order is that of commissariat; what will be the appropriate sources of provisions? Of course, the sources from which societies in general can be provisioned are varied and numerous, twice as numerous, at least, as those open to our citizens, since a Greek population, as a rule, draws its food supply from land and sea alike, whereas ours is confined to the land.   So far as the legislator is concerned, this makes his work lighter; the number of laws necessary for adequacy will be reduced not merely to one-half, but within still narrower compass, and those which are required will also be fitter for free-born men.   The maker of our city's code is free to turn his back on the regulation of commerce water-borne or land-borne, of retail trading, inn-keeping, tolls and customs, mining operations, interest simple and compound, and a thousand such details; his statutes will be made for husbandmen, graziers, bee-keepers, custodians of such stock, and users of the implements connected with it; his principal task has already been achieved by his regulation of marriage, procreation and rearing of children, education, appointment of civic officials; he has now to turn his attention to regulations for those who raise the food-supply or are concerned in its preparation.

We shall begin, then, with a number of statutes under the rubric *Of Agriculture*.   At their head shall stand a law of the sacred landmark, and it shall run thus: No man shall move his neighbour's landmark, whether that neighbour be a fellow-citizen, or the property lie on the border marches and the neighbour be thus an alien; the act must be held to be a literal 'moving of the not-to-be-moved'; and every man must be readier to venture the shifting of the heaviest boulder that marks no boundary than to move the tiny stone, consecrate by oath to heaven, that marks off the land of a friend or a foe.   For Zeus the god of common clanship is witness to one of these sanctities, Zeus protector of the stranger to the other, and when

843

---

[1] For the differences between the systems of Crete and of Sparta, cf. Aristot. *Pol.*, 1271 *a* ff, and Athenaeus iv, p. 143   The main difference is that in Sparta the expense of the meals fell upon the individual citizens, who consequently lost their franchise if unable to keep up their contributions; in the Cretan cities the cost was defrayed by the community as a whole.

the wrath of these powers is awakened, deadliest hostilities ensue. He that is obedient to the law shall feel none of its penalties, but he that sets it at nought shall be guilty at more bars than one, first and foremost at the bar of Heaven, and next at that of the law. None, I say, shall move a neighbour's boundary-stone of his own free purpose; if they are so moved, he that will may lay an information before the husbandman, who shall bring the matter into court. If a man be cast in such a suit, he shall be held for one that seeks by stealth or violence to assail freehold, and the court shall assess the penalty the culprit shall suffer or the mulct he shall pay.

Further, little repeated torts between neighbours by their frequency engender a heavy burden of ill-will and make neighbourhood a grievous and bitter hardship. Hence neighbour must take every care to do nothing exceptionable to neighbour; must keep himself strictly from all such acts, and above all from encroachment on a neighbour's lands; for whereas by no means every man can do his neighbour a service, to cause him hurt is easy enough, and any man can do it. He that disregards boundary-marks and works soil that belongs to his neighbour shall make the damage good to him, and shall moreover, by way of medicine for his churlish insolence, pay a further sum of double the amount of the damage to the sufferer. In all such cases the inspection, conviction, and assessment of penalties shall be in the hands of the Rural Commissioners—action being taken, as has already been said,[1] in graver cases with the whole staff for the district, in the lighter with their commanders. If any man graze his cattle on a neighbour's land, they shall likewise decide the case and fix the penalty by ocular inspection of the damage done. If a man appropriate the bees of another's hive by humouring their tastes, and so beat down the swarm and make it his own, he shall pay for the damage done. If in making a bonfire he take no precaution for the timber of his neighbour's land, he shall pay such fine as the magistrates think good. And so, likewise, if in planting trees he should set them at an insufficient space from his neighbour's land. These matters have received competent treatment from many legislators, and we should adopt their regulations; we must not expect the great author of our social order to make statutes for all these numerous little matters with which any and every legislator can deal. Thus, to take one instance, there are 844

---

[1] At 761 *e*, where the duties of this force of rural police under its commissioners were described.

sound old laws extant concerning the farmer's *water-supplies*.
There is no need that they should be distilled in our discourse,
but any who is minded to bring water to his steading may draw
it from the public water-courses, so long as he does not tap
exposed springs owned by another private person, and may
conduct it in any channel he pleases, provided he avoids houses,
temples, and tombs, and causes no damage beyond the cutting
of the channel itself. If certain districts are naturally arid
from failure to retain rain-water, and so there is a scarcity of the
needful supply, the owner may dig on his own land down to the
clay; if he should find no water at that depth, he shall be furnished by his neighbours with just so much as he needs for the
drinking supply of his domestic staff; if the distress extends to
the neighbours also, he shall procure an order for his ration of
water from the Rural Commissioners, and receive that quantity
daily by contribution from the neighbours. If a man causes
damage to the occupant of the farm or dwelling-house immediately above his own by impeding the outflow of rain-water, or
again to the occupant of a lower site by careless discharge of the
efflux from a higher, with the consequence that the parties
decline to oblige one another in the matter, either may obtain
an order for the conduct of both from an Urban Commissioner,
if the case arise within the town, or a Rural Commissioner, if it
occur in a country district; a party who disregards such an order
shall render himself liable to proceedings by his grudging and
unaccommodating spirit, and on conviction shall pay the sufferer
double the amount of damage caused as a penalty for his refusal
to comply with the magistrate's directions.

As to the *fruit-harvest*, there must be an accepted general
understanding to some such effect as this. Two gifts are
bestowed on us by the bounty of the goddess of harvest, one
the 'ungarnered nursling [1] of Dionysus', the other destined for
storage; so our law of fruits shall impose the following rules.
If a man taste the common sort of fruit, whether grapes or figs,
before Arcturus have brought round the season of vintage,
whether on his own ground or on that of another, he shall incur
a fine in honour of Dionysus, of fifty drachmas for fruit culled

[1] The two gifts, as explained below, are the 'common' or 'coarse' grapes,
figs, etc., which are dried or made into *vin ordinaire* in bulk, and the
choice fruit specially preserved for eating. I have kept the MSS. reading
παιδείαν Διονυσιάδα (844 *d* 6), '*nursling* of D', against the emendation
παιδιὰν, 'plaything of D.', adopted by Burnet and others (Stallbaum,
Ritter), on the ground of the Euripidean description of the lotus-plant as
πλεκτὰν Αἰγύπτου παιδείαν (*Troades*, 128).

in his own grounds, a mina for that taken from his neighbour's, two-thirds of a mina for fruit gathered elsewhere. As for what we commonly call 'choice' grapes or choice figs, if a man has a mind to harvest them and takes them from his own plants, he shall be free to gather them as and when he will, but if they are taken from another's plants without the owner's consent, he shall be fined for each such act conformably to the law which forbids him to 'take up what he did not lay down'. If it is 845 actually a slave who touches such things without permission from the owner of the land, he shall receive a stripe for every grape of each cluster taken, or every fig taken from the tree. A resident alien who buys the choice produce may gather it at his pleasure. As for the alien on a temporary visit, who may desire to eat the fruit as he travels the roads, he and a single attendant may, if he so pleases, take the choice fruit without payment, as a gift of national hospitality, but the law must prohibit the foreigner from meddling with our 'common' fruits and the like; if they are taken in ignorance by master or slave, the slave shall suffer a whipping, the free man shall be dismissed with a warning and an admonition only to touch such fruit as is unfit to be set apart for use as raisins, wine, or dried figs. As for pears, apples, pomegranates, and the like, it shall be no felony to filch them, but should any man under thirty years of age be taken in the act, he shall be punished by blows which must not draw blood, and a free man shall have no remedy at law against such blows. An alien shall be free to take his share of this produce, as of the grapes and figs; if they are taken by a citizen over the age of thirty, he may share in them on the same terms as the alien, provided he eat the fruit on the spot and carry none away, but disobedience to the law shall render him liable to disqualification from seeking distinctions, when the time comes, if such conduct is brought to the notice of the acting judges.

Water, above all things, is exceptionally necessary for the growth of all garden produce, but is easily corrupted. It is not easy to affect the other contributory causes of the growth of products of the ground, the soil, the sunlight, the winds, by doctoring, diverting, or intercepting the supply, but water can be tampered with in all these ways, and the law must accordingly come to the rescue. So we shall meet the case by enacting as follows: if one man intentionally tamper with another's supply, whether of spring-water or standing water, whether by way of drugging, of digging, or of abstraction, the injured party shall put the amount of the damage on record, and proceed at law before the Urban Commissioners; a party convicted of poisoning waters, shall, over and above the payment of the fine imposed, undertake the purification of the contaminated springs or reservoir in such fashion as the canon law may direct this purification to be performed in the individual case.

As to the *bringing home* of the fruits of the seasons, it shall be 846 open to any man to fetch in his crop by the route he pleases, provided either that he cause no damage to another, or that the profit to himself is threefold of the damage to his neighbour: the determination in these cases shall lie with the magistrate, as generally in other cases where intentional damage is done to any man's person or property without his consent by a second party or a chattel of such party; information shall be given to a magistrate and redress awarded for damage to the amount of three minae or under; when the claim is for a greater sum, the complainant shall carry the case before the public courts and seek redress of the injury from them. If any magistrate is judged to have shown injustice in an award of compensation, he shall be liable to forfeit double the amount to the aggrieved party; an unfair decision about any charge may be brought before the public courts by either party to the suit. These countless minor formalities about methods of judicial procedure —the institution of a process, the issuing of a summons, the number of witnesses, whether two or some other number, required to its service, and the like—cannot be left without legal regulation, and yet are beneath the attention of an aged legislator. His younger imitators should prescribe them on the model of his antecedent and more important rules; they should make an experimental use of such rules where they are forced to employ them, until they are satisfied that they have a complete and adequate collection of them; then, when the rules have been got into shape, and not before, they should treat them as final and live by them.

As to the *arts and crafts* we should proceed as follows. In the first place, no native, and no servant of a native, is to practice a craft as his calling. A citizen has already a calling which will make full demands on him, in view of the constant practice and wide study it involves, in the preservation and enjoyment of the public social order—a task which permits of no relegation to the second place. But human capacity, we may fairly say, is never equal to the finished exercise of two callings or crafts; nay more, none of us has the gift of following one craft himself while he superintends another's practice of a second. Hence we must from the start take this as a principle of our society: no one shall be smith and carpenter at once, and further, no one who is a carpenter shall be permitted to superintend others who are engaged in smiths' work, to the neglect of his own craft, on the plea that as overseer of so many employees who are working for his profit, he naturally supervises them the more carefully because his revenue from their labours is so much greater than his income from his own trade. 847 Each artisan in the society must have his single craft, and must earn his living by that trade and no other. The Urban Commissioners must exert themselves to keep this law in force. If a native stray from the pursuit of goodness into some trade or craft, they shall correct him by reproach and degradation until he be brought back again into the straight course; if an alien follow two crafts, there shall be correction in the shape of imprisonment, fine, or expulsion from the city to constrain him to play one part, not several. Disputes about wages due to workmen or refusal (?) [1] of work done by them, and complaints of injustice done to them by others, or to others by them, shall be decided by the Urban Commissioners where the sum involved is not more than fifty drachmas; where it is greater, the public courts shall deal with the case as the law may direct.

No dues shall be paid in our city either on *exports* or on *imports*. There shall be no importation of frankincense or other such foreign perfumes for the purposes of religious ceremonial, nor yet of purple and other dye-stuffs not produced in the country, nor of the materials of any other industry dependent on foreign importation and serving no necessary purpose. Further there shall be no exportation of any commodities which it is indispensable to retain at home. The jurisdiction and supervision in all these matters shall be with the twelve Curators of Law who stand at the head of the board when its five senior members are exempted.

[1] The meaning of ἀναιρέσεων τῶν ἔργων (847 b 3) is uncertain. On the analogy of the juristic use of ἀναίρεσις for the *repeal* of a law, the meaning should be *refusal* to accept unsatisfactory work. On the other hand, on the analogy of the use of the word to mean the 'taking up', 'recovery', of the slain after a battle, it may mean here either the 'acceptance' of work done to an order, or (?) the 'taking-up' of a contract to do a certain piece of work. (I do not even feel sure that England is wrong in suggesting that Plato wrote ἀνακρίσεων, the 'scrutiny' of a piece of work produced by the artisan. This would cover both the possible cases of complaint that the work had been wrongfully rejected and that it had been 'passed' and then not paid for.) On the whole, however, I think the rendering I have adopted the most probable.

As to *weapons of war* and military equipment of all kinds; if military purposes require the importation of any industry, vegetable, mineral substance, material for rope-making, or animal, the cavalry commanders and generals shall have the control of such importation and exportation,[1] the State being both seller and buyer, and the proper and sufficient regulations for the proceeding being imposed by the Curators of Law: there shall be no retailing of these or any other materials for profit anywhere within our territory or among our citizens.

When we come to *supplies* and the *distribution* of natural produce, a rule much like that followed in Crete will probably be found to serve our turn. All should divide the total produce of the soil into twelve parts, as it will in fact be divided in consumption: each twelfth—that of the wheat and barley, for example, and all the produce of the seasons as well as all sale-
848   able livestock in the various districts must, of course, be subject to the same law of division—should be subdivided into three proportional shares, one for the free citizens, another for their servants, while the third shall be for artisans and other non-citizens, whether permanent residents requiring the necessities of life or temporary visitors brought in by the business of the State or of private citizens, and the third part of all the necessaries of life shall be the only part which shall be forced into the market; there shall be no compulsion to sell any portion of the remaining two-thirds. Now what will be the right way of making this division? For one thing, it must obviously be equal in one way, though not in another.

Clin. A word in explanation, please.

Ath. Why, you know, some of these products are bound to be inferior in strain and condition and others superior.

Clin. Of course.

Ath. Well, in that respect none of the three subdivisions, neither that for the masters, nor that for the slaves, nor yet that of the aliens, shall have any advantage over the other; the distribution shall secure the same equality of similarity for all. Each citizen shall receive the two-thirds and be authorized to distribute them among the slaves and free persons of his household in such quantity and quality as he pleases. The residue shall be distributed by number and measure in manner following; the distribution shall proceed upon a computation

---

[1] The *exporting* is mentioned because the imported 'war material' would have been paid for by exportation. The main point of the law is that the State is to be the dealer in these transactions; they are not to be undertaken by 'private enterprise .

of the whole livestock which will have to be supported by the produce.

Next, we must provide our *personnel* with individual *dwelling-houses* properly grouped, and the following disposition will be appropriate for the purpose. There should be twelve villages, each standing in the centre of one of our twelve regional districts. Our first proceeding should be, in each of these villages, to set apart temples, with a market-square, for the gods and super-human beings under them, taking care that any local deities of the Magnetes, or sanctuaries of other powers of venerable memory which may be left, receive the same honours as in earlier ages. In each of the twelve regions we shall found shrines of Hestia, Zeus, Athena, and the god, whoever he may be, who is to be patron of the district. We should then begin by building dwellings on the highest ground, in the neighbour-hood of these temples, as the strongest lodging we can find for the garrison. The whole of the rest of our territory will be furnished with workmen, who will be divided into thirteen sections. One of these will be appointed to dwell in the capital (this section itself, in its turn, will be divided into twelve parts, like the capital itself, who will be distributed through all the suburbs) while we shall collect in the several villages the classes of hands whom farmers will find useful. The supervision of them all is to be in the hands of the chiefs of the Rural Com-missioners, who shall decide what workers each district requires, and how many of them, and where they can live with least discomfort to themselves and most benefit to the farmers. The workmen in the capital shall, in like manner, be placed 849 and remain under the supervision of the board of Urban Commissioners.

The details of the conduct of the *market* must, of course, rest with the Commissioners of the Market. After their vigilance to protect the temples in the market-place from all violation, their second concern must be with the supervision of the human traffic, and in this charge they shall take careful note of decency and indecency of behaviour, and inflict correction where it is called for. They are, first of all, to take note whether the sales of the articles which citizens are required to vend to aliens are in all cases conducted as the law commands. For each such article the law will be that on the first of the month the quantity which is to be sold to the aliens shall be produced by the agents —that is, aliens or slaves appointed by the citizens for this purpose—beginning with the monthly twelfth portion of corn, and an alien shall at this first market purchase corn and all that belongs to it for the whole month. On the tenth the parties shall respectively conduct the sale and purchase of liquids sufficient for the full month. On the twentieth there shall be a third sale [1] of such livestock as it meets the requirements of the parties to buy or sell, and also of such manufactured goods and articles as farmers have for sale, and foreigners can only acquire by purchase; for example, hides, wearing apparel, woven stuffs, felts. As to the *retailing* of those goods, of wheat or barley in the form of flour, or of any foodstuffs whatsoever, there shall be absolutely no selling to citizens or their slaves in this way, and no purchasing from them, though an alien, selling to artisans and their servants, in the market for foreigners,[2] may drive a trade in wine and corn, a 'retail business', as it is commonly called; butchers also may cut up carcases and dispose of the joints to aliens, artisans and artisans' servants. As for *firewood*, an alien shall be free, if he pleases, to buy it in bulk daily from the agents of the district, and may then retail it in such bulk and at such times as he pleases to other aliens. As for all other goods or manufactured articles of which various parties may be in need, they shall be brought to the general market,[3] each article to the proper quarter, and there offered for sale on the site appointed for traffic, and furnished with convenient stalls by the Curators of Law and the Commissioners of Market and City. The sale is to be by actual exchange of currency for goods and goods for currency, and neither party shall waive the receipt of a *quid pro quo*. A party who acts thus, by way of giving credit, shall put up with the consequences, whether he receives that for which he has bargained or not, as 850 no action will lie in the case of such transactions. If the property bought or sold, in quantity or value, violate the law which fixes the limits of increase and decrease outside which both transactions are prohibited, the excess must be at once recorded

[1] I depart, with some hesitation, from Burnet's text by adopting τρίτη (W. R. Paton) for the MSS. τρίτη in 849 c 1. With the MSS. text, the sense may be either that the cattle-market shall be held 'on the twenty-third', or that it shall be held 'on the third twentieth' (which presumably would mean rather 'every other month' than 'every quarter'). But the choice of the day is wholly arbitrary with the first interpretation: on the second, the cattle-market is, to judge from the practice of our own dealers, not held often enough.

[2] The 'market for foreigners' is (of course) to be distinguished from the three 'stated markets' just described, at which citizens, as well as aliens, do business.

[3] This is apparently to be distinguished from both the markets already mentioned, since it is implied that it is held every day.

in the court of curators, or the deficit cancelled.[1] The same
rule shall apply to the inscription of the property of aliens.
Any foreigner who pleases may become a resident in the country
on certain express conditions. It shall be understood that we
offer a home to any alien who desires to take up his abode
with us and is able to do so; but he must have a craft, and his
residence must not be prolonged more than twenty years from
the date of his registration. He shall pay no personal dues as
an alien, however small, beyond good behaviour, and no toll
on the transactions of sale and purchase, and when the period
of his stay has expired, he shall take his property with him on
his departure. Should it be his good fortune, during this
period, to have distinguished himself by some signal service
to the State, and have hopes of satisfying the council and
assembly of his claim to an official prorogation of his departure,
or even to lifelong residence, he may appear and plead his case,
and any claims of which he can convince the State shall receive
full satisfaction. For the children of such aliens, provided they
possess a handicraft and have reached the age of fifteen, the
period of residence shall be computed from their fifteenth year;
when one of them who fulfils these conditions, has completed
his twenty years, he shall depart whither he pleases, or if he
prefer to remain, he must obtain permission as already provided
for. At a man's departure, the entries which previously stood
against his name in the magistrates' register shall be cancelled.

[1] The meaning is that if any sale or purchase results in bringing a citizen's
wealth above the upper, or below the lower, limits legally permissible,
the fact is to be at once recorded. The 'excess', in the former case,
would, by Plato's requirements in Book V, be confiscated: whether the
'cancelling of the deficit' in the contrary case, means that the man who
has been thus impoverished by a contract contrary to the spirit of the
law, is to be recouped in some way, or that the sale or purchase itself is to
be pronounced invalid is not stated. Common sense surely suggests
the second interpretation.

BOOK IX

Ath. The next place in a digest of law will naturally fall to judicial processes arising from all the activities we have so far studied. What will inevitably be the matter of actions at law we have, indeed, already explained in a measure, viz., the affairs of the farm and the business connected therewith. But the main topic has not yet been broached; to handle it in its details—to say what punishment an offence must receive and before what court it must be brought—will be the next subject for our consideration.

Clin. And rightly so.

Ath. In a way, to be sure, it is to our shame to be framing any such legislation as we are now on the point of undertaking at all in such a society as we contemplate, one which, we hope, will have all advantages and enjoy all the right conditions for the practice of virtue. Why, the very assumption that a man will ever be born in such a society who will be stained by the graver turpitudes of other States, that we consequently need to anticipate the appearance of such characters by minatory legislation and enact statutes for their warning and punishment in the expectation that they will be found among us—the mere imagination, as I say, is, in a way, to our shame. But after all, we are not in the position of the legislators of earlier days, whose codes were framed for an age of heroes: they, if the current tales may be believed, were sons of gods and their laws were made for men of the same celestial ancestry; we are but men, and the law we are imposing is meant for slips of humanity. So we may well be pardoned for the apprehension that some 'hard-shell'[1] may be found among our citizens whose native stubbornness will be proof against all softening, and that such characters should yield no more to the mollifying influence of our laws, effective as they are, than the tough bean to the heat of the fire. So for their ungracious sake I will begin with a law against *temple-robbery*, should any one commit so brazen a crime. It is not to be wished, and hardly to be imagined,

---

[1] I assume that Stephanus was right in inserting a και befor καθάπερ in *d* 3. (Burnet follows the MSS.)

that any rightly nurtured citizen should ever take the infection, but attempts in this way may not infrequently be made by servants, or by aliens and their slaves. For their benefit, in the first instance, though also from concern for our universal human frailty, I shall propound my statute against *sacrilege* 854 and other such desperate, or well-nigh desperate crimes generally. But I must first, on the principle we have already accepted, deliver myself of the briefest of preambles to this whole class of laws.

To him, then, who is driven by the voice of some unhappy passion that besets him by day and wakes him from his sleep at night, to go a-temple-robbing we may address some such words of reasoning and exhortation as these: 'Poor soul, this evil prompting which now moves you to go a-robbing temples comes neither from man nor from God; 'tis an infatuate obsession that is bred in men by crime done long ago and never expiated, and so runs its fatal course. You should strain every nerve to guard yourself from it; how you are to do so, you are now to be told. When thoughts of such things assail you, hasten to the rites that baffle the evil chance, hasten in supplication to the altars of the gods who give deliverance from curses, hasten to the company of your men of virtuous repute; listen to them as they tell you, yes and do your best to tell the story to yourself, how all are bound to revere the good and the right. From the company of the evil run, and look not once back. If such action bring relief from your malady, well; if not, think on the better way of death, and take your leave of life.'

In such strains we shall couch our preludes for the behoof of such as purpose any of these accursed deeds whereby a society is undone. The actual law shall be left without a voice for him who hearkens to us, but for him who will not listen it must follow up our prelude in ringing tones. Whosoever shall be taken in sacrilege, shall, if slave or alien, have his misfortune branded on hands and forehead, be scourged with such number of stripes as the court shall think proper, and be cast forth naked beyond the borders. For if he suffer that judgment, he may perchance be made a better man by his correction. For truly judgment by sentence of law is never inflicted for harm's sake: its normal effect is one of two; it makes him that suffers it a better man, or, failing this, less of a wretch. If ever a citizen be detected in such an act, in gross and horrible crime against gods, parents, or society, the judge shall treat

him as one whose case is already desperate, in view of the education and nurture he has enjoyed from a child and the depth of shame to which he is sunk. Whence his sentence shall be death, the lightest of ills for him, and he shall serve
855 as an example for the profit of others, being buried in silence [1] and beyond the borders. But children and family, if they forsake their father's ways, shall have an honourable name and good report, as those that have done well and manfully in leaving evil for good. 'Twill not be proper that there should be any forfeiture of such men's estates in a society where patrimonies must remain for ever unchanged and of undiminished number. And when a man has done a wrong which is judged to be met by a fine, he may meetly be made to pay such fine to the amount of whatever property may remain to him when his patrimony has been stocked, but no more. The Curators shall ascertain the exact facts of each case from their register and report them to the court in due course of procedure, that no estate may go out of working for want of means. If a man's case be judged to call for a heavier fine than this, then if he have no friends who are ready to be bound for him and discharge their part of his debt, his punishment shall take the form of long terms of prison, pillorying, and marks of degradation. For no offence whatsoever shall any man be made a hopeless outlaw, not even though he have fled beyond our borders: death, prison, stripes, ignominious postures of sitting or standing, or exposure at sanctuaries on the frontiers, fines, in cases where, as we have said, their payment is a proper sentence—these shall be our penalties. In a case of life and death the judges shall be Curators of Law acting together with the court selected for merit from the magistrates of the preceding year; [2] it shall be the business of the junior Curators to attend to the bringing-in [3] of the case, the issuing of citations and similar details, the observance of rules of procedure; we

---

[1] i.e. not only must the offender, after execution, be refused a grave in his native land, but his very name must never be mentioned.

[2] For the method of appointing this court, see *supra* 767 *b* ff. It corresponds to the Athenian Areopagus, but its jurisdiction is extended to all capital cases [not confined to those of homicide, and in these trials it is augmented by the addition of an unspecified number of the senior νομοφύλακες].

[3] εἰσαγωγάς (855 *d* 1) means the formal laying of the case before the jury, and involves seeing that all the proper proceedings have been taken in the formulation of the charge and the defendant's reply to it, that the depositions of witnesses, any documents to be used in evidence, and the like are in order, and so on. This was, at Athens, the business of the magistrate who presided over a trial in one of the Heliastic courts.

as legislators must prescribe the manner of taking the vote. The votes, then, shall be given openly, and before they are given the judges shall one and all, in order of seniority, take their seats in a compact body, facing prosecutor and defendant, and all citizens who have the necessary leisure shall be present and give attentive hearing to the pleadings in such cases.

The prosecutor shall state his case and the defendant reply to it, each in a single speech. When the speeches have been delivered, the senior judge shall first state his view of the case, discussing the statements of the parties in full and sufficient detail. When he has finished, the rest of the judges, each in his order, shall review any omissions or errors they find to complain of in the pleadings of either party, a judge who has no complaint to make leaving the right of speech to his neighbour; the written record of all statements pronounced to be relevant shall be confirmed by the seals of all the judges and deposited 856 on the altar of Hestia.[1] They shall meet again the next day at the same place to continue the review of the case, and once more affix their seals to the documents. When this has been done for a third time, due weight being allowed to the evidence and witnesses, each judge shall give a solemn vote, swearing by the altar to pronounce just and true judgment to the best of his power, and this shall be the end of that trial.[2]

To turn from cases of religion to cases of *treason* to the State.[3] Whosoever seeks to put law in chains and the State under the control of faction by subjecting them to the domination of persons, and further serves these ends and foments civil strife by revolutionary violence, must be counted the deadliest foe of the whole State, and he that, being in high office, though himself no party to such plottings, neglects to avenge his country on the plotter—whether it be that he detects them not, or that he detects them indeed, but is a craven at heart—such citizen must be held second only to the other in guilt. Any man of worth, however slight, must reveal the matter to the

---

[1] Or—which comes to the same thing—on the sacred *hearth* of the court-room.

[2] The proceedings are largely modelled on those of the Areopagus, but with the important addition that the verdict is not reached by a secret ballot, but after a reasoned pronouncement from each member of the court. The extension of the length of a trial to three days, itself apparently based on Areopagitic procedure, to *all* capital cases, is another important reform.

[3] κατάλυσιν τῆς πολιτείας (856 *b* 1), 'subversion of the established constitution'.

magistrate by bringing the plotter to trial for revolutionary and illegal violence. The judges in the case shall be the same as in those of sacrilege, and their whole procedure shall follow the same rule; death to be inflicted by a majority of their sentences. But once for all, in no case shall a father's disgrace or sentence descend to his children, save only when father, grandfather, great-grandfather have all, without break, incurred judgment of death: in that case the State shall deport them to their original native place with all their property beyond the whole stock of their patrimonial holding.[1] Ten names shall be chosen by lot from the families of citizens who have more than one son over ten years of age, on the nomination of a father or grandfather on either side, and sent to Delphi; the nominee preferred by the god shall be constituted heir to the derelict house—let us pray, with brighter hopes!

Clin. An admirable proposal.

Ath. There is yet a third class to be covered by a single law [2] prescribing the judges who shall sit upon them and the process of their trials, those who may be brought into court on the 857 charge of *traffic with the enemy*. In like manner our proposed law concerning the retention of their children in the country or expulsion therefrom shall be the same for all three, the trafficker with the enemy, the temple-breaker, the violent subverter of the State's laws. For the *thief*, again, there shall be one law, alike whether his theft be a great one or a small, and one legal penalty for all cases. For first, he must pay twice the value of the thing stolen if convicted on such a charge, and if he have sufficient property besides his patrimonial holding to make the payment. If he have not, he shall lie in prison until the sum be either paid or remitted by the successful prosecutor. He that is convicted of theft from the public shall be released from durance on obtaining his grace from the State, or making payment of double the sum.

Clin. Pray, sir, how can we rule that it shall make no difference to a thief's case whether the stolen property be of great value or little, whether it be taken from a consecrated spot or an unconsecrated, or how the circumstances of a theft may differ in other respects? A lawgiver should surely adapt himself to

---

[1] The repeated prohibition of *forfeiture*, as a method of punishment by which the innocent suffer in perpetuity for the guilty, is aimed at a marked blemish in the Attic legal system.

[2] I would read τρίτοις in *e* 5, '*one* law is to be common to still a third class of offenders', i.e. common to them with the traitors and temple-breakers already dealt with.

the variety of these particulars by attaching widely different penalties to the several offences.

Ath. A sound observation, Clinias. I fear I was letting myself drift when the collision with you woke me up. You remind me of the observation I made a while ago, that the business of legislation, if I may speak on the spur of the moment, has never yet been thoroughly worked out on right lines. But what, you may ask, do I mean by this? That was no unhappy simile by which we likened all existing legislation to the treatment of unfree patients by unfree physicians.[1] You may be sure that were one of these empirical practitioners of the healing art, so innocent of the theory of it, to discover a free physician conversing with his free patient, to hear him talking almost like a philosopher, tracing the disorder to its source, reviewing the whole system of human physiology, his merriment would be instantaneous and loud. His language would be no other than that which comes so pat from the lips of most of our so-styled physicians. 'This is not to treat the patient, fool, but to educate him—as though he wanted to be made a medical man, not to recover his health!'

Clin. Well, and would not the speaker be in the right of it?

Ath. He might be so, if only he also understood that any man who treats of law in the style we are now adopting, *means* to educate his fellow-citizens rather than to lay down the law to them. That, too, would be a pertinent remark, would it not?

Clin. It might be.

Ath. And how fortunate for us that our present position is what it is!

Clin. In what way fortunate?

Ath. Because we are under no obligation to lay down the law; we are free to pursue our own reflections on all points of political theory, to set ourselves to discover how to effect either the best possible result, or the indispensable minimum. In the case under discussion, for example, it is open to us, I take it, to ask either what would be the ideally best legislation, or what is indispensably requisite as a minimum, according to our preference. So we must make our option.

Clin. A singular pair of alternatives, sir. We should be in the position of the statesman driven by the stress of some dire necessity to produce his laws on the instant, because to-morrow will be too late. Our case, please God, is more like that of stonemasons or some such workers at the beginning of their

858

---

[1] *Supra,* 720 *a.*

operations. We are free to collect our materials in the mass before we proceed to select those which will suit the future construction, and we can make the selection itself at our leisure. So we will take ourselves to be erecting our present edifice, not under pressure, but with undiminished leisure to lay up some of our material for future employment while we work the rest into our fabric. Thus we may rightly think of our body of law as composed partly of statutes actually imposed, partly of material for statutes.

Ath. At all events, Clinias, our digest of law will be the more scientific so. For here is a point I beg we may observe in connection with the legislator.

Clin. And what may it be?

Ath. Our societies, we may say, abound in literary works by various authors, and of this literature the productions of the legislator form part.

Clin. Certainly.

Ath. Well then; are we to give serious attention to the compositions of others, poets and others who have left a written record of their counsels for the conduct of life, in prose or in verse, and none to the legislator's? Should not they have our first attention?

Clin. Decidedly.

Ath. And can we suppose that the legislator alone among authors is to give us no counsel about honour, good, or right, not to tell us what they are, and how they must be cultivated by one who would have a happy life?

Clin. Of course he must tell us.

Ath. Then if it is discreditable in Homer, or Tyrtaeus, or another poet, to have laid down bad precepts for the conduct of life in his verses, is the discredit less in Lycurgus, or Solon, or any other author of a legislation? Surely a society's law-book should, in right and reason, prove, when we open it, far the best and finest work of its whole literature; other men's com-
859 positions should either conform to it, or, if they strike a different note, excite our contempt. How should we imagine the rightful position of a written law in a society? Should its statutes disclose the lineaments of wise and affectionate parents, or should they wear the semblance of an autocratic despot—issue a menacing order, post it on the walls, and so have done? Here, then, is the immediate question for us: shall we try to take this line [1] in uttering our thoughts on law, or, at least,

[1] i.e. the line of wise and affectionate counsel.

make an earnest effort to do so, be its success as it may? And
if there are hazards to be run on the road, shall we risk them?
But may all be for the best—as it will be, God willing!

Clin. Well said, indeed; we must act as you propose.

Ath. Then we must, in the first place, go on with the investigation we had begun; we must look closely into our law of sacrilege,
theft in general, and injuries as a class. We must not be discouraged to find that though some matters have been disposed
of in the course of our still unfinished legislation, others still
demand further consideration. We are still on our way to
become legislators, but as yet have not reached the goal, as
we may perhaps do in time. With your approval, then, we will
discuss the points I have specified on the lines I suggest.

Clin. With all my heart.

Ath. Then here is the point where we must make an effort
after clarity of vision in all discussion of the good and right.
What amount of agreement and what amount of disagreement
is actually to be found, among ourselves (who, you know,
would own at least to an aspiration to surpass the common
herd), and again among the mass of mankind among themselves?

Clin. Of what disagreements between us are you thinking?

Ath. Let me try to explain. When we think of right in
general, or of upright men, right deeds, right conduct, we are
universally agreed in a way that they are one and all comely.
Thus, however strongly a man should insist on the point that
even upright men who may be physically ugly are perfectly
comely, in respect of their eminent uprightness of character,
his language would never be thought out of place.

Clin. And rightly not, surely.

Ath. No doubt. But I would have you observe that if all
that is characterized by rightness is comely, this 'all' must
include what is *done to* us, no less than what we *do*.

Clin. And what then?

Ath. The right thing we do, just so far as it has its share of
rightness, equally partakes of comeliness.

Clin. Certainly.

Ath. Well then, if our language is to be kept clear of in-
consistency, we must also admit that the thing *done to* us is 860
comely just so far as it has its share of rightness.

Clin. True enough.

Ath. But if we grant that something may be done to us which
is unseemly, though right, there will be a discord between the

right and the comely; we shall have pronounced a right thing
a shame.

Clin. But the point of your remark?

Ath. Quite a simple one. The laws we were just now laying
down look like a proclamation of the direct contrary of our
present doctrine.

Clin. Where does the discrepancy come in?

Ath. Why, you know, we laid it down that a temple-robber
or a man at war with an excellent law is rightly put to death.
And we were on the point of enacting a host of similar rules
when we were checked by the discovery that we have here the
infliction of a host of severe penalties, and that these inflictions
are at once supremely right and superlatively shameful.[1] Thus
we seem to assert first an absolute identity and subsequently an
utter opposition between the right and the comely.

Clin. It looks dangerously like it.

Ath. And this is what brings the discordance and confusion
into the popular employment of the epithets *comely* and *right*
in such cases.

Clin. So it should seem, sir.

Ath. Well then, Clinias, let us turn to ourselves. How far
are *we* consistent in our language about the matter?

Clin. Consistent? Consistent with what?[2]

Ath. I fancy I have already[3] said in so many words—or if
I have not, you may now take me as saying that——

Clin. That what?

Ath. That bad men universally are always bad against their
own will. Now on that presupposition a further consequence
inevitably follows.

Clin. And that consequence is——?

Ath. Why, the doer of a wrong, you will grant, is a bad man,
and a bad man is what he is against his will. But it is mere
nonsense to talk of the voluntary doing of an involuntary act.
Ergo, he who declares the doing of a wrong involuntary must

---

[1] The connection of thought is this. A legal penalty is always a πάθυς
or 'infliction', something *done to* a man. In popular language, it is said
both that it is **right** that we should do the thing to him, and that it is
shameful, degrading, unseemly that he should have it done to him. What
it is right, and therefore seemly, in us to do to him, it is 'an ignominy'
that he should undergo. And yet, when we come to think of it, if it is
seemly that we should inflict the penalty, it cannot also be unseemly that
it should be undergone.

[2] πρὸς ποίαν (860 *c* 6) could only mean πρὸς ποίαν συμφωνίαν, and this
makes no good sense. As a makeshift, I render Ast's πρὸς ποῖον or
Baiter's πρὸς ποῖα.

[3] e.g. at 731 *c* 2, 734 *b* 4.

regard the doer of it as acting contrary to his own will, and I in particular am bound at this moment to accept the position. I grant, in fact, that those who commit wrongs always act against their own will. (There may be those who are led by contentiousness or the desire to shine into saying that while there are involuntary wrong-doers, there are also many whose wrong-doing is voluntary, but for my part, I hold to the first statement and reject the second.) Well then, I ask you, how am I to be consistent with my own avowals? Suppose you, Clinias and Megillus, put this question: 'The case being as you say, sir, how would you advise us about framing a code for our Magnesian State? Shall we make one or not?' 'Make one, by all means,' I answer. 'Then will it draw a distinction between involuntary wrongs and voluntary? Will it inflict heavier penalties for a voluntary transgression or wrong, and lighter for an involuntary? Or should they all be treated alike, 861 on the ground that there is no such thing as a voluntary act of wrong?'

Clin. Indeed, sir, you are very right. What are we to make of our statements?

Ath. Well demanded. Well, the first thing to be made of them is this.

Clin. What?

Ath. We shall remind ourselves of the truth of our recent remarks about the bewildering confusion and contradiction in our views of rights. Bearing this in mind, we shall go on to ask ourselves a further question. 'We have never extricated ourselves from our perplexity about this matter; we have never achieved any clear demarcation between these two types of wrongs, the voluntary and the involuntary, which are recognized as distinct by every legislator who has ever existed in any society and regarded as distinct by all law: and is the formula we have just pronounced to dispose of the business by an *ipse dixit*, like some oracular response? Is it, so to say, to stifle opposition by decree, without one syllable of justification?' Surely not. Before we come to the legislating we are bound to show that the cases are distinct and the difference between them other than supposed, to ensure that when we prescribe the penalty for an offence of either kind, every one shall follow our reasoning and be capable of a more or less competent judgment on the appropriateness of the infliction.

Clin. Your audience is with you, there, sir. Of two things, one; either we must deny the thesis that all wrongful acts are involuntary, or else, before we assert it, we must establish its soundness by making a distinction.[1]

Ath. One of your alternatives, the denial of the thesis, I must absolutely decline to admit. Convinced as I am of its truth, to deny it would be unlawful and impious. But how do the two cases differ, if not as the involuntary and the voluntary? Of course we must try to find some other principle of distinction.

Clin. Assuredly, sir, we can think of no other possible course.

Ath. Well, I will try to do so. Consider: citizens, of course, frequently cause mutual *damage* in their various associations and relations with one another, and the damage is often enough voluntary and also often enough involuntary.

Clin. Exactly.

Ath. Now we should not regard all these cases of causation of damage as *wrongs*, and so come to the conclusion that the *wrong* done in such acts may be of two kinds, voluntary, or again involuntary—involuntary *damage*, as a form of damage, is as common and serious as voluntary—what you must con-
862 sider is whether there is any truth or none at all in what I am next to say. What I maintain, Clinias and Megillus, is not that when one man causes hurt to another unintentionally and of no set purpose, he does him a wrong, but an involuntary wrong (and so I shall not propose to treat the act legally as an involuntary wrong); I shall not regard such causing of detriment, serious or trifling, as a *wrong* at all; also, if my view carries the day, the author of a benefit will often be said to do a *wrong*, when that benefit is not rightfully conferred. Speaking generally, my friends, we cannot call it a right act without further qualification when one man gives another something, nor a wrong when he takes something from him. What the legislator has to ask himself is whether the agent of the beneficial or detrimental act is acting with a rightful spirit and in a rightful manner. There are thus two considerations he must keep in view, the *wrong* committed and the *detriment* occasioned. He must do all he can by his laws to make damage good, to recover the lost, rebuild the dilapidated, replace the

---

[1] Plato means that the really important distinction for the jurist, which is misapprehended when a court is invited to base its verdict on the voluntariness or involuntariness of detriment caused, is that between the violation of a *right* (which involves wrongful *intention*), and the mere infliction of loss or detriment. There is here no unlawful *intention*, and therefore no *wrong* at all.

slaughtered or wounded by the sound; he must aim throughout in his legislation at reconciling the minds of the authors and sufferers of the various forms of detriment by award of compensation, and converting their difference into friendship.

Clin. Admirable, so far.

Ath. And then as to *wrongful* detriment—or gain, either, in the case that a man should cause another to profit by a wrongful act—such things, as we know, are maladies of the soul, and we must cure them whenever they are curable. And the line our cure for wrong must follow, I say, is this.

Clin. What?

Ath. The line whereby law will both teach and constrain the man who has done a wrong, great or small, never again, if he can help it, to venture on repetition of the act, or to repeat it much more rarely—and he must make the damage good to boot. And so, if we can but bring a man to this—to hatred of iniquity, and love of right or even acquiescence in right—by acts we do or words we utter, through pleasure or through pain, through honour bestowed or disgrace inflicted, in a word, whatever the means we take, thus and only thus is the work of a perfect law effected. But should our legislator find one whose disease is past such cure, what will be his sentence or law for such a case? He will judge, I take it, that longer life is no boon to the sinner himself in such a case, and that his decease will bring a double blessing on his neighbours; it will be a lesson to them to keep themselves from wrong, and will rid society of an evil man. These are the reasons for which a legislator is bound to ordain 863 the chastisement of death for such desperate villainies, and for them alone.

Clin. All you have said seems, in its way, sound enough. But there is a point on which we should still be thankful for clearer explanations. How comes the distinction between wrong and detriment to be complicated in these cases with that between voluntary and involuntary?

Ath. Well, I must do what I can to give the explanation you require of me. I am sure that when you talk together about the soul there is one point assumed by speaker and listener alike, the presence in it of a native character—or, if you like, part—*of passion,* a contentious and combative element which frequently causes shipwreck by its headstrong violence.

Clin. Yes, of course.

Ath. You must observe further that we draw a distinction between passion and *pleasure*; the empire of pleasure, we say, is based on an opposite foundation; it regularly gets its will by a combination of seduction with cunning deception.[1]

Clin. Assuredly.

Ath. And we should not be wrong if we spoke of *ignorance* as a third source of misconduct. Though you should note that the legislator will do well to make two kinds of it, ignorance pure and simple, which he will regard as a cause of venial offences, and the more complicated condition in which a man's folly means that he is suffering not from ignorance alone, but also from a conceit of his own wisdom, and supposes himself to know all about matters of which he knows nothing whatsoever. When such ignorance is accompanied by exceptional capacity or power the lawgiver will regard the combination as a source of grave and monstrous crime; when it is conjoined with impotence, since the consequent misconduct is puerile or senile, he will treat it as an offence, indeed, and make laws against its perpetrator as an offender, but those laws will be the mildest and most indulgent of his whole code.

Clin. That is no more than sense and reason.

Ath. Now we all talk of one man as the master of his pleasures or his passion, of another as a slave to them, and this language describes real facts.

Clin. Most certainly it does.

Ath. But we have never heard it said that so-and-so is the master of his ignorance, or so-and-so a slave to it.

Clin. We certainly have not.

Ath. And yet we speak of all three as frequently impelling a man in one direction at the very time his own will is urging him in the opposite.

Clin. Ay, times out of mind.

Ath. Now at last I am in a position to explain precisely what I mean by right and wrong without any complications. *Wrong* is the name I give to the domination of the soul by passion, fear, pleasure or pain, envy or cupidity, alike in all cases, 864 whether damage is the consequence or not. But where there

---

[1] The βιαίον, 'violent,' of the MSS. text (printed by Burnet) can hardly be right (πειθοῖ μετὰ ἀπάτης βιαίον, 863 b 8). The whole point is the contrast between the furious *violence* of θυμός and the *seduction* of ἡδονή. (Cf. for the same sort of distinction, *Rep.* 413 b ff.) England's οὐ βίᾳ, a most ingenious suggestion, which merely presupposes that the οὐ was accidentally omitted and subsequently inserted above the line a little too much to the right, may be the true correction; or βιαίον may be a scribe's error for λαθραίον. Just as at *Herc. Fur.* 1351 all MSS. read ἐγκαρτερήσω θάνατον, though Euripides must have written ἐγκαρτερήσω βίοτον, as given by recent editors.

is the conviction that a course is *best*—wherever a society or private individuals may take that best to lie [1]—where that conviction prevails in the soul and governs a man's conduct, even if unfortunate consequences should arise, all that is done from such a principle, and all obedience of individuals to it, must be pronounced *right* and for the highest good of human life, though detriment thus caused is popularly taken to be involuntary wrong. Our business at present is not to contend about words, but, in the first place, to get a still surer mental grasp on the three classes of error which have already been indicated. One of these, you will remember, had a principal source of which we spoke as passion and fear.

Clin. Just so.

Ath. The second had its origin in pleasures and cupidities, and the third, which is of a very different kind, in the loss [2] (?) of sound anticipations and convictions about the good. Since the last has itself been sub-divided into three, we get a total of five classes,[3] as we may now observe, and for all five we have now to make distinct laws, under two principal heads.

Clin. And what are they?

Ath. Under one head fall all cases of deeds of open violence, under the other those of dark and crafty contrivance; there are also cases of acts in which both are employed, and it is, of course, these with which the law will deal most severely, if it is to have its proper effects.

Clin. Yes, to be sure.

Ath. So we may now revert to the point at which this digression began and continue our law-making. If I am not mistaken, we had already legislated against robbery of heaven and treasonable traffic with the public enemy, and also against subversion of the established constitution by tampering with the laws. Now a man might conceivably commit an act of one of these

---

[1] For the unintelligible τούτων of 864 *a* 2, I adopt Hermann's simple emendation τοῦτό γ'.

[2] Since the 'third' case is that of 'ignorance', discussed above, the MSS. text (left by Burnet as it stands) in 864 *b* 7, δόξης τῆς ἀληθοῦς περὶ τὸ ἄριστον ἔφεσις, must be wrong somewhere. There are objections, I think, to all the proposed corrections, but as a stop-gap, which at least gives the general sense, I take Grou's ἄφεσις for ἔφεσις. (Unfortunately the word is not elsewhere found in the sense here required, *loss*, though it is used for *dismissal, release*.) H. Jackson's ὕφεσις, *remission*, suits the context, but the word occurs nowhere else in Plato.

[3] The five classes of offences are thus: (1) those prompted by furious passions; (2) those caused by the seductions of pleasure; (3) those due to ignorance which may be (*c*) mere ignorance, or ignorance complicated with a false conceit of knowledge, and may again be found either (*d*) in important and powerful or (*e*) in insignificant persons.

kinds from insanity, or when so disordered by disease, so extremely aged, or of such tender years, as to be virtually insane. If one of these pleas can be established to the satisfaction of the court selected for the trial of the case, on the representations of the culprit or his advocate, and the verdict should be that the accused committed his transgression in such condition, he shall in any case pay full compensation to any party endamaged by his act, but the rest of the sentence shall be remitted, unless, indeed, he have taken a life and incurred the pollution of homicide. In that case, he shall remove to an abode in some other country, and remain there in exile for a full year; if he return before the legal term be expired, or set foot on any part of his native soil, the Curators shall commit him to prison, and he shall not be released therefrom for two years.

865   As we have entered on the subject of *homicide*, we may attempt a complete statute dealing with all its forms; we will treat first of the case of unintentional violence. If a man unintentionally cause the death of a person with whom he is on friendly terms, in a competition or at the public sports, whether the death be immediate or result later from injuries received, or similarly if he cause such death in war or in some military exercise, whether unarmed practice or sham fight with armour, he shall, on accomplishing such purifications as may be directed by a law for these cases received from Delphi, be esteemed clear of pollution. In the case of all medical practitioners, if the patient meet his end by an unintentional act of the physician, the law shall hold the physician clear. And if one man take the life of another by his own act but without intention, whether with his naked hands, with weapon or missile, by administration of meat or drink, by application of heat or cold, by deprivation of air, by his own physical agency alone or by that of other persons, in all cases the deed shall be held his personal act, and he shall pay the penalty hereinunder stated. If the slain man be a slave, he shall consider that it is just as though one had made away with a slave of his own and indemnify the owner of the deceased for his loss, or shall, in default, be condemned in double the value of the deceased— the said value to be estimated by the court—and shall be put to purifications more burdensome and numerous than those enjoined on those who cause loss of life at the sports, authority to prescribe these rights being vested in the interpreters of religious law whom the oracle shall nominate. If the slain man be his own slave, he shall be clear on accomplishing the

purifications required by law. If one have unintentionally
slain a free man, he shall be cleansed with the same purifications
as the slayer of a slave, but let him take heed not to despise
the teaching of the venerable and primitive myth. It tells us
how he that is done to death with violence, as one that has
lived his days in all the pride of a free man, has his wrath
kindled against the author of his death in the days while the
deed is still fresh, how he is likewise filled with fear and horror
by his bloody fate, how he is aghast to see his murderer haunting
walks that were once familiar and his own, how in his own
distraction of soul, he allies himself with the doer's own memories
to bring all possible distraction upon him and all his works.
Whence it is truly but right that the homicide should avoid his
victim's path through the round of a full year, and leave all
homely spots of his native land clear of his presence; and if
the deceased be an alien, he must likewise be forbidden the
alien's native country for the same space of time. If a man 866
comply with this law of his own motion, the next of kin to the
deceased, who shall take note of his obedience, shall pardon
his act, and will do no more than right to keep the peace with
him. If a man disobey, if, in the first place, he venture to
enter the sanctuaries with the stain of blood on his hands and
do sacrifice there, or again, if he decline to expatriate himself
for the full time appointed, the next of kin shall bring his
action of homicide against the slayer, and if conviction follow,
all the penalties shall be doubled. But if the next kinsman do
not prosecute the case, though the blood [1] now lies at his door,
inasmuch as the dead man demands atonement for his death,
any who will may proceed against him at law and drive him by
legal sentence to five years' banishment from his land. If an
alien slay an alien resident in the State, he who will may prosecute the suit under the same law, and if the defendant be a
resident settler, he shall go into exile for a year; if he be wholly
an alien, whether the slain man were alien, resident alien, or
citizen, he shall, after his purification, be excluded from the
land to which these laws belong for the term of his natural life.
If he return in violation of the law, the Curators shall visit
him with death, and shall deliver any effects he may possess to
the next of kin of the sufferer. [2] If the return be involuntary,

[1] τὸ μίασμα (866 b 3-4), lit. 'the pollution'. The bloodshed is thought of
as a kind of physical taint (or infection) clinging to the family to which the
deceased belonged.

[2] The 'sufferer' (the παθών), I take it must mean the alien who under-
goes the sentence of death just prescribed. Any property he leaves behind

he shall, if shipwrecked on our coasts, take up his quarters where the sea wets his feet and wait for a boat to remove him; if he be brought back by land by *force majeure*, the first official into whose hands he may come shall release him and send him over the border under safe conduct.

If one slay a free man by one's own act but the deed be done in *passion*, there are first two cases to be distinguished. It is an act of passion when a man is done away with on the impulse of the moment, by blows or the like, suddenly and without any previous purpose to kill, and remorse instantly follows on the act; it is also an act of passion when a man is roused by insult in words or dishonouring gestures, pursues his revenge, and ends by taking a life with purpose to slay and without subsequent remorse for the deed. I take it we cannot treat these as two distinct forms of homicide; both may fairly be said to be due to passion and to be partially voluntary, partially involuntary. Not but what each of them has a resemblance to one extreme. The man who nurses his passion and takes his revenge not at the moment and on the spot, but afterwards and of set purpose, bears a resemblance to the deliberate man-slayer; he who does not bottle up his wrath but expends it all at once, on the spot, without premeditation, is like the involuntary homicide, still we cannot say that even he is altogether an involuntary agent, though he is like one. Hence the difficulty of deciding whether homicides of passion should be treated in law as intentional or, in some sense, unintentional. However the best and soundest procedure is to class each sort with that which it resembles, discriminating the one from the other by the presence or absence of premeditation, and legally visiting the slaughter where there is premeditation as well as angry feeling with a severer, that which is committed on the spur of the moment and without purpose aforethought with a milder, sentence. That which is like the graver crime should receive the graver punishment, that which resembles the lighter a lighter. Our own laws, then, will of course be on these lines.

Clin. Most assuredly.

Ath. Then let us return to our code and continue it thus. If a man slay a free-born person by his own act, but the deed

---

will be handed over to the relatives he may leave behind him, not forfeited, on the principle already announced that forfeiture is to have no place in our code. Plato can hardly mean that the property is to go as compensation to relatives of the man whom the alien had *killed*, since he is speaking here only of a penalty for return from the banishment inflicted for the original homicide.

be done in angry passion and without purpose aforethought, his sentence shall be in all other respects the same as that proper for him who has slain without passion, but the offender shall be made to spend two years in exile, to learn to bridle his temper. He that slays in passion, but with the addition of premeditation, again shall have the same sentence, in other respects, as the former, but three years of exile in the place of the other's two; as his passion was the more grievous, so the term of his punishment shall be the longer. The rule for their restoration from banishment shall be as follows. (It is hard to lay it down in the law with precision, as there are cases in which the criminal reckoned by the law the more dangerous proves the more tractable and the more tractable, as the law considers him, the more dangerous, the act of the latter being at times the more barbarous, that of the former the more humane, though in general the distinction already drawn holds good. The last word on these and similar matters must rest with the Curators.) When the term of banishment, then, is expired in either case, the Curators shall send twelve of their own number to the frontier to sit upon the case; the twelve must, during this interval, have subjected the exile's actions to still closer scrutiny, and they are to judge about giving the criminals their grace and receiving them home again—the parties to be finally bound by this official verdict. If an offender of either kind ever after his restoration give way to rage and 868 repeat his crime, he shall go into exile never to be recalled, and if he return, shall meet the same end as the returned alien. The man who slays a slave in his passion shall, if the slave be his own, purify himself, if another man's, pay his owner twice what he has lost. If any homicide of any class, in defiance of the law, shall pollute, by his presence still uncleansed, market-place, public sports, or other hallowed assemblies, he that will may bring his action against both the kinsman who is executor for the deceased and the homicide, and compel exaction and payment of money and all else that is due twice over,[1] and the sum so paid shall be awarded by law to the informer himself. If a slave slay his owner in his passion, the kinsmen of the deceased shall deal with the slayer as they please and be clean of guilt—only that in no case shall they spare his life.[2] If a free man be killed in

[1] i.e. apparently the 'purification' required will be twice as elaborate, and therefore cost twice as much, as would have been the case without the attempt to ignore the law.

[2] This rather barbarous enactment is out of keeping with the general considerateness of Plato's regulations about slaves. It is in keeping,

passion by a slave not his own, such slave shall be delivered by
his owner to the kinsmen of the deceased, who shall be bound
to put the slayer to death, but the manner of his death shall be
in their own choice. If—for though unusual, the case does
occur—father or mother take the life of son or daughter in
passion, by stripes or other violence, the purificatory rites shall
be as in other cases, and the period of exile shall be three full
years. When the slayers have been received back, there shall
be a divorce of wife from husband, husband from wife; procreation between them must cease; there must be no part in
the family or its worship for one who has robbed it of a son and
brother. He that impiously refuses to comply with this ordinance shall be open to an action for impiety at the suit of any who
will charge him. If a man slay his wedded wife in passion, or
a woman do the like by her husband, there shall be the same
rites of purifying, and the term of banishment shall be three
years. When the criminal returns, he shall be cut off from
joining in worship with his children, or sitting at one table with
them for ever. If father or child disregard this law, once more
it shall be open to him who will to bring them to trial for impiety.
If brother or sister slay a brother or sister in passion, the purifications and term of exile shall be as ordained in the former
case of parent and child—no man shall share one board or join
in one worship with the brother he has robbed of a brother, or
the parents he has robbed of a child—and if the command is
disobeyed, the disobedient shall be liable to answer to the afore-
869 said law of impiety, as is just and right. If ever any man should
harbour such unbridled passion against those that gave him
being that he should presume in the frenzy of his fury to slay
a parent, then, if the deceased, before his end, freely forgave
the criminal his death, he shall be clear when he has accomplished the same purification imposed on the unintentional
homicide and performed what else is prescribed for that case.[1]
But if such forgiveness be not given, the criminal in this sort
shall lie in the danger of more laws than one. He shall lie open
to heaviest judgment for violent outrage, and for impiety, and
sacrilege to boot; he has done despite to the temple of a parent's

apparently, with Roman republican practice, but not with Attic. The
exceptional harshness is, no doubt, explained by the fact that where
slavery is a recognized institution, the murder of a master by a slave has
the character of mutiny. This explains also the hard treatment of the
slave who in self-defence kills a free man (869 d).

[1] i.e. the law about the period of banishment shall be the same as for
the unintentional homicide.

soul, whence, were it possible a man should die more than once, it were perfect justice to put the parricide or matricide whose crime was done in passion to repeated deaths. In this sole case, when a man's life is in danger from his parents, no law will permit slaying, not even in self-defence—the slaying of the father or mother to whom his very being is due. The law's command will be that he must endure the worst rather than commit such a crime; how then can he, under the law, fitly receive any judgment but one? Let death, then, be the penalty prescribed for him who in passion takes the life of father or mother. If brother slay brother in a faction fight or some like case, and the act be done in self-defence and the slain man the aggressor, he shall be clear of guilt, as though the slain had been an enemy in arms; the same shall hold in such case for slaying of citizen by citizen, or alien by alien. If citizen slay citizen, in self-defence, he shall likewise be clear, and so also slave who slays slave. But if the slave take the life of a free man in his own defence, he shall fall under the same laws as the parricide. All we have said of the father's forgiveness of his own death shall hold also for all forgiveness of the act; if any party soever freely forgive any party soever his death, and treat it as undesigned, the law shall enjoin on the homicide performance of the prescribed purifications and one year's absence from the country. So much may serve for a reasonably full treatment of violent, unintentional, and passionate homicide. We are next to deal with the case of acts in this kind done with intent, in downright wickedness, and of deliberate design,[1] at the dictation of overmastering pleasures, cupidities, and jealousies.

Clin. Very true.

Ath. Then let us once more begin with an attempt to enumerate their sources.[2] First and foremost there is concupiscence 870 with its domination over a soul stung to savagery by unsatisfied lusts. Now this is chiefly found concerned with that on which most men's longing is most permanently and sharply set— wealth, with the power wealth gets alike from native bias and pernicious wrong education to breed countless cravings for insatiate and unbounded possession of itself. And the source of this perverse education is the credit given to false praise of

---

[1] Stallbaum seems to me right in adding <ἐξ> before ἐπιβουλῆς in 869 *e* 7.

[2] τῶν τοιούτων (869 *e* 10) refers to the 'pleasures', etc. just mentioned. What is proposed is an enumeration of the *motives* which commonly lead to deliberate murder. They are said to be, in the order of their prevalence: (1) greed, (2) envy and jealousy, (3) fear.

riches alike by Greek and non-Greek; they promote wealth to
the first place among good things, whereas in truth it holds but
the third, and thus they deprive not only themselves but their
posterity. 'Twere for the truest good and glory of all societies
that the truth should be told of riches; they are for the service
of the body, as the body itself for the service of the soul; since,
then, there are goods to which wealth is but a means, it must
hold a third place, after goodness of body and soul. From this
doctrine we should learn that the aim of him who would be
happy must be not to get riches, but to get such riches as
rectitude and self-command will permit; that lesson learned,
society will no longer see homicide calling for still further
homicide in expiation, whereas, to-day, as we said at first, this
greed of riches is one source, and the chief source, of the most
aggravated charges of wilful homicide. A second is the spirit
of rivalry with its brood of jealousies, dangerous company
that they are for the envious man himself in the first instance,
and only less dangerous to the best of his fellow-citizens. And
a third cause of too many homicides may be found in craven
and guilty terrors; there are acts of a man's present or past to
which he would wish none but himself to be privy, and so the
informer in such a case is removed by murder, if all other
methods fail. All this shall be dealt with in our preludes;
they will also state a truth firmly believed by many who have
learned it from the lips of those who occupy themselves with
these matters at the Mysteries, that vengeance is taken on
such crimes beyond the grave, and when the sinner has returned
to our own world once more, he must infallibly pay Nature's
penalty—must be done by as he did—and end the life he is now
living by the like violence at another's hands. If our mere
prelude move any to obedience and proper fear of such a judg-
871 ment, for them the note of formal command need not be struck,
but for the disobedient the statute shall run thus in writing:
If a man take the life of a fellow-tribesman by his own act,
wrongfully, and of set purpose, he shall in the first place be
excluded from every place of lawful assembly, and forbidden
to pollute with his presence temples, markets, harbours, or
other places of public resort whatsoever, and that none the less
whether any man have given the slayer public notice of the
ban or not: the law itself gives notice of it and proclaims it on
behalf of the community at large, now and to all time. If any
man of the deceased's kin within the limits of cousinship, on
either father's or mother's side, shall neglect his duty to in-

stitute proceedings, or to make proclamation of the excommunication first, on his own head be the pollution and—for the law's
curse brings the evil omen with it—the wrath of heaven.[1]
Next, he shall be open to prosecution by any man who is minded
to avenge the deceased. He that has a mind to avenge him
shall fulfil with due care the washings and other observances
the oracle may prescribe in such cases, and give formal notice
of the excommunication; he shall then proceed to compel the
culprit to submit to execution as required by the law. That
this process should be attended by prayers and sacrifices to gods
whose function is to preserve societies from homicides the legislator may declare without trouble to himself: what gods these
should be and what manner of conducting such trials will best
suit with religion shall be determined by the Curators of Law,
in concert with canonists, seers, and the oracle, before they
institute the trials. The court shall be the same to which we
gave authority to decide in charges of sacrilege. The convicted offender shall be put to death, and shall not receive
burial in the land of his victim—for that would add insult to
impiety. If he flee the land and decline to submit to judgment,
his banishment shall be everlasting. If any such exile[2] set foot
in the country of his victim, the first kinsman of the murdered
man, or indeed the first fellow-citizen, who may fall in with
him, shall slay him, with the law's permission, or else put him
in bonds and deliver him for execution to the magistrates
presiding over the court in which the case was tried. He that
enters the case for prosecution shall also at the same time
demand security from the accused, who shall produce his sureties,
men whom the court of judges constituted for these cases shall
pronounce sufficient, three substantial sureties pledged to surrender him for his trial. In the case of refusal or inability to
find such surety, the court shall arrest the accused, keep him
prisoner, and produce him at the trial. If a man be not the
actual assassin, but have purposed the death of another and 872
brought him to his end by design and contrivance, and then
continue to reside in the State a guilty man with the stain of
homicide on his soul, the procedure in the trial of such charges

---

[1] The procedure is taken from that current in Attica, where the first
step in proceeding against a man for φόνος, homicide, was to serve the
'excommunication' just described upon him in the presence of witnesses.
Plato improves on Athenian law by permitting any citizen to take the
necessary steps, if there is no kinsman able and willing to do so.

[2] Here I feel sure we must read with Cornarius τούτων (871 *d* 7) for the
που τῶν of the MSS. (and Burnet's text).

shall be the same, only that security shall not be demanded, and that the convicted may find burial in his native soil; in all other respects this case shall be treated precisely like the other. The procedure shall be the same in cases both of homicide where both parties are aliens, or one party a citizen and the other an alien, or both parties slaves, and of plotting homicide, except as concerns giving of security; as to that point, the party who advances the charge of homicide shall at the same time demand security from the accused in such cases, exactly as it has been prescribed to be required from the assassin.[1] If a slave cause the death of a free man with intent, either as the actual homicide or as the plotter of it, the common executioner shall conduct him towards the burial-place of the victim and to a spot from which the tomb is visible, when he shall be scourged with as many stripes as the prosecutor shall enjoin, and, if he survive the infliction, be put to death. If a man slay a slave who has committed no crime, from apprehension that he may inform against his own shameful misdeeds, or some similar motive, he shall stand his trial for the homicide of such slave precisely as though the slain had been a citizen.

Should there arise cases for which it is a grim and repulsive task even to provide in a legislation, though impossible to ignore them, I mean cases of deliberate and purely wicked homicide by act or contrivance between kinsmen—they are mostly to be found in States where the way of life or the system of training is corrupt; still such a thing may happen even in a land where we could least expect it—why, we can but repeat the doctrine we uttered but now, in the hope that it will by its appeal dispose a hearer the more readily to eschew of his own free choice this most abominable of all forms of homicide. That tale, or doctrine—call it what you please—comes to us on the authority of priests of ancient days, and it tells us expressly that there is a justice watching to avenge a kinsman's blood, and that the law followed by this justice is no other than that we even now stated; it is appointed that he who has dealt in such guilt shall infallibly be done by as he has done: if any man have slain his father, there shall come a time when he shall have to suffer the same violent end at the hands of a child; if his mother, his certain doom in later days is to be born himself

---

[1] I am satisfied by Dr. England's note that the comma of Burnet's and other texts after εἴρηται (872 b 2) should be deleted, and that the δὲ in the next line should either be deleted also or regarded as an unintentional oversight on the part of the writer.

a female creature and, in the end, to have his life taken by those whom he has borne. When pollution has been brought on the common blood, there is no other way of purification but this; the stain refuses to be effaced until the guilty soul have paid 873 life for life, like for like, and this atonement lulled the wrath of the whole lineage to sleep. Thus a man's hand should be stayed by dread of such vengeance from heaven, but should there be wretches so whelmed in misery that they of malice prepense rend father's, mother's, brother's or child's soul from body, our human legislator's statute provides for their case as follows: The regulations for making proclamation of excommunication and taking of security shall be as appointed in the former cases. If a man be found guilty of such homicide, that is of slaying any of the aforesaid, the officers of the court with the magistrates shall put him to death and cast him out naked, outside the city at an appointed place where three ways meet; there all the magistrates, in the name of the State, shall take each man his stone and cast it on the head of the corpse as in expiation for the State; the corpse shall then be carried to the frontier and cast out by legal sentence without sepulture.

But what of him who takes the life, that is, as they say, 'nearest and dearest' to himself? What should be his punishment? I mean the man whose violence frustrates the decree of Destiny by *self-slaughter* though no sentence of the State has required this of him, no stress of cruel and inevitable calamity driven him to the act, and he has been involved in no desperate and intolerable disgrace, the man who thus gives unrighteous sentence against himself from mere poltroonery and unmanly cowardice. Well, in such a case, what further rites must be observed, in the way of purifications and ceremonies of burial, it is for Heaven to say; the next of kin should consult the official canonists as well as the laws on the subject, and act according to their direction. But the graves of such as perish thus must, in the first place, be solitary; they must have no companions whatsoever in the tomb; further they must be buried ignominiously in waste and nameless spots on the boundaries between the twelve districts, and the tomb shall be marked by neither headstone nor name.

If a beast of draught or other animal cause homicide, except in the case when the deed is done by a beast competing in one of the public sports, the kinsman shall institute proceedings for homicide against the slayer; the case shall be heard by such and as many of the Rural Commissioners as the next of kin may appoint; on conviction, the beast shall be put to death and cast out beyond the frontier. If an inanimate thing cause the loss of a human life—an exception being made for lightning or other such visitation of God—any object which causes death by its falling upon a man or his falling against it shall be sat upon in judgment by the nearest neighbour, at the invitation of

874 the next of kin, who shall hereby acquit himself and the whole family of their obligation; on conviction the guilty object to be cast beyond the frontier, as was directed in the case of a beast.[1]

But if a man have manifestly been murdered, and the murderer is unknown or cannot be discovered after careful inquiry, notice of prosecution shall be given as in other cases, but the prosecutor shall address the notification to 'the author of the homicide', and after establishing his right to prosecute shall give public warning in the market-place to 'the criminal slayer of so-and-so' to set no foot in the sanctuaries or any other place within the country of his victim, with the threat that if he makes an appearance and is recognized, he shall be put to death and cast out of the country of the victim unburied.[2] This, then, shall form one chapter in our law—the statutes of homicide.

So much then on these matters: the cases wherein and conditions whereon a slayer shall rightly be held guiltless shall be these following: he that slays a thief entering the house by night with intent of robbery shall be guiltless; he that in his own defence slays a footpad shall be guiltless. He that offers lustful violence to a free woman or boy may be slain without fear of the law by the object of his violent rape, or by father, brother, or son of such party; if a man take one in the act of enforcing his wedded wife and slay him, he shall be clear in the eye of the law. If a man slay in defence of a father's life—the father not being engaged in a criminal act—or in like defence of child, brother, or mother of his children, he shall be altogether clear.

Thus much then for the law of the living soul and that nurture and education which it must needs enjoy if it is to live, and

[1] This solemn 'trial' of the animal or thing which has caused a death is taken over from Attic law, where, as in the similar instances in medieval Europe, the practice is a consequence of the view of the shedding of man's blood as involving religious pollution.

[2] Here again, Plato is thinking of Attic procedure. At Athens, in the case of a murder by a 'person or persons unknown', the ceremonial was that the legal representative of the dead addressed the formal warning to abstain from frequenting a place of public resort, τοῖς δεδρακόσι καὶ κτείνασι, to 'the murderer, whoever he may be' ([Demosth.], xlvii, 69).

without which it must die, and the vengeance to be taken for death by violence. The law of the nurture and training of the body has been stated, and it will next, I take it, be right to proceed to a kindred topic, to classify and enumerate to the best of our ability the various intentional or unintentional violent assaults committed by man on man, and to prescribe the penalties properly to be attached to their several kinds.

Wounds and *maims*, then, will be placed next after manslaughter by the veriest dabbler in legislation. Thus, like homicides, wounds must be divided into the involuntary, wounds inflicted in passion, those inflicted in fear, those that are intentional and deliberate. Hence we should begin our treatment of all classes with a prefatory statement to the following effect. Mankind must either give themselves a law and regulate their lives by it, or live no better than the wildest 875 of wild beasts, and that for the following reason. There is no man whose natural endowments will ensure that he shall both discern what is good for mankind as a community and invariably be both able and willing to put the good into practice when he has perceived it. It is hard, in the first place, to perceive that a true social science must be concerned with the community, not with the individual—common interest tending to cement society as private to disrupt it—and that it is to the advantage of community and individual at once that public well-being should be considered before private. Again, even one who had attained clear perception of this principle as a point of scientific theory, if subsequently placed in a position of irresponsible autocratic sovereignty, would never prove loyal to his conviction, or spend his life in the promotion of the public good of the State as the paramount object to which his own advantage must be secondary. His frail human nature will always tempt such a man to self-aggrandizement and selfseeking, will be bent beyond all reason on the avoidance of pain and pursuit of pleasure, and put both these ends before the claims of the right and the good; in this self-caused blindness it will end by sinking him and his community with him in depths of ruin. I grant you readily that if ever, by God's mercy, a man were born with the capacity to attain to this perception, he would need no laws to govern him. No law or ordinance whatever has the right to sovereignty over true knowledge; 'tis a sin that understanding should be any creature's subject or servant; its place is to be ruler of all, if only it is indeed, as it ought to be, genuine and free. But, as things

are, such insight is nowhere to be met with, except in faint
vestiges, and so we have to choose the second-best, ordinance
and law. Now they can consider most cases and provide for
them, but not all, and this is why I have said what I have.
You and I are about to fix the penalty or fine to be inflicted on
him who wounds another or does him a hurt. Now it is, of
course, a proper and obvious comment to make at this point,
to say: 'Wounds? Yes, but wounds whom, and where and
how and when? The different cases are countless and their
circumstances are widely unlike'. So it is equally impossible to
leave everything to the discretion of the courts and to leave
nothing. One issue, indeed, we cannot avoid leaving to their
discretion in all cases, that of the occurrence or non-occurrence
of the alleged event. And it is quite impossible to the legislator
to leave the courts no discretion at all on the further question of
876 the amount of the fine or penalty to be imposed on the perpetrator of this sort of wrong, but deal with all cases himself,
light or grave, by statute.

Clin. What line, then, are we to take up now?

Ath. Why, this: something must be left to the discretion of
the courts, but not everything; there are things which the law
must itself regulate.

Clin. Then which are the points to be thus dealt with by
statute, and which should be entrusted to a court's discretion?

Ath. The proper step to take next is to point out that in a
State where the courts of law are poor-spirited and inarticulate,
where their members keep their convictions to themselves and
reach their verdict by a secret vote,[1] where, worst of all, they
do not even listen to the case in silence but make the walls
ring with the voice of their applause or censure of the alternate
speakers, like the audience at a play, the community finds
itself in a difficult position. Where the courts are so constituted, to be sure, the legislator's hand is forced by an unfortunate
but very real necessity; he is compelled to restrict the court's
discretion to assess penalties to cases of the most insignificant
kind and to do most of the work himself by express statute, if he
has the misfortune to be legislator for such a society. But in

---

[1] Three defects in the procedure of the Attic δικαστήρια are singled out
for censure: (1) There is no discussion and comparison of views between
the individual dicasts who form a jury; (2) the vote is a secret one, care
being taken to prevent any discovery how the individual dicast has voted;
(3) the court, which ought to maintain an impartial and judicial silence,
encourages or discourages plaintiff and defendant by manifestations of
its sympathies, the θόρυβος we find the orators so frequently deprecating.

a community where the constitution of the courts is thoroughly
sound, and the persons who will have to exercise the judicial
function have been properly trained and made to pass the most
exacting tests, it will be entirely right and fitting that such
courts should be allowed a wide discretion in assessing the fines
or other penalties of offenders. So we may well be excused, in
the present instance, if we do not impose on them by statute
the numerous and important rules which may be discovered
by the insight of judges with a training inferior to theirs for
attaching to the particular offences the penalty merited by
the wrong committed and hurt inflicted. Indeed, as we believe
the persons for whom we are making our statutes likely to
prove particularly capable judges in such matters, we shall
trust most of them to their discretion. Not that we were not
perfectly right in the doctrine we have repeatedly stated and
observed in practice in the preceding part of our own legislation; an outline of the law with samples of penalties should be
set before the judges as a model to keep them from any infringement of the bounds of right. I shall, in fact, act so again
in the present case; and this brings me back to the work of
law-making. The statute of *wounding*, then, shall run thus.
If any one intend and purpose the death of a person with whom
he is on friendly terms, such person not being one against whom
the law arms his hand, and fail to kill, but inflict a wound, he
who wounds with such intent deserves no mercy, and shall be
made to stand his trial for homicide with as little scruple as 877
though he had killed. But the law will show its reverence for
his not too wholly unpropitious fortune and the tutelary power [1]
which has, in mercy to both wounder and wounded, preserved
the one from a fatal hurt and the other from incurring a curse
and a disaster; it will show its gratitude and submission to that
power by sparing the criminal's life and dooming him to life-
long banishment to the nearest State [2], where he shall enjoy his
revenues in full. He must make payment of whatever damage
he have caused to the wounded, the amount being fixed by the
court before which the case is tried, and this court shall be
composed of the same persons as would have tried the homicide
had death followed as a consequence of the wounds inflicted.

---

[1] δαίμων—in effect an imaginative personification of the 'not wholly
unpropitious fortune' just mentioned.

[2] There is no real difficulty about the definite article τὴν in 877 *b* 1,
τὴν γείτονα πόλιν means 'whatever State is nearest' exactly as τὸν ἐλεύθερον
at 882 *a* 2 means '*a* free man', or as ἡ δοθεῖσα εὐθεῖα, in the language of
Greek mathematics, means '*a* given straight line'.

If a son wound his parents or a slave his master with the like intent, the penalty shall be death; so also if brother or sister wound brother or sister in like fashion, and be found guilty of wounding with intent, the penalty shall be death. If a wife wound her husband, or a husband his wife, with design to kill, they shall go into perpetual banishment: as for the estate, if there are sons or daughters who are still minors, it shall be in the hands of the guardians, who shall be charged with the care of the children as though they were orphans; if the family be of full age, there shall be no liability of the offspring to support the banished man,[1] and the estate shall be their property. If the victim of the calamity be childless, the kinsmen of the exile within the degree of second-cousinship on both male and female sides shall meet to appoint an inheritor for the house in question—the five-thousandth-and-fortieth of the State—in consultation with the Curators and priests, and they shall do so with this thought before their minds: there is no house of the five thousand and forty that belongs so truly to its occupant or his whole kin as to the State, and that by every right of ownership; it is for the State, then, to keep its house in all purity and good fortune. When a house, then, is visited with such guilt and misfortune at once[2] that the owner leaves no sons to succeed to it, but dies unwedded or wedded but childless, under conviction of wilful homicide, or other sin against heaven or human society for which the pain of death stands expressly prescribed in the law, or again when a childless man is under doom of perpetual exile, the house itself shall first be purified and exorcised as the law directs; next the household shall meet,
878 as provided even now, along with the Curators, to consider what house of all in the State is at once of the first repute for goodness, favoured by fortune, and possessed of more children than one. From such a house they shall adopt one person as a son and successor to the father of the deceased and his line before him, naming him after one of the lineage for the omen's

---

[1] I translate the MSS. text retained by Burnet. As I understand the passage, Plato is thinking of the law of Solon which required an Athenian citizen to support his parents in their old age: the point is that the man who has made a murderous assault on his own parents, is punished in kind by forfeiting his claim for such support on his children. Hence I cannot follow Dr. England in accepting W. Jenstedt's alteration of ἄνδρες, μὴ (877 c 6) to ἄνδρες ἤδη, with the sense that 'if the sons are already grown men, they shall be obliged to support the exile, though the estate shall be in their possession'.

[2] δυστυχηθῇ (877 e 2) may be a bold formation of Plato's own suggested by the following ἀσεβηθῇ, but it looks very much as though H. Richards were right in suggesting δυστυχήσῃ.

sake, and offering prayers that they may all find in him by this means a progenitor of issue, a preserver of the hearth, and a minister in things secular and sacred with fairer fortunes than his father.[1] They shall then constitute him legal heir to the estate, while the criminal shall be left without name, children, or portion when such calamity overtakes him.

It should seem that boundary is not in all cases immediately adjacent to boundary; where there is a border-land, this interposing belt touches either region first and is common ground to both. In particular we have said that deeds of passion form such a border-land between the unintentional and the intentional. Hence our law of *wounding in anger* shall run thus. On conviction, first the offender shall repay the damage done two-fold, if the wound prove curable, four-fold for an incurable hurt. And if the wound, though curable, cause the injured man some grave and shameful disfigurement, the payment shall be [2] three-fold. In a case where the assailant causes detriment not only to the victim, but to the State as well, by incapacitating the wounded for national defence, he shall further, in addition to all other penalties, compensate the State for the loss. That is, in addition to his personal military service he shall also discharge that of the disabled and take his place in the ranks; failure to perform the task shall render him legally liable to prosecution at the instance of any man who pleases for evasion of military duty. The rate of compensation—whether it shall be two-fold, three-fold, or even four-fold—shall be determined by the court who found the verdict of guilty. If kinsman wound kinsman in the ways aforesaid, the parents and kinsfolk of both sexes and on both sides, within the degree of second cousins, shall meet, find a verdict, and commit the fixing of penalty to the natural parents of the parties. If their assessment be called in question, the male progenitors shall be authorized to make an assessment; if they fail to reach a decision for themselves, the matter shall be finally committed by them to the Curators of Law. In the case of such wounding of parents by their children, the judges shall be required to be persons of over sixty years of age who have children, not by adoption, but of their own begetting. On conviction, it shall

---

[1] i.e. the adoptive father, who has the misfortune that his actual son is a life-long exile.

[2] I depart here from Burnet's text which has τετραπλασίαν (878 c 4), four-fold, the reading of the MSS. The context makes Hermann's τριπλασίαν a certain emendation.

be for the court to determine whether the offence shall be
punished by death or some other sentence, more, or possibly
slightly less, heavy. No kinsman of the culprit shall be a
879 member of the court, even if he have attained the age required
by law. If a slave wound a free man in anger, the owner of
such slave shall deliver him to the wounded man to be used
at his pleasure; failing to deliver him, he shall himself make
good the damage. If the defendant allege that the case is one
of conspiracy between the slave and the wounded man, he
must sustain his allegations; if he lose his suit, he shall pay
the damage three-fold, if he gain it, he shall have an action for
kidnapping [1] against the party who so conspired with the slave.
He that wounds another without intent shall pay the simple
damage—no legislator can be expected to prescribe rules to
chance; the judges shall be as directed for the case of parents
wounded by their children, and they shall fix the amount of
compensation.

Assault and battery, in its various forms, is, like the cases of
which we have treated, an offence of violence. Apropos of
such conduct, it should never be forgotten by any one, man,
woman, or child, that seniority is held in highest consideration
alike by gods and by men who intend a long and happy life.
Hence the public assault of a younger man on his senior is a
shameful spectacle and abominable in the eye of heaven; if
the younger man is struck by the elder, the seemly course is
ever that he should meekly give place to his anger, and thus lay
up a capital of the same consideration for his own old age.
Hence our rule shall run thus. All shall show their reverence
for their seniors in act and speech. A man shall stay his hand
from any that is twenty years older than himself, be it man or
woman, as he would from his own father or mother; he must
spare all who are of an age to have begotten or borne him, in
duty to the gods of birth. He must likewise keep his hand from
the alien, old-established resident and recent arrival alike;
neither in aggression nor in self-defence shall he ever permit
himself to admonish one of that class by a blow. If the alien
strike him a wanton and insolent blow and he think correction
called for, he shall seize him and carry him before the court of
the Urban Commissioners, without striking him back, that he
may be taught never more to presume to beat a native. The

---

[1] I think it plain that ἀνδραποδισμοῦ (879 *a* 8) is a genitive of the charge
on which the collusive complainant is to be indicted, and that the interpretation 'an action of which the result will be that the defendant is sentenced
to slavery' is impossible.

commissioners shall take the accused and examine into his case, but with all due regard for the god who watches over the alien: if the alien be judged to have struck the native wrongfully, they shall give him as many lashes of the scourge as he has himself struck blows, to break him of his abuse of his position; if to have done no wrong, they shall warn and censure the apprehender and so dismiss both parties. If a man be struck by another of his own age, or a senior but childless man 880 by a junior, whether the parties be both old or both young, he shall defend himself with the arms nature has given him, his unweaponed naked fists (but if a man above forty years of age permit himself to fight another, whether he be assailant or attacked, he will meet no more than his desert if punished by being ill-reputed as a ruffian and a boor). With him that is amenable to this counsel we shall have no difficulties; the refractory, who care nothing for our preamble shall find a law ready to meet their case to this effect. If a man strike one that is his senior by twenty years or more, first, any bystander who is neither of the same age as the combatants nor younger shall come between them, on pain of proclamation as a coward; if the bystander be of the same years as the party struck, or younger, he shall defend the attacked as he would his own brother, father, or still older kinsman. Furthermore, he that presumed to strike his senior, as already said, shall stand his trial for assault and battery and, if convicted, shall lie in prison for a full year at the least; or if the court propose a longer sentence, its determination of the period shall be binding. If a foreigner or resident alien strike one who is his senior by twenty or more years, the same legal provision for assistance from bystanders shall be in force, and he that is condemned on this count, if an alien and non-resident among us, shall purge that offence [1] by two years of imprisonment, if a resident, shall be imprisoned three years for his violation of our laws, unless the court award sentence of a longer term. Further a fine shall be laid in all such cases on a bystander who does not render the assistance required by the law, the amount to be one mina for members of the first property-class, fifty drachmas for those of the second, thirty for those of the third, twenty for those of the fourth. The court, in such cases, shall be composed of the generals, infantry commanders, phylarchs, and hipparchs.

Laws, we may say, are made in part for the virtuous, to

---

[1] I think England right in suggesting that αὐτὴν (880 c 7) is an error for αὖ (due to accidental duplication of the letters of the following τὴν).

teach them what rule they should follow in their intercourse with one another, if they are to live in peace and good will; partly also for men who have shunned instruction, men whose stubborn tempers have yielded to none of those melting influences that might hold them back from utter debasement. It is to their account you must lay what I have now to utter, for them that a legislator will be driven to enact laws for which he could wish no need might ever arise. If any should ever presume to offer violent assault to father, mother, or one of their progenitors, 881 should so far forget his fear of the wrath of heaven and the punishments of which men tell beyond the grave as to be led by his conceit of knowing where he is utterly ignorant, and his scorn of the venerable and universal tradition into that trespass —some last deterrent is wanted for his case. Now the 'last penalty' is not death, and as for the pains said to be inflicted on such sinners in the world to come, though they are more extreme than any on earth and threaten in the tones of truth itself, they effect nothing for the deterrence of these criminal souls; were it otherwise, we should hear of no mishandlings of mothers or other cursed and presumptuous striking of progenitors. Hence we must make the chastisements for such crime here in this present life, if we can, no less stern than those of the life to come. Our next proclamation, then, shall be as follows: If a man, not being afflicted with insanity, presume to strike father, mother, or their parents, first, the bystanders shall come to their aid, as in cases already disposed of; the resident alien [1] who intervenes thus shall be offered a seat in the front rank at the public sports, he who fails in this duty shall go into perpetual banishment from our soil: a non-resident alien affording such help shall receive public commendation, and who witholds it, public censure; a slave who affords it shall have his freedom, a slave who withholds it shall suffer a hundred lashes with the scourge, to be administered by the Commissioners of the Market, if the offence is committed in the market-place; if committed in the city but elsewhere than in the market-square the correction to be inflicted by the Urban Commissioner in residence, if in some rural district by the commanders of the Rural Commission. Every bystander of native birth, child or woman or man, shall join in the rescue, crying out on the assailant as wretch and monster, and any that takes no part shall be held by the law under the curse of the god of kindred

---

[1] At 881 *c* 1, the MSS. and Burnet's text have μέτοικος ἢ ξένος, but the context shows that England is right in deleting the ἤ.

and family. If a man be convicted of assault on a parent, first he shall be perpetually relegated from the capital city to another region of the country and excluded from all holy places; if he do not observe the exclusion, the Rural Commission shall correct him with stripes, or in any way they please; if he returns he shall be condemned to death. If any free person eat, drink, or have any dealings whatever with the criminal, or so much as take his hand on meeting him wittingly, he shall enter neither place of worship, market-square, nor any part of the city whatsoever, without first purifying himself, as one that has been infected by contact with an accursed horror, and if he disobey and pollute holy places and city by infraction of the law, any magistrate informed of the fact and not proceeding against the guilty party shall have the fact charged against him as a point of first moment at 882 his audit. If a slave strike a free man, alien or citizen, a by-stander shall come to his aid or incur the specified fine, according to his status; the bystanders shall assist to bind the striker of the blow and shall deliver him to the injured party, who shall then lay him in fetters, scourge him with as many stripes as he pleases, provided no detriment to his master's interests ensue, and deliver him up to the master as his rightful owner. The words of the law shall run: If a slave strike a free man, except by order of a magistrate,[1] the owner of such slave shall receive him in fetters from the aggrieved party, and shall not release him therefrom until such slave have satisfied the aggrieved that he deserves to be at large. These same rules of law shall hold good for cases of the same kind when both parties are women, or where either is a woman and the other a man.

---

[1] The precaution is necessary to meet the case of a free man condemned to whipping by a court of law. The functionaries who administer the whipping will be slaves of the community.

BOOK X

884   *Ath.* Now that we have dealt with assault, we may enunciate a single and comprehensive principle of law in respect of cases of violence, to the following effect.   No man shall lift the goods and chattels of others, nor yet make use of a neighbour's property without the owner's permission, since such conduct is the beginning whence all the aforesaid mischiefs, past, present, or future, derive by consequence.   Now the gravest mischiefs of them all are the licenses and outrages of youth, and the affront is gravest when done to consecrated things, and most singularly grave again when the objects affronted are not only sacred but public, or partly public, as common to a tribe or 885 some similar group.   Second in order and in gravity are offences against private shrines and private tombs, and third impieties to parents other than the crimes already enumerated.[1]   A fourth form of outrage is the case when a man shows contempt for magistrates by lifting their goods or chattels, or using anything that is theirs without permission obtained, and a fifth branch will be such violation of the civil rights of the private citizen as calls for legal redress.   Hence we must provide a law applicable to all these branches alike.   Now as for actual sacrilege, open and forcible or secret, we have already said succinctly what the penalty for its commission should be [2]; we are now to prescribe a punishment for all verbal or practical outrage offered to the gods by speech or act.   But first our legislator must introduce his usual admonition, and it shall run to this effect. 'No man who believes in gods as the law would have him believe has ever yet of his own free will done unhallowed deed or let slip lawless discourse; if a man acts thus, 'tis from one of three causes; either, as I say, he does not believe, or again, he believes that they are, but are regardless of mankind, or lastly, that they are lightly to be won over by the cajoling of offerings and prayers.'

Clin. Then how are we to treat such men, or what should we say to them?

---

[1] The acts of physical violence dealt with in the last book.
[2] *Supra* 854 *d.*

274

Ath. Nay, my dear sir, let us begin by giving a hearing to the mockeries in which, as I conceive, their scorn of us would find utterance.

Clin. And what form would this mockery take?

Ath. Why, their satire might well run to this effect: 'Gentlemen of Athens, Lacedaemon, and Cnossus, you are in the right of it. Some of us, in fact, recognize no gods whatsoever, and others gods such as you describe. So we make the same demand of you that you have yourselves made of the laws: before you come to the severities of threats, it is for you to try persuasion; to convince us by sufficient proof that there really are gods, and that they are too good to be diverted from the path of justice by the attraction of gifts. As things are, that, and more to the same effect, is what we have heard from those who have the repute of being our first-rate poets, orators, prophets, and priests, and countless thousands of others, and this is why most of us follow the path not of refusing to do wrong, but of committing it and trying to patch it up. So we expect you, as legislators who make a profession of humanity rather than severity, to try persuasion on us in the first instance. Your case for the existence of gods may not be much better than that of the other side, but persuade us that it *is* better in the one point of *truth*, and you may perhaps make converts of us. So if you think our challenge a fair one, you must try to answer it.'

Clin. Why, surely, sir, it looks easy enough to speak the truth in saying that gods exist.

Ath. And on what grounds? 886

Clin. Why, to begin with, think of the earth, and sun, and planets, and everything! And the wonderful and beautiful order of the seasons with its distinctions of years and months! Besides, there is the fact that all mankind, Greeks and non-Greeks alike, believe in the existence of gods.

Ath. My dear friend, I have a fear—I will never call it an *awe*—of these evil men; a fear that they may despise us. You and our friend, in fact, do not understand the ground of their controversy [1] with us; you imagine that what impels their souls to irreligion is incontinence of pleasures and lusts, and nothing more.

Clin. Why, sir, what further cause can there be in the case?

[1] Or, if we adopt Cornarius's plausible emendation διαφθορᾶς for the διαφορᾶς of 886 *a* 9, 'the cause of their depravity'.

Ath. One of which your friend and you can be expected to know nothing; you fail to remark it because it does not touch your lives.

Clin. Now I wonder what it can be to which you allude.

Ath. Why, folly of a deadly sort that conceits itself to be the height of wisdom.

Clin. And what is that?

Ath. We have in my own community literary narratives— the excellence of your civic institutions, I am informed, prevents their appearance among you—which treat of the gods, some of them in verse, and others again in prose: the most ancient of these narratives relate that the primitive realities were the sky, and so forth; when the story has got a little way past this starting-point it recounts the birth of the gods, and their subsequent conduct towards each other. Now whether in other respects the effect of these stories on those who hear them is good or the reverse is not lightly to be decided, in view of their antiquity, but as concerns their bearing on the tendance and reverence due to parents, I could certainly never commend them as salutary, nor as true at all. However, we may dismiss the primitive stories without more ado; let them be told in any way Heaven pleases. But the theories of our modern men of enlightenment must be held to account for the mischief they cause. Now the effect of their compositions is this. When you and I produce our evidence of the existence of gods, and allege this very point—the deity or divinity of sun and moon, planets and earth—the converts of these sages will reply that they are but earth and stones, incapable of minding human conduct, however plausibly we have coated them over with a varnish of sugared eloquence.

Clin. A dreadful theory this that you are talking of, sir, even if there were only one such; how much more dreadful our present age, when such doctrines are so rife.

Ath. Well, what answer have we, then? What course should we take? Must we look on ourselves as, so to say, indicted at the bar of the ungodly and defend our incriminated legislation 887 from the charge that it has no right to assume the existence of gods? Or should we drop the subject and return to our lawmaking for fear our preamble may actually prove longer than the enactments to follow it? The discourse, to be sure, will run to considerable length, if we are first to furnish the undevoutly disposed with adequate proofs on the points which they said we were bound to treat, and so put the opponent in fear, only proceeding to the enactment of suitable regulations after we have thus created a disrelish for irreligion.

Clin. Well, sir, in the little while we have spent together we have repeatedly had occasion to remark that there is no reason to prefer brevity of speech, in our present business to length— the proverbial 'pursuer' is not on our traces; so we should make but a sorry and ludicrous show if we chose the shorter course rather than the best. And 'tis of the first importance to give our plea for the existence of gods, and good gods with a super-human reverence for right, such persuasiveness as we can; such a preamble would, in fact, be the noblest and best defence for our whole legislation. Let us, then, show neither reluctance nor impatience, but unreservedly employ whatever gifts of persuasion we may possess in such matters on the task of adequate exposition to the utmost of our powers.

Ath. The earnestness and passion of your speech are, I feel, an invitation to prayer; they leave no further room for post-ponement of the argument. Come then; how shall we plead for the existence of gods dispassionately? To be sure, no man can help feeling some resentment and disgust with the parties who now, as in the past, impose the burden of the argument on us by their want of faith in the stories heard so often in earliest infancy, while still at the breast, from their mothers and nurses— stories, you may say, crooned over them, in sport and in earnest, like spells—and heard again in prayers offered over sacrifices, in conjunction with the spectacle which gives such intense delight to the eye and ear of children, as it is enacted at a sacrifice, the spectacle of our parents addressing their gods, with assured belief in their existence, in earnest prayer and supplication for themselves and their children. Then, again, at rising and setting of sun and moon, they have heard and seen the universal prostrations and devotions of mankind, Greeks and non-Greeks alike, in all the varied circumstances of evil fortune and good, with their implication that gods are no fictions, but the most certain of realities, and their being beyond the remotest shadow of a doubt. When we see all this evidence treated with contempt by the persons who are forcing us into our present argument, and that, as any man with a grain of intelligence will admit, without a single respectable reason, how, I ask, is a man to find gentle language in which to combine reproof with instruction in the initial truth about the gods— 888 that of their existence? Still, the task is to be faced; we can never permit one party among us to run mad from lust of pleasure, and the rest equally mad from fury against them. So our dispassionate preliminary admonition to minds thus depraved shall run to this effect: (we will suppress our passion and use gentle language, imagining ourselves to be addressing a single person of the type). 'My lad, you are still young, and as time advances it will lead you to a complete reversal of many of your present convictions; you should wait for the future, then, before you undertake to judge of the supreme issues; and the greatest of these, though you now count it so trivial—is that of thinking rightly about the gods and so living well, or the reverse. I may begin with a single word of significant warning which you will assuredly find to be no mistake, and it is this. You yourself and your friends, are not the first nor the only persons to embrace this tenet as your doctrine about gods; nay, in every age there are sufferers from the malady, more or fewer. Hence I, who have had the acquaintance of many such, can assure you that no one who in early life has adopted this doctrine of the non-existence of gods has ever persisted to old age constant to that conviction, though there have been cases—not many, certainly, but still some few—of persistence in the other two attitudes, the belief that there are gods but that they are indifferent to human conduct, and again, that, though not indifferent, they are lightly placated by sacrifice and prayers. If you will be ruled by me, then, you will wait for the fullness of clear and confident judgment on these matters to come to you, and inquire whether truth lies in one direction or another, seeking for guidance in all quarters, and above all from the legislator. Meanwhile, beware of all impiety towards gods. For he who is framing the law for you must make it his business, hereafter as well as now, to instruct you in the truth of this matter.'

Clin. Admirably said, sir, so far as we have gone yet.

Ath. Just so, Megillus and Clinias; but we have unconsciously embroiled ourselves with a portentous theory.

Clin. And what theory may that be?

Ath. One which is widely held to be the last word of wisdom.

Clin. You must be still more explicit.

Ath. We are told, you know, that everything whatever which comes, has come, or will come into existence is a product either of nature, or of art, or of chance.

Clin. And rightly so told, are we not?

Ath. Why, there is, of course, a presumption that what wise 889 men tell us is true. But suppose we follow up their traces, and ask ourselves what the real meaning of the spokesmen of that party may be.

Clin. With all my heart.

Ath. Evidently, so they say, all the grandest and fairest of things are products of nature and chance, and only the more insignificant of art. Art takes over the grand primary works from the hands of nature, already formed, and then models and fashions the more insignificant, and this is the very reason why we all call them 'artificial'.

Clin. You mean to say?——

Ath. Let me put it more plainly still. Fire and water, earth and air—so they say—all owe their being to nature and chance, none of them to art; they, in turn, are the agents, and the absolutely soulless agents, in the production of the bodies of the next rank, the earth, sun, moon, and stars. They drifted casually, each in virtue of their several tendencies; as they came together in certain fitting and convenient dispositions—hot with cold, dry with moist, soft with hard, and so on in all the inevitable casual combinations which arise from blending of contraries—thus, and on this wise, they gave birth to the whole heavens and all their contents, and, in due course, to all animals and plants, when once all the seasons of the year had been produced from those same causes; not, so they say, by the agency of mind, or any god, or art, but, as I tell you, by nature and chance. Art, the subsequent late-born product of these causes, herself as perishable as her creators, has since given birth to certain toys with little real substance in them, simulacra as shadowy as the arts themselves, such as those which spring from painting, music, and the other fellow crafts. Or if there are arts which really produce anything of genuine worth, they are those which lend their aid to nature, like medicine, husbandry, gymnastic. Statesmanship in especial, they say, is a thing which has a little in common with nature, but is mainly a business of art; legislation, likewise, is altogether an affair not of nature, but of art, and its positions are unreal.

Clin. Unreal—but how so?

Ath. Why, my dear sir, to begin with, this party assert that gods have no real and natural, but only an artificial being, in virtue of legal conventions, as they call them, and thus there are different gods for different places, conformably to the convention made by each group among themselves when they drew up their legislation. Then they actually declare that the really and naturally laudable is one thing and the conventionally laudable quite another, while as for right, there is absolutely no such thing as a real and natural right, mankind are eternally disputing about rights and altering them, and every change 890 thus made, once made, is from that moment valid, though it owes its being to artifice and legislation, not to anything you could call nature. All these views, my friends, come from men who impress the young as wise, prose-writers and poets who profess that indefeasible right means whatever a man can carry with the high hand. Hence our epidemics of youthful irreligion—as though there were no gods such as the law enjoins us to believe in—and hence the factions created by those who seek, on such grounds, to attract men to the 'really and naturally right life', that is, the life of real domination over others, not of conventional service to them.

Clin. What an awful creed you describe, sir! What a general corruption of the young people of whole cities and private households!

Ath. Too true, Clinias, too true. But how would you have the legislator act where such a situation is of long standing? Should he be content to stand up in public and threaten people all round that unless they confess the being of gods, and believe in their hearts that they are such as his law declares—(and the case is the same with the laudable, the right, and everything of highest moment; and all that makes for virtue or vice;[1] action must conform in all cases to the convictions prescribed by the text of the legislation)—is he to threaten, I say, that those who will not lend a ready ear to the laws shall in some cases suffer death, in others be visited with bonds and whipping, in others with infamy, and in yet others with poverty and banishment, but to have no words of persuasion with which to work on his people, as he dictates their laws, and so, it may be, tame them?

Clin. Far from it, sir, far from it. If there are indeed persuasives, however weak, in such matters, no legislator who deserves the slightest consideration must ever faint. He should strain every nerve, as they say, to plead in support of the old traditional belief of the being of gods and of all you have just recounted. In especial also, he should defend the claim of law itself and of art to be natural, or no less real than nature, seeing that they are products of mind by a sound argument which I take you to be now propounding and in which I concur.

[1] I follow Burnet's general punctuation of the sentence, but agree with England that it requires the change of ὅσα δὲ at 890 c 1 to ὅσα τε (Stephanus), or possibly ὅσα γε. I adopt the former change in the translation.

Ath. Why, Clinias, here is zeal indeed! But pray, are not statements thus made to a multitude hard to support by argument, and do they not entail an interminable deal of it?

Clin. Well, sir, and what then? We bore with one another through all those long discourses of the wine-cup and of music, and are we to show less patience now we are treating of gods and kindred themes? And, mark you, such argument will be a most valuable aid to intelligent legislation, because legal enactments, once put into writing, remain always on record, 891 as though to challenge the question of all time to come. Hence we need feel no dismay if they should be difficult on a first hearing, since even the dull student may recur to them for reiterated scrutiny. Nor does their length, provided they are beneficial, make it less irrational than it is, in my opinion at least, impious for any man to refuse such discourse his heartiest support.

Meg. What Clinias says, sir, has my fullest approval.

Ath. And mine, too, Megillus, and we must do as he bids us. To be sure, if such theories had not been so widely broadcast, as we may fairly say, throughout all mankind, there would have been no need for arguments to defend the being of gods, but, as the case stands, they cannot be dispensed with. So with the highest laws in risk of perishing at the hands of wicked men, whose function can it be to come to the rescue before the legislator?

Meg. Why, no man's.

Ath. Well then, Clinias—for you must be my partner in the argument—let me hear *your* opinion once more. Presumably one who reasons thus holds that fire and water, earth and air, are the most primitive origins of all things—*nature* being just the name he gives to them—but the soul is a later derivative from them. Or, more probably, it is no case of a presumption; his argument is an actual declaration to that effect.

Cin. Precisely.

Ath. Why, in God's name then, have we traced the unreason and error of all who have ever busied themselves with research into nature back to what we may call its source? Pray consider the point with careful attention to all their positions, as it will make a vast difference if we can show that those who have taken up with irreligious doctrines and set the tune for others to follow have actually argued their case ill and fallaciously. And I honestly believe this to be the fact.

Clin. Excellent; but you must try to explain where the fallacy lies.

Ath. Then I am afraid I shall have to treat of rather unfamiliar matters.

Clin. There is no need for your hesitation, sir. I see you apprehend you will be going outside the limits of legislation if we are to deal with such matters. But if that is the one and only way to accordance with the truth about gods, as now stated in our law, why, my good man, our argument must take it.

Ath. Then it seems I must propound my none too familiar thesis at once, and here it is. In the doctrine of which the soul of the ungodly is the product, the primal cause of all coming to be and ceasing to be is pronounced to be not primal but secondary and derivative, the secondary primitive. Hence their error about the veritable being of gods.

892 *Clin.* I am still in the dark.

Ath. Soul, my friend, soul is that of whose nature and potency all but the few would seem to know nothing; in this general ignorance of it they know not in particular of its origin, how it is among the primal things, elder-born than all bodies and prime source of all their changes and transformations. But if this is indeed so, must not all that is akin to soul needs be of earlier birth than all that is proper to bodies, seeing that soul herself is older than body?

Clin. Why, necessarily.

Ath. And so judgment and foresight, wisdom, art and law, must be prior to hard and soft, heavy and light; ay, and the grand primal works and deeds, for the very reason that they are primal, will prove to be those of art; those of nature, and nature herself—wrongly so called—will be secondary and derivative from art and mind.

Clin. 'Wrongly so called'; why wrongly?

Ath. Why, by *nature* they mean what was there to begin with; but if we can show that soul came first—that it was not fire, nor air, but soul which was there to begin with—it will be perfectly true to say that it is the existence of soul which is most eminently *natural*. Now this is the case if it can be proved that soul is more ancient than body, and not otherwise.

Clin. How true that is!

Ath. Then our next step must be to address ourselves to the proof of that point.

Clin. Yes, of course.

Ath. Good; then let us be on our guard against the extreme

subtleties of the argument; we are elderly, and it a lusty
stripling who may slip through our fingers by a feint; then we
shall make ourselves a laughing-stock, and be judged to have
failed even of the little in our eagerness to reach after the
greater. So reflect a moment. Suppose the three of us had
to cross a river with a strong current, and I, being the youngest
of the party and having a wide experience of such currents,
were to say: 'I must first try the crossing by myself, leaving
you in safety, to see whether the water is equally fordable for
you, my elders, or not; if it proves so, afterwards I must call to
you and help you across it by my experience, but if it turns out
to be out of the depth of men of your years, the risk will have
been all mine', you would think this a reasonable suggestion.
Well, it is even so with the waters of discourse which confront
us now; the current is strong, and the passage perhaps too
much for your strength. So to save you from being dizzied
and staggered by the rush of questions you are unpractised in 893
answering, and the consequent unpleasantness of an undignified
and unbecoming situation, I propose that I should act in this
same fashion now: I will first put certain questions to myself
while you listen in safety, and then once more give the answers
to them myself; this plan will be followed throughout the
argument until our discussion of the soul is completed, and its
priority to body proved.

Clin. An admirable proposal, sir; pray, act upon it.

Ath. To the work, then, and if we are ever to beseech God's
help, let it be done now. Let us take it as understood that
the gods have, of course, been invoked in all earnest to assist
our proof of their own being, and plunge into the waters of the
argument before us with the prayer as a sure guiding-rope for
our support. If put to the proof, then, on such a subject, the
safest course, I take it, is to meet the following questions with
the following answers. Sir—so someone may say—are all
things at rest, and nothing in motion? Or is the truth the very
reverse? Or are some things in motion, others at rest? Of
course, I shall reply, some are moving and others at rest. And
those which move are moving, just as those which are at rest
are resting, in a space of some kind? Of course. And some
of them, you will grant, do this in a single situation, others
in more than one? When you speak of moving in a single
situation, I shall reply, you refer to things characterized by the
immobility of their centres, as is the case with the revolution of
so-called 'sleeping' circles? Yes. And we observe, in the case

of this revolution that such a motion carries round the greatest
and the smallest circle together, dividing itself proportionately
to lesser and greater, and being itself proportionately less and
greater.[1] This, in fact, is what makes it a source of all sorts
of marvels, since it supplies greater and smaller circles at once
with velocities high or low answering to their sizes—an effect
one might have imagined impossible.[2] Just so. And by things
which move in several situations I suppose you mean those
which have a motion of translation and shift at every moment
to a fresh place, sometimes having a single point of support,
sometimes, in the case of rolling, more than one.[3] In their
various encounters one with another, collision with a stationary
object disintegrates, while impact upon other moving objects
coming from an opposite quarter integrates them into new
combinations which are betwixt and between the original
components?[4] Yes, I grant the facts are as you state them.
And further with integration goes augmentation in bulk, and
reduction of bulk with disintegration—provided, that is, the
894 pre-established constitution of the object persists; if it does not,
both processes give rise to dissolution.[5] But the condition

[1] e.g. in the revolution of a circular disk every point on the disk, except
the centre, is describing a circle. All the circles complete their revolutions
in the same time, but they are of different circumference, according to the
distances of the several points from the centre, hence the velocities also
differ in the same proportion.

[2] England observes that Plato 'must have had some special reason for
enlarging on this peculiarity of circular motion'. He had, and it is this.
Until Eudoxus devised his famous astronomical hypothesis of concentric
spheres, the planetary motions were thought of, as they are always by
Plato himself, on the analogy of the revolution of wheels or disks spun
round their centre. The 'orbit', as we call it, was thought of as carrying
round the planet, as a ring turned round the finger carries the stone set
in it. This is, for example, the picture presupposed in the myth of Er in
Rep. X, and throughout the *Timaeus*. The thought in Plato's mind is
that the velocity of a planet in its orbit is proportional to its distance from
the centre of the system.

[3] The distinction is between *gliding* and rolling. As my pencil glides
over the paper, the *same* point of the pencil is successively in contact with
different points in the paper; it would be otherwise if the pencil were
allowed to roll.

[4] The meaning is that when a moving mass collides with a stationary,
the former is disintegrated; the result of collision between two masses
moving in different directions is taken to be coalescence of the two into a
single moving mass, which Plato speaks of as, in some sense, 'betwixt and
between' its components. I suppose him to mean that the direction and
velocity of the new movement are intermediate between those of the
original motions.

[5] What is meant by the 'pre-established condition' (καθεστηκυῖα ἕξις,
893 e 7) of the moving things? England says hesitatingly (and Bury
without hesitation) its physical state, as solid, liquid, or gaseous. This,
I believe, is an error. Plato is describing the results of various combina-

under which coming-to-be universally takes place—what is it?
Manifestly 'tis effected whenever its starting-point has received
increment and so come to its second stage, and from this to
the next, and so by three steps acquired perceptibility to
percipients.[1] 'Tis ever by such change and transformation of
motion that a thing comes to be; it is in veritable being so long
as it persists; when it has changed to a different constitution,
it is utterly destroyed. Perhaps, my friends, we have now
classed and numbered all the types of motion—except, indeed,
two?

Clin. And what are those two?

Ath. Why, the very pair, my good sir, with an eye to which
our whole discussion is now in progress.

Clin. I must ask you to be plainer.

Ath. The discussion began with a view to soul, did it not?

Clin. To be sure, it did.

Ath. Then let us take for one of our pair the motion which
can regularly set other things in movement but not itself; as
a second single type in the scheme of motions in general we will
take that which can regularly set itself going as well as other
things, alike in processes of integration and disintegration, by
way of augmentation and its opposite, or by coming into and
perishing out of being.

Clin. And so we will.

Ath. We may proceed, then, to place the type which regularly
moves some object other than itself, and is itself induced by
such an object, ninth on our list; that which moves itself as
well as other things—it finds its place in all doing and all
being-done-to, and is veritably called transformation and motion
of all that is—this we will reckon as tenth.

Clin. Yes, certainly.

Ath. Now of these ten motions which should we be most
right to pronounce most powerful of all, and most superlatively
effective?

Clin. Why, of course, we are bound to say that that which

tion of motions from a purely kinematical—not a physical—point of view.
I take him, therefore to mean that so long as the same *kinematical configuration*, or pattern of motion, is preserved, the 'integration' of which
he has spoken gives rise to increase in bulk.

[1] The language is purposely brief and slightly obscure, being meant to
be a little 'over the heads' of the two old men. The key to it is τρίτη
αὔξη, a mathematical technicality for 'third dimension'. To be per-
ceptible to sense a thing must have *volume*. *Volumes* are regarded as
generated by the motion of a surface, surfaces by motion of a line or lines,
and lines by that of a point.

can move itself is infinitely most effective, and all the rest posterior to it.

Ath. Excellent. Then we should perhaps find one or two mistakes in what has just been said?

Clin. And what mistakes are they?

Ath. We were wrong, I think, in using that word 'tenth'.

Clin. But why wrong?

Ath. It is demonstrably *first* in procedure, as in power, and the next in order is, as we hold, *second*, though we have just called it—oddly enough—ninth.

Clin. How am I to understand you?

Ath. Why, thus. When we have one thing making a change in a second, the second, in turn, in a third, and so on—will there ever, in such a series, be a first source of change? Why, how can what is set moving by something other than itself ever be the first of the causes of alteration? The thing is an impossibility. But when something[1] which has set itself moving alters a second thing, this second thing still a third, and the motion is thus passed on in course to thousands and tens of
895 thousands of things, will there be any starting-point for the whole movement of all, other than the change in the movement which initiated itself?

Clin. Admirably put, and the position must be conceded.

Ath. Besides, let us put the point over again in this way, once more answering our own question. Suppose all things were to come together and stand still—as most of the party have the hardihood to affirm—which of the movements we have specified must be the first to arise in things? Why, of course, that which can move itself; there can be no possible previous origination of change by anything else, since, by hypothesis, change was not previously existent in the system. Consequently as the source of all motions whatsoever, the first to occur among bodies at rest and the first in rank in moving bodies, the motion which initiates itself we shall pronounce to be necessarily the earliest and mightiest of all changes, while that which is altered by something else and sets something else moving is secondary.

Clin. Unquestionably.

Ath. Then, now that the discussion has reached this point, we may answer a further question.

Clin. And what question is it?

In 894 *e* 7 Apelt's ὅ γ' ἂν seems to me a certain emendation of the MSS. ὅταν.

Ath. When we see that this motion has shown itself in a thing composed of earth, water, or fire—separately or in combination—how should we describe the character resident in such a thing?

Clin. Am I right in supposing you to ask whether, when the thing moves itself, we speak of it as *alive?*

Ath. Certainly.

Clin. Alive? Of course it is alive.

Ath. Very well, and when we see soul in a thing, the case is the same, is it not? We must allow that the thing is alive.

Clin. Precisely.

Ath. In Heaven's name, then, hold; you will grant, I presume, that there are three points to be noted about anything?

Clin. You mean?

Ath. I mean, for one, the reality of the thing, what it *is*; for another the *definition* of this reality; for another, its *name*. And thus you see there are two questions we can ask about everything which is.

Clin. And what are the two?

Ath. Sometimes a man propounds the bare name and demands the definition; sometimes, again, he propounds the definition by itself and asks for the corresponding name. In other words, we mean something to this effect, do we not?

Clin. To what effect?

Ath. There is, as you know, bisection in numbers, as in other things. Well, in the case of a number, the *name* of the thing is 'even', and the definition 'number divisible into two equal parts'.

Clin. Certainly.

Ath. That is the sort of case I have in mind. We are denoting the same thing, are we not, in either case, whether we are asked about the definition and reply with the name, or about the name, and reply with the definition? It is the same thing we describe indifferently by the name 'even', and the definition 'number divided into two equal parts'?

Clin. Identically the same.

Ath. Well then, what is the definition of the thing for which *soul* is the name? Can we find any but the phrase we have just used, 'the motion which can set itself moving'? 896

Clin. You mean that the self-same reality which has the name *soul* in the vocabulary of all of us has *self-movement* as its definition?

Ath. I do. But if this is indeed so, is there anything we can desiderate, anything further towards complete demonstration of the identity of soul with the primal becoming and movement of all that is, has been, or shall be, and of all their contraries, seeing it has disclosed itself as the universal cause of all change and motion?

Clin. No, indeed. Our proof that soul, since it is found to be the source of movement, is the first-born of all things is absolutely complete.

Ath. Then must not the motion which, wherever it arises, is induced by something else, but never confers the power of self-motion on anything, come second in the scale, or as low down as you please to put it, being, in fact, change in a truly soulless body?

Clin. Rightly argued.

Ath. Consequently it will be a right, decisive, true and final statement to assert, as we did, that soul is prior to body, body secondary and derivative, soul governing in the real order of things, and body being subject to governance.

Clin. Indeed it would.

Ath. But we have not, I imagine, forgotten our earlier agreement that if soul could be proved older than body, the characters of soul must also be older than those of body.

Clin. Not in the least.

Ath. And so moods and habits of mind, wishes, calculations, and true judgments, purposes,[1] and memories, will all be prior to physical lengths, breadths, and depths, in virtue of the priority of soul itself to body.

Clin. Inevitably so.

Ath. Hence we are driven, are we not, to agree in the consequence that soul is the cause of good and evil, fair and foul, right and wrong; in fact of all contraries, if we mean to assert it as the *universal* cause?

Clin. Certainly we are.

Ath. Well then, if indwelling soul thus controls all things universally that move anywhere, are we not bound to say it controls heaven itself?

Clin. Yes, of course.

Ath. And is this done by one single soul, or by more than one? I will give the answer for both of you, 'by more than one'.

---

[1] ἐπιμέλειαι (896 *d* 1) 'tendances', acts of 'caring for' some object. Hence, as coupled with μνῆμαι, purposes for the future, in antithesis with recollections of the past.

At least we must assume not fewer than two, one beneficent, the other capable of the contrary effect? [1]

Clin. Decidedly you are in the right of it.

Ath. So far, so good. Soul, then, by her own motions stirs all things in sky, earth, or sea (and the names of these motions are wish, reflection, foresight, counsel, judgment—true or false 897 —pleasure, pain, hope, fear, hate, love), stirs them, I say, by these and whatever other kindred, or primary, motions there may be. They, in turn, bring in their train secondary and corporeal movements, and so guide all things to increase and decrease, disgregation and integration, with their attendant characters of heat and cold, weight and lightness, hardness and softness, white and black, dry and sweet. By these and all her instruments, when wisdom is her helper, . . . [2] she conducts all things to the right and happy issue, whereas when she companies with folly, the effect is clean contrary. Shall we set it down that this is so, or have we still our doubts that it may be otherwise?

Clin. Nay, there is no doubt whatsoever.

Ath. Then which manner of soul, must we say, has control of heaven and earth and their whole circuit? That which is prudent and replete with goodness, or that which has neither virtue? Shall we, if you please, give the question this answer?

Clin. What answer?

Ath. Why, man, if the whole path and movement of heaven and all its contents are of like nature with the motion, revolution, and calculations of wisdom, and proceed after that kind, plainly we must say it is the supremely good soul that takes forethought for the universe and guides it along that path.

Clin. True.

---

[1] It was on these words that Plutarch and Atticus in antiquity, like some modern interpreters, based their theory that Plato believed in two 'souls of the world', or at least two conflicting factors in the 'soul of the world', a good and an evil. But there is nothing said here about an evil 'soul of the world'. The question is only whether *all* that takes place can be due to the initiation of one and the same soul, and the answer is NO, on the ground that good and evil, right and wrong, are equally actual. Thus the minimum number of souls required to account for this would be two, one good, and one 'capable of the contrary'.

[2] I omit the words ἀεὶ θεὸν ὀρθῶς θεοῖς of 897 b 2, as the MSS. text is both uncertain and corrupt. As a makeshift, we might adopt Winckelmann's ὀρθῶς θέουσα for ὀρθῶς θεοῖς, which give the sense that when 'wisdom which is ever a god' is her helper 'soul, running her course rightly, conducts things to the right and happy issue'. A has a marginal variant θεὸς οὖσα for θεὸν ὀρθῶς θεοῖς, but ψυχή, as distinct from νοῦς, is never spoken of by Plato as a god.

Ath. But the evil, if the procedure is distraught and without order.

Clin. That is true, too.

Ath. Then of what nature, pray, is the movement of wisdom? There, my friends, we reach a question hard to be answered with due understanding. So it is only fair that I too should have a hand in your present reply.

Clin. A welcome proposal.

Ath. Then let us beware of creating a darkness at noonday for ourselves by gazing, so to say, direct at the sun as we give our answer, as though we could hope to attain adequate vision and perception of wisdom with mortal eyes. 'Twill be the safer course to turn our gaze on an image of the object of our quest.

Clin. You mean to say——?

Ath. Let us take as that image the motion in our list of ten to which wisdom bears a resemblance. We will all recall it, as I join you in giving our answer.

Clin. An excellent proposal.

Ath. Then do we still remember this much of what we said, that we decided that some things are in motion and others at rest?

Clin. We do.

Ath. And that some of those in motion move in one place, 898 others in more than one?

Clin. Certainly.

Ath. Of these two movements, that confined to one place must in every case be performed about a centre, after the fashion of a well-turned cartwheel, and it is this which must surely have the closest affinity and resemblance that may be to the revolution of intelligence.

Clin. Your meaning is——?

Ath. Why, of course, that if we say that intelligence and movement performed in one place are both like the revolutions of a well-made globe, in moving regularly and uniformly in one compass about one centre, and in one sense, according to one single law and plan, we need have no fear of proving unskilled artists in imagery.

Clin. Very true.

Ath. And again, motion which is never regular or uniform, never in the same compass, nor about the same centre, or in one place, motion which has no order, plan, or law, will have kinship with folly of every kind.

Clin. Indeed it will.

Ath. *Now* there can be no further obstacle to positive assertion, since we have found that it is soul which conducts the
revolutions of all things, and are also bound to say that the
soul by which the circle of the heavens is turned about with
all foresight and order is either the supremely good, or its
contrary——[1]

Clin. Nay, sir, if what has gone before is true, it were blasphemy to ascribe the work to aught but a soul or souls—one
or more than one—of absolute goodness.

Ath. You have followed the argument to good purpose
indeed, Clinias, but I would have you follow it a step farther
still.

Clin. And what is that step?

Ath. Take sun, and moon, and the other heavenly bodies:
if the revolution of all is due to soul, so also is that of each
singly, is it not?

Clin. Why, of course.

Ath. Thus we may take one of them in particular as the
subject of an argument we shall find no less applicable to all
these celestial bodies.

Clin. And which of them shall we take?[2]

Ath. The sun, whose body can be seen by any man, but his
soul by no man, any more than that of any other creature's
body is to be seen, during life or at the time of death. We
have every reason to believe that it enfolds us in a fashion
utterly imperceptible to all bodily senses, and is only to be
discerned by the understanding. So here is a relevant consideration which we must apprehend by an act of pure understanding
and thought.

Clin. And what is it?

Ath. Since soul guides the sun on his course, we cannot well
go wrong in saying that she must act in one of three ways.

Clin. And what are the three?

Ath. Either she dwells within this visible round body and
conveys it hither and thither, as our soul carries us wherever
we go; or, as some hold, she provides herself a body of her
own, of fire, or it may be, of air, and pushes body from without 899
forcibly by body; or finally, she is herself naked of body, and

---

[1] I follow England in the view that the intended speech of the Athenian
is interrupted by Clinias.
[2] Taking, with Burnet and most editors, the reading τίνος from Eusebius
in 898 *d* 8. But the τίνας of the MSS. also gives an excellent sense.
'What argument is this?—The sun's body is visible to every one, but his
soul to no one, any more than . . .'

does this work of guidance by some other most miraculous faculties of hers.

Clin. Yes, one of these ways is that by which soul transacts the whole business; so much is sure.

Ath. . . .[1] this soul, whether we take it to bring light to the world by driving the sun as its car, or from without, or in what way soever, each of us should esteem a god, should he not?

Clin. He should, if not sunk in the very depths of folly.

Ath. Of all the planets, of the moon, of years and months and all seasons, what other story shall we have to tell than just this same, that since soul, or souls, and those souls good with perfect goodness, have proved to be the causes of all, these souls we hold to be gods, whether they direct the universe by inhabiting bodies, like animated beings, or whatever the manner of their action? Will any man who shares this belief bear to hear it said that all things are not 'full of gods'?

Clin. No man, sir, can be so much beside himself.

Ath. Then, my dear Megillus and Clinias, we may state our terms to him who has hitherto declined to acknowledge gods and dispose of him.

Clin. What terms shall we offer?

Ath. Either he must show us that we are wrong in pronouncing soul the primary source of all things, and in the further consequences we drew, or if unable to get the better of our reasoning, he must yield to us and live henceforth a believer in gods. Let us consider, then, whether our defence of the being of gods against the unbeliever is now duly complete or defective.

Clin. Defective, sir? Anything but that.

Ath. Then, so far as concerns that party, let our discourse come to its end; we are now to admonish him who confesses the being of gods but denies that they take any heed of the affairs of men. 'Fair sir,' we will say, 'as to your belief in gods, 'tis perhaps some kinship with the divine that draws you to your native stock in worship and acknowledgment; on the other side there are private and public fortunes of ill and wicked men—fortunes truly unblessed, but passionately, though tastelessly, extolled as blessed by the voice of public repute—and these draw you towards irreligion when you hear them wrongly harped upon in poetry and literature of all kinds. Or, it may

---

[1] I have left untranslated the opening words of 899 *a* 7, αὐτοῦ δὴ ἄμεινον. They make neither sense nor satisfactory grammar, and the proposed 'emendations' are unhappy. With misgiving I suggest as a possibility αὐτοῦ δὴ ἄμεινον <ὄν> or ἀμείνονα, 'a man should regard this soul, a thing so much better than himself, as a god.'

be, you remark men who have come to the grave in fullness of days and left sons and sons' sons after them in high honours, and now you are dismayed when you find, from what you have heard from others or from your own personal observation of sundry deeds of impiety and horror in their histories, that some of the number have risen by these very crimes from obscurity to pre-eminence and a throne. The visible consequence of it all is that at such moments, while your kinship with the gods will not permit you to charge them with the responsibility for this, ill reasoning and inability to reproach the gods have together brought you to your present pass, your conviction that though they indeed exist, they despise and disregard humanity. So, that your present creed may lead you to no worse pitch of impiety, that the spectre, as we may say, may happily be laid, as it approaches, by the power of argument, we must try to connect what now remains to be said with our original rejoinder to the complete atheist, and so have the benefit of that also.' You, Clinias—and you too, Megillus —must, as before, take the young man's place as respondent. And if the argument should chance to miscarry, I will once more take the task off your hands and put you across the waters.

Clin. A sound proposal. Act on it, then, and we, too, will do our best to carry out your suggestions.

Ath. Well, perhaps it would not be hard to establish as much as this, that the gods are more, not less, careful for small things than for great. The man was present, you know, at our recent discussion and was told that the gods, who are good with perfect goodness, have the universal charge of all things as their special and proper function.

Clin. He was most certainly told so.

Ath. Then let them join us in asking what we mean by the goodness in virtue of which we confess the gods to be good. Come, now; prudence, may we say, and understanding belong to goodness, their opposites to badness?

Clin. We may.

Ath. And again that valour is part of goodness, cowardice of badness?

Clin. Assuredly.

Ath. And the latter qualities we shall call shameful, the former noble?

Clin. No doubt we must.

Ath. And all the baser qualities, we shall say, belong, if to any one, to ourselves; gods have no part in them, great or small.

Clin. That, too, will be universally conceded.

Ath. Well, then, shall we set down negligence, indolence, petulance as goodness of soul? How say you?

Clin. Nay, how could we?

Ath. As its opposite, then?

Clin. Yes.

901 *Ath.* Then *their* opposites will be referred to *its* opposite?

Clin. They will.

Ath. Very well, then. Any one who is petulant, negligent, or indolent must be pronounced such a character as that the poet [1] called 'most like a stingless drone'.

Clin. And an excellent comparison it is.

Ath. Then it must never be said that God has such a character as this, a character God himself abhors, or if any one ventures on such a speech, we must forbid him.

Clin. Indeed we must; how could we do otherwise?

Ath. If one has the office of action and peculiar care of some charge, and his mind, though careful in great matters, is negligent in small, what ground could we find for commendation of such a one that would not ring false? We may look at the case thus. The conduct of him who behaves thus, be he god or man, may take either of two forms, may it not?

Clin. Either of what two forms?

Ath. Either he thinks neglect of little details makes no difference to the total result, or if it makes a difference which he disregards, he shows indolence or petulance. Can we, in fact, ascribe negligence to any other causes? For, of course, where concern for a whole is *impossible*, it is no negligence of the little or the great, in god or in ordinary mortal, to make no provision for that to which one's powers are not equal, and for which one is thus unable to provide.

Clin. Of course not.

Ath. Very well; now for an answer to the interrogation of the three of us from the two parties who both confess the being of gods, but gods whom the one holds to be venal and the other negligent of little details. You both admit, to begin with, that the gods perceive, see, and hear everything, that nothing within the compass of sense or knowledge can fall outside their cognizance. That is your position, is it not?

Clin. It is.

---

[1] The poet is Hesiod, *Works and Days*, 303 ff. 'Gods and men alike are wroth with him who lives without working, with a temper like the stingless drones'.

Ath. And further that they can do all that is possible to be done by mortal or immortal?

Clin. Why, of course, they will concede that admission too.

Ath. Besides, all five of us have already agreed that they are good, and superlatively good.

Clin. Beyond all doubt.

Ath. Must we not then confess it a sheer impossibility that there should be any indolence or petulance in their conduct, so long as their character is such as we concede it to be. In ourselves, you know, want of courage gives birth to sloth, and sloth and petulance to indolence.

Clin. True, indeed.

Ath. No god, then, can be negligent from sloth or indolence, for none, we may presume, has any lack of courage.

Clin. Rightly argued, indeed.

Ath. Then if they indeed neglect the trivial matters and 902 minor details of the universe, we must conclude either that they do so with the knowledge that there is no need whatsoever of attention to such points or—what other alternative is left but the contrary of knowledge?

Clin. None whatever.

Ath. Well, then, my dear good man, which view must we take you to hold? That they act in ignorance and neglect due to ignorance where attention ought to be shown, or that they are aware that attention is needed, and yet behave as the sorriest sort of men are said to do—men who know a better course than that they actually take, but leave it alone from some inferiority to pleasures or pains?

Clin. Out of the question altogether.

Ath. Well, then, is not human life a part of animated nature, and man himself moreover the most god-fearing of all living creatures?

Clin. Why, yes, to all appearances.

Ath. And surely we hold that all living creatures, like the world as a whole, are chattels of the gods?

Clin. To be sure we do.

Ath. 'Tis all one, then, whether a man counts such things small or great in the eyes of Heaven; in neither case can it become our owners, provident and all-good as they are, to neglect them. For here is a still further point for our consideration.

Clin. And what may it be?

Ath. Whether there is not a natural opposition between perception and power in respect of their ease or difficulty.

Clin. In what way?

Ath. Why, that 'tis harder to see or hear the little than the great, whereas every one finds it easier to move, wield, superintend the small and few than their contraries.

Clin. Emphatically so.

Ath. But suppose a physician who has the task of treating a whole body is willing and able to give his attention to the large masses but neglects the minor members and parts, will his whole subject ever be in good condition?

Clin. No, never.

Ath. Nor yet will seamen, captains, householders, or again statesmen, as they are called, or persons with any other such functions make a success of the many or the great tasks apart from the few and the little; why, even the hedger will tell you that the large stones will not lie well without the small.

Clin. Of course they will not.

Ath. We are never, then, to fancy God the inferior of human workmen. The better they are at their work, the more exactly and perfectly do they accomplish their proper tasks, small or great, in virtue of one and the same skill, and we must never suppose that God, who is at once supremely wise and both 903 willing and able to provide, makes no provision for the small matters, which we have found it easier to care for, but only for the great, like some idle fellow or faint-heart who shirks his work from fear of exertion.

Clin. Nay, sir, let us never entertain such a belief about gods; the thought would be wholly impious and utterly false.

Ath. And now, I take it, we have had quite enough of controversy with him who is prone to charge the gods with negligence.

Clin. We have.

Ath. I mean so far as forcing him by argument to confess his error will go. Still something more, I believe, needs to be said by way of a charm for him.

Clin. And what shall it be, my friend?

Ath. Why, our discourse must persuade the young man that he who provides for the world has disposed all things with a view to the preservation and perfection of the whole, wherefore each several thing also, so far as may be, does and has done to it what is meet. And for each and all there are, in every case, governors appointed of all doing and being done to, down to the least detail, who have achieved perfection even to the minute particulars. Thine own being also, fond man, is one such fragment, and so, for all its littleness, all its striving is ever directed towards the whole, but thou hast forgotten in the business that the purpose of all that happens is what we have said, to win bliss for the life of the whole; it is not made for thee, but thou for it. For any physician or craftsman in any profession does all his work for the sake of some whole, but the part he fashions for the sake of the whole, to contribute to the general good, not the whole for the part's sake. And yet thou dost murmur because thou seest not how in thine own case what is best for the whole proves best also for thyself in virtue of our common origin. And seeing that a soul, in its successive conjunction first with one body and then with another, runs the whole gamut of change through its own action or that of some other soul, no labour is left for the mover of the pieces but this—to shift the character that is becoming better to a better place, and that which is growing worse to a worser, each according to its due, that each may meet with its proper doom.

Clin. Shift it—but how?

Ath. Why, I believe I can show you how universal superintendence may be easy enough for gods. In fact, if in his constant regard for the whole, an artificer were to mould everything by new transformations—fashioning fire, for example, into (?) cold[1] water, instead of producing variety from unity or unity from variety, by the time things had reached a first, second, or third generation the variations in the changing configuration would be infinitely numerous; but as it is, he who provides for the universe has an admirably light task. 904

Clin. Once more—your meaning?

Ath. I mean this. Since our King perceived that all our actions have soul in them and contain much virtue and likewise much vice, and that the complex of soul and body when once it has come to be, though not eternal, is, like the gods recognized by law, imperishable—for there would be no procreation of living creatures were either of the pair to be destroyed—and since he considered that 'tis ever the nature of such soul as is good to work blessing and of such as is evil to work harm—since he saw all this, I say, he contrived where to post each several item so as to provide most utterly, easily, and well for the triumph of virtue and rout of vice throughout the whole. Thus

[1] ἐκ πυρὸς ὕδωρ ἔμψυχον, 903 *e* 6. If the word ἔμψυχον is sound here—and I do not see how it could otherwise have got into the text—I think it probably means not 'animate' (from ἐν and ψυχή), but 'cold' (from ἐν and ψῦχος). ἔμψυχος, in this sense, is a genuine Greek word.

he has contrived to this universal end the seat or regions which must receive either type of soul as it is formed in their inhabitants; but the causes of the formation of either type he left free to our individual volitions. For as a man's desires tend, and as is the soul that conceives them, so and such, as a general rule, does every one of us come to be.

Clin. 'Tis a fair presumption.

Ath. Thus all things that have part in soul change, for the cause of change lies within themselves; and as they change they move in accord with the ordinance and law of destiny. If their changes of character are unimportant and few, they are transferred over the surface of the soil; if they are more and in the direction of grave wickedness, they fall into the depths and the so-called underworld, the region known by the name of Hades and the like appellations, which fill the fancy of quick and departed alike with dreams of dismay. If a soul have drunk still deeper of vice or virtue, by reason of its own volition and the potent influence of past converse with others, when near contact with divine goodness has made it itself especially godlike, so surely is it removed to a special place of utter holiness, and translated to another and a better world, or, in the contrary case, transported to live in the opposite realm. This, my boy—or my lad—who deemest thyself forgotten by Heaven,

is the doom of the gods who dwell on Olympus,[1]

that he that grows better shall make his way to the better souls and he that has grown worse to the worser, and so, in life, and throughout the series of deaths, do and have done to him what it is meet the like-minded should do to their likes. 905 This doom of heaven be sure neither thyself nor any other that has fallen on ill ways shall ever claim to have escaped; 'tis that which the fashioners of doom have established before all others and that which should be shunned with utter dread. It will never leave thee forgotten; though thou make thyself never so small and creep into the depths of earth, or exalt thyself and mount up to heaven, yet shalt thou pay them the due penalty, either while thou art still here among us, or after thy departure in Hades, or, it may be, by translation to some yet grimmer region. 'Twill be the same, thou must know, with them also whom thou hast seen raised from small beginnings to greatness by deeds of sacrilege or the like, and fancied to have passed from misery to blessedness, whence thou thoughtest their for-

[1] *Odyssey*, τ 43.

tunes a mirror wherein to behold the utter carelessness of the gods, knowing not how their contribution plays its part in the whole. Yet how, thou hardiest of men, canst thou doubt thy need of the knowledge? Nay, if a man has it not, he will never catch so much as a vestige of the truth, or be in case to say a word of life's happiness or disasters. If friend Clinias and the rest of our band of elders here assembled can convince thee of this much, that thou sayest of the gods thou knowest not what, why, 'tis well, and God's grace be thy aid! But if thou shouldst perchance need further argument, then listen, if thou hast any understanding, while we reason with our third antagonist. For that gods there are, and that they are concerned for mankind, has, I would maintain, been shown by no contemptible proofs. But that gods can be perverted by the receipt of gifts from the wicked, that again is what none must admit and we must dispute to the best of our power.

Clin. Well said; let us do so.

Ath. Why, then, I ask you, in the name of these same gods, what can be the mode of the perversion, if indeed they are to be perverted? And what or what manner of beings must they be themselves? Governors, to be sure, they must be supposed to be, if they are to have effective control of the whole universe.

Clin. No doubt.

Ath. But what kind of governors are they like? Or what kind whom we can by any possibility compare rightly with them, as less with greater, are like them? Would drivers of contending teams, or captains of competing vessels, be a proper parallel? Or we might perhaps compare them with commanders of armies in the field, or they may even resemble physicians defending the body from the onslaughts of disease, or husbandmen anxiously apprehending recurrent seasons of danger for 906 their crops, or again overseers of flocks and herds. For since, as we have agreed among ourselves, the world is full of good things, but no less full of their contraries, and those that are amiss are the more numerous, the fight we have in mind is, we maintain, undying and calls for a wondrous watchfulness; gods and spirits are our allies in the warfare and we, moreover, the property of these gods and spirits. Wrong, arrogance, and folly are our undoing, righteousness, temperance, and wisdom our salvation, and these have their home in the living might of the gods, though some faint trace of them is also plainly to be seen dwelling here within ourselves. Yet it should seem there are souls inhabiting our earth in possession of unrighteous spoil—bestial souls, these, beyond a doubt—who grovel before the souls of our guardians—watch-dogs, shepherds, supreme masters of all, alike—and would fain persuade them by fawning speeches and witcheries of supplication—such is the tale told by the wicked—that it is lawful for them to encroach upon mankind without grievous consequence. But our contention, I take it, is that this vice I have just named of encroachment when found in bodies of flesh and blood is what is called *disease*, when found in seasons and whole years, *pestilence*, while in societies and politics it shows itself once more under the changed designation of *iniquity*.

Clin. Just so.

Ath. So the case of one who teaches that the gods are always indulgent to the unrighteous and the wrong-doer, if a share of the plunder is assigned them, comes inevitably to this: 'tis as though the wolf should assign some small part of his spoil to the sheep-dog, and the dog, pacified by the present, agree to the ravaging of the flock. That is the case of those who hold the gods to be venal, is it not?

Clin. It is indeed.

Ath. Well, then, with which of our former list of guardians can a man compare the gods without absurdity? With seamen who are 'turned from their course by "flow and fragrance" of wine'[1] and overturn vessel and crew?

Clin. Surely not.

Ath. And surely not with charioteers placed for the race but won over by a bribe to forfeit the victory to another team?

Clin. Nay, your comparison will be a shocking one if you say that.

Ath. And certainly not with commanders, physicians, or husbandmen, nor yet with herdsmen nor with sheep-dogs on whom wolves have cast a spell?

907 *Clin.* Flat blasphemy! Quite impossible!

Ath. Now are not the gods, one and all, our chiefest guardians, and the interests they guard our chief interests?

Clin. Ay, and by far.

Ath. And shall we pronounce those who have the noblest of things to guard and are themselves supremely skilful in the task of guarding inferior to sheep-dogs or average men, who will never betray the right for the sinful offer of a bribe from the unrighteous?

[1] *Iliad*, I 500 (from the famous speech of Phoenix).

Clin. Assuredly not; the thought is not to be borne. Of all reprobates who are given to any form of ungodliness the defender of such a creed may well be most righteously condemned as the very worst and most ungodly.

Ath. Then I presume we may say our three propositions, that there are gods, that they are mindful of us, that they are never to be seduced from the path of right, are sufficiently demonstrated.

Clin. Indeed you may, and my friend and I concur with your arguments.

Ath. Still I confess they have been delivered with some heat due to eagerness to triumph over these bad men. But the source of this zeal, my dear Clinias, was apprehension that if they get the better of the argument, the wicked may fancy themselves free to *act* as they will, seeing how many strange ideas they entertain about the gods. This is what prompted me to speak with more than common vigour; if I have done never so little to influence such men towards self-reprobation and attraction towards the opposite type of character, the prelude to our laws against impiety will have been spoken to good purpose.

Clin. Well, let us hope so; but if not, at least the cause will bring no discredit on a legislator.

Ath. So our preamble may properly be followed by a sentence which will express the sense of our laws, a general injunction to the ungodly to turn from their ways to those of godliness. For the disobedient our law against *impiety* may run as follows: If any man commit impiety of word or act, any person present shall defend the law by giving information to the magistrates, and the first magistrates under whose notice the matter comes shall bring the case before the court appointed to deal with such offences as the law directs. Any official failing to take action on information received shall himself be liable to be proceeded against for impiety at the suit of any one willing to vindicate the law. In the case of conviction, the court shall impose a particular penalty on the offender for each act of impiety. Imprisonment [1] shall form part of the penalty in all cases. And whereas there are three prisons in the State, a *common gaol* in 908 the market-place for the majority of cases, for safe custody of

---

[1] This is a departure from Attic practice which has, therefore, to be specially noted. Imprisonment, except in the form of detention until a fine inflicted by the courts has been discharged, was not a penalty inflicted on Attic citizens. The proposed grading of prisons is an interesting anticipation of an important modern reform.

the persons of the commonalty, a second attached to the
Nocturnal Council[1] and known as the *house of correction,* and a
third in the heart of the country in the most solitary and wildest
situation available, and called by some designation suggestive
of *punishment*; and whereas also there are three causes of impiety,
those we have already specified, and each such cause gives rise
to two types of offence, there will be in all six classes of offenders
against religion to be discriminated, who require different and
dissimilar treatment.   For though a man should be a complete
unbeliever in the being of gods, if he have also a native uprightness of temper, such persons will detest evil men; their repugnance to wrong disinclines them to commit wrongful acts; they
shun the unrighteous and are drawn to the upright.   But
those in whom the conviction that the world has no place in
it for gods is conjoined with incontinence of pleasure and pain
and the possession of a vigorous memory and a keen intelligence share the malady of atheism with the other sort, but are
sure to work more harm, where the former do less, in the way
of mischief to their fellows.   The first man may probably be
free-spoken enough about gods, sacrifices, and oaths, and perhaps, if he does not meet with his deserts, his mockery may
make converts of others.   But the second, who holds the same
creed as the other, but is what is popularly called a 'man of
parts', a fellow of plentiful subtlety and guile—that is the type
which furnishes our swarms of diviners and fanatics for all
kinds of imposture; on occasion also it produces dictators,
demagogues, generals, contrivers of private Mysteries, and the
arts and tricks of the so-called 'sophist'.   Thus there are
numerous types of these atheists, but two which legislation
must take into account, the hypocritical, whose crimes deserve
more than one death, or even two, and the others, who call for
the combination of admonition with confinement.   Similarly,
the belief in divine indifference gives rise to two further types,
and that in divine venality to another two.   These distinctions
once recognized, the law shall direct the judge to commit those
whose fault is due to folly apart from viciousness of temper or
909 disposition to the house of correction for a term of not less than
five years.   Throughout this period they shall have no com-
munication with any citizen except the members of the Nocturnal

---

[1] This is the first allusion in the *Laws* to this body, which acts as a sort
of extraordinary 'Committee of Public Safety' in permanent session.
It gets its name from the provision that its daily meetings are to be held
before daybreak.   Its constitution will be described later at XII, 951 *c–e*,
and 961 *a, b*.

Council, who shall visit them with a view to admonition and their soul's salvation. When the term of confinement has expired, if the prisoner is deemed to have returned to his right mind, he shall dwell with the right-minded, but if not, and he be condemned a second time on the same charge, he shall suffer the penalty of death.[1] As for those who add the character of a beast of prey to their atheism or belief in divine indifference or venality, those who in their contempt of mankind bewitch so many of the living by the pretence of evoking the dead and the promise of winning over the gods by the supposed sorceries of prayer, sacrifice, and incantations, and thus do their best for lucre to ruin individuals, whole families, and communities, the law shall direct the court to sentence a culprit convicted of belonging to this class to incarceration in the central prison, where no free citizen whatsoever shall have access to him, and where he shall receive from the turnkeys the strict rations proscribed by the Curators of the Laws. At death he shall be cast out beyond the borders without burial, and if any free citizen has a hand in his burial, he shall be liable to a prosecution for impiety at the suit of any who cares to take proceedings. But should he leave children fit to be citizens, the guardians of orphans shall provide for them also, no worse than for other orphans, from the date of the father's conviction.

Moreover we must frame a law applicable to all these offenders alike, and designed to alleviate the sin of most of them against religion in word or act—to say nothing of the folly of the sinners—by the prohibition of illegal ceremonial. In fact the following law should be enacted for all cases without exception. No man shall possess a shrine in his private house; when a man feels himself moved to offer sacrifice, he shall go to the public temples for that purpose and deliver his offerings to the priests of either sex whose business it is to consecrate them. He may join with himself in the prayers any persons whose company he may desire. This regulation shall be adopted for the reasons following. The founding of a sanctuary or cult is no light task; to discharge it properly demands some serious

---

[1] This may mean that the offender who is not believed to have been converted by the imprisonment and the admonitions addressed to him is pronounced contumacious at the end of his term of confinement, and put to death as an obstinate heretic. But since even the hypocritical villain of 909 *c* is allowed to die in the course of nature, more probably Plato means that the milder offence is presumed to have been purged by imprisonment, and death only inflicted if a repetition aud a second conviction prove a man not to have been 'brought back to sanity'.

thought. But it is the common way, especially with all women, with the sick universally, with persons in danger or any sort of distress, as on the other hand with those who have enjoyed a stroke of good fortune, to dedicate whatever comes to hand 910 at the moment and vow sacrifices and endowments to gods, spirits, and sons of gods, as prompted by fears of portents beheld in waking life, or by dreams. Similarly, the recollection of endless visions and the quest of a specific for them commonly leads to a filling of every house and village with shrines and altars erected in clear spaces or wherever such persons are minded to place them. All these are grounds for conformity with the law now proposed, and there is the further ground that it serves as a check on the ungodly. It prevents them from fraud in this matter itself, from setting up shrines and altars in their own houses, under the delusion that they are winning the privy favour of Heaven by offerings and prayers, thus indefinitely aggravating their criminality and bringing guilt before God on themselves and the better men who tolerate their conduct, until the whole community reaps the harvest of their impiety—as in a sense it deserves. Our legislator, in any case, shall be clear before God, for his enactment shall run thus: No citizen to possess a shrine in his private dwelling-house; in the case of proved possession, or worship at any shrine other than the public, if the possessor, whether man or woman, have committed no serious act of impiety, he that discovers the fact shall proceed to lay an information before the Curators of the Law, who shall direct the private shrine to be removed to a public temple, and, in the case of disobedience, impose penalties until the removal is effected. Any person proved guilty of a sin against piety which is the crime of a grown man, not the trivial offence of a child, whether by dedicating a shrine on private ground or by doing sacrifice to any gods whatsoever in public, shall suffer death for doing sacrifice in a state of defilement. What offences are or are not puerile shall be decided by the Curators, who shall bring the offenders accordingly before the courts and inflict the penalty.

BOOK XI

Ath. Our next need will, of course, be a proper regulation 913 of our business transactions with each other. A simple general rule, I take it, might be expressed thus. I would have no one touch my property, if I can help it, or disturb it in the slightest way without some kind of consent on my part; if I am a man of sense, I must treat the property of others in the same way. We will take as a first instance *treasure* which someone, not being an ancestor of my own, has amassed as store for himself and his descendants. I must never pray to find such treasure; if I do find it, I must not meddle with it, I must breathe no word of it to diviners, as they are called, who are certain to recommend me [1] to appropriate what has been committed to earth's keeping. If I appropriate it, the benefit to my fortunes will assuredly be more contracted than the expansion I shall gain in moral goodness and rectitude by leaving it alone. Purchase for purchase, I shall have made a better bargain in a better cause, if I choose to get rectitude for my soul rather than wealth for my pocket. The wise proverb which forbids moving what is better left alone has a wide range of application, and this is one of the cases to which it applies. Besides, one should give credence to the current tradition that such things are no blessing to a man's descendants. The man who is so careless for his posterity and deaf to the voice of the legislator that he takes up what neither he nor any of his fathers' fathers ever laid down, and that without the depositor's permission, in violation of one of the best of laws, that straightforward enactment of an illustrious man [2] which runs: 'What thou hast not laid down, take not up'—the man, I repeat, who does despite to both these legislators and takes up what he has not himself laid down, and not on a petty scale either—often it is a vast heap of treasure—what shall be done to him? What Heaven will do to him, of course, is God's concern; but the first

[1] Accepting Stephanus's συμβουλεύσουσιν for συμβουλεύουσιν (MSS. and Burnet) at 913 *b* 3.
[2] The author to whom the saying was popularly ascribed is Solon (Diog. Laert. I. 57). The 'two legislators' of the next words are, of course, Solon and the legislator of the supposed Cretan city.

person to discover the fact shall report it, if the thing happen in the capital, to the Urban Commissioners, or if in the market-square of the capital, to the Commissioners of the Market, or, 914 if it occur outside the capital, shall bring it to the notice of the Rural Commission and their heads. On receipt of the information, the State shall send a deputation to Delphi: accordingly as the god shall pronounce about the property or the disturber of it, so the State shall act by the mandate of the oracle. If the informer be a free man, he shall be commended for his virtue, and censured as vicious if he neglects to give information; if a slave, he shall receive his well-earned freedom as a gift from the State, which shall pay his owner his price, but be punished with death if the information is withheld. It follows by consequence that we must have this same rule alike in small matters as in great. If a man leave his property behind him in any place, voluntarily or not, he that lights upon it must let it alone undisturbed: he must regard such things as placed under the protection of the Spirit of the wayside, to whom they are deemed consecrate in law. Any person who appropriates such things and carries them home with him, in contravention of the law, shall, if a slave and the article of little value, receive a sound beating from any, not being under thirty years of age, who may fall in with him. If he be a free man, he shall be pronounced a churl unfit to consort with law-respecting men, and shall furthermore pay the owner of the goods he has disturbed their value ten times over. If a man charge another with being in possession of his property, great or small, and the man so charged admit possession of the object but dispute the ownership, the complainant shall, in the case of articles entered by legal requirement on the magistrates' register, summon the party in possession before the magistrates, to whom he shall produce the article. If, upon such exhibition, such article is found to be recorded in the register as the property of either litigant, he shall be put in possession of it and so dismissed. If it prove to belong to a third party who is not in court, either party, on providing sufficient sureties, may remove it on behalf of the absent owner and in his right, for delivery to him. If the article in dispute be not recorded in the register, it shall be in the custody of three senior magistrates until the suit is decided. And if the thing so hypothecated be a beast, the loser in the suit shall pay the authorities the cost of its keep. The magistrates shall dispose of the case within three days.

Any man, provided he be sane, shall be at liberty to lay hands on his own slave for such purpose as he may please in the way of lawful business, and at liberty likewise to lay hands on the fugitive slave of any kinsman or friend, with a view to his safe-keeping. If a man be thus seized as a slave and any person claim him as free and resist his detention, the captor shall let the man go, and the party opposing the detention shall provide three substantial sureties and stay the detention on these conditions aforesaid, and on no others. If capture is stayed otherwise than on these conditions, there shall be an action for assault, and the defendant, if convicted, shall pay the 915 party whose right has been stayed twice the value of the article, as shown by the register. There shall be the like right of seizure of a freedman who pays no homage, or insufficient homage, to the authors of his freedom. Homage shall be deemed to mean that the freedman repair thrice in the month to the hearth of his emancipator and make proffer of all such services as are right and possible, and likewise that in the matter of marriage he act only with the approval of his former owner. It shall be illegal for the freedman to possess more wealth than the emancipator, and any surplus shall belong to the master. A man thus receiving his freedom shall not prolong his residence beyond twenty years, but depart, like all aliens, with his estate in full, unless he can gain permission from the magistrates and the master who enlarged him. If the estate of a freedman or other alien come to exceed the census of the third class, he shall within thirty days from the day on which the excess first began, take up his property and depart, and in this case the authorities shall have no power to grant any extension of residence. Any person brought before the courts for non-compliance and convicted shall receive sentence of death, and his goods shall be forfeit to the State. Suits of this kind shall come before the court of a tribe, save when the counter-allegations of the parties have been previously disposed of before the neighbours, or before judges appointed by themselves.

If a man claim any other man's beast, or any other of his goods, as his own property,[1] the party in possession shall return the article to the vendor, responsible and lawful donor, or person who otherwise made valid delivery of that article, where such person is a citizen or resident alien, within thirty days, or in

---

[1] In 915 *c* 8 it seems to me we must write αὐτοῦ (Ast, Stallbaum), against the αὑτοῦ of our MSS. and many editors, including Burnet. In any case, the pronoun stands for the party who is in possession of the article but whose right to it is disputed.

the case where delivery was made by a foreigner, within a period of five months, of which months [1] the midmost shall be that of the summer solstice. In all reciprocal exchange by means of sale and purchase, goods exchanged are to be delivered on the sites appointed in the market-square for the various articles, and the price is to be received at the time; exchange shall not be permitted in any other locality, and there shall be neither selling nor buying on credit. If any citizen make any exchange whatever, for any return whatsoever, with another under other conditions or in a different locality, because he trusts the party with whom he is dealing, he must do so on the understanding that the law permits no action in respect of articles not vended under the conditions here specified.[2] As to subscriptions to clubs,[3] any one who pleases shall be free to raise them as between friends, but if a difference arise about a subscription, the parties must conduct their affairs with the understanding that the law will in no case grant an action on such grounds. If the vendor of an article receive a price of fifty drachmas or more, he shall be bound to remain in the territory for a space of ten days, and 916 the purchaser shall be informed of the vendor's lodging with a view to the making of complaints such as are common in such cases, and satisfying the legal regulations about restitution. The legal requirements in question shall be as follows. In the case of the vending of a slave affected by phthisis, stone, strangury, or by the so-called 'holy distemper',[4] or other disorder of body or mind which readily escapes ordinary observation and is inamenable to treatment, if the sale were made to a physician or trainer, there shall be no right to return the article to the vendor; there shall likewise be none, if the defect was truth-fully mentioned at the time of sale. But where a professional man vends such an article to a layman, the purchaser shall have the right to return it within six months, except in the case of

---

[1] In 915 *d* 5 I assume England to be right in substituting οἷς for the ἧς of the MSS. and the other editors; the antecedent must surely be μηνῶν. It is assumed that business with overseas traders will be confined to the summer. For this cf. what is said of these traders as 'birds of passage' at 961 *d–e*.

[2] Or possibly we should transfer the comma in 915 *e* 4 to follow ταῦτα, and translate, 'he must trust to the other party to the exchange in acting thus, since the law will not grant an action', etc.

[3] Ἔρανοι, 'clubs', means associations of a kind common at Athens; their ostensible outward and visible purpose was the social and religious one of a common dinner, but they also served as 'benefit-clubs', which advanced loans to members to set them up in business.

[4] i.e. epilepsy, a disorder which might go undetected longer than the others.

the 'holy distemper', for which the period allowed for the
return shall be one year. The case shall be brought before a
body of physicians, to be nominated and selected by agreement
between the parties, and a convicted vendor shall pay a sum
double of the price at which he sold. If both parties be lay-
men, the regulations as to right of return and the trial of the
issue shall be as in the former case, but the convicted vendor
shall pay only the actual price received. If a man vend a
slave who is a homicide, and both parties are aware of the fact,
there shall be no right of return in respect of the transaction.
If the purchaser be unaware, there shall be a right to return the
purchase forthwith when the buyer shall discover the fact, and
the case shall be heard before the five junior Curators. The
vendor who is adjudged to have made such sale willingly shall
purify the dwelling of the purchaser as the canonists' rules
require, and shall repay the price three-fold.

He that exchanges against coin other coin or any article
whatsoever, animate or inanimate, shall be expected by the law
in all cases to give genuine value and demand the same. But,
as elsewhere in our code, let us make room for a preamble dealing with roguery of this sort at large. Every one should understand that imposture, false pretences, fraud, are all things of
one kind, the kind which is unhappily credited in current
popular parlance with being often enough an excellent thing
'if practised at the proper juncture'. When and where this
juncture occurs is left vague and indefinite, and thus the proverb
works no little mischief to the believer and the rest of society.
A legislator cannot be allowed to leave the point in this uncertainty. He should always draw definite boundary-lines,
wider or narrower, as we shall now proceed to do. No man
shall practise any imposture or fraud of word or act with the
name of a god on his lips, but one that would encounter God's 917
reprobation; and such is he who swears lying oaths in contempt
of Heaven, and, in a lesser degree, he who lies to his superior.
Now good men are the superiors of worse, the aged, speaking
generally, of the youthful, and, by consequence, parents of their
offspring, husbands, again, of their wives and children, magistrates of their subjects. Universal reverence is no more than
the proper due of all who are in any of these positions of authority,
and most of all the due of the authorities of the State, and it is
of them we are now discoursing. A man who practises an
imposition in the market is lying, cheating, and calling Heaven
to witness by his oaths in the face of all the laws and *caveats*

of the Commissioners of Markets; he has no more respect for man than fear of God. Now undoubtedly it is a becoming habit to be careful of taking divine names in vain, to show the same regard for them that most of us commonly and customarily show for ceremonial purity and cleanness in matters of worship, but if there should be any disobedience, here is our law. He that sells any article whatsoever in the market shall in no case put two prices on his wares. He shall ask one price, and if he do not get it, he will do right to take his goods away again, and shall not, that same day, set a higher or lower price on them. Also there shall be no puffing of wares offered for sale, or vouching for them by an oath. In case of breach of this statute, any citizen present, not being under thirty years of age, shall have the law's permission to chastise the swearer of such oath by blows; a citizen making light of the matter and disregarding this provision shall be liable to censure as a traitor to the law. The vendor of a spurious article, who cannot be persuaded by our present discourse, shall be exposed before the authorities by any person present with the knowledge requisite for his detection; such person, if a slave or resident alien, shall have the counterfeit article for his own use; if a citizen and neglecting to expose the cheat, shall be declared guilty of defrauding Heaven; if he expose it, he shall publicly dedicate the article to the gods of the market.[1] And the party found offering such wares for sale shall be deprived of the counterfeit goods, and shall moreover be scourged in the market-square, and receive a stripe for each drachma of the price he set on his goods, proclamation being first made by a crier of the cause for the scourging. To counteract the impostures and knaveries of vendors, the Commissioners of the Market and Curators shall inform themselves by inquiry from experts in different trades, and draw up rules of what the vendor may and may not do; these rules shall be engraved on a column to be erected in front of the offices of the Commission of the Market as regulations 918 for the more precise direction of persons doing business in the market. The functions of the Urban Commission have been described sufficiently already; if further regulations are thought needful, the Commissioners shall consult with the Curators of Law and draft the necessary supplement; both the earlier and later rules for their official procedure shall be posted on a column in front of the offices of the Commission.

---

[1] The dedicated object would be set up in public view; this is the reason for the clause.

The consideration of fraudulent practices and business leads direct to that of *retail trade*. We shall first deal with the subject as a whole in the way of reasoned counsel, and then propose legal regulation for it. Internal retail trade, when one considers its essential function, is not a mischievous thing, but much the reverse. Can a man be other than a benefactor if he effects the even and proportionate diffusion of anything in its own nature so disproportionately and unevenly diffused as commodities of all sorts? This, we should remind ourselves, is the very result achieved by a currency, and this, as we should recognize, the function assigned to the trader. Similarly the wage-earner, the tavern-keeper, and other callings, some more and some less reputable, all have the common function of meeting various demands with supply and distributing commodities more evenly. What, then, can be the reason why the calling is of no good credit or repute? What makes it generally unpopular? We must look into the question if we are to provide a partial remedy (a total cure would be beyond us) by our legislation. The thing is well worth doing, I fancy, and calls for no common abilities.

Clin. How so?

Ath. Why, Clinias my friend, 'tis but a small section of mankind, a few of exceptional natural parts disciplined by consummate training, who have the resolution to prove true to moderation when they find themselves in the full current of demands and desires; there are not many of us who remain sober when they have the opportunity to grow wealthy, or prefer measure to abundance. The great multitude of men are of a clean contrary temper: what they desire they desire out of all measure; when they have the option of making a reasonable profit, they prefer to make an exorbitant one. This is why all classes of retailers, business men, tavern-keepers, are so unpopular and under so severe a social stigma. And yet, only suppose—an impossible supposition and Heaven forbid it should be anything else!—but suppose the very best of men could be compelled—the fancy will sound ludicrous, I know, but I must give it utterance—suppose they could be compelled to take for a time to inn-keeping, or retail trade, or some such calling; or suppose, for the matter of that, that some unavoidable destiny were to drive the best women into such professions: then we should discover that all are humane and beneficent occupations; if they were only conducted on principles of strict integrity, we should respect them as we

do the vocation of mother or nurse. But look at the actual
919 facts! For purposes of commerce a man sets up his quarters
in some solitary spot remote from everywhere; there he entertains the famished traveller and the refugee from tempests
with welcome lodging, and provides them with calm in storm
and cool shelter in heat. But what comes next? Where he
might treat his customers as so many friends, and add an
hospitable banquet to the entertainment, he behaves as though
he were dealing with captive enemies who had fallen into his
hands, and holds them to the hardest, most iniquitous, most
abominable terms of ransom. These malpractices, and others
like them, are to be found in all these callings, and it is they
which have brought catering for the wants of the distressed
into merited ill-repute. This is the malady in them all for
which law must find a specific. Now it is a sound old adage
that it is hard to fight against two enemies at once—even
when they are enemies from opposite quarters; we see the truth
of this in medicine and elsewhere. And in the battle we are
at this moment waging against the evils of these professions
we have two such enemies, penury and opulence; the one rots
souls with luxury, the other, with its distresses, drives them
into sheer insensibility to shame. What remedy, then, can be
found for the disease in an intelligent society? Well, the remedy
is, in the first place, that the numbers of those employed in
trade be kept as low as possible; next that such occupations
be assigned to the sort of men whose corruption will do not great
mischief to society; thirdly, some means must be found to
prevent the characters of those actually engaged in these
callings from readily taking the contagion of complete abandonment and baseness. So our preface shall at once be followed
by a law—and the blessing of Providence go with it!—to this
effect. In the Magnesian city which Heaven is restoring from
its decay, no one of all the five thousand and forty landowners
who are our householders shall follow a trade, by his own will
or against it, nor even engage in merchandise; neither shall he
discharge menial services of any kind to a private employer
who renders no like services to himself, save for services performed, without derogation to gentle blood, to father, mother,
remoter ancestors, or to any man of gentle birth senior to
himself.[1] What services are thus consistent with gentle lineage
and what are not can hardly be stated with precision in a law;

[1] I agree with England that the comma in 919 *e* 2 should be placed after
ἐλεύθεροι, not after πρεσβυτέροις (as in Burnet's text).

the point shall be decided by those who have won distinction
for abhorrence of the base and devotion to the gentle. If a
citizen, on any pretext, engage in sordid trade, he shall be
liable to an indictment for tainting the blood, to be preferred
by any who will, and to come before a jury of men who have
attained the first distinction for goodness; if found to have
defiled the ancestral hearth by an unworthy pursuit, he shall
suffer a year's imprisonment as a lesson to avoid such conduct,
or, for a repeated offence, two years' imprisonment; on each 920
subsequent conviction the term inflicted for the last offence
shall be regularly doubled.[1] Now for a second law. A person
proposing to follow a retail business shall always be a resident
alien or a foreigner. And there shall be yet a third: to ensure
that there shall be as much virtue, or at least, as little vice, as
is possible among these associates in the life of our society, the
Curators must not be regarded merely as guardians of the
class whom it is easy to protect from falling into crime or vice,
the favourably born and properly educated and trained; still
more careful guard must be kept over those who have not
these advantages, and follow callings which have a marked
tendency to predispose to vice. So to effect this result for
retail trade with its numerous branches and the many debasing
employments it embraces—I mean those of them which we
shall permit to subsist in our society because we have found
their presence absolutely necessary—the Curators will once more
be required in this case to consult with the experts in all departments of trade, exactly as they have been enjoined to do in
connection with the allied business of the prevention of fraud;
they shall ascertain by consultation what scale of payment
and expenditure will secure the trader a modest profit, and this
scale of outlay and receipts shall be publicly displayed and
enforced by the Commissioners of the Market and Urban and
Rural Commissioners in their respective spheres. Under such
regulation we may expect our retail trade to produce general
benefit for all classes with the minimum of harm to the class
who follow it as their vocation.

In the case of failure to execute an admitted contract—save
and except a contract to do what is prohibited by statute or
by executive decree of the Assembly, a contract extorted by
wrongful constraint, a contract unintentionally frustrated by

[1] The text of the MSS. (and Burnet) may just possibly be construed, but
I think it more probable that we should, with Ast, read τοῦ χρόνου for
τὸν χρόνον in 920 a 2-3.

unforeseen circumstances—there shall be an action for *non-fulfilment of contract* before the tribal courts, unless settlement can be previously reached before arbitrators or a court of the local neighbours. The class of artificers whose crafts have equipped us for the daily needs of life will be under the patronage of Hephaestus and Athena, while the other class who provide for our safety by a second group of crafts—those which subserve defence—will have Ares and Athena as their patrons. (There are as good grounds for this divine protection in the second case as in the other. All alike are engaged in continuous service of country and people; the one sort in taking charge of our struggles in the field, the other in producing implements and commodities for hire.) Reverence for their divine progenitors will thus make it unseemly in such men to break their 921 word about their work. If a craftsman, then, culpably fail to complete a task within the specified time, and thus forget the reverence due to the god from whom he gets his living, fancying, in his ignorance, that God is a mate who will make allowances, he shall, first, answer for it to the god, and, next, there shall be a law to suit the case. If a man break his word to the employer with whom he has contracted for any piece of work, he shall be indebted in the value of the work and shall execute it again gratis from the beginning within the time agreed on. The law will further give the same counsel to contractors for such performances as was given to vendors. The vendor was advised to take no advantage by asking too high a price, but to price his goods with all candour at their true worth, and the law gives the same injunction to the contractor, who, of course, as a craftsman is aware of the true value of his work. In a city of free men, then, the craftsman of all men may never use his expert knowledge, in itself an honest and straightforward thing, to take advantage of the layman by the tricks of the trade, and persons wronged by such tricks must have a legal remedy. On the other side, if the party contracting with a workman fail to pay his wages strictly as stipulated in an agreement valid in law, this is to dishonour Zeus, our national defender, and Athena, who are both partners in our society, and to dissolve the supreme social bonds for the sake of petty profit, and there shall be a law to champion the Heaven-ordained civic tie to this effect. If a man, having received delivery of work contracted for, do not pay the price within the stipulated time, the said price shall be recoverable from him twofold: if payment be not made within the year,

whereas all other moneys out upon loan shall bear no interest,
a defaulter in this kind shall pay an interest of one obol on the
drachma for each month in arrear; actions under this head to
be taken in the tribal courts.

As we *have* raised this topic of artificers, it is only right to
say a passing word about the artificers of our preservation in
war, generals and other military experts. In their case also—
for they too, like the others, are craftsmen, though of a different
sort—if any of them undertake work for the public, whether
as a volunteer or under orders, and perform it well and truly,
the law will never tire in commendation of the citizen who
loyally pays him the soldier's wages—honours; but if the
citizen receive delivery of the fine piece of military work and
withhold the payment, the law shall censure him. We shall
accordingly enact, and couple with our commendation of these
heroes, the following law, which we address to the populace
rather by way of counsel than by way of compulsion: The brave
men who preserve our whole State by deeds of valour or 922
military skill shall receive honours of the second class. (Our
supreme distinctions must be understood to have been assigned
to those who stand first of all in merit, those who have
proved pre-eminent in reverence for the precepts of good
legislators.)

We have now, we may say, completed our regulation of the
more important business relations of man with man, except for
those which concern orphans and their supervision by their
guardians. These are the sphere we are next driven to regulate
as best we can. The foundations of the whole subject are laid
by the desire of the dying to make a disposition of their estates
and the accident of deaths without any such settlement; and
the reason why I spoke of being 'driven' to treat of it, Clinias,
was that I saw the intricacies and difficulties involved. We
certainly cannot leave such matters without all regulation.
Were we to concede the unqualified validity of any testamentary
disposition made at the end of life, irrespective of the testator's
condition, men would often make disposals inconsistent in
themselves and repugnant to law, or to the moral sense of the
living, or of the testator himself at an earlier time of life. For
in most of us, as you know, when in imminent expectation
of death, the mental powers are in abeyance, broken, as I
may say.

Clin. Yes, sir, and what of it?

Ath. A man at the point of death, Clinias, is not easy to handle;

he is full of a notion which must give a legislator grave concern
and perplexity.

Clin. How so, pray?

Ath. He wants to have his own way about everything, and
so there is commonly a touch of passion in his language.

Clin. Language—what language?

Ath. 'Lord!' he will say, 'I call it a shame if I am not to be
perfectly free to give my own property to a man or not, exactly
as I please, and not free to give more of it to one man, less to
another, according as I have found them treating me well or ill
under the searching test of sickness, old age, and the other
varied circumstances of life.'

Clin. A perfectly proper thing to say, too, sir; don't you
think so?

Ath. Why, Clinias, I think our legislators in the past have
been too soft; their codes have been based on short views of
human life and imperfect understanding of it.

Clin. But in what way?

Ath. Why, my dear sir, they were afraid of such complaints,
and that is why they made the law which permits of the absolute
923 disposition of property entirely as the testator pleases. You
and I must pitch our reply to the dying in this society of yours
in a more suitable key. 'Friends, who have, in literal fact,
only a day to live'—this is what we shall tell them—'in your
present condition it is hard enough for you to know what
is your own property; what is more, it is hard, as the inscription at Delphi says, to know what you are yourselves. So I,
speaking as legislator, pronounce that neither your own persons
nor the estate are your own; both belong to your whole line,
past and future, and still more absolutely do both lineage and
estate belong to the community. This is so surely so that I
shall never, if I can help it, permit you, when shaken by age
or infirmity, to be cajoled into evil testamentary dispositions
by the insinuating arts of the flatterer. My law will be made
with a general view to the best interests of society at large
and your whole line, as I rightly hold the single person and his
affairs of minor importance. Depart from us in peace and
good will on the journey you are now to take, as all flesh must;
what you leave behind you shall be our concern; we will take
all the thought for it we may, and that with no partial care'.
Such exhortations alike to living and dying shall form our
preamble, Clinias; our statute shall be to this effect: A person
making written testamentary disposition of his effects, shall,

if he have issue, first set down the name of such son as he judges
proper to inherit;[1] if he have another son whom he offers for
adoption by a fellow-citizen, he shall set his name down also;
if there be still a son left, not already adopted as heir to any
patrimony, who may expect in course of law to be sent to some
overseas settlement, it shall be free to him to bequeath to such
son such of his goods as he sees fit, other than his patrimonial
estate and its complete plenishing; if there be more such sons
than one, the father shall divide his possessions, other than his
patrimony, among them in such proportions as he pleases.
But if a son already possess a house,[2] no portion of such goods
shall be bequeathed to him, and the same shall hold in the case
of a daughter; a daughter not contracted to a husband shall
receive her share, but a daughter already so contracted shall
receive none. If a son or daughter be found to have come into
possession of an allotment of land subsequent to the date of
the will, such party shall leave the bequest in the hands of the
testator's heir.[3] If the testator leave only female issue without
male, he shall by will provide one daughter, selected at his
pleasure, with a husband and himself with a son, and shall
name such husband as his heir. If a man's son, naturally
begotten or adopted, die in infancy before reaching the age of
manhood, the testator shall further make provision for this 924
contingency by naming a child to succeed such son with happier
omens.[4] If the party making his testament be absolutely childless, he may set aside one tenth part of his *acquired* [5] possessions
for the purpose of legacies to any persons he pleases; all else
shall be left to the adopted heir whom he shall make his son,
in all integrity on the one part and gratitude on the other,

[1] i.e. to inherit the family landed estate, which, as we learned in Book V,
is never to be either alienated or divided. The law in this respect is like
our own of primogeniture, except that the selection of the heir is left to
the father's discretion.
[2] 'House', οἶκος (923 *d* 8), means 'family', not 'dwelling-place'. The
sense is that a son who is either adopted under the will as *heir to the patrimony of a citizen*, or has been so adopted during his father's life, is already
provided for, and so has no rightful claim to any part of the 'personal
property'.
[3] This is to meet the case of a son adopted by some landholder, or daughter
contracted to such landholder, after the making of the will. The spirit
of the law demands that a legacy shall, in this case, 'revert to the testator's
estate'.
[4] i.e. a testator who names as his heir a son under full age is to provide
for the possibility of the heir's dying a minor, by naming an eventual
successor.
[5] i.e. exclusive of the patrimony and its 'plenishing'. This is the only
case of free bequest permitted by Plato's law.

with the law's approval. Where the children require a *guardian*,[1] if the deceased have stated in his will how many guardians he desires for his children and whom, and the parties named consent to act, the nomination of guardians in the will shall be final. If a man die wholly intestate, or without selecting such guardians, the lawful guardians shall be the nearest kinsmen on both sides, two from the father's side, two from the mother's, together with one personal friend of the deceased, the appointment to be made for an orphan in such case by the Curators. The whole department of wardships and orphans shall be under the supervision of fifteen of the Curators, the senior members of the board, who shall regularly divide themselves into groups of three, in order of seniority, one such group acting for one year and another for the next, until the five yearly periods are discharged; no avoidable breach shall be permitted in this rotation.

If a man die absolutely intestate but leaving children who need the care of a guardian, his children's distress shall share the benefit of these same laws. But if he meet his end by some incalculable accident and leave daughters behind him, he must make allowances for the legislator's disposal of his daughters' hands if it takes two points out of three into account, nearness in blood, and protection of the patrimony; the third point— and this is what would have engaged a father's attention—the selection of the person out of the whole citizen-body most congenial in character and disposition as a son for himself and bridegroom for his daughter, the legislator will pretermit as an impossible task. Here, then, is the best law we can devise for the case. If an intestate person leave daughters, a brother of the deceased on the father's side, or a brother on the mother's side having no patrimony of his own, shall take his daughter and inherit his patrimony; the same shall be the case if there be a brother's son but no brother, provided the parties are of suitable age; if there be none of these, the rule shall hold for a sister's son. Father's brother shall be fourth in succession, his son fifth, father's sister's son sixth. In all cases where female 925 issue is left, the family succession shall proceed in this regular order of proximity in blood through brothers and sisters and their offspring, males having the precedence over females in the same generation. The suitability or unsuitability of the match in point of years shall be determined by inspection, and

---

[1] i.e. when there are no relatives near enough to have a *right* to the position by kinship.

the judge shall view the males stripped and the females stripped to the navel. If there be a failure of kin within the family, as far as brother's grandsons, and likewise grandsons of grandfather's sons, the maiden shall be free, with her guardians' assent, to make her choice among the citizens, the person so chosen, if he consent, becoming heir to the deceased and bridegroom to his daughter. Further, life is full of accidents, and it may well happen at times that an heir is still harder to find within the State. So if a maiden can find no husband on the spot, but have her eye on some party previously dispatched to a colony, whom she is minded to make her father's heir, that party, if a kinsman, shall come to the inheritance as the law appoints; if outside the family, provided there be no kinsmen within the State, consent of the daughter of the deceased and her guardians shall empower him to make the match and return home to take up the succession to the intestate person. If a man decease intestate leaving no issue, male or female, in all other respects the law above stated shall apply to the case, but a female and male from the family shall mate, as we may express it, and be placed in the deserted homestead, the patrimony being legally assigned to them: the order of succession shall be: (1) sister, (2) brother's daughter, (3) sister's daughter, (4) father's sister, (5) father's brother's daughter, (6) father's sister's daughter; these shall be settled on their kinsmen, in accord with the provisions of the foregoing statute, as consanguinity and religion demand. Of course we must not forget that such laws can prove burdensome; it is sometimes a hardship that they require a blood-connection of the deceased to marry his kinswoman, but appear to overlook the numerous obstacles which will make any man reluctant to comply with the command and ready to face any consequence rather than obey, cases like those of bodily or mental disorder or deficiency in a party whom the law requires us to take as wife or husband. Hence it might be supposed that the legislator is indifferent to those considerations, but that would be a misconception. So you must take my remarks as a preamble delivered in the interests alike of the legislator and the parties for whom he legislates; they are meant to bespeak the indulgence of such parties for the legislator, if his concern for the public good hardly leaves him equally free to control the fortunes of private individuals, and a like indulgence for the recipients of his laws, 926 if they sometimes, no less naturally, find themselves unable to execute orders laid on them in ignorance of the facts.

Clin. Then, let me ask you, sir, what would be the fairest way to act in such a situation?

Ath. In such a case, Clinias, we must appoint arbitrators between the law and the persons it commands.

Clin. Pray explain yourself.

Ath. Sometimes a nephew whose father is a wealthy man might make difficulties about marrying his uncle's daughter because he has high notions and aspires to a more splendid match. Sometimes, again, a man might be driven to disobey the law because what the legislator requires is disastrous, as when he would constrain you to connect yourself with a house in which there is insanity, or other grievous bodily or mental affliction, such as renders life positively intolerable. So what I have to say on the subject shall be couched in the form of a law to this effect: If a party complain of being aggrieved by the laws now enacted, the law of testamentary dispositions or another, and in particular by the law of marriage, and emit a solemn declaration to the effect that the legislator, if now alive and present in person, would never have required the action— the taking or giving in marriage—of either party from whom it is now demanded; and if a relative or guardian make affirmation to the contrary: the law shall take the view that the legislator has bequeathed the fifteen Curators to our orphans of both sexes as arbitrators and parents; litigants on these issues shall have recourse to them for the determination of their disputes, and shall act on their verdict as final. If the powers thus conferred on the Curators be deemed too extensive by any party, he shall bring the Curators before the court of selected judges and take its decision on the issue. If he lose his case, the legislator shall visit him with censure and disgrace, penalties heavier in the judgment of intelligence than the most grievous fine.

Our orphan children will thus experience a kind of second birth. How they should all be reared and trained after their first birth has already been explained. What we have to do after this second birth, a birth without a parent, is to discover the plan by which their unfortunate bereavement will entail least distress on the sufferers. First, then, to make laws for their conduct, in place of their fleshly begetters we appoint the Curators, parents at least as good as they; moreover we especially charge [three of?][1] them every year to care for them

[1] It is not necessary, but highly tempting, since the reference is to the annual acting committees of three of whom we heard at 924 *c*, to follow Susemihl in assuming the numeral τρεῖς (Γ) to have fallen out of the text in this clause.

as their own, and we add a preamble on the up-bringing of
orphans apposite to these officers, as to all guardians. I believe,
in fact, there was something really opportune in all we said
before of a power of taking an interest in human life retained 927
by the souls of the departed after death. The tales which
convey this moral may be lengthy, but they are true, and we
ought to give our credence to general tradition on the subject,
when we consider how abundant and how very venerable that
tradition is, but particularly to legislators who lend their
sanction to such beliefs—unless, indeed, we account them men
of no judgment at all. If all this be truly so, there should be
fear, first and foremost, of the gods in heaven, who behold the
orphan in his loneliness, and next of the parted spirits whose
native instinct is to keep especial watch over their own offspring, to show good will to him who respects them and ill to
him who neglects; fear, in the third place, of the souls of men
still alive, but of advanced years and high distinction. Where
the laws of a State are good and its fortunes blessed, children's
children delight to lavish affection on such men; their sight
and hearing in such matters is quick; their good will is assured
to him who walks uprightly in them, and their wrath hot against
the despoiler of the defenceless orphan; they count him a
solemn and sacred trust. Guardians and magistrates, if men
of discretion, howsoever slight, should stand in awe of all these
powers and bear themselves warily in all that concerns the
orphan's upbringing and education; they should do them all
they good they may in every way, even as though the benefit
were bestowed on themselves and their own sons. So he that
will give ear to the words of our preamble and keep himself
from all spoiling of the orphan shall learn nothing of the legislator's naked wrath against these crimes; but he that will not
hear, and wrongs fatherless or motherless shall pay two-fold
the full compensation demanded of him who misconducts
himself towards those whose parents are both in life. As
touching a general legislation for guardians of orphans, or
magistrates who have charge of the guardians, had they no
model already of an upbringing for the sons of the gently-born
in their upbringing of their own children and management of
their own estates, or had they not moreover a sufficient law
prescribed them for such matters, 'twould be no more than
reason to propound a law of wardships with a special character
of its own, and to make a distinction of the orphan's life from
others by various special rules. As the case is, in our society

the orphan's status is not very different in all these respects from that of the child under its father's care, though the two are commonly on such different levels in public estimation and in respect of the care bestowed. 'Tis, indeed, because of this 928 very difference that our law has been so earnest with its exhortations and threats in its regulations concerning the orphan. We may add this further and most seasonable threat: The guardians of male or female infant, and the Curator appointed to exercise surveillance of such guardian, shall show no less concern for the bereaved orphan than for his own children, and shall pay the same zealous attention to the estate of the ward under his care as to his own—or indeed more. This shall be the law, and the only law, under which guardianship of an orphan shall be exercised: in the case of any contravention of this law, a guardian shall be fined by the magistrate; a defaulting magistrate shall be cited by the guardian before the court of the select judges, and fined twice the amount of his defalcations as assessed by the court. If the family, or any fellow-citizen, charge a guardian with negligence or dishonesty, the case shall be brought before the same court; any defalcation proved shall be repaid four-fold, half the sum to go to the orphan child, and half to the successful prosecutor in the case. If an orphan who has attained his majority believe his guardian's administration to have been faulty, it shall be open to him to institute proceedings in respect of the guardianship at any date within five years from the expiry of said guardianship. If a guardian be convicted, the court shall determine the penalty or fine; if a magistrate, and the injury to the orphan be found due to negligence, the court shall determine the sum payable to the ward, but if the verdict be one of malversation, the offender shall, in addition to payment of the fine, be removed from the office of Curator, and the authorities shall provide country and State with a new Curator in his stead.

Graver differences are found to arise between fathers and sons, sons and fathers, than ought to be possible; as a consequence, fathers are disposed to take the view that the legislator should empower them, if they see fit, to make public and legal notification through the crier that they will no longer hold a son as their son, and sons, on their part, to expect legal authorization to take proceedings in lunacy against a father discredited by years or disease. The cause of such variance is commonly to be found in utter unqualified badness of character; where the badness is on one side only, as where the son is an ill man but his father not so, or vice versa, such dissensions are not pushed to the point where they issue in disaster. Now in any society but ours a disinherited son would not necessarily lose his citizenship, but in the State for which these our laws are intended, a man whose father has cast him off has no option but to expatriate himself to some distant land, as we permit 929 no addition whatsoever to our number of five thousand and forty households. Hence to be legally repudiated, a man must be disowned not merely by his father, but by the whole kindred. Thus our law will in such cases provide some such process as this: If, with just cause or without it, unhappy passion assail a man with the desire to cast out of his kin the son of his own begetting and breeding, he shall have no licence to do the act incontinently, without due form. He shall first summon his own kin, as far as his cousins, and his son's kin by the mother's side in like manner, and lay his charges before them, in proof that expulsion from the kindred is no more than the accused's desert at the hands of all, and shall grant the son equal facilities of pleading that he deserves no such thing. If the father prevail and can carry the suffrage of more than one-half of the kinsmen—those excepted who shall have no vote, the father, the mother, the defendant himself, and such other persons, male or female, as have not yet reached maturity [1] —the father shall have leave to renounce his son—on these terms and conditions stated, and upon no others. If a citizen be minded to adopt one thus repudiated into his own house there shall be no bar in law to the adoption (life commonly, works frequent changes in a young man's temper); but if no one, within ten years, show desire to adopt the disowned son, the officers charged with the care of supernumerary children whom we destine for our settlement abroad shall take his case also under their charge, that he may duly receive his place there. If disease, age, sullen temper, or all together derange a man's mind with more than common violence, though the fact go undiscovered by all but those who share his daily life, so that he waste the family estate as one that is absolute lord of it, while his son knows not where to turn, and scruples to bring his action of lunacy; in such case, the law shall be that

---

[1] Some small correction needs to be made in the MSS. text (that given by Burnet). Paleographically the most probable correction, I believe, is to read διαψηφιζομένους for διαψηφιζομένον in 929 b 7 (Ast), and to insert <μὴ> before τέλειοι in c 2 (England). The sense is fortunately certain.

he must first have recourse to the eldest of the Curators and tell them his father's case; they shall make diligent inquiry, and then counsel him whether the action shall be brought or no; if their counsel be to bring it, they shall, when the case comes on, serve the complainant both as witnesses and as advocates. The father who loses such action shall thereafter have no power to make any disposition of his goods in the smallest particular, but shall be treated as a child for the rest of his life.

If *man and wife be utterly estranged* by their unhappy temper, 930 the matter should in every case be referred to ten men—Curators intermediate between the extremes in point of age—and ten women, of those who have charge of wedlock. If they are able to effect an accommodation, the arrangements thus made shall hold good, but if the storm rages too high within, they shall seek the best mate they can find for either party. The temper in these cases is like to be none too gentle, whence we try to match them with partners of more sedate and gentle mood. When the discordant parties have no children, or too few, an eye shall be had also in the new alliance to procreation; where there are already children in sufficient number, the end of the separation and new conjunction should be companionship in age and mutual care of one another. If a woman die leaving children male and female, our law shall counsel, but shall not compel, her husband to bring up the children he has and give them no stepmother; if there be no children, the husband shall be bound to marry again, until he have begotten children in number sufficient for the house and for the State. If the husband die leaving children in sufficient number, their mother shall remain in the household to bring them up. But if she be deemed unduly youthful to live without a man and keep her health, her kinsmen shall communicate with the women who have charge of wedlock and act as shall seem good to themselves and them. If there be a lack of children, that point also shall be considered; the lowest number which shall constitute a sufficiency in law shall be one boy and one girl. When *the parentage of issue is admitted* and it is to be determined *which parent the off-spring shall follow*, if a slave woman have had to do with slave, free man, or freedman, the offspring shall, in every case, belong to her owner; if a free woman lie with a slave, the offspring shall be his owner's; if master have a child by his slave-woman, or mistress by her slave, and the fact be notorious, the woman's child shall be sent, along with its father, by the women functionaries, the man's, with its mother, by the Curators, to another land.[1]

Neglect of parents is that to which neither god nor right-thinking man will ever counsel any. A man should have the wit to see how pat the preamble now to be delivered on divine worship is like to fit this theme of respect and disrespect of parents. All the world over the primitive rules of worship are two-fold. Some of the gods of our worship are manifest to 931 sight; there are others in whose likeness we set up images, believing that when we adore the lifeless image, we win the bountiful favour and grace of the living god for whom it stands.[2] If, then, a man have a father or mother, or a parent of either, safe kept within-doors in the last frailty of age, he should remember that while there is such a figure to hallow his hearth at home, no image can be so potent for good, if only the owner give it the rightful worship he should.

Clin. Now what may you mean by this 'rightful' worship?

Ath. Why, I will tell you; indeed, my friends, 'tis a theme well deserving our attention.

Clin. Say on, then.

Ath. Oedipus, so we commonly say, called down a curse on his sons when they showed him disrespect, and it is a familiar tale with us all, as you know, how fully heaven answered his prayer. And we have the stories of the cursing of Phoenix by his angry father Amyntor,[3] and of Hippolytus by Theseus, with many another to the same effect—plain proof that heaven will listen to a parent's prayers against his children. In fact, the curse of the parent on the offspring is more effectual than any other, and 'tis only right it should be so. If, then, 'tis the order of things that God is so exceeding quick to hear the prayer of father or mother when their children show them dishonour, let none conceit himself that when the parent receives his honours, rejoices and delights in them, and is moved to fervent prayer for blessings on the children—must we not think, I say, that Heaven hears that prayer no less than the other, and

[1] The object is, in the first instance, to prevent children of servile origin from getting any footing in a citizen family. Plato is also anxious to discourage clandestine concubinage itself; hence the deportation of the slave lover or mistress.

[2] Cf. the similar distinction at *Timaeus*, 41 *a*, *Epinomis*, 984 *d*. The visible divinities are the stars, the 'invisible' the beings of the popular mythology.

[3] See *Iliad*, I, 447 ff. for the story of Amyntor and Phoenix. The curse inflicted on Phoenix was that of childlessness.

dispenses the blessing?   Were it not so, its blessings would not
be fairly dispensed, a thought most unworthy of it.

Clin. Most unworthy indeed.

Ath. And so, as I have just said, we must believe that no
image we can procure is more precious in Heaven's eye than a
father or forefather in the weakness of his age, or a mother in
like case; when a man does them worship and honour, there is
joy in Heaven, or their prayers would not be heard.   An ancestor's person is, in truth, an image of God more marvellous than
any lifeless statue; these living images will always second our
prayers for ourselves when we pay them worship, and pray in
the opposite sense when we show them dishonour, but the
others can do neither the one thing nor the other.   And so the
man who bears himself as he ought to father, father's father,
and the rest of his ancestors will find no other image so effectual
to assure the favour of heaven as this which he has got.

Clin. Most admirably said.

Ath. And thus all right-thinking men treat a parent's prayer
with fear and reverence; they know how time and again such
932 petitions have been effectual.   This being nature's appointment, a good man finds his aged progenitors treasure-trove to
the last breath of their lives, and when they depart, the loss to
their juniors [1] is most heavy; to evil men they are cause for real
and deep alarm.   Wherefore I would have all men listen to our
present pleadings and show their parents all lawful honour.
If there should be any whom 'fame attaints' of deafness [2] to
a prelude to such strains, 'twould be a fitting law against such
men to decree as follows: *If any person in our State be less mindful
of his parents than he ought*, not showing himself more careful
to consider and comply with all their wishes, more than those
of his sons and other posterity whatsoever and his own also,
he that lies under such neglect may report it, in person or by
deputy, to the three senior Curators and three of the women who
have charge of wedlock; they shall deal with the complaint, and
chastise the criminal with stripes and imprisonment, if still
young, that is, in the case of a man, not over thirty years; the
penalty for a woman that offends shall be the same for a further
ten years.   If persons beyond these years still persistently
neglect their parents, or, it may be treat them ill, they shall
cite them before a court of one hundred and one citizens, the

---

[1] I depart here by one letter from the text of the MSS (and Burnet).
Winckelmann's νέοις for νέοι in 932 *a* 3 seems to me nearly certain.

[2] England's emendation of κωφή (932 *a* 6) to κωφὸν seems to me certain.

most ancient we have. In case of conviction the court shall determine the fine or other penalty, and shall not hold themselves debarred from the infliction of the utmost a man can be made to suffer or pay. If a person so ill-treated be unable to complain, any who shall become aware of the facts shall report them to the authorities, or else be deemed a craven, and lie open to action at any man's suit for the mischief.[1] If the informer be a slave, he shall receive his freedom; if his owner be the party inflicting or suffering the injury, the magistrate shall pronounce him free; if another citizen, his price shall be paid to his owner from the public purse. The authorities shall take care that no wrong be done him in revenge for his information.

To come to injury inflicted by *poisons*: we have dealt at large with the cases where death results, but not, as yet, with lesser injuries arising from deliberate and intentional administration of articles of meat or drink, or unguents. What gives us pause here is that mankind practice poisoning in two different ways. The form we have just expressly named is that in which the body is hurt by the action of some other body in normal ways. 933 There is another form which works by art magic, incantations, and spells, as they are called, and breeds in the minds of the projectors the belief that they possess such powers of doing harm, in those of the victims the conviction that the authors of their suffering can verily bewitch them. Now as to all such matters the true facts are hard to learn, nor, if one could learn them, would it be an easy task to convince another. And it would be labour lost to try to bring conviction to minds beset with such suspicions of each other, to tell them, if they should perchance see a manikin of wax set up in the doorway, or at the cross-roads, or at the grave of a parent, to think nothing of such things, as nothing is known of them for certain. We shall therefore divide the law of *poisons* into two chapters, according to the mode in which the poisoner makes his attempt. But first we shall publish our request, desire, or counsel that no such attempt be made, that there be among us no working on the terrors of mankind—the most part of whom are as timorous as babes—and no constraint upon legislator or judge to find a remedy for these terrors. The would-be poisoner, we shall say, *imprimis* knows nothing of what he does, nothing, unless he be expert in medicine, of treatment of the body, nothing, unless he be prophet or diviner, of sorcery. The law of *poisons*,

---

[1] i.e. for the ill-treatment against which he might have given information. His silence about it is treated as making him responsible for it.

then, shall run to this effect: Any man administering a poison
to another, or to persons employed by him, without fatal effect,
or with effects fatal or otherwise to his cattle or bees, and convicted of the offence of poisoning shall, if a physician, suffer
death, and if a layman, such penalty or fine as the court shall
impose. And any found to have brought himself under suspicion
of doing a mischief by the practice of spells, charms, incantations, or other such sorceries whatsoever, shall, if prophet or
diviner, have sentence of death; if the conviction be for sorcery
without any help of prophetic art, he shall be dealt with as in
the former case—the court, as before, shall determine his
sentence or fine at its discretion.

In all cases of injury by *theft or robbery with violence*, the
culprit shall pay compensation to the party injured, greater or
less, according to the gravity of the mischief done, but in any
case sufficient to cover completely the whole loss occasioned by
his act; further, each such culprit shall pay a penalty imposed
934 upon the offence by way of correction.[1] The correction shall
be lighter when the offender has been led astray by the folly of
another to whose over-persuasion he has yielded by reason of
youth, or some other such cause, heavier when the crime is due
to folly of his own, failure to resist pleasure or pain, or the
pressure of desperate lust, envy, or rage. The purpose of the
penalty is not to cancel the crime—what is once done can never
be made undone—but to bring the criminal and all who witness
his punishment in the future to complete renunciation of such
criminality, or at least to recovery in great part from the dreadful
state. For all these reasons, and since it has all these ends in
view, the law must take careful aim at its mark; it must be
exact in determining the magnitude of the correction imposed on
the particular offence, and, above all, the amount of compensation to be paid. The judge must have the same task before him,
and lend his services to the legislator, when the law leaves it
to his discretion to fix a defendant's fine or sentence; the
legislator, in this case, is like a draughtsman who must design
the outlines of cases which answer to the code. This is, in fact,
Megillus and Clinias, what you and I are now to do to the
fullest extent of our ability: we have to specify the penalties
to be imposed on thefts and robberies of every kind, so far as
the gods and their sons permit us to legislate on the subject.

---

[1] In 933 *e* 10 I think we should probably delete πρὸς ἑκάστῳ (as suggested
by England). I suspect the words originated from a form of the text in
which the προσεκτεισάτω of the next line was placed here.

No *lunatic* shall be allowed to be at large in the community; the relatives of such persons shall keep them in safe custody at home by such methods as they can contrive, on penalty of fine. The fine for failure to control the lunatic, whether slave or free man, shall be for offenders of the highest property-class one mina,[1] for the second four-fifths of that sum, for the third three-fifths, for the fourth two-fifths. Now there are many lunatics and their lunacy takes many different forms. In the case just mentioned it springs from disease, but there is another sort of lunatics who owe their madness to unhappy native tendency to angry passion further strengthened by ill training, a kind of men whom any trifling dissension will provoke to clamorous and scurrilous reviling of each other, conduct always and totally out of place in a well-ordered society. We shall therefore have one single law of *defamatory words* to deal with all such men, and that law shall be this: No person shall use defamatory words of any other. A party to a dispute of any kind shall listen to his adversary's contention, and put his own before the adversary and the company present without scurrility of any sort. When disputants begin to invoke imprecations on one another and bandy foul names, like wrangling vixens, 935 the first result is that such words, in themselves trifles light as air, yield a heavy harvest of deeds of spite and hatred. Passion is an ill-favoured thing, and the speaker who does his wrath the favour to feast it on the poison it craves turns all the humanity education has fashioned within him into brutishness once more; persistence in his morose rancour makes him a wild beast, and that sorry return is all the return passion makes him for his favours. And besides, 'tis the common way with all men in such encounters to be ever turning to the utterance of scoffs at the adversary, a practice to which no man ever yet formed himself, save at the cost of losing all gravity of character or the better part of his dignity. For all these reasons no single scoffing word shall be uttered by any man in any temple or at any public sacrifice, nor yet at the public sports, nor in market-place, court of justice, or any place of public resort. The offence shall be in every case punished by the official in charge,[2] on pain of disqualification from all claims to distinction, as one that has no regard for the law and neglects to execute the legislator's injunctions. If a man indulge in such scurrilities elsewhere,

---

[1] 1 mina = 100 drachmas.
[2] I have followed England in omitting the word ἀνατί (935 *b* 8), 'with impunity'. It makes no good sense here and was absent from the original text of A and O.

whether he begin the reviling or retort it, any bystander, being
an older man, shall uphold the law and drive out with blows
him who humours his bad companion,[1] temper, or else shall be
subjected to the appointed fine. Now mark my point; when
a man is entangled in a scolding-match, he can say nothing
without seeking to raise a laugh, and it is the resort to this
trick at the prompting of angry passion which I denounce.
But what follows? Are we lending our countenance to the
comedians' efforts to raise a laugh against mankind, provided
the object of their comedies is to attain their result, to turn
the laugh against their fellow-citizens, without such passion?
Shall we draw the line between sport and earnest, permitting
men to jest upon one another in sport and without anger, but
absolutely forbidding all such jesting, as we have already done,
where it is in downright earnest and charged with passion?
That proviso must certainly not be withdrawn, but the law will
proceed to specify the persons to whom permission shall or
shall not be granted. No composer of comedy, iambic or lyric
verse [2] shall be permitted to hold any citizen up to laughter,
by word or gesture, with passion or otherwise; in case of dis-
936 obedience the Presidents of the festival shall give orders for the
offender's expulsion from the State's territory within the course
of the day, on pain of a fine of three minae to be paid to the
deity in whose honour the festival is held. The persons to whom
permission has already been granted by an earlier arrangement
to compose personal satire [3] shall be free to satirize each other
dispassionately and in jest, but not in earnest or with angry
feeling. The actual drawing of the distinction shall be left to
the Minister in charge of the system of juvenile education.
If he approve a piece, its composer shall have licence to produce
it in public; if he disapprove the composer shall neither appear
in it himself nor train any other person, slave or free, to perform
it, on pain of being declared a bad citizen and a law-breaker.

The true object of pity is not the man who is hungry or in
some similar needy case, but the man who has sobriety of soul

---

[1] In 935 *c* 6 England's ἐταίρῳ seems to me a necessary emendation for
the ἑτέρῳ of the MSS. and previous editors. If ἑτέρῳ is kept, the sense
seems to be 'him who humours his angry passion by *another evil* thing'
(viz. mockery of his adversary).   But this is intolerably frigid.
[2] 'Iambic' verse is specified as a form historically appropriated to lampoons.
There is apparently some small error in the text of 935 *e* 4, and Ast's trans-
position of the τινος (to stand before μουσῶν) is highly attractive.
[3] See 829 *c supra*. The uncertainty whether the comma should be
placed after ποιεῖν, as by Burnet, or after ἀλλήλους, does not affect the sense
of the regulation.

or some other virtue, or share in such virtue, and misfortunes to boot. Whence in a State where constitution and citizens alike are even middling good, it will be strange to find any such man, slave or free, so wholly neglected that he comes to utter beggary. Such men will be in no danger if the legislator enact the following statute. There shall be no *begging* in the State; if any one attempt it and seek to scrape up a living by his incessant entreaties, he shall be expelled the market-place by the Commissioners of the Market and the city by the Urban Commission, and escorted over the borders by the rural police, that our land may be entirely cleaned of such creatures.

If *damage be done to a man's property of any kind by another's slave, male or female,* such person not being himself contributory to the charge by awkwardness or other ill-management,[1] the owner of the party causing the damage shall either make compensation in full, or surrender the person of the culprit. If such owner allege that the charge is made by collusion between the parties causing the mischief and the party sustaining it, with intent to defraud him of his slave, he shall take proceedings against the person alleging himself to have sustained damage; if he win the suit, he shall receive twice such price as the court may set upon the slave, if he lose it, shall pay compensation for the damage and further surrender the slave. Likewise, if harm be done to a neighbour's property by draught-animal, horse, dog, or other animal, the owner shall pay compensation for the damage.

If a man *refuse to give evidence,* he shall be served with a citation by the party desiring his testimony, on receipt whereof, he shall present himself at the trial of the case. If he have knowledge of the facts and is ready to depose to them, he shall then make his deposition; if he deny all knowledge, he shall profess his denial on oath by three gods, Zeus, Apollo, and Themis, and be dismissed from the case. Any person cited in evidence and not answering to the citation shall be legally liable to action for damage. If a judge in the case be called up to give evidence, he shall do so and shall have no vote in the determination of such case. A free woman shall be qualified to give evidence and support a case,[2] if she have attained the age of forty; if she have no husband, she shall further be qualified

937

---

[1] 'Other ill-management', as England says, means here much what we call 'culpable negligence'.

[2] The 'support of the case' (συνηγορεῖν, 937 a 9) appears to mean the support given to it by the very act of making a deposition, since all 'advocacy' is expressly forbidden.

to initiate a process at law, but if she have a living husband, to
give evidence only. A slave of either sex, or a child, shall be
qualified to give evidence and support a case only in proceedings
for homicide, and provided sufficient security is given that in
case a demurrer is lodged against the deposition as false, the
deponent will await his trial.[1] A plaintiff or defendant making
an allegation of perjury shall put in his demurrer to the whole
or part of the testimony before the decision in the case is
reached; the pleas of demurrer shall receive the seals of both
parties to the suit and be in the custody of the officials for
production at the hearing of the charge of perjury. A person
twice convicted of bearing false witness shall be under no legal
obligation to give evidence in the future, a person convicted
thrice shall be in future disqualified to bear witness. Any who
shall have the front to do so after three convictions shall be
summarily arrested upon information as to fact by the magistrates, who shall deliver him to a court, for sentence of death
if convicted. Whenever depositions have been thus judicially
condemned by a decision that the victory of the successful
litigant was due to false evidence, if the condemnation affect
half or more of such depositions, the suit so decided against a
litigant shall be annulled, and the issue shall be raised and
determined whether or not the suit was decided by these
depositions; the result of the inquiry, either way, shall finally
dispose of the original suit.

Life abounds in good things, but most of those good things
are infested by polluting and defiling parasites. Justice, for
example, is undeniably a boon to mankind; it has humanized
the whole of life. And if justice is such a blessing, how can
advocacy be other than a blessing too? Well, both blessings
are brought into ill-repute by a vice which cloaks itself under
the specious name of an 'art'. It begins by professing that
there is a device for managing one's legal business—in fact
that it is itself a device for managing such business of one's
own and assisting another to manage his—and that this device
will ensure victory equally whether the conduct at issue in the
case, whatever it is, has been rightful or not. And it then adds
that this art itself and the eloquence it teaches are to be had as

---

[1] The procedure is Attic. A party to a case claiming that testimony
put in at the 'pre-cognition' by the other side is false enters a demurrer
(ἐπίσκηψις ψευδομαρτυρίου) against it, and the issue thus raised has to be
tried. The 'trial' which the slave or minor has here to give security to
await is that on this allegation of perjury, not that of the original issue in
connection with which the incriminating deposition was made.

a gift by any one who will make a gift in money in return. Now 938
this device—be it which it may, art or mere artless empiric
knack—must not, if we can help it, strike root in our society.
The legislator will call for obedient silence in the presence of
Right and departure to some other territory; to him who complies the law will have nothing more to say, but to the disobedient its language will be this: Any who shall fall under
suspicion of *attempting to pervert the influence of justice* upon
the mind of a judge, of *wrongfully multiplying suits at law*, or
wrongfully aiding others to such suits, shall be liable to prosecution by all who choose on the charge of *perversion of justice*
or *abetment* of such perversion, as the case may be. The charge
shall be tried before the court of select judges, and if it result in
conviction, the court shall determine whether the defendant, in
its judgment, acted from ambition, or from greed of lucre. If
from the former, the court shall fix a space of time during which
the guilty party shall have no right to enter a suit against any
man, nor assist any man in a suit. If the offence be found due
to greed of gain, the culprit shall, if an alien, be expelled the
country on pain of death in the case of return, and, if a citizen,
suffer death for his insatiate love of lucre. Also a second
conviction of commission of the same offence from the motive
of ambition shall lead to sentence of death.

BOOK XII

941   *Ath.* *If an ambassador or envoy to a foreign State behave dis-loyally in his office,* whether by falsification of the despatch he is commissioned to deliver or by proved distortion of messages entrusted to him by such State, friendly or hostile, as ambas-sador or envoy, all such persons shall lie open to impeachment of the crime of sacrilege against the function and ordinances of Hermes and Zeus, and it shall be determined what sentence or fine shall follow conviction.

Larceny is a sordid thing and open robbery a flagitious.[1] No son of Zeus has ever had dealings in either; neither fraud nor force is to their liking. So let none of us, if he offends in this sort, suffer himself to be gulled by the fictions of the poets and fabulists; let him never fancy his pilfering or robbing no deed of shame, but an act such as is done by the very gods themselves. That is a tale with neither truth nor semblance of truth about it, and he that transgresses so is no god, nor the son of any god at all. In these things 'tis the legislator's business to know better than all the poets together. So, if a man will obey our counsel, 'tis well with him (and may it ever be well!), but if he will not, why, then he shall find a law up in arms against him, to this effect: *For all theft of public property,* great or small, there shall be one and the same judgment. For he that steals a little thing does his thieving with weaker hand but not with less lust, and he that takes up a greater, when he had not laid it down, is guilty of the whole law. This is why the law deems it fit that one offender should be visited with a lighter doom than the other—not that what he stole was a lesser thing, but because one may yet be recovered perchance, and the other is beyond cure. Whence, if a conviction for theft of the public property be gained in the courts against an alien or slave, seeing he may yet, in all likelihood, be recovered, the court
942 shall decide what sentence he must serve, or what fine he shall

[1] Theft from private persons has already been dealt with; the present paragraph is concerned with the graver crime of peculation from the State. But it is noticeable that the severity of 942 *a* is quite inconsistent with the milder anticipatory treatment of the crime of theft from the public at 857 *b*.

pay; a citizen, one trained as our citizens will be trained, found guilty of plundering or deforcing his native country, whether taken red-handed or no, shall suffer death as one beyond curing.

The organization of our forces is a thing calling in its nature for much advice and the framing of many rules, but the principal is this—that no man, and no woman, be ever suffered to live without an officer set over them, and no soul of man to learn the trick of doing one single thing of its own sole motion, in play or in earnest, but, in peace as in war, ever to live with the commander in sight, to follow his leading, and take its motions from him to the least detail; to halt or advance, to drill, to bathe, to dine, to keep wakeful hours o' nights as sentry or despatch-carrier, all at his bidding; in the stricken field itself neither to pursue nor to retire without the captain's signal; in a word, to teach one's soul the habit of never so much as thinking to do one single act apart from one's fellows, of making life, to the very uttermost, an unbroken consort, society, and community of all with all (a wiser and better rule than this man neither has discovered, nor ever will, nor a truer art of military salvation and victory). 'Tis this lesson of commanding our fellows and being commanded by them we should rehearse in the times of peace, from our very cradles; *anarchy*—the absence of the commander—is what we should expel root and branch from the lives of all mankind, ay, and all beast-kind that is under man's dominion. In especial, all the choric dances our people are to learn must look to gallantry in the field; the same must be the end of all their training in easy and nimble movement, all their endurance of hunger and thirst, cold and heat, and lying hard; above all, they must, to the same end, learn not to corrupt the native strength of the head and feet by swathing them in artificial coverings, and so tampering with the growth and function of the head-cover and footwear of nature's providing. For head and feet are the body's extremities, and due care of them affects the whole body most potently for good, neglect for ill; the foot is the whole body's servant of servants, the head the master-member made by nature to contain all its principal organs of sense. So much, 943 then, for the praise of the warrior's life we would have a young man listen to [in fancy][1]—now for the relative laws. A man put on the roll or assigned to any arm of the forces shall perform

---

[1] I enclose the words 'in fancy' in square brackets to indicate my feeling that Stallbaum was right in regarding the δοκεῖν of 943 *a* 2 as a scribal error for δεῖν.

his service. If a man absent himself from cowardice without a discharge from his commanders, he shall, on the return of the forces from the field, be impeached before the officers of the army *for evasion of military duty*, and the verdict shall be given by some one branch of the forces—infantry, cavalry, or other arm—in separate session. Thus an infantryman shall be brought before the infantry, a cavalryman before the cavalry, a member of some other force similarly before his comrades. A convicted person shall, *imprimis*, be disqualified for life for all competitions for distinction, and prohibited from laying an impeachment of the same kind against another, or speaking as accuser in such cases; the court shall, moreover, determine what further sentence or fine shall be inflicted. Next, when the charges of evasion of service have all been heard, the officers shall hold a second review of all arms, and the claims of all candidates for awards of distinction shall be settled before a body of their own mates; all evidence and commendatory testimonials proferred by candidates shall relate exclusively to the campaign just terminated, and to no previous service. The prize in each branch of the service shall be a wreath of olive; the winner shall dedicate this wreath in such temple of a god of war as he may prefer, as evidence for a future award of first, second, and third-rank distinctions for the conduct of a whole life. A man going on service but returning prematurely before the commanders have withdrawn the forces shall be liable to impeachment for *desertion* before the same court in which cases of evasion are heard, and the penalties for conviction shall likewise be as in that case. A person bringing a charge against another must, of course, be most scrupulously careful neither intentionally nor unintentionally to bring him to unmerited punishment. (Justice is, indeed, as she has been called, the virgin daughter of Conscience, and Conscience and Justice both are heart-haters of the false charge.) I say a man must keep himself from this and other offences against justice, and in especial in the matter of loss of arms in war, a man must be tender of bringing unmerited judgment on the innocent, by mistaking an enforced loss for a shameful, and so making it a reproach. 'Tis truly no easy matter to draw the line of distinction between the two cases, and yet the law 944 should do what it can to distinguish them. And so we will help ourselves out by recalling a legend. If Patroclus had come to himself in the tent when he had been carried there without his arms—and the thing, we know, has happened to thousands

—while the gallant armour he had been wearing—by the poet's tale it came to Peleus with Thetis as a nuptial gift from the gods—was in Hector's hands, the baser sort of that day would have had their chance to taunt the brave son of Menoetius with casting away his arms.[1]   And then there are all the cases of those who have lost their arms by falls from heights, at sea, or when suddenly swept off their feet, under stress of weather, by a swirl of waters—or countless other excuses may be conjured with, to put a fair face on a suspicious misadventure. So we must do our best to discriminate the graver and uglier mischance from the lesser.   There is a distinction, then, to be made when such epithets are used in reproach.   It would not be fair in all cases to call the man one who has *flung his shield away*, though he may be said to have *lost* his arms.   A man who is stripped of his shield by a considerable exertion of force cannot be said to have flung it away with the same truth as one who drops it of his own act; there is all the difference in the world between the cases.   So we shall give our law this wording: If a man surrounded by the enemy, and having arms in his hands, do not turn to try and defend himself but intentionally throw down his weapons, or cast them away, and thus choose to purchase a life of shame by his cowardice rather than fair and glorious death by his valour, there shall be judgment for the loss of arms thus flung away; in the other case abovementioned, the judge shall hold careful inquiry.   Correction must always be meted to the bad—to make a better man of him—not to the unfortunate; on him it is wasted.   Now what shall we call a fitting punishment for the coward who throws away weapons so formidable for his defence?   A human judge cannot, indeed, invert the transformation which is said to have been wrought on Caeneus [2] of Thessaly; he, we are told, had been a woman, but a god changed him into a man.   Were the reverse process, transformation from man to woman, possible, that, in a way, would be of all penalties the properest for the man who has flung his shield away.   To come as near as we may to this in our treatment of the craven's pitiful clinging to his life, and that he may have no risks to take for the future, but prolong his life of infamy to the last minute possible, our law in these cases shall run thus: If a man be judicially convicted of the shameful

---

[1] In the well-known story of the *Iliad*, Patroclus is, of course, only brought back to the tent of Achilles as a corpse. The armour which was stripped from his body by Hector was that of Achilles.

[2] For the transformation of the girl Caenis into the man Caeneus, see Ovid, *Met.* xii. 189-209.

casting away of his weapons of war, he shall not again be employed as a soldier nor assigned to any military post whatever 945 by any general or other military officer. In case of disregard of this provision, the officer who so employs the coward shall be mulcted by the auditor of his official accounts to the amount of one thousand drachmas,[1] if he belong to the wealthiest class, five minae if to the second, three minae if to the third, or one, if to the fourth. And the convicted coward shall not only be discharged, as befits his unmanly spirit, from all the dangerous services that become a true man, but shall further pay a price, of a thousand drachmas if he come from the wealthiest class, five minae if from the second, three if from the third, or, if from the fourth class one, as in the previous clause.

Now as to *auditors*,[2] what plan will be the proper one for us, whose magistrates have been appointed, some for a year and by the chance of the lot, some for years together and by selection from a leet? Who will be competent to put the crooked in such officers straight, if one of them should perchance act awry under the crushing weight of his office and his own inequality to its dignity?[3] 'Twill indeed be no light task to find an officer of such supereminent merit to set over our officers themselves, and yet the attempt to discover auditors of such more than human quality must be made. For the matter, in fact, stands thus. A polity is like a ship or a living organism. The dissolution of the fabric hangs on a multitude of devices of one character under all their various forms, to which we give different names in the different cases, such as stays, girders, tendons of the sinews; one such, and not the least momentous, in the case of a polity, critical for its preservation or utter dissolution, is that now under our consideration. For if the censors who are to approve our magistrates are better men than themselves, and do their work with flawless and irreproachable justice, then there will be prosperity and true happiness for the whole of nation and society; but if aught is amiss with the auditing of our magistrates, then the bonds of right which hold all branches of our social fabric together in one will be loosened;

---

[1] 1000 dr. = 10 minae.

[2] The regulation is taken from Attic practice, but Plato's method of appointing his auditors, and the extraordinary powers and honours he bestows on them are his own.

[3] The text of 945 b 6–7 seems to me not capable of absolutely certain reconstruction. With some hesitation, I follow England in accepting Baiter's πη for εἴπη in b 6, rejecting Cornarius's addition of <ἦ> at the end of the same line, and the τὴν ἀρχὴν (absent from the original text of A and O) in b 7.

every office will be dismembered from every other, and all will
no longer conspire in one effect; the State will no longer be one
but many, will be filled with conflicting factions and, ere long,
destroyed. So we must see to it that these auditors are, one
and all,[1] eminent in every sort of excellence. And so we shall
contrive their creation in some such fashion as this. The whole
body of citizens shall annually, after the day of the summer
solstice, assemble in a precinct jointly dedicate to the sun and
to Apollo for the purpose of presenting before the god three
men, each citizen presenting the man of not less than fifty years
of age whom he judges in all respects (himself excluded) the 946
best. From those thus first elected they shall then select those
for whom most votes have been cast, to the number of one
half (if the total number be even—if it be odd, they shall omit
the one name for which fewest votes have been given), so that
half the names, as determined by the number of votes cast, are
retained. (If several names receive an equal number of votes,
and the half thus becomes too large, they shall reduce it by
excluding the youngest names and retaining the others.) The
voting shall then be repeated until only three names are left,
with an unequal number of votes. (If the votes cast for all
three, or for two of them, be equal, they shall commit the issue
to Providence and good fortune, and decide it by lot.) They
shall then crown the first, second, and third competitors with
olive; when this distinction has been awarded, public proclamation shall be made in this form: The State of the Mag-
nesians, now providentially restored to its old prosperity,
hereby presents its three most worthy citizens to the sun, and
dedicates them, in accord with its ancient usage, as a choice
offering of first-fruits, to Apollo and the sun in common for so
long as they shall give themselves to their work as judges.
Twelve[2] such auditors shall be created in the first year, each
to hold office until attaining the age of five-and-seventy; thereafter three more shall be created annually. They shall divide
the magistracies into twelve groups and scrutinize all by the
application of every test to which a gentleman can be subjected.
For their term of office they shall have their residence in the

---

[1] According to England πάντας, not the πάντως of earlier editions, is the
reading of A in 945 *e* 2, as it certainly makes the better sense.

[2] It is plain that the meaning is that at the first institution of the proposed
system *twelve* of these officials are to be elected, but annually in future only
three in any one year, and that there is no question, as has been sometimes
supposed, of an original election of three men, who then co-opt others.
Hence I believe England right in reading τ<οι>ούτους for τούτους in 946 *c* 2.

same precinct of Apollo and the sun in which their election was held. They shall individually, or in some cases conjointly, hold a scrutiny into the conduct of all out-going officers of State, and declare by publication in writing in the market-square what sentence or fine each official should incur in the judgment of the board of Auditors. Any official claiming that their judgment upon him is unfair shall summon the auditors before the court of select judges, and if acquitted of their censures, may, if he so pleases, bring his action against the auditors themselves; if he lose his case, and the sentence previously pronounced against him by the auditors be that of death, it shall simply stand, as no more can be done to him, but any other sentence which can be doubled in the infliction shall be exacted two-fold. You must next be told what audit will be appointed for the auditors themselves, and how it will be conducted. While they are still alive, as men whom the whole community has pronounced worthy of its supreme distinction, they shall have the foremost 947 seat at all festivals, and further, the heads of all delegations dispatched to inter-Hellenic sacrifices, religious gatherings, and other such international solemnities, shall always be taken from among them. They shall be the only citizens permitted to decorate themselves with the laurel-wreath. They shall all hold priesthoods of Apollo and the sun, while the chief priest-hood shall every year be enjoyed by the member of the college placed first at the election of that year, and the year shall be officially registered under his name, as a means of dating, so long as our society survives. When they decease, the lying-in-state, the procession to the grave, and the grave itself shall be more distinguished than in the case of other citizens. All the draperies shall be white, and there shall be neither dirges nor lamentations, but the bier shall be surrounded by a choir of fifteen maidens and another of fifteen lads; these choirs shall alternately chant a eulogy on the priests in the form of a hymn, and this lyrical panegyric shall be kept up throughout the day. At dawn the next day the bier shall be conducted to the tomb, the actual escort being one hundred of the young men from the gymnasia, to be selected at their pleasure by the deceased's kinsmen. At the head of the procession shall march the young bachelors, all apparelled in their accoutrements—the horsemen having their chargers, the infantry their arms, and the rest in the like array; the bier shall be immediately preceded by the boys, who will sing their national chant, and followed by the maidens, and such married women as are past the time of procreation. In the rear shall come priests and priestesses; even though they are debarred from accompanying other funerals, they may follow this, as one that imparts no defilement, if the Pythian prophetess will add her sanction to our proposal. The tomb shall be made in the form of an oblong underground vault of tufa, the most indestructible procurable, and provided with couches of stone set side by side. When the blessed dead has been laid to rest there, they shall cover the place with earth and plant a grove of trees round it, but leaving one end free, that the burial-place may admit of extension at this end, where there will never be earth over the interred. And they shall hold an annual contest in music, athletic exercises, and horse-racing in their honour. These, then, shall be the guerdons to be bestowed on those who have stood their audit and come out clear. But if any of them presume on his election and prove himself but too human after all by degeneration after his appointment, the law shall ordain that he may be impeached by any who will, and the court before which the issue shall be tried shall be formed as follows. It shall be constituted of (1) Curators of Law, (2) surviving members of the board of Auditors itself, (3) the panel of select judges. The 948 verbal form of the prosecutor's impeachment shall be: 'Such a one is unworthy of his distinctions and the office he holds.' If the impeached be convicted, he shall forfeit his office, as well as the public burial and other honours granted to him; but if the prosecutor cannot obtain a fifth part of the votes, he shall pay a fine, if of the wealthiest class, of twelve minae, if of the second, of eight, if of the third, of six, if of the fourth, of two.

We may well admire one thing in Rhadamanthys' manner of deciding issues at law, as the tale describes it—his perception that the men of his day were so confident of the manifest existence of gods—as well they might be, according to the story, since most of them at that time, and Rhadamanthys among them, had gods for their parents. Apparently he held that a judge's work should not be entrusted to any mere man, but only to gods, and this is why he could decide the cases that came before him so simply and rapidly. He put the litigants in a case to their oath about their assertions, and so had his business speedily and surely despatched. In these days of ours, when, as we have said, some men have no belief whatever in gods, others hold that they give themselves no concern about us, and the creed of the worst, who are the majority, is that if they pay the gods a trifle in the way of sacrifice and flattery, they will lend their help in vast frauds and deliver the sinner from all sorts of heavy penalties, in this present-day world, of course, the juristic methods of Rhadamanthys are no longer in place. Men's beliefs about gods have changed, and so the law must be changed too. A thoughtful legislator should abolish the oath taken by either litigant in the institution of a private action; the party instituting proceedings should state his charges in writing, but take no oath to their truth; similarly the defendant should deliver his denial of the charge to the magistrate in writing, without swearing to it. It is surely an awful thing, in a city where lawsuits are common, to know perfectly well that half or nearly half of the inhabitants are forsworn, and yet have no uneasiness about associating with each other at common meals and on other occasions of public and private intercourse. Our law, then, will require an oath to be taken by a judge before delivering his sentence; it will command the citizen who gives his vote for the appointment of a public official to do so in all cases either upon oath, or by using a ballot 949 fetched from a consecrated spot;[1] similarly, it will require an oath from judges of choirs or other musical performers, and presidents and umpires of gymnastic and equestrian sports, and persons in any similar position, where a false oath brings nothing men commonly regard as profit to the swearer. But wherever there is great and manifest profit (so esteemed) in denying the truth and standing to the denial on oath, the decision between the various contending parties must be reached by legal process requiring no oaths. And more generally, the presiding authorities of the court shall permit the litigant neither to court credence by swearing to his assertions, nor to support them by imprecations upon himself and his house, nor to indulge in degrading appeals for mercy or unmanly pathos; they shall see to it that he confines himself entirely to the statement of the rights he claims, in decent and reverent language, and gives a like decent hearing to his opponent; in case of breach of this rule, the presiding officers shall regard him as out of order, and recall him to relevance to the matter in hand. In a case between aliens, however, the parties shall be legally permitted to tender an oath to the opponent, or accept such a tender from him, at their pleasure. (Remember that they will not, as a rule, live to old age among us, or make themselves a nest

---

[1] i.e. to use for voting purposes a pebble brought from a god's altar, a 'consecrated' pebble. This is tantamount to the taking of an oath, as it equally exposes the voter to the wrath of the god whose altar has been profaned, if the vote is corruptly given.

where others of their own type will be bred up to be naturalized in our country.) We shall decide how all such parties are to initiate private suits against each other on the same principle.

In cases of *disobedience to the State on the part of a free citizen* —I mean cases not grave enough to call for whipping, imprisonment, or death—neglect to present oneself at the meetings of a choir, or to take part in a procession, or some other ceremonial or act of public service[1] (e.g. a sacrifice in peace time, or the payment of a special levy in time of war)—in all such cases, I say, the first requisite shall be that the †[2] loss be made good to the State, and the disobedient party shall be required to give a pledge to the officials empowered by the State's laws to demand it. If the disobedience continue after the pledge has been deposited, the articles so deposited shall be sold, and the proceeds confiscated to the State. If still further penalties be required, they shall be suitably imposed by the officers empowered to deal with the case in question, who shall cite the refractory parties before the courts, until they consent to obey orders.

A State which has no revenues except those it derives from its own soil, and no commerce is bound to make up its mind what course it should take as regards *foreign travel* on the part of its citizens and admission of aliens to its own dominions. So a legislator has to open his treatment of the subject with counsels which he must make as persuasive as he can. Now free intercourse between different States has the tendency to produce all manner of admixture of characters, as the itch for innovation is caught by host from visitor or visitor from host. Now this 950 may result in the most detrimental consequences to a society where public life is sound and controlled by right laws, though in most communities, where the laws are far from what they should be, it makes no real difference that the inhabitants should welcome the foreign visitor and blend with him, or take a jaunt into another State themselves, as and when the fancy for travel takes hold of them, young or old. On the other side, to refuse all admission to the foreigner and permit the native no opportunity of foreign travel is, for one thing, not always

---

[1] *Lit.* 'liturgy' (λητουργιῶν, 949 *d* 1), i.e. a public burden of any kind laid upon the richer citizen as due to the State on account of his superior affluence.

[2] The MSS. text of 949 *d* 2–3, given by Burnet, τὴν πρώτην ἀνάγκην ἰατὴν εἶναι τῆς ζημίας, can hardly be correct, unless ἰατὴν is the accusative of an otherwise unknown ἰατής. I suggest ἰατῆρ', 'the first necessity must be to make good the loss'.

possible, and, for another, may earn a State a reputation for barbarism and inhumanity with the rest of the world; its citizens will be thought to be adopting the ill-sounding policy of 'exclusion of aliens' and developing a repulsive and intractable character; but reputation, for good or ill, with the outer world ought never to be under-valued. Mankind at large may come far short of the real possession of virtue, but they are by no means equally deficient in the power to judge of the vice or virtue of others; there is a wonderful sagacity among the wicked themselves by which the very wickedest of them are often enabled to discriminate better men from worse accurately enough in their thought and language. Hence it is sound advice to give to most societies if one counsels them to prize a good reputation with the wider world. The one absolutely right, supreme rule, in fact, is first to be genuinely good and then to pursue repute for goodness, never, if we mean to be perfect, mere reputation by itself; so it will be only proper for the State we are now founding in Crete, like others, to earn the highest and most illustrious reputation for virtue with all its neighbours, and we may have every reasonable hope that if our plan is carried out, ours will be one of the few well-governed States and countries that enjoy the beams of the sun and his fellow gods. Our course in respect of *travels in foreign* parts and *admission of aliens to our territory* should therefore be as follows. First, no permission of foreign travel shall, in any circumstances whatsoever, be granted to any person under the age of forty; further, such permission shall be granted to no person for his private occasions, but only to those travelling on business of State, envoys, embassies, and deputations to divers ceremonies of religion. (It will not be proper to reckon absences in war or field-service among these occasions of State.) As it will be our duty to send deputations to Apollo of Pytho and Zeus of Olympia, as well as to Nemea and the Isthmus, to take their part in the sacrifices and games with which these gods are honoured, we must do our utmost to make these deputations as numerous, noble, and distinguished as we can; they must be composed of men who will make our city illustrious in the gatherings of religion and peace, and 951 cover her with a glory to match her renown in the field; on their return they shall explain to their juniors how inferior are the ways of other nations to the institutions of their own land. There are other commissioners who should—with the Curators' licence be sent abroad; they are these: If we should have citizens desirous to investigate the affairs of other peoples with

ampler leisure, no law shall stand in their way. A State unacquainted with mankind, bad and good, will never in its isola-
tion attain an adequate level of civilization and maturity, nor
will it succeed in preserving its own laws permanently, so long
as its grasp of them depends on mere habituation without
comprehension. Among the great mass of men there are always,
in fact, some, though few, of a superhuman quality; they are
to be found in States with defective laws no less than in States
with good, and their society is priceless. An inhabitant of a
well-governed State whose own character is proof against corruption should follow their trail over sea and land with a view
to the confirmation of such practices in his own community as
are sound and the amendment of any that are defective. Indeed
without observation and inquiry of this kind, or if it is ill conducted, no scheme of polity is perfectly stable.

Clin. Then how would you secure this pair of results?

Ath. Why, thus. This observer of whom we are speaking
shall, in the first place, be a man of fifty or upwards. Next, if
our Curators are to let him reach other lands as a sample of
what they can produce, he must be of high repute, military and
otherwise; and the period of his observations shall not be prolonged beyond his sixtieth year. He shall spend such part of
these ten years as he pleases in his observations, and, on his
return from them, shall report himself to the Council entrusted
with supervision of the laws. This shall be a body composed
of younger and senior members, and shall be required to hold
daily sessions from daybreak until after sunrise. It shall
contain, first, the priests who have won distinctions of the first
rank; [1] next the ten senior acting Curators; next the last elected
Minister of Education and any retired holders of that office.
Each of these shall not merely attend in person but associate
with himself such younger person of the age of thirty to forty
years as he deems best. The matter of the discourse held at
their conferences shall always be the laws of their own community, with such relevant suggestions of moment as they may 952
learn from other quarters, and, in especial, all branches of study
they may judge to advance their inquiries by shedding light on
points of law that would be left unduly dark and perplexed if
these studies were neglected. The junior members shall give
all diligence to pursue any such studies approved by their
seniors, and if any of these assessors prove unworthy, the whole

---

[1] For further details about this perpetual 'Council of Public Safety',
see 961 *infra*.

Council shall reprimand him who invited his presence. Such of them as obtain a good repute shall be a target for the observation of the whole community; they shall be the object of its particular care and regard, and receive marks of honour or more than common disgrace, according as they do themselves credit or fall below the general average in their conduct. Now the observer returned from his travels about the world is to present himself incontinently before this Council. If he have met with persons possessed of any information about legislation, education, or the management of children, or, as may also happen, have brought back personal reflections of his own, the results shall be laid before the whole Council. If they judge him to have come back neither the worse nor the better, he shall still receive their commendations for his trouble and industry. If much better, he shall, while still living, be commended much more warmly, and at his death shall be honoured with appropriate distinctions by the authority of the Council. But should he appear to have come home corrupted by his travels, he shall not make his assumed 'wisdom' a pretext for conferences with young or old. If he will obey orders in this matter, he shall live out his life in privacy; if not, he shall have sentence of death—I mean, if a court convict him of meddling in any matter of education or legislation. If the magistrates neglect to bring such offender before the court, where cause for proceedings has been given, the fact shall be remembered to their discredit at the award of distinctions.

So much, then, of parties who shall have leave of foreign travel and the terms of their leave; we are next to consider the welcome to be given to a visitor from abroad. The foreign visitors of whom account must be taken are of four sorts. First, and everlastingly, a guest who will pay his incessant calls, for the most part, in the summer, like a bird of passage; most of his kind are, in fact, just like winged creatures in the way they come flying overseas, at the proper season, on their profitable business errands. He shall be admitted by officials appointed for his benefit, to our market-place, harbours, and certain public buildings erected near the city but outside its walls. 953 The officials will take care to prevent the introduction of novelties by these guests, and will administer proper justice to them, but shall keep their intercourse with them within the strict bounds of necessity. The second sort are observers in the literal sense of the word; they come for the sights to be beheld by the eye and the musical displays to be enjoyed by the ear. Lodging shall be provided for all such visitants at the temples with a generous hospitality, and they shall receive the attention and solicitude of our priests and sacristans during a sojourn of reasonable length, but when they have seen and heard what they purposed, they must depart without harm done or received. In case of wrongs done or suffered by them, the matter shall be adjudicated upon by the priests, when the claim does not exceed fifty drachmas; where the sum claimed is higher, the case shall come before the Commissioners of the Market. A third sort, who must be entertained as guests of the State, are those who come from other countries on business of State. They shall be entertained by the generals and commanders of cavalry and infantry divisions, and by no other persons, and the business of their entertainment shall be confined to the particular commander in whose house such a guest receives lodging, acting in concert with the *prytanes*.[1] In the case of a visitant of the fourth sort—the event will be indeed uncommon, but if we should be visited by a counterpart of our own observers from some other country—he must, in the first place, have attained the age of fifty at least, and further, his avowed object must be either to see for himself some excellent features superior to the beauties to be found in other societies, or to reveal something of the sort to another State. Such a visitor, then, shall need no bidding to enter the doors of our men of 'wealth and wisdom', being himself a man of these same qualities. I mean, he may go to the house of the Minister of Education, confident of his fitness to be guest to such a host, or to that of some man who has won the award for virtue. He shall pass his time with some of these, imparting knowledge and acquiring it, and when he departs, it shall be as a friend from friends, with suitable parting presents and distinctions. These, I say, are the laws by which our citizens should manage all reception of foreign visitors, male or female, and despatch of their own countrymen to foreign parts. They should show their reverence for Zeus, the stranger's patron, not make meats and sacrifices a device for repelling the alien, as we see the 'dusky brood of Nilus'[2] doing to-day, or banish him by barbarian edicts.

Any person *giving a security* shall do so in explicit terms; he shall set down the whole transaction in a legal document, and

---

[1] The persons intended by this Attic technical name are the members of the committees described above at 758 *b–d*.

[2] Cf. *Genesis*, xliii 33: 'the Egyptians might not eat bread with the Hebrews; for that is an abomination unto the Egyptians.'

in the presence of witnesses, to the number of three at the least, if the sum concerned be not more than a thousand drachmas, or five at the least if it be higher.   Also the broker at a sale shall be security for a seller who has no sound title to the article sold, or cannot guarantee delivery, and an action shall lie against broker no less than against vendor.

954

A person proposing to *search for stolen goods* on another's premises shall first strip to his shirt and lay aside his belt, and shall also have made oath by the gods, as required by law, that he honestly expects to find his goods.   The other party shall permit the search, which shall extend to sealed, as well as to unsealed, receptacles.   If one party desire to make a search and the other refuse permission, the party so repelled shall lay an action, specifying the value of the missing goods, and the defendant shall, on conviction, pay twice the amount as specified.   If the owner of the house be absent from home, the occupants shall permit the search of unsealed receptacles; sealed receptacles shall be countersealed by the searcher and left for five days under such guard as he pleases.   If the absence of the owner is further prolonged, the searcher shall call in the Urban Commissioners and prosecute his search; the sealed receptacles themselves shall be opened, but shall be afterwards re-sealed as before in the presence of the household and the Commissioners.

In cases of *disputed title* there shall be the following [1] limits of time, beyond which a possessor's title shall no longer be liable to question.   In this Cretan city there can be no such thing as a disputed title to a landed estate or a dwelling-house; as to other property of which a man may be possessed, when the possessor of an article makes open use thereof in town, market-square, and temples no counter-claim being advanced, then, if another profess to be looking for the article during this period, while the possessor is plainly making no concealment thereof, if the possession on the one side and search on the other have continued for a year, after the expiry of such year no one shall have legal right to claim such article.   If the article be in open use on a country estate, though not in town or market-place, and no claimant appear within five years, no man's claim to such article shall thenceforth be entertained.   If the article be in use within-doors, and in the town, the term of prescription

---

[1] The sentence as it stands in the MSS. has no predicate, and would have to be regarded as a mere 'heading', *Prescription*.   But the δὲ found after χρόνον in 954 c 3 seems to be, as remarked by W. R. Paton, the trace of a predicative ὅδε, and I translate accordingly.

shall be three years, or for an article thus held in undisclosed possession on a man's country estate, ten. If the article be in some other country, at whatever time it may be found, prescription shall be no bar to the claim of the finder.

If a man *forcibly hinder the presence of a litigant or his witnesses in the courts*, and the party thus hindered be a slave, his own or another's, the suit shall be declared null and void; if the party 955 hindered be a free man, the offender shall further undergo a year's imprisonment, and shall be liable to action for kidnapping at the instance of any who pleases. If a man forcibly prevent the presence of a rival competitor at any gymnastic, musical, or other contest, any who may please shall inform the Presidents of the contest, and they shall set the intending competitor free to enter the contest. In a case where this is impossible, if the party hindering the appearance of a competitor prove victorious, the Presidents shall award the prize to the competitor so hindered, and inscribe his name as victorious in such temples as he pleases; the party causing the hindrance shall be forbidden to commemorate such a contest by dedication or inscription, and shall be equally liable to an action for damage whether he be defeated in the competition or successful.

If a man *knowingly receive stolen goods*, he shall be liable to the same penalties as the thief; the sentence for *reception of an exile* shall be death.

All citizens shall regard a friend or enemy of the State as their own personal friend or enemy. Any person *making peace or war* with any parties independently of the commonwealth shall likewise incur the pain of death. If a section of the State make peace or war with any on its own account, the generals shall bring the authors of the measure before a court, and the penalty for conviction shall be death.

The *servants of the nation* are to render their services *without any taking of presents*, and there shall be no glosing of the practice, nor accepting of the principle that 'a present should be taken for a good deed, though not for an ill'. To form your judgment and then abide by it is no easy task, and 'tis a man's surest course to give loyal obedience to the law which commands 'do no service for a present'. The disobedient shall, if convicted, die without ceremony.

As *concerns payment to the public Treasury*, every man must have his estate valued, and that for more reasons than one, but the members of every tribe shall also furnish the Rural Commission with a written record of each year's produce that the exchequer may be free to choose at its pleasure, between the two methods of raising its revenue, as the authorities will consider annually whether they shall exact some fraction of the capital valuation or some part of the annual income, exclusive of the cost of the public table.

A modest man's *gifts in the way of offerings to the gods* should themselves be modest. Now the soil and the household hearthstone are sacred, in our universal conviction, to all gods that are. No man, then, shall reconsecrate what is dedicated already. In other societies you will find gold and silver in temples as well as in private houses, but they are possessions which breed 956 ill-will against their owner; ivory—a body that soul has forsaken—is no clean offering; bronze and iron are tools of battle. But any man, at his pleasure, may dedicate in our public temples, an image of wood, carved in one piece, or of stone similarly fashioned, or a piece of woven work, not exceeding what one woman can finish in a month. White is the colour most proper for the gods, in tapestry as in other materials; dyes are not to be used except for military adornment. The most pious presents we can offer the gods are birds and figures on such scale that they can be finished by one artist in one day; our other offerings shall be on the model of these.

We have now spoken of the sections into which our whole city must be divided—their number and nature—and done what we may to prescribe laws for all its chief business transactions; it remains to *constitute our justiciary*. Our tribunal of first instance will consist of judges appointed by the concurrent choice of defendant and plaintiff; arbitrators would be a more appropriate name for them. The second court shall be formed from fellow-villagers and tribesmen (each tribe being subdivided into twelve). If no decision can be reached at the first stage, the litigants shall continue their contention before these judges, but the stake will be increased; the defendant, if worsted a second time, shall pay the award imposed in the original suit with an additional fifth. If he be ill-content with his judges and desire to contest the case a third time, he shall take it before the select judges, and shall, if worsted once more, pay the original award with an additional half. A plaintiff who will not sit down with a defeat in the primary court but carries the case to the second shall, if successful, receive the additional fifth, but, if defeated, shall pay the same fraction of the sum under dispute. If the antagonists refuse to submit to the earlier judgments and take the case to the third court, the defeated party shall pay, if he be the defendant, the first award with an additional half, as already enacted, and if plaintiff, the half only. For what concerns balloting for juries and filling vacancies on them, the provision of a staff for the different courts and the intervals at which sessions shall be held, the manner of taking the vote, the adjournment of the court, and other such necessary details of the administration of justice (as, for example, determination of the order in which suits shall be heard, the rules of compulsory answers to interrogatories and compulsory attendance in court,[1] and the like generally), the matter has been dealt with already,[2] but 'tis no ill deed to repeat a sound maxim or even to state it a third time. In a word, all such minor and simple details of legal procedure may be left by our aged legislator for his younger successors to fill in. Here, then, we have a fair model for the composition of courts to adjudge private disputes; for tribunals in affairs of common and public concern and courts which are to subserve the magistrate in the exercise of his function, many communities already possess decorous institutions derived from excellent authors and our Curators must construct out of this material a scheme suited to the polity now in process of birth. They shall compare these institutions and amend them in the light of their personal experience until they judge them to be all sufficiently perfected; then only will they take the last step, stamp them as wholly immutable, and put them into practice for all time to come. For the silence and decorum of speech to be observed by the judges, and their contrary, as for our divergences from the various standards of right, good, honour in other societies, something has been said of this already, and we shall find more to say in the close. He that would show himself a righteously equal judge must keep these matters before his eyes; he must procure books on the subject, and must make them his study. There is, in truth, no study whatsoever so potent as this of law, if the law be what it should be, to make a better man of its student—else 'twould be for nothing that the law that so stirs our worship and wonder bears a name so cognate with that of understanding. Furthermore, consider all other discourse, poesy with its eulogies and its satires, or utterances in prose (whether in literature or in the common converse of daily life), with their contentious disagreements and their

957

---

[1] The meaning of the word used here, παρακαταβάσεων, a word which occurs nowhere else, is not certainly known.
[2] See especially 846 b–c.

too often unmeaning admissions: the one certain touchstone of all is the text of the legislator. The good judge will possess the text within his own breast as an antidote against other discourse, and thus he will be the State's preserver as well as his own. He will secure in the good the retention and increase of their rectitude, and in the evil, or those of them whose vicious principles admit remedy, will promote, so far as he can, conversion from folly, from profligacy, from cowardice, in a word, from all forms of wrong. As for those who are fatally attached to such principles, if our judges and their superiors prescribe death as the cure for a soul in that state, they will, as has been more than once said already, deserve the praise of the community for their conduct.

958

When the suits of the year have been carried through to their final adjudication, the law as to *execution* of judgment shall be this. First, the magistrate delivering judgment shall make an assignment to the successful litigant of all the goods of the unsuccessful party, except such as he must necessarily be allowed to retain, and this shall be done, in every case, immediately upon the delivery of the verdict, through the crier of the court, in the presence of the judges. On the expiry of the month following that wherein a suit is tried, if no discharge have been obtained from the victorious litigant to the satisfaction of both parties, the magistrate before whom the suit was tried shall, at the instance of the victor, enforce delivery to him of the goods of the loser. If these prove insufficient to meet the obligation, and the deficiency amount to one drachma or upwards, the loser shall be deprived of all right to institute a suit against any person whatsoever, until he have first discharged in full his debt to the victor, other parties retaining their full rights to institute proceedings against such debtor. Any person thus cast *obstructing the action of the court* which condemned him shall be brought by the magistrates so obstructed before the court of the Curators, and any person convicted on such a charge shall suffer death as one that would undo our whole society and its law.

Now to proceed: when a man has been born into the world and brought up to manhood, has begotten his children and brought them up, has played his part duly in the transaction of affairs, offering compensation to any to whom he had done an injury and accepting [1] such compensation from another, and

----

[1] As a point of syntax ought not ἐκλαβόντι (958 *d* 2) to be corrected to ἐκλα$<\mu>$β$<άν>$οντι.

has so come in due course to law-respecting old age, the natural close will be his decease. As to the *deceased*, then, whether male or female, full authority to prescribe the offices of piety it will be proper to perform towards deities of the underworld or of our own shall be given to the interpreters of religious law. But there must be no grave or tomb, whether great or small, on any site capable of cultivation: they must fill up the places where our soil is naturally fitted only for this one purpose of receiving and concealing the bodies of the departed with least inconvenience to the living; where earth, a true mother to us in the matter, is minded to yield sustenance for us, our living shall not be cheated of the benefit by any man, living or dead. The mound of earth shall not be made higher than can be done by five men within five days, and no stone shall be erected upon it larger than is needed to receive, at the outside, the customary four hexameter verses in commendation of the life of the deceased. The lying-in-state in the house shall, in the 959 first place, be prolonged only for the time needed to distinguish between a swoon and a genuine death; the general rule will thus be that a man may properly be conveyed to the grave on the third day after his decease. And our faith in the legislator should extend particularly to his statements when he tells us that soul is utterly superior to body, and that what gives each one of us his being is nothing else but his soul, whereas the body is no more than a shadow which keeps us company; so 'tis well said of the deceased that the corpse is but a ghost, the real man —the undying thing called the soul—departs to give account to the gods of another world, even as we are taught by ancestral tradition—an account to which the good may look forward without misgiving, but the evil with grievous dismay. Whence, the legislator will add, we can do very little to help a man when he is once dead. The help should have been given by all connected with him while he was still alive, and it should have aided him to pass life, while it lasted, in all rectitude and purity, and at death to escape the vengeance of the world to come on grave sin. Now since things stand thus with us, we should never waste our substance in the fancy that he who was so much to us is this bulk of flesh that is being committed to its grave, and not the real man—the son, or brother, or other lamented kinsman we fancy ourselves to be burying— who has left us, to continue and fulfil his own destiny; our duty, we must think, is rather to make the best of the case and to keep expenditure on what is, as it were, an altar of the dead about which no spirit hovers, within modest bounds, and the oracle which may best declare what modesty is is the voice of the legislator. Our law, then, shall be this: Modest expenditure shall mean an outlay upon the whole ceremonies of burial which must not exceed five minae for a person of the wealthiest class, three for one of the second, two for one of the third, one for one of the fourth. It will be by no means the least of the many inevitable duties and cares of Curators to give their life to the supervision of children, adults, and persons of all ages; in especial, at his death every man shall be put under the care of a particular Curator to be called in as supervisor by the household of the deceased, to whose credit it shall count if the funeral ceremonies are conducted with propriety and moderation, and who shall be discredited by any impropriety. The lying-in-state and like matters shall be regulated by the custom in such things, but custom must bow to the legislation of the statesman in the points I shall now specify. To command or 960 forbid tears to be shed over the departed would be unseemly, but it shall be forbidden to utter dirges over him, or to let the noise of the mourning be audible outside the house; we shall also prohibit the carrying of a corpse through the public streets and the raising of cries as the mourners traverse them, and the party must be beyond the city-wall before daybreak. These are the regulations we shall impose in the matter; compliance therewith will secure a man from all penalty, disobedience shall be visited by one of the Curators with a penalty to be approved by the whole body. Further rites of sepulture, as also the acts which involve loss of the right to sepulture—parricide, sacrilege, and others—have already been made matters of legislation, and we may accordingly say that our code is substantially completed. But the end of an enterprise is never reached by the mere performance of the act, acquisition of the possession, or establishment of the foundation; we must never take ourselves to have done all there was to do until we have provided a complete and permanent guarantee for the preservation of our work; until then we should regard our whole achievement as unfinished.

Clin. Very true, sir. But I could wish for further light on the application of that last observation.

Ath. Why, look you, Clinias, there is good sense in many of our old household phrases, and not least in the designations men have given to the Fates.

Clin. How so?

Ath. We are told that the first of them is called Lachesis, the second Clotho, and the third, she who, in fact, makes the result fast, Atropos, with an allusion to the . . .[1] which makes the spinning irreversible. So likewise, the need of a State or constitution is not merely for provision for bodily health and preservation, but for the presence of loyalty to law in the soul, or rather for the abiding preservation of its law. And this, I believe, is the one thing still manifestly lacking to our own laws, some means of ensuring, so far as we can, this rightful irreversibility.

Clin. A serious deficiency, too, in any achievement, if it is really impossible to give it such a character.

Ath. Nay, the thing is certainly possible, as I can now see quite plainly.

Clin. Then we must on no account relinquish our work without performing this same service for our proposed code; you know it is always ridiculous to waste one's pains by building on insecurely laid foundations.

Ath. Well reminded; you will find me in accord with you there.

Clin. I am very glad to hear it. Well then, what, let me ask you, is to be this safeguard for our system and its laws? How do you propose to effect it?

Ath. Why, did we not say that our State must have a Council 961 which would be constituted in some such fashion as this? The ten senior acting Curators of Law and the whole body of persons who had won supreme distinction were to meet in council; further, any persons who had travelled into foreign parts to inquire into any capital invention for the preservation of law they might hear of, and had returned, were to be examined by this body and pronounced, on approval, worthy of association with it.[2] Furthermore, each member was to bring with him one younger man, not being under the age of thirty, and present him to his colleagues, though not until he had personally judged him worthy of the honour by his parts and education: if the approval of the whole board were obtained, the young man was to be received as an associate; if not, his original nomination

---

[1] ἀπηκασμένα τῇ τῶν κλωσθέντων τῷ πυρι τὴν ἀμετάστροφον ἀπεργαζομένων δύναμιν, 960 *c* 9–*d* 1. The words cannot be construed and there is some corruption. I believe Ast was right in reading ἀπεργαζομένῃ, and that otherwise the text is sound except for the unintelligible τῷ πυρι. No 'emendation' of these words convinces me, and I therefore leave a gap.

[2] In 961 *a* 6 I retain the text of the MSS. with Burnet, but remove his comma after δόξαι.

was to be kept a profound secret from every one, and particularly from himself. The Council was to hold its meetings before daybreak, the time, above all others when a man is always freest from all other business, private or public. I think this was much the substance of what we said.

Clin. You are right, it was.

Ath. Then I will go back to the subject of this Council and this is what I would affirm about it. If it is cast out, so to say, as a sheet-anchor of State, furnished with all its proper appurtenances, it will prove the safeguard of all our hopes.

Clin. And how so?

Ath. Ah, there is the critical point at which you and I have to do our uttermost to advise rightly.

Clin. Admirably said; but pray put the purpose into execution.

Ath. Well then, Clinias, we have to discover what is the fitting protector for anything in all its various activities. In a living organism, for instance, it is, above everything else, the soul and head which are designed to this function.

Clin. Once more, how so?

Ath. Why, you know, it is the perfection of these two that guarantees the preservation of the whole creature.

Clin. How so?

Ath. By the development of intelligence in the soul and vision and hearing in the head as the crowning endowment of each. To put it concisely, when intelligence is fused into a unity with these noblest of the senses, they constitute what we have every right to call a creature's salvation.

Clin. That certainly sounds like the truth.

Ath. If does indeed. But what in particular is the object envisaged by the blended intelligence and sense which is to be the salvation of a vessel in storm and calm? In this case of the ship, it is the fusion of the sharp senses of captain and crew alike with the captain's intelligence that preserves ship and ship's company together, is it not?

Clin. To be sure.

Ath. Well the point surely calls for no great number of illustrative examples. Take the case of a military expedition; we have to ask ourselves what must be the mark aimed at by its commanders—or again, by any medical service—if they are to
962 aim at 'salvation', as they ought to do. In the first case, I take it, the target is victory and superiority to the enemy, in that of the physicians and their staff, the preservation of bodily health?

Clin. Why, of course.

Ath. Well then, if a physician knew nothing of the nature of bodily health, as we have just called it, or a commander nothing of the nature of victory and the other results we mentioned, it would surely be clear that he had no understanding of his subject whatsoever.

Clin. Why, certainly.

Ath. Well, then, to come to the case of a State: if a man plainly knows nothing of the mark a statesman must keep before his view, has he, for one thing, any right to the style of a magistrate, and will he, for another, have any capacity for the preservation of that of whose aim he is so utterly ignorant?

Clin. None whatsoever.

Ath. Why then, mark the inference. If our present disposition of our territory is to be completed, it must provide for the presence there of some body which understands, in the first place, the true nature of this mark of statesmanship, as we have called it, and next, the methods by which it may be attained, and the counsels—emanating principally from the laws themselves, secondarily from individual men—which make for or against it. If a State leave no room for such a body, we should not be surprised that a society so unintelligent and so imperceptive habitually finds itself drifting at the mercy of circumstance in its various undertakings.

Clin. Just so.

Ath. Now where in our society, in which of its sections or institutions as so far prescribed, have we made any adequate provision for such a safeguard? Can we specify anything of the kind?

Clin. No indeed, sir, not with any certainty. But if I may hazard a guess, your observations seem to be pointing to the Committee which, as you just said, will be expected to meet in the small hours.

Ath. You understand me perfectly, Clinias. That body, as our present observations prefigure, will, indeed, need to be equipped with all virtue. And the first point of such virtue will be that its aim must not wander from object to object; it must have a single mark always before its eye and make it the target of all its shafts.

Clin. Assuredly it must.

Ath. Now we have reached this point, we shall understand that there is nothing surprising in the fact that the laws of our various societies should be all at sea, seeing that the aims of the legislators in each of them are so conflicting. In general, we must not be surprised that the standard of rights with some men is the restriction of power to a certain group, no matter whether better or worse in reality than others, with others the acquisition of riches, no matter whether or not at the cost of enslavement, and yet others make 'liberty' the object of their passion; others, again, combine two objects in their legislation and keep an eye on both together, liberty and empire over other societies, while the wisest of all, as they fancy themselves, pursue all these aims and others like them at once; they set no one object of a particular devotion before them to which they might point as the proper aim of all other pursuits.

963   *Clin.* Surely then, sir, the position we took so long ago was the sound one. We said there was one end to be kept in view in all our own laws, and we were agreed, I believe, that the right name for the thing is *virtue*.

Ath. We were so.

Clin. And virtue, as I remember, we said has four parts.

Ath. Precisely.

Clin. But the chief of them all is understanding, and it should be the aim of the three other parts, as well as of everything else.

Ath. You follow my argument perfectly, Clinias; pray keep me company in the next step. As to this matter of the single aim, we have specified the mark on which the understanding of navigator, physician, military commander should direct its gaze and are now in the act of examining that of the statesman. If we like to personify his wisdom, we may address it with these words: 'In the name of all that is wonderful, what is it you have in view? What is your one aim? The physician's wisdom can give us a definite answer: you, the wisest of all the wise, by your own account, have you no answer?' Now Megillus and Clinias, can you, between you, act as his spokesmen? Can you give me a definition stating what you take this object to be, like the definitions I have so often given you as spokesman for other parties?

Clin. Nay sir, there we are at a loss.

Ath. Now what is it that we must be so anxious to discern, in itself as in its various manifestations?

Clin. I should like some illustration of what you mean by 'manifestations'.

Ath. As an illustration, then, take our language about the four types of virtue. If there are four of them, obviously we must hold that each type by itself is one.

Clin. Obviously.

Ath. And yet we give one name to all of them. In fact, we speak of courage as virtue, of wisdom as virtue, and similarly with the other two, and this implies that they are not really several things, but just this one thing—virtue.

Clin. Certainly.

Ath. Now it is easy enough to point out where these two, or the others, differ and why they have received two distinct names; it is not so light a matter to show why we have given both of them, and the rest, the one common name, *virtue.*

Clin. Now what is your point?

Ath. One which I can explain readily enough. Suppose we divide the parts of questioner and respondent between us.

Clin. Again, I must ask you to explain yourself.

Ath. Ask me the question why we first call both things by the one name *virtue,* and then speak of them as two—*courage* and *wisdom.* I will give you the reason. One of them—courage —is concerned with fears, and so is to be found in the brutes and in the behaviour of mere infants. In fact, a soul may attain to courage by mere native temperament independently of discourse of reason, but without such discourse no soul ever comes by understanding or wisdom; none has ever done so, and none ever will; the cases are utterly different.

Clin. That is true enough.

Ath. Very good; my statement has told you where the things 964 differ and why they are two; it is now your turn to tell me in what respects they are one and the same. Remember that you will also have to explain in what way the four things can be one thing, and that when you have given your explanation you are once more to ask me in what way they are four. And there will be still a further point to investigate: if a man is to have competent knowledge of anything whatsoever which has not only a name but a definition, is it enough that he should know its bare name, but be unaware of its definition? Is not any such ignorance in a man of any account disgraceful, when the matter at issue is one of paramount importance and dignity?

Clin. So I should presume.

Ath. In the eye of an author or custodian of law, a man who believes in his own pre-eminence in virtue and has won the prize for the very qualities of which we are treating, can there be anything of greater importance than these qualities themselves, valour, purity, justice, wisdom?

Clin. There surely cannot.

Ath. Then where these are the issues at stake, is it to be believed [1] of our interpreters, our teachers, our legislators, the very men who have the rest of us in their keeping—can it be believed, I say, when it comes to the provision for one who needs to learn and know, or to be corrected and rebuked for his faults, that a man such as we have in mind will not show himself pre-eminent as a teacher of the characteristic quality of virtue and vice and generally as an instructor? Can we suppose that some poet or pretended 'educator of youth' who has come to our city will get the credit of superiority to one who has won the palm of a perfect virtue? In a State like this, where there are no custodians competent in act as in thought from their competent acquaintance with virtue—is it surprising, I ask you if a State left so unguarded has the fortunes of too many of our States of to-day?

Clin. Why no, I suppose not.

Ath. What follows? Shall we act, as we are now proposing, or how? Shall we equip our guardians with a more finished mastery in the theory and practice of virtue than the mass of their neighbours? How else is our own city to resemble an intelligent man's head with its sense-organs in its possession of such a defence within itself?

Clin. Pray, sir, how are we to understand the comparison? In what does the likeness consist?

Ath. Why manifestly the city at large is the trunk of the body: the younger guardians—we selected them for their superior parts, for the quickness of all their faculties—are stationed, so to say, at its summit, their vision ranges over the whole compass of the State, they commit what they perceive in their watch to memory, and serve their elders as scouts in
965 every branch of affairs. Those senior men—we may compare them with the understanding for their special wisdom in so many momentous matters—sit in council, where they avail themselves of the services and suggestions of their juniors, and thus, by their united action, the two parties are, between them, the real salvation of the whole State. Is this to be our project, or are we to find some other arrangement for ourselves? Are

[1] The sentence as Plato appears to have left it has no main finite verb, the δεῖ of 964 c 2 being apparently a 'corrector's emendation of δέ.

we to leave all our citizens [1] on one level of training and education, with no more sedulously trained class among them?

Clin. My dear sir! We cannot possibly take such a course.

Ath. Then we shall have to proceed to an education of a more exacting kind than we have so for contemplated.

Clin. I dare say we shall.

Ath. And that on which we have just touched may perhaps prove to be the very one we need?

Clin. Indeed it may.

Ath. I believe we said that a consummate craftsman or guardian in any sphere will need the ability not merely to fix his regard on the Many, but to advance to the recognition of the One and the organization of all other detail in the light of that recognition?

Clin. Yes, and it was the truth.

Ath. Now whose vision and view of his object can be more intimate than his who has learned to look from the dissimilar Many to the One Form?

Clin. You may be right.

Ath. Not 'may be', bless you! There *is* no surer path for a man's steps, and can be none.

Clin. Well, sir, I admit it on your assurance; so we may let the argument take that course.

Ath. Then it looks as though the guardians of our god-given constitution too must be constrained, first and foremost, to see exactly what is the identity permeating all the four, the unity to be found, as we hold, alike in courage, in purity, in rectitude, in wisdom, and entitling them all to be called by the one name, *virtue*. This, my friends, if you please, is what we must now close upon with a firm and unyielding grip, until we are content with our account of the real character of the mark on which our gaze shall be fixed, whether it prove to be a unit or a whole, or both at once, or what you please. If we let this slip through our fingers, can we suppose we shall ever be fully equipped for a virtue of which we cannot tell whether it is many things, or four, or one? No, if we are to follow our own advice, we must find some other way of securing this result in our society. But of course we must consider whether we should leave the whole subject alone.

Clin. Nay, sir, in the name of the god of strangers, you cannot

---

[1] The MSS. κεκτημένους in 965 *a* 6 gives a satisfactory sense, and I therefore translate it. But it is very possible that Wilamowitz-Moellendorf's κεκτημένην should be accepted. ('Is *the city* to have all its members on one level, etc.')

let such a matter drop; we find your remarks full of truth. But how is the thing to be compassed?

966 *Ath.* Ah, that is a question we are not yet ready to ask. We must first be sure we are agreed whether or not the thing must be done.

Clin. Indeed it must, if only it can be done.

Ath. Then what say you to this? Do we take this same view when it comes to the *fine*, or to the *good*? Will our guardians have merely to know that each of them is many, or must they know further how and in what way each is a unit?

Clin. Why, we seem fairly driven to hold that they will actually have to understand their unity.

Ath. And suppose they can perceive this, but are unable to give any articulate demonstration of it?

Clin. Out of the question! A condition only fit for a slave!

Ath. Well, once more, must we say the same of all matters of moment? Men who are to be real guardians of the law [1] will need a real knowledge of them all; they must be able to expound this knowledge in their speech and to conform to it in their practice, to discern the true intrinsic demarcations of good and evil?

Clin. Indubitably.

Ath. Now among these matters of high import is not the subject of divinity which we treated so earnestly pre-eminent? 'Tis of supreme moment for us, is it not, to know with all the certainty permitted to man that there are gods, and with what evident might they are invested? In the great mass of our citizens we may tolerate mere conformity to the tradition embodied in the laws, but we shall do well to deny all access to the body of our guardians to any man who has not made it his serious business to master every proof there is of the being of gods. And by denial of access I mean that no man who is not divinely gifted or has not laboured at divinity shall ever be chosen for a Curator, nor ever be numbered among those who win the distinction for virtue.

Clin. As you say, it will be only right that the slothful or incompetent in such matters should be hopelessly excluded from high distinction.

Ath. May we say, then, that we know of two motives—those we have already rehearsed—of credibility in divinity?

---

[1] The 'real guardians' are the more select body constituting the 'Nocturnal Council', as distinguished from the thirty-seven magistrates *officially* entitled νομοφύλακες 'Curators of the Laws'.

Clin. And what are these two?

Ath. One of them is our theory of the soul, our doctrine that it is more ancient and more divine than anything that draws perennial being from a motion that once had a beginning; the other our doctrine of the orderliness in the movements of the planets and other bodies swayed by the mind that has set this whole frame of things in comely array. No man who has once turned a careful and practised gaze on this spectacle has ever been so ungodly at heart that its effect has not been the very reverse of that currently expected. 'Tis the common 967 belief that men who busy themselves with such themes are made infidels by their astronomy and its sister sciences, with their disclosure of a realm where events happen by stringent necessity, not by the purpose of a will bent on the achievement of good.

Clin. And what is the true state of the matter?

Ath. As I told you, the situation has been precisely reversed since the days when observers of these bodies conceived them to be without souls. Even then, they awakened wonder, and aroused in the breasts of close students the suspicion, which has now been converted into an accepted doctrine,[1] that were they without souls, and by consequence without intelligence, they would never have conformed to such precise computations; even in those days there were persons bold enough to hazard the actual assertion that it is mind to which the heavens owe all their ordered array. And yet these same thinkers went astray about the soul; they took it to be junior to body, not senior, and their error, as I may say, wrecked the whole scheme, or, to speak more accurately, wrecked themselves. For on a short-sighted view, the whole moving contents of the heavens seemed to them a parcel of stones, earth, and other soulless bodies, though they furnish the sources of the world-order! It was this that involved the thinkers of those days in so many charges of infidelity and so much unpopularity, and further inspired poets to denounce students of philosophy by comparing them with dogs baying the moon, and to talk a world of folly besides; but, as I told you, to-day the position has been reversed.

Clin. In what way?

Ath. No son of man will ever come to a settled fear of God until he has grasped the two truths we are now affirming, the soul's dateless anteriority to all things generable, her immortality

---

[1] The contrast is between the spirit of the early 'pre-Socratic' cosmology and that of the astronomy and cosmology of Plato's Academy. The 'thinker' alluded to in what follows is Anaxagoras.

and sovereignty over the world of bodies, and moreover that presence among the heavenly bodies of a Mind of all things of which we have spoken so often already. He must also possess the requisite preliminary sciences, perceive the links which connect them with music, and apply his knowledge meetly to his moral and legal behaviour; also he must be able to give a 968 reasoned account of all that admits thereof. He that adds not these endowments to his possession of the popular virtues will never be a sufficient magistrate of a whole community, but only a magistrate's underling. Thus the time has now come, Megillus and Clinias, when we must ask ourselves whether we shall add one more statute to all hitherto rehearsed, a law instituting the Nocturnal Council of magistrates, duly furnished with the whole education we have described, as the State's custodian and preserver. How shall we act, think you?

Clin. How, my dear friend, can we do other than make the addition, if we have the power, in however low degree?

Ath. Then let us indeed, one and all, throw our powers into so worthy an undertaking. This at least is a task in which you will find me eager to help—and I may possibly discover other co-operators besides myself—from my copious experience of such matters and meditation upon them.

Clin. Out of all question, sir, we must take the road along which God himself is so plainly guiding us. But what is our right way to set about it? That is what our present conference has to discover.

Ath. As to laws on such a point, Megillus and Clinias, it is impossible to lay them down now, before the institution has been framed—it will be time to define its statutory powers when it exists—all that can be done at present towards fashioning such a body, if the work is to be done rightly, is instruction by repeated conferences.

Clin. How so? What is the meaning of that remark?

Ath. Well, we must obviously begin by compiling a list of persons qualified for the post of guardian in respect of age, intellectual ability, character and habits. When we come to the next point, that of the subjects to be studied, it is no easy matter to invent them ourselves, nor yet to go to school to some other inventor.[1] Further, it would be futile to give regulations

---

[1] Because the mathematics necessary for dealing with the problems are still only in course of creation—an allusion to the progress being actually made in the study by the Academy. So the allusion in the phrase about 'modern legislators' in 969 *c* below is to the scientific jurisprudence which was being created in the Academy.

either for the length of time to be given to the single subjects or for the order in which they shall be taken up; the student himself will not discover which of his studies is relevant until scientific knowledge of the subject has found a settlement in his soul. Thus you see that while it would be wrong to call these various subjects incapable of *description*, it is very right to call them incapable of *prescription*, for prescription can throw no light on their contents.

Clin. Why, sir, if the case stands so, what, I ask you, are we to do?

Ath. As the phrase goes, my friends, we have a 'fair field and no favour'; if we are ready, as they say, to stake the whole future of our polity on a throw of triple six or triple ace, why, so we must, and I, for one, will take my share in the risk; my 969 part shall be the statement and exposition of my own convictions about the scheme of education and training which our conversation has thus started for the second time. But the hazard we run, mind you, is no slight one; there are not many others to be compared with it. I would advise you, Clinias, in particular, to lay the matter deeply to heart. For you the alternatives are to construct this State of Magnesia—or whatever name God will have it called after—on right lines and cover yourself with glory, or to incur the abiding reputation of a temerity not to be equalled in all future ages. But if we can once create this admirable Council, then, my good friends and colleagues, we must deliver the State into its keeping, and there will be hardly one modern legislator to disagree with us. The dream on which we touched a while ago in our talk, when we painted our picture of the partnership of the mind and the head, will have found its fulfilment in real and working fact, if and when we have seen our men scrupulously selected, duly educated, settled at the end of the process in the nation's central fortress and established there as guardians whose likes we have never seen in our whole lives for perfection as protectors.

Meg. My dear Clinias, after all that has now been said, we shall either have to abandon the foundation of your city or else to be deaf to our friend's excuses, and try every entreaty and inducement to secure him as a co-operator in the foundation.

Clin. Very true, Megillus. I will do as you wish, and you must assist me.

Meg. Count upon me.

INDEX

INDEX